BRITAIN'S HIGHEST MOUNTAIN WALKS

Published by Collins
An imprint of HarperCollins Publishers
Westerhill Road, Bishopbriggs, Glasgow G64 2QT

First Edition 2013

Printed in China by South China Printing Co. Ltd

British Library Cataloguing in Publication Data
A catalogue record for this book is available from the British Library

978 0 00 748821 6
978 0 00 793597 0
Imp 001

All mapping in this publication is generated from Collins Bartholomew digital databases.
Collins Bartholomew, the UK's leading independent geographical information supplier,
can provide a digital, custom, and premium mapping service to a variety of markets.
For further information:
Tel: +44 (0) 208 307 4515
e-mail: collinsbartholomew@harpercollins.co.uk
or visit our website at: www.collinsbartholomew.com

If you would like to comment on any aspect of this book, please write to:
Collins Maps, HarperCollins Publishers, Westerhill Road, Bishopbriggs, Glasgow G64 2QT
e-mail: collinsmaps@harpercollins.co.uk
or visit our website at: www.collinsmaps.com

 Follow us @collinsmaps

Contents

Introduction

In this book you will find detailed all the main routes to the highest peaks of England, Scotland and Wales. Most of the routes are essentially mountain walks, though a number of the logical lines of approach cross ground of a more precipitous nature and therefore are classified as scrambles. The information provided is based around a series of 3-D maps, which cover each route separately, together with overview 3-D maps, crag diagrams, photographs and text. Each route describes an ascent and, where safe, a descent. Link routes between adjacent peaks are also described.

PEAK SELECTION

The initial idea for this guidebook was to select and detail the most significant peaks in England, Scotland and Wales, which could be most accurately described as Britain's highest peaks. After much consideration I decided that peaks over 3000ft in England and Wales gave a suitable cross section, while Scotland, with hundreds of mountains over 3000ft, warranted a higher contour. I therefore chose the 4000ft mark, which isolated a manageable selection of fine peaks.

It is widely accepted that in England there are four 3000ft mountains with four subsidiary tops. Since the introduction of metric mapping, nine distinct 4000ft mountains with seven subsidiary tops can be identified in Scotland. For the purposes of this guide I judged that Sgòr an Lochain Uaine was so close to Cairn Toul that it should be treated as part of the same mountain to save undue route duplication. Scotland therefore has eight mountains listed.

Wales, however, has traditionally claimed fourteen 3000ft peaks (fifteen since metric mapping). For the purposes of this book, I am following Irvine Butterfield's lead by adopting the same criteria for re-classifying the Welsh 3000ft mountains and tops as described in his excellent book *The High Mountains of Britain and Ireland* (Diadem Books, 1986): 'To qualify as a separate mountain a "top" must have 250ft [76m] of ascent on all sides or, alternatively, must be separated from another

The aim of this guide is to provide a flexible approach to route planning. Sufficient information is given to allow various combinations of ascent, descent and links between peaks to be plotted on a map (Ordnance Survey, Harvey, or British Mountain Maps) so that a selection of routes over your choice of peak (or peaks) may be compiled. The book comes in both print and digital formats and although the smaller print and digital versions are easily carried on the hill they should not be used as a navigational tool. Correctly used, only a map and compass can provide the level of navigational information to safely traverse potentially dangerous mountain terrain.

mountain by an interval exceeding 2 miles [3.2km].' This gives a total of eight distinct mountains for Wales without the confusing overlap of routes had the full fifteen been detailed.

Nearing the top of the Carn Dearg (Southwest Path) on Ben Nevis

USING THIS GUIDE

This guide is designed to be used in conjunction with Ordnance Survey or Harvey maps to aid in the selection of routes up and down Britain's highest mountains. The relevant maps for use on each peak are listed at the beginning of each chapter. The 1:50 000 OS Landranger series gives good general coverage but for the more complicated approaches the 1:25 000 Outdoor Leisure/Explorer, Harvey Superwalker, or British Mountain Maps (1:40 000) are recommended. The nomenclature is derived from the latest Ordnance Survey mapping on general release. Some of the names and spellings on Ordnance Survey maps may differ from those known locally; however, for purposes of cross-reference and accurate navigation it was deemed safer to be consistent with the best mapping available at the time of writing.

The peaks in this guide are broken down into national sections, and then into chapters in order of height. Within each chapter information is provided by a combination of illustrations, photographs and text.

Illustrations

Relief maps: Relief maps, drawn in perspective, outline the course of each route denoted by a red dashed line (alternative route shown by a red dotted line).

Crag diagrams: Line illustrations generally highlighting the course of routes over ground of a confusing or difficult nature.

Photographs

Photographs are used at two levels: first to give an overall impression of each peak so that it can be identified, and second to highlight its most attractive features. The majority of these photographs were taken during spells of settled or clear weather and so can be a little misleading – such conditions being the exception rather than the rule on Britain's highest mountains.

Star rating

The star rating is my attempt to give an indication of quality in order to help with route choice. All routes in this book are worthwhile undertakings otherwise they would not have made the cut.

★   above average routes
★★   routes of notable quality
★★★   best routes in Britain

My ratings are, however, very subjective and only my personal opinion after 30 years' experience of climbing these mountains. Weather, time of year, friends and my particular preference for mountaineering-style routes will all have influenced my ratings.

Route Title

For ease of cross-reference with the maps, illustrations and photographs, each route is individually named. Where there is no obvious evidence of an existing name one has been contrived either from the main feature it ascends or from its general compass direction.

Grades

Routes in this guidebook are graded by their three key elements. These are strenuousness, navigation and technicality. Each element has a level between 1 and 5, the easiest being 1 and the hardest being 5. The grades are allocated to routes under normal ground and weather conditions. However, as with all mountain activities, ground and weather conditions can deteriorate dramatically and make the routes considerably harder or, in some cases, impossible.

Strenuousness

How much time and effort will this route demand of me?

●○○○○ Part day – a morning, afternoon or a summer evening.

●●○○○ Short day – will take most of the day but you will be able to start late in the morning or finish early in the afternoon.

●●●○○ Full day – you will need to start promptly in the morning and will not be finished until teatime.

●●●●○ Very full day – an early start and it will be into evening by the time you have finished.

●●●●● An epic day route or a multi-dayer – routes that could straddle a couple of days.

Navigation

How difficult is the route to follow?

●○○○○ Roads, unmade roads, forest and woodland roads and way-marked paths. All easy to follow.

●●○○○ Valley, moor, hill or mountain paths, which are normally clear but low cloud could affect your ability to follow paths.

●●●○○ Almost pathless in valleys; less clear paths on moors, hills and mountains, but generally following clearly defined hill shapes.

●●●●○ Some paths but not clear, not well used or some confusion possible.

●●●●● Open moorland, mountain plateau or crag without paths. Route confusion likely and close attention to navigation needed at all times.

Scafell and Scafell Pike from summit of Little Stand

Technicality – Walks
How tricky will I find it?

●○○○○ Easy walks in gentle countryside.

●●○○○ Unthreatening slopes with no exposure.

●●●○○ Typical fell walk – rough, rocky ground, bogs and steeper slopes.

●●●●○ Steep, rough ground and scree. Occasional exposure.

●●●●● Hands required for at least one move – airy and steep throughout.

Scramble/Climbs
Specific scrambling or winter climbing grades have been added where appropriate.

●○○ Grade 1 scramble: simple route that has difficulties, which are short and/or avoidable.

●●○ Grade 2 scramble: more sustained difficulties with greater exposure.

●●● Grade 3 scramble: serious routes, which are exposed and can involve easy rock climbing.

●○ Grade 1 winter climb: simple snow climb up gullies or buttresses, which may carry cornices.

●● Grade 2 winter climb: more serious route involving minor pitches on snow, ice and rock.

Route Descriptions

 Start: Located at the most convenient road head; indicated by name and by a six-figure grid reference (the relevant maps are listed at the beginning of each chapter).

 Time: The times listed are for *ascent only* – it is safe to assume that the descent will take a similar time, particularly if you have no prior knowledge of it. A combination of personal experience and Naismith's Rule – 5km per hour plus half an hour for every 300m of ascent (3 miles per hour plus half an hour for every 1000ft of ascent) – has been used to calculate the times.

 Height gain: The total amount of ascent involved.

Terrain: A brief listing of the typical terrain encountered along the route.

 Variation: A description of possible alternative starts, finishes or detours.

Summary: Brief outline of the route, to aid selection.

Ascent: Point-to-point description, so that the route can be identified on the relevant map.

Descent: Point-to-point description reversing the ascent, although the route may vary slightly to avoid dangerous ground which cannot be seen from above. **If the route has not been described in descent it cannot be recommended as such by the author.**

MOUNTAIN SAFETY
Mountain walking, scrambling and climbing are potentially very dangerous pursuits and no more so than when carried out on Britain's highest mountains. The terrain and weather conditions encountered can vary from easy-angled grassland to thousand-foot cliffs and from sweltering sunshine to blizzards of arctic proportions. It is possible to experience such ranges of terrain and conditions in one day and on one mountain, and it is therefore essential that you have the experience and equipment to deal with them.

For those new to mountaineering it is recommended that they, either take a basic course, join a club or enlist the assistance of experienced friends. To start with they should build up to the peaks detailed in this book by attempting hills or mountains that are less demanding.

The potential for accidents is always present and it is important that you take every step to prepare for them. To deal with them on the hill it is important that you carry basic survival and first-aid equipment. Apart from normal mountaineering clothing and equipment you should carry the following:

- Map of the relevant area and compass. GPS devices and smartphones can prove to be useful navigational tools and are worth taking; however, because of reception issues and the relative shortness of battery life they should not be relied upon alone.
- First-aid kit.
- Survival bag – 2.4m x 1.2m (8ft x 4ft) 500 gauge polythene bag.
- Whistle – the International Alpine Distress Signal is six blasts followed by a pause of a minute then a repetition; the reply is three blasts.
- Torch – the International Alpine Distress Signal is six flashes followed by a pause of a minute then a repetition; the reply is three flashes.
- Emergency rations.

To help rescue services find you, should you be unable to deal with an accident yourself, you should leave the following information with a responsible person:

- Name and home address.
- Times of departure and expected arrival.
- Planned route with grid references and basic directions.
- Any possible route variations.
- Possible escape routes.
- Details of medical problems.

Avalanches
On routes listed in this guide the risk of avalanche or cornice collapse is a real danger in winter. Assessing the risks involved and avoiding danger areas are key skills for anybody venturing onto Britain's mountains in the winter. Winter skills courses or time spent with a mountain guide/instructor are good approaches in building the necessary skill sets. There are also numerous specialist books on the topic. In Scotland during the winter season avalanche forecasts are issued by the Sport Scotland Avalanche Information Service and are posted at key road heads or with outdoor providers. Forecasts are also available on line at www.sais.gov.uk. For England and Wales there is no specific service although national park rangers in both the Lake District and Snowdonia sometimes issue warnings.

THE ENVIRONMENT
Britain's highest mountains are among the finest examples of mountain wilderness in western Europe and it is the responsibility of every mountain user that they remain so. Compared with the activities of agriculture, industry and commerce, the effect on this sensitive environment by mountaineers is small but nevertheless significant.

When embarking on a trip to the mountains we should carefully consider the environmental consequences of our activities. It should be easy enough to follow simple practices such as taking our waste home, but it is far harder, for example, not to disturb breeding birds (which may involve a long detour) or to use public transport instead of the more convenient car.

As regular users of the mountain environment, mountaineers are in an ideal position to monitor any abuses of it. If we genuinely wish to ensure the survival of the small amount of wilderness we have, it is important both to minimise our own impact on the environment and to campaign vigorously against its abuse by others.

ACCESS AND RIGHTS OF WAY
Although every care has been taken in the preparation of this guidebook, the representation of any route in no way constitutes evidence of the existence of public access or a right of way. If in any doubt, either check the Definitive Maps, which are held by the appropriate County Councils and National Park Authorities, or seek the landowner's permission.

The Scottish Mountaineering Trust in conjunction with the Scottish Landowners' Federation has produced a useful book, *Heading for the Scottish Hills* (ISBN 0-907521-24X), which provides names and contact addresses of landowners. It covers all the Scottish mountains dealt with in this guide. Useful addresses for the English and Welsh peaks are: Lake District National Park Authority, Murley Moss, Oxenholme Road, Kendal, LA9 7RL and Snowdonia National Park, National Park Office, Penrhyndeudraeth, Gwynedd LL48 6LF.

. . . AND FINALLY
Please remember that mountains can be dangerous places and are ventured onto at your own risk. This book is *not* an instruction manual and neither the author nor the publishers accept any responsibility for any accident, injury, loss or damage sustained while following any of the routes or procedures described.

Seemingly benign slopes can hold considerable risk; this slope on the west side of Coire an Lochain in the Cairngorms has been the site of numerous avalanches

England's 3000ft Mountains

England has four mountains that can claim to be separate 3000ft (914m) peaks. They all lie within the boundaries of the Lake District National Park and form three separate groupings. Scafell Pike and Scafell are part of the Scafell massif which lies in the southern fells. Helvellyn, within the eastern fells, lies adjacent to the main Ambleside to Keswick road. Skiddaw lies north of Keswick in the northern fells.

The three distinct groupings of mountains, each with very different terrain, create a wide network of individual routes, from easy walks over the grassy flanks of Skiddaw to the hardest grade of scrambling on Scafell's mighty crags.

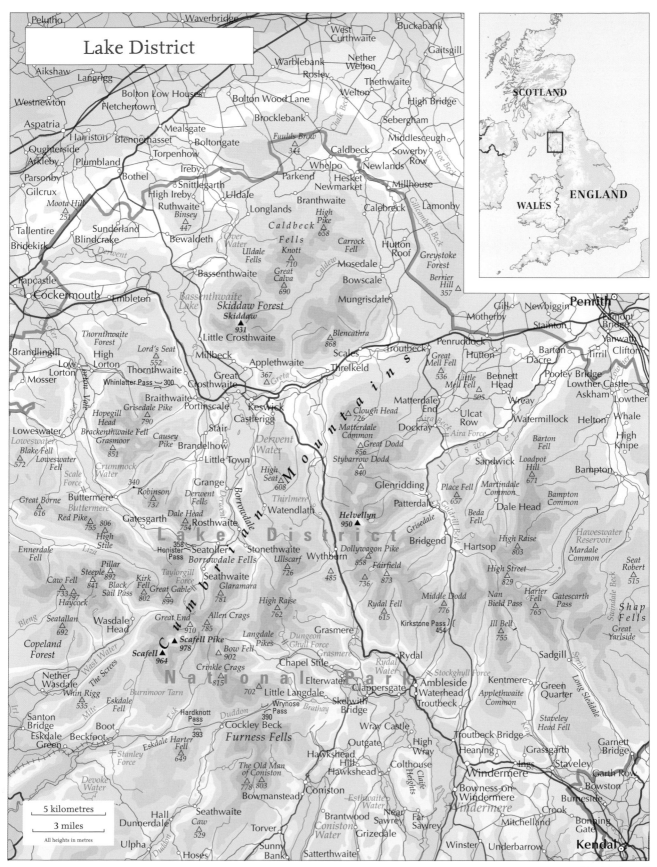

Lake District

SCOTLAND

ENGLAND

WALES

Scafell Pike
978m (3208ft)

Ill Crag 935m (3068ft)
Broad Crag 934m (3064ft)

Scafell Pike is England's highest mountain; it is suitably grand, suitably rocky and suitably inaccessible. At the very heart of the Lake District's central mountain range it lies adjacent to Esk Hause from where all the main valleys radiate. The closest valley to Scafell Pike's summit is Wasdale, which lies to the northwest. Next nearest on the south and east side is Eskdale, while Borrowdale and Langdale share a watershed to the north and east at Esk Hause.

Scafell Pike is a distinct domed peak on a high rocky ridge, and it shares this main ridge with Ill Crag, Broad Crag and Great End. To the southwest along the same ridge line, but across the deep gap of Mickledore, it is linked to Scafell, England's second-highest mountain. The length of this ridge is predominantly exposed rock. Each of the individual peaks has its own set of crags and Scafell Pike is no exception: the Wasdale face is occupied by the broken columns and narrow gullies of Pikes Crag, while at a slightly lower level on the Eskdale side, presiding over the marshy flats of Great Moss, is Esk Buttress.

Each of the approach routes to Scafell Pike has a special quality, none of which could be described as easy. The shortest route, directly up the moraine of Brown Tongue, is an unremitting slog which

When you arrive

Ordnance Survey: Explorer OL4 & OL6 (1:25 000); Landranger 89, 90 & 96 (1:50 000).
Harvey Mountain Maps: Western Lakeland (1:25 000)
British Mountain Maps: Lake District (1:40 000)

Tourist Information Centres: Windermere: *Brockhole*; Ambleside; Keswick.

Youth Hostels: Eskdale: *Boot*; Wasdale: *Wasdale Hall*; Borrowdale: *Longthwaite*; Langdale: *Elterwater*.
Hotels and B&B: Eskdale: *Boot* and *Eskdale Green*; Wasdale: *Wasdale Head, Nether Wasdale* and *Santon Bridge*; Borrowdale: *Seathwaite, Seatoller, Stonethwaite, Rosthwaite* and *Grange*; Langdale: *Elterwater, Chapel Stile, New Dungeon Ghyll* and *Old Dungeon Ghyll*.

Camp sites: Eskdale: *Boot* and *Eskdale Green*; Wasdale: *Wasdale Head, Nether Wasdale* and *Santon Bridge*; Borrowdale: *Seathwaite, Seatoller, Longthwaite* and *Grange*; Langdale: *near the Old Dungeon Ghyll (National Trust)* and *Chapel Stile*.

Bothies and Howffs: Hollow Stones, GR NY208070 – built-up boulder that provides a very rough bivouac shelter. Sampson's Stones, GR NY218054 – numerous built-up boulders that provide rough bivouac shelter.

Scafell Pike's trig point

Burnthwaite
Wasdale Head
Brackenclose
Wast Water
Burnm
Tarn
Bo
Dalegarth
Sta.

Scafell Pike

has the advantage of leading to Hollow Stones, a magnificent setting right at the base of Pikes and Scafell Crags. From the north the routes either follow the Corridor Route, which traverses a rough terrace high above the upper reaches of Wasdale, or take the main ridge direct. The main ridge can be gained at a number of points, most popularly by Calf Cove; for the more adventurous a combination of Skew Gill and Cust's Gully gives a circuitous but excellent scramble. For those who do not mind a bit of a trek there are the wilderness delights of Upper Eskdale. This northerly extension to Eskdale has not been penetrated by roads and has not suffered the agricultural tinkering apparent in other valleys.

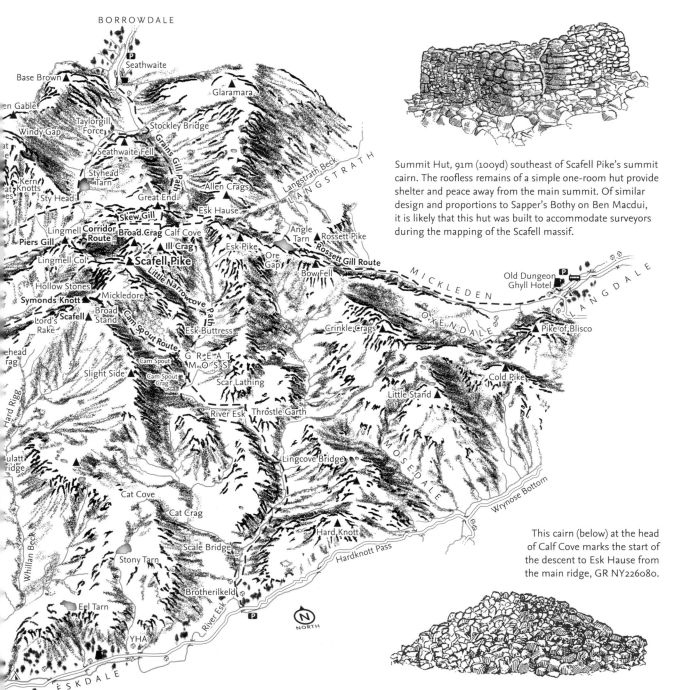

Summit Hut, 91m (100yd) southeast of Scafell Pike's summit cairn. The roofless remains of a simple one-room hut provide shelter and peace away from the main summit. Of similar design and proportions to Sapper's Bothy on Ben Macdui, it is likely that this hut was built to accommodate surveyors during the mapping of the Scafell massif.

This cairn (below) at the head of Calf Cove marks the start of the descent to Esk Hause from the main ridge, GR NY226080.

Little Narrowcove Path SCAFELL PIKE

'Wild and remote' ★★

Summary: Remote and wild, Little Narrowcove provides a fine route to Scafell Pike. It is reached by an approach along Upper Eskdale and a traverse across the bogs of Great Moss.

Ascent: Follow the lane towards the farm then take the narrow path alongside the River Esk. Head NE along Upper Eskdale to Lingcove Bridge. Cross it ascending the path N to Scar Lathing veering W onto Great Moss. Head N to an old wall and follow it alongside the River Esk past Esk Buttress to where the beck issuing from Little Narrowcove enters the river. Ford the Esk and climb the fellside on the southwest side of the beck to a shallow gully which is followed NW into Little Narrowcove proper. Continue NW up through the cove to the col, then turn L and climb the rocky path SW to Scafell Pike.

Descent: Head NE down to the col dropping SE into Little Narrowcove. Near the bottom the path becomes vague and is followed down a shallow gully on the southwest side of the cove. Drop down the fellside then ford the River Esk (difficult in spate) and turn S alongside the river and old wall to Scar Lathing. Follow the

path E along the south side of Scar Lathing then head S to drop down to Lingcove Bridge. Cross it and follow the path SW along Upper Eskdale to Brotherilkeld.

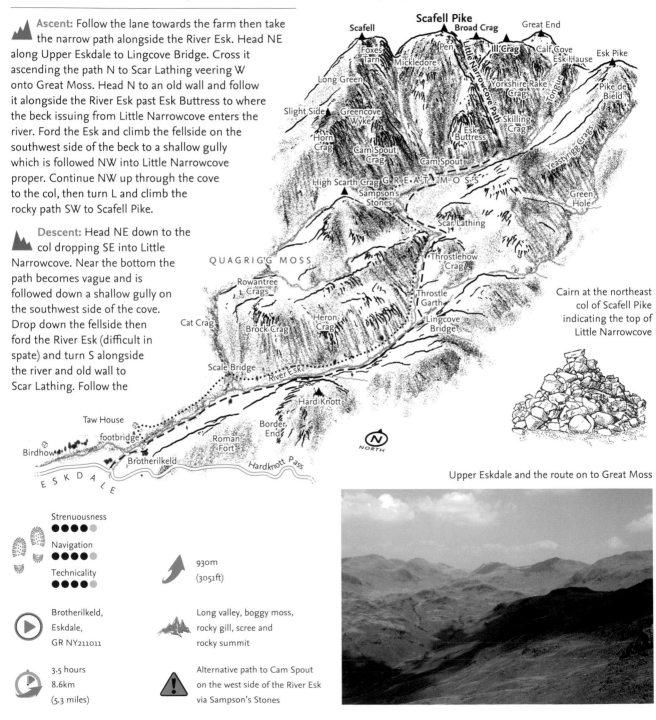

Cairn at the northeast col of Scafell Pike indicating the top of Little Narrowcove

Upper Eskdale and the route on to Great Moss

Strenuousness ●●●●○

Navigation ●●●●○

Technicality ●●●●○

930m
(3051ft)

Brotherilkeld,
Eskdale,
GR NY211011

Long valley, boggy moss, rocky gill, scree and rocky summit

3.5 hours
8.6km
(5.3 miles)

Alternative path to Cam Spout on the west side of the River Esk via Sampson's Stones

Cam Spout Route SCAFELL PIKE

'Remote easy scramble' ★ ★ ★

Summary: An easy scramble at the side of the spectacular Cam Spout Force is reached by an approach along Upper Eskdale and a traverse across the bogs of Great Moss. Above Cam Spout, Scafell Pike is reached via Mickledore.

▲ **Ascent:** Follow the lane towards the farm taking the narrow path alongside the River Esk. Head NE along Upper Eskdale to Lingcove Bridge. Cross it and climb the path N to Scar Lathing turning W onto Great Moss. Head N to an old wall and follow it to where How Beck enters the River Esk. Ford the river (difficult in spate) and head NW to Cam Spout. Climb the rocks on the east side of the waterfall continuing up the gill to Mickledore. At the stretcher box turn R and follow the rough path NE to Scafell Pike.

▲ **Descent:** Take the rough path SW down to Mickledore turning SE and descend the gill to the top of Cam Spout. Scramble down the northeast side of the waterfall then follow How Beck until it joins the River Esk. Ford the river and then turn S alongside an old wall to Scar Lathing. Follow the path E along the south side of Scar Lathing

then head S dropping down to Lingcove Bridge. Cross it and follow the path SW along Upper Eskdale to Brotherilkeld.

Strenuousness
● ● ● ● ○

Navigation
● ● ● ● ○

Technicality
● ● ● ● ○

Brotherilkeld, Eskdale, GR NY211011 ▶

3.5 hours
8.3km
(5.1 miles)

945m
(3100ft)

Long valley, boggy moss, rocky gill, scree and rocky summit

Alternative path to Cam Spout on the west side of the River Esk via Sampson's Stones ⚠

Cam Spout and Scafell Pike from Sampson's Stones on Great Moss

Brown Tongue Path SCAFELL PIKE

'A slog with a view'

Summary: Follows the course of Lingmell Beck then climbs the steep, unremitting moraine of Brown Tongue. Hard work, but a fine route with ever-expanding views of Pikes Crag and Scafell Crag.

Ascent: Take the permissive path past Brackenclose then cross Lingmell Gill by the footbridge. On the other side follow the path E alongside the beck to the ford at the foot of Brown Tongue. Cross the ford and climb the steep path up Brown Tongue to the boulders at Hollow Stones. Take the constructed path NE to Lingmell Col. Turn R and follow the pitched path as it snakes SE to Scafell Pike.

Descent: Take the rough path NW down to Lingmell Col then turn SW and descend the constructed path to Hollow Stones. Make the steep descent down Brown Tongue to the ford, cross this and head W on the north side of Lingmell Gill to the footbridge. Cross this and take the permissive path past Brackenclose onto the camp site.

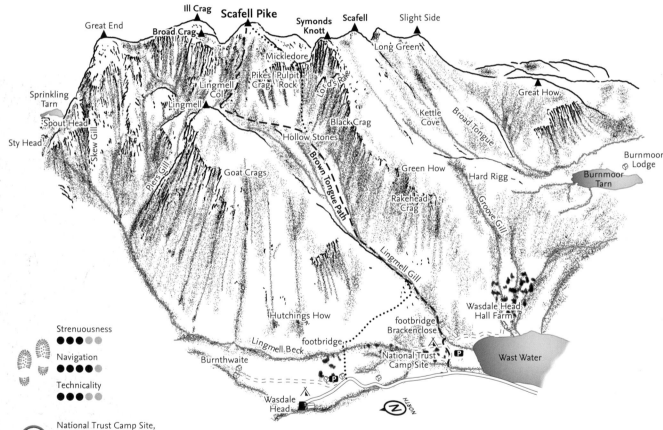

Strenuousness

Navigation

Technicality

 Gill, steep moraine, boulders, scree and rocky summit

 Alternative start from Wasdale Head (GR NY186083) via footbridge over Lingmell Beck

National Trust Camp Site, Wasdale Head, GR NY181074

2.5 hours
4km
(2.5 miles)

910m
(2986ft)

Brackenclose on the south side of Lingmell Gill, southeast of the National Trust Camp Site at Wasdale Head, GR NY184073. The permissive path at the side of the FRCC climbing hut provides access to the Brown Tongue Path.

RIGHT
Brown Tongue and Pikes Crag

Corridor Route SCAFELL PIKE

'Ingenious traverse' ★ ★ ★

Summary: Traverses the northwest side of the main Scafell Pike ridge from Sty Head to Lingmell Col then climbs direct to the summit. A particularly fine route taking in some of England's finest mountain scenery.

Ascent: Take the bridleway S to Stockley Bridge, cross it and climb the steep zigzags W then head SW alongside Styhead Gill to Styhead Tarn. Turn E at the stretcher box and follow the bridleway a short distance to a fork. Take the R branch and descend onto the Corridor Route which is followed as it climbs steadily SSW to Lingmell Col. Turn L and follow the pitched path over scree and boulders SE to Scafell Pike.

Descent: Head NW down the boulders and scree (pitched path) to Lingmell Col and join the Corridor Route

(care should be taken at this point to establish you are on the Corridor Route, particularly in mist, as it is easy to stray onto the Piers Gill path, or even into Piers Gill) which is taken NNE to the Sty Head bridleway. Turn W and follow the bridleway to Sty Head. From Sty Head take the bridleway NE alongside the gill then E down to Stockley Bridge. Cross the bridge and head N to Seathwaite.

Strenuousness
● ● ● ○ ○

Navigation
● ● ● ● ○

Technicality
● ● ● ○ ○

Seathwaite,
Borrowdale,
GR NY235121

3–3.5 hours
7.2km
(4.5 miles)

895m
(2936ft)

Valley, rocky gill,
rough craggy fellside,
scree and rocky summit

⚠ Can be gained from Wasdale Head (GR NY187088) by following either the bridleway to Sty Head or the path alongside Lingmell Beck then on the east side of Piers Gill. The main ridge at a point between Great End and Ill Crag can easily be reached from the Corridor Route via either Greta Gill or Lambfoot Dub.

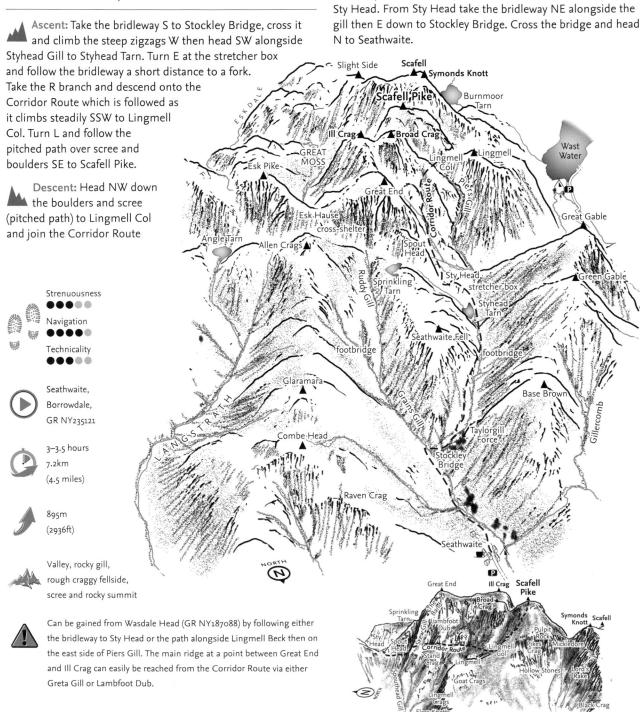

Skew Gill and Great End SCAFELL PIKE

'Atmospheric scramble' ★★

Summary: An adventurous approach to the main Scafell Pike ridge via the terminal peak of Great End. Skew Gill, which holds one steep section, gives access to The Band, a broad ridge that climbs the north end of Great End Crag. Along the way you can peer down into the impressive depths of Cust's Gully capped with its famous chockstone.

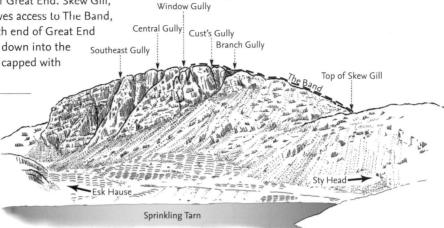

G R E A T E N D
Window Gully
Central Gully
Cust's Gully
Southeast Gully
Branch Gully
The Band
Top of Skew Gill
Esk Hause
Sty Head
Sprinkling Tarn

Ascent: Take the bridleway S to Stockley Bridge, cross it and climb the steep zigzags W then head SW alongside Styhead Gill to Styhead Tarn. Turn E at the stretcher box and follow the bridleway a short distance to a fork. Take the R branch and descend onto the Corridor Route which is followed to Skew Gill. Climb SE up the bed of Skew Gill to the steeper section which is passed on the L and continue to the col. From the col scramble the broad ridge above, SSE to the summit rocks of Great End. Descend SE to the head of Calf Cove then join the main ridge path past Ill Crag and Broad Crag to Scafell Pike.

Great End from Sprinkling Tarn

The stretcher box at Sty Head – a major crossroads for access to the central fells

Stockley Bridge, 1.2km (0.75 miles) south of Seathwaite, indicates the start of both the Grains Gill Path and the Sty Head bridleway.

Strenuousness
●●●●●

Navigation
●●●●○

Technicality
●●●●●

Scramble/Winter climb
●●○/●●

Seathwaite, Borrowdale, GR NY235121

4 hours
7.7km
(4.8 miles)

1030m
(3379ft)

Valley, rocky gill, gullies, rough mountain ridge and rocky summit

Grains Gill SCAFELL PIKE

'Efficient descent' ★

Summary: Direct route from Borrowdale to the north end of the Scafell massif via Esk Hause. Useful as a descent route or to avoid the crowds at Sty Head.

Ascent: Take the bridleway S past Stockley Bridge then L up Grains Gill to join the Esk Hause bridleway, turn L and follow it to the shelter near Esk Hause. Turn R and take the path W over Esk Hause and up through Calf Cove. At the top of the cove turn SW and follow the path past Ill Crag and Broad Crag to Scafell Pike.

Descent: Head NE along the main ridge past Broad Crag and Ill Crag to the top of Calf Cove. Drop down through the cove and follow the path to Esk Hause, then turn NE to join the bridleway by the shelter. Follow it NW to the head of Grains Gill which is then descended N past Stockley Bridge to Seathwaite.

Strenuousness
●●●●○○

Navigation
●●●●●○

Technicality
●●●○○○

Seathwaite,
Borrowdale,
GR NY235121

3 hours
7km
(4.3 miles)

925m
(3035ft)

Steep-sided valley, exposed col, stony cove, rough mountain ridge and rocky summit

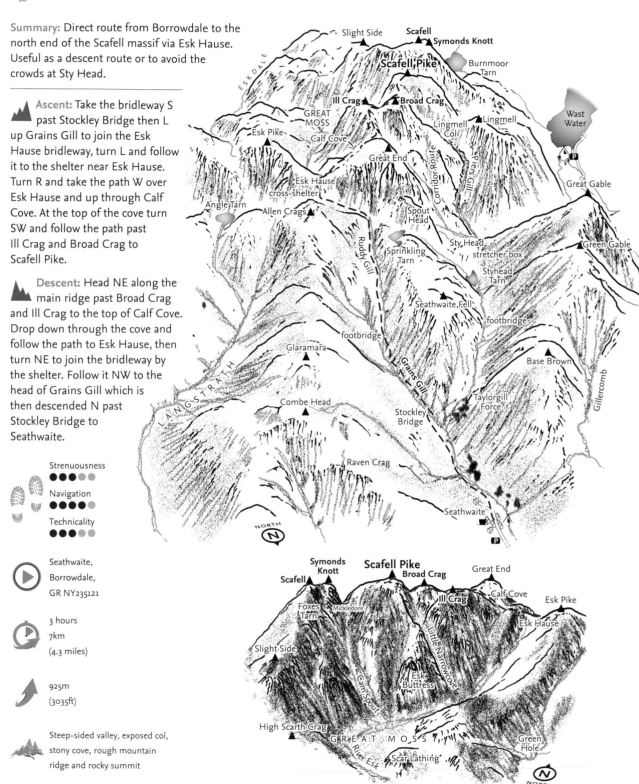

From Langdale via Rossett Gill

SCAFELL PIKE

'Epic test piece' ★★

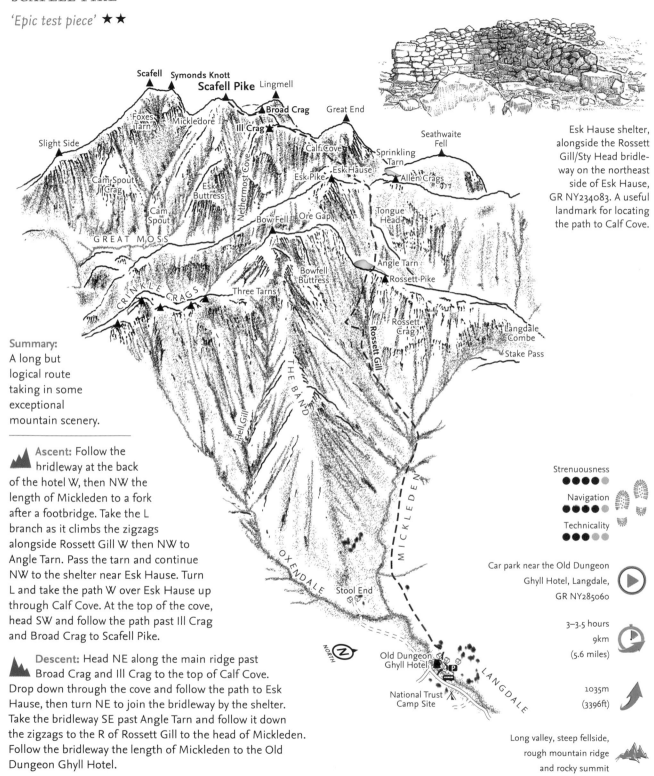

Esk Hause shelter, alongside the Rossett Gill/Sty Head bridleway on the northeast side of Esk Hause, GR NY234083. A useful landmark for locating the path to Calf Cove.

Summary:
A long but logical route taking in some exceptional mountain scenery.

Ascent: Follow the bridleway at the back of the hotel W, then NW the length of Mickleden to a fork after a footbridge. Take the L branch as it climbs the zigzags alongside Rossett Gill W then NW to Angle Tarn. Pass the tarn and continue NW to the shelter near Esk Hause. Turn L and take the path W over Esk Hause up through Calf Cove. At the top of the cove, head SW and follow the path past Ill Crag and Broad Crag to Scafell Pike.

Descent: Head NE along the main ridge past Broad Crag and Ill Crag to the top of Calf Cove. Drop down through the cove and follow the path to Esk Hause, then turn NE to join the bridleway by the shelter. Take the bridleway SE past Angle Tarn and follow it down the zigzags to the R of Rossett Gill to the head of Mickleden. Follow the bridleway the length of Mickleden to the Old Dungeon Ghyll Hotel.

Strenuousness
●●●●○

Navigation
●●●●○

Technicality
●●●○○

Car park near the Old Dungeon Ghyll Hotel, Langdale, GR NY285060

3–3.5 hours
9km
(5.6 miles)

1035m
(3396ft)

Long valley, steep fellside, rough mountain ridge and rocky summit

Scafell

964m (3163ft)

Symonds Knott 959m (3146ft)

Although not as high as Scafell Pike, Scafell is by far the more impressive of the two peaks. Its long southern ridge dominates Upper Eskdale and the wilderness of Great Moss, while Scafell Crag's great north face is one of the most awe-inspiring cliffs in Britain. It draws the eye with its steep and complex geometry of dihedrals, blank walls and deep gullies. A mecca for climbers in both summer and winter, it has produced routes of particularly high quality. From the very first days of climbing, routes have been put up on Scafell Crag which set the standard of the time, both on rock and on snow and ice.

Walkers too can find adventure among the acres of rock of Scafell's north face, for although the cliffs may seem impossibly steep, there are a number of breaks and weaknesses which can be followed without recourse to ropes and belays. Most popular of these is Lord's Rake, which follows a diagonal line across the top of Shamrock Buttress. A variant to this is West Wall Traverse, which takes an exposed line into the secretive depths of Deep Gill. Infamous, rather than famous, is Broad Stand, a fierce little scramble, which climbs the low rocks at Mickledore. Many people have come to grief on this short but problematic section of rock.

The western side of Scafell is unrecognisable as the same mountain. Essentially one huge grassy slope it descends uninterrupted to the bleak moorland plateau occupied by Burnmoor Tarn. The routes up this side are easy but a little monotonous. However, this does not detract from their quality, for although there is little of interest close at hand the views are superb. In the middle distance towards the west is the restless prospect of Wast Water tucked behind the screes and crags of Illgill Head, while to the south is the wooded softness of Eskdale. Filling the horizon is the Irish Sea. On clear days the mountains of Snowdonia, the Isle of Man and the Solway Firth are all visible.

When you arrive

Ordnance Survey: Explorer OL4 & OL6 (1:25 000); Landranger 89, 90 & 96 (1:50 000).

Harvey Mountain Maps: Western Lakeland (1:25 000)

British Mountain Maps: Lake District (1:40 000)

Tourist Information Centres: Windermere: *Brockhole*; Ambleside; Keswick.

Youth Hostels: Eskdale: *Boot*; Wasdale; Wasdale Hall; Borrowdale: *Longthwaite*; Langdale: *Elterwater*.

Hotels and B&B: Eskdale: *Boot* and *Eskdale Green*; Wasdale: *Wasdale Head*, *Nether Wasdale* and *Santon Bridge*; Borrowdale: *Seathwaite*, *Seatoller*, *Stonethwaite*, *Rosthwaite* and *Grange*; Langdale: *Elterwater*, *Chapel Stile*, *New Dungeon Ghyll* and *Old Dungeon Ghyll*.

Scafell's summit rocks are marked by a scrappy cairn. Many people mistakenly head for the more spectacularly situated but lower cairn on Symonds Knott.

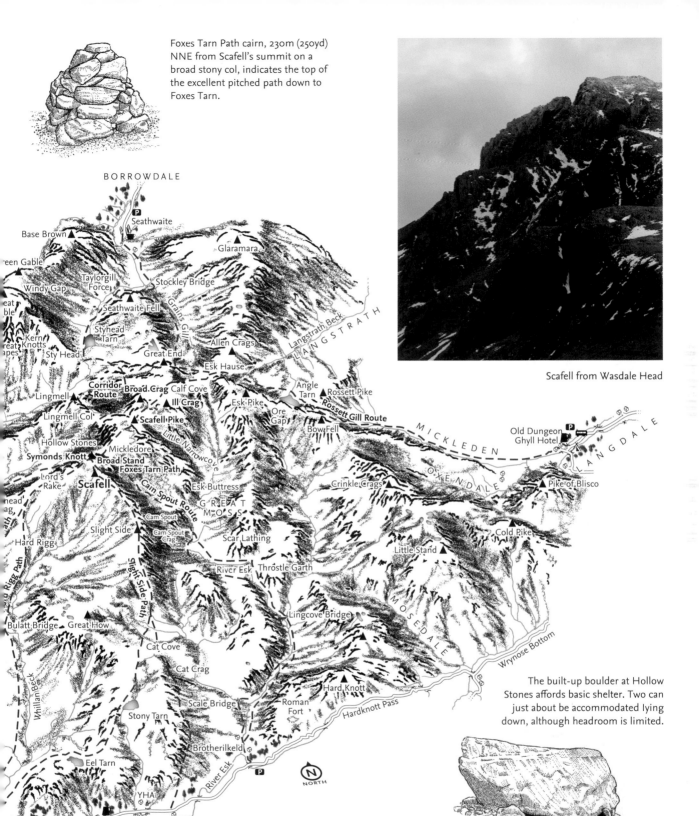

Foxes Tarn Path cairn, 230m (250yd) NNE from Scafell's summit on a broad stony col, indicates the top of the excellent pitched path down to Foxes Tarn.

Scafell from Wasdale Head

The built-up boulder at Hollow Stones affords basic shelter. Two can just about be accommodated lying down, although headroom is limited.

BORROWDALE

Base Brown
reen Gable
Windy Gap
Seathwaite
Taylorgill Force
Seathwaite Fell
Glaramara
Stockley Bridge
Grains Gill
Langstrath Beck
LANGSTRATH
Kern Knotts
reat
apes
Sty Head
Styhead Tarn
Great End
Allen Crags
Esk Hause
Lingmell
Corridor Route
Broad Crag
Ill Crag
Calf Cove
Esk Pike
Angle Tarn
Rossett Pike
Rossett Gill Route
MICKLEDEN
Old Dungeon Ghyll Hotel
LANGDALE
Lingmell Col
Scafell Pike
Ore Gap
Bow Fell
Hollow Stones
Mickledore
Little Narrowcove
OXENDALE
Symonds Knott
Broad Stand
Foxes Tarn Path
Lord's Rake
Scafell
Cam Spout Route
Esk Buttress
Crinkle Crags
Pike of Blisco
head
ag,
GREAT MOSS
Cam Spout
Cam Spout Crag
Scar Lathing
Cold Pike
Little Stand
Slight Side
Slight Side Path
Hard Rigg
River Esk
Throstle Garth
MOSEDALE
Rigg Path
Lingcove Bridge
Bulatt Bridge
Great How
Cat Cove
Wrynose Bottom
Whillan Beck
Cat Crag
Scale Bridge
Roman Fort
Hard Knott
Hardknott Pass
Stony Tarn
Brotherilkeld
N
NORTH
Eel Tarn
YHA
ESKDALE

Scafell **21**

Hard Rigg Path SCAFELL

'Steep but rewarding' ★

Summary: The steep western slopes of Scafell have few features, and of these few the most pronounced is Hard Rigg. This grassy ridge is separated from the fellside by Hardrigg Gill and gives easy access to the summit slopes.

Ascent: Take the Burnmoor Tarn bridleway N to a fork just over Bulatt Bridge. Take the vague R branch which climbs Hard Rigg NNE to a levelling near the top of Hardrigg Gill. The path then swings NE then E and is followed up the steep fellside to the summit rocks of Scafell.

Descent: Head W and descend the scree and grass to a levelling at the top of Hardrigg Gill. Descend the grassy ridge on the northwest side of the gill to Bulatt Bridge. Join the bridleway at Burnmoor Tarn and follow it S to Boot.

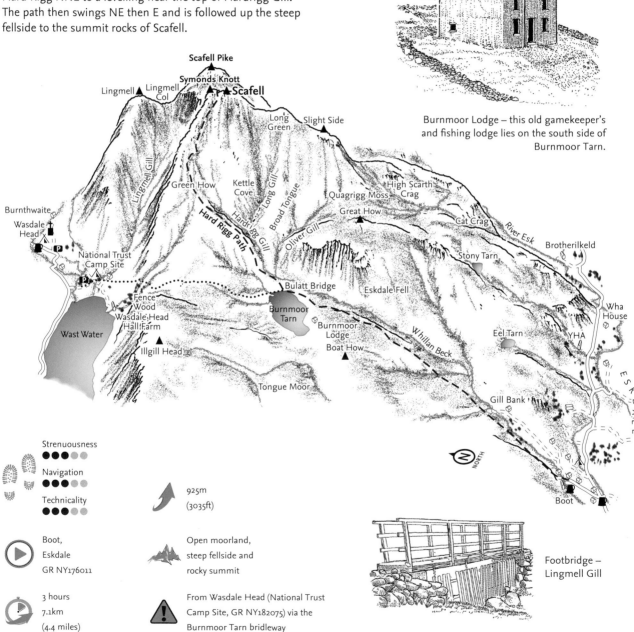

Burnmoor Lodge – this old gamekeeper's and fishing lodge lies on the south side of Burnmoor Tarn.

Footbridge – Lingmell Gill

Strenuousness
●●●○○

Navigation
●●●○○

Technicality
●●●○○

925m
(3035ft)

Boot,
Eskdale
GR NY176011

Open moorland,
steep fellside and
rocky summit

3 hours
7.1km
(4.4 miles)

From Wasdale Head (National Trust
Camp Site, GR NY182075) via the
Burnmoor Tarn bridleway

Slight Side Path SCAFELL

'Long high-level approach' ★★

Summary: Slight Side lies on the long southern ridge of Scafell which extends to the craggy broken fells of Eskdale. It provides a direct and straightforward route useful as a descent route to Eskdale.

 Ascent: From the road head NE along the top of the intake wall then N to Catcove Beck. Ford the beck and make the steady climb N across open fell; the gradient steepens as the path skirts the west side of Horn Crag. A short section of scree and rock steps leads NE onto Slight Side. The ridge line becomes more distinct and is followed NNW to Scafell.

 Descent: Follow the path SSE from the summit rocks to the rocky knoll of Slight Side. A vague path descends SE through the rocks and is then followed S across fellside to Catcove Beck. Cross the beck and continue S along the path. Among the rocky fells the path becomes vague but swings SW to the top of the intake wall and is then followed down to the road.

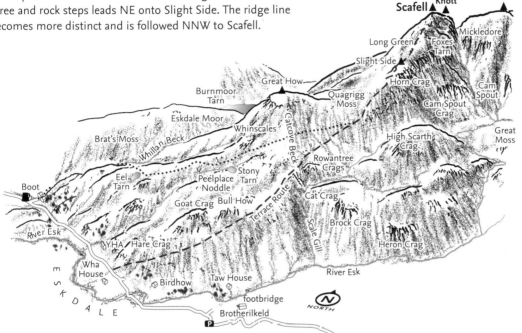

Strenuousness

●●●○○

Navigation

●●●○○

Technicality

●●●○○

Near Wha House Farm in Eskdale, GR NY200009

3 hours 6.3km (3.9 miles)

925m (3035ft)

Craggy fellside, steep-sided ridge and rocky summit

Via Eel Tarn and Stony Tarn from Boot, GR NY176011

Scafell and Slight Side from Eskdale

Brown Tongue Path SCAFELL

'Path slog with a view'

Summary: Follows the course of Lingmell Gill then climbs the steep unremitting moraine (pitched path) of Brown Tongue. Hard work but a fine route rewarded by the ever-expanding views of Scafell Crag and Pikes Crag.

Ascent: Take the permissive path past Brackenclose then cross Lingmell Gill over the footbridge. Once on the other side follow the path E alongside the beck to the ford at the foot of Brown Tongue. Cross the ford and climb the steep path up Brown Tongue to the boulders at Hollow Stones. Lord's Rake starts S at the top of the scree. Follow it first up a loose gully then along a narrow path over two cols to the top of Scafell Crag. Head SE up the final steep and loose slope to a col between Scafell and Symonds Knott. Turn R and make the short pull S to Scafell. Following recent rock slides there is loose rock in the rake and care should be taken to avoid dislodging it and to avoid any dislodged by other parties.

Alternatively, West Wall Traverse can be followed (Grade 1 scramble/Grade 1 winter climb). It starts just below the first col of Lord's Rake and follows a very narrow path L into Deep Gill. Once in the bed of Deep Gill climb direct to the top of Scafell Crag, then head SW across the col to Scafell.

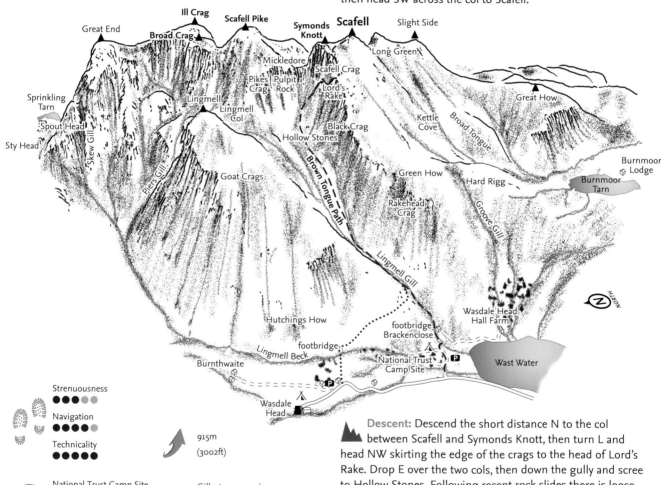

Strenuousness
●●●●○

Navigation
●●●●○

Technicality
●●●●●

 National Trust Camp Site, Wasdale Head, GR NY181074

2.5 hours
3.9km
(2.4 miles)

915m
(3002ft)

 Gill, steep moraine, boulders, scree, crags and rocky summit

⚠️ Alternative start from Wasdale Head (GR NY186083) via footbridge over Lingmell Beck

Descent: Descend the short distance N to the col between Scafell and Symonds Knott, then turn L and head NW skirting the edge of the crags to the head of Lord's Rake. Drop E over the two cols, then down the gully and scree to Hollow Stones. Following recent rock slides there is loose rock in the rake and care should be taken to avoid dislodging it and to avoid any dislodged by other parties. Turn W and make the steep descent down Brown Tongue to a ford, cross this and continue W on the north side of Lingmell Gill to the footbridge. Cross this and take the permissive path past Brackenclose onto the camp site.

Green How Path SCAFELL

'Rewarding descent' ★

Summary: Scafell's north face extends west from Scafell Crag through Shamrock Buttress and Black Crag then peters out among the broken rocks of Rakehead Crag. Running along the top of this long line of crags is the Green How Path which gives a steep direct approach from Wasdale Head – a good descent route.

Ascent: From the camp site take the Burnmoor Tarn bridleway SE then S up through Fence Wood. After the gate turn L off the bridleway and follow the vague path E up the steep fellside to Green How. Continue climbing E as the path becomes more distinct some way back from the edge of Scafell's north-facing crags. The last section ascends scree to arrive at a col between Scafell and Symonds Knott. Turn R and make the short pull S to Scafell.

Descent: Descend the short distance N to the col between Scafell and Symonds Knott, then turn L and head W down the scree. The path continues to descend W (well back from the edge of Scafell's north-facing crags) to the Burnmoor Tarn bridleway at Fence Wood. Join it and follow it N then NW to the camp site.

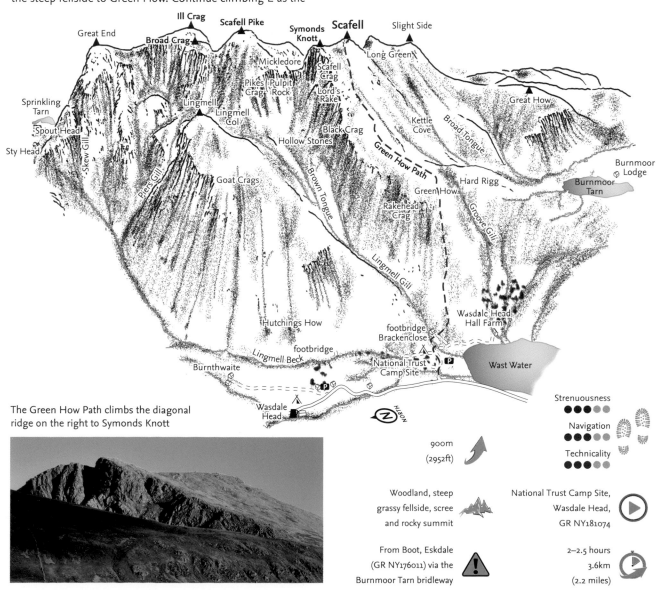

The Green How Path climbs the diagonal ridge on the right to Symonds Knott

900m
(2952ft)

Woodland, steep grassy fellside, scree and rocky summit

From Boot, Eskdale (GR NY176011) via the Burnmoor Tarn bridleway

Strenuousness
●●●●○

Navigation
●●●●○

Technicality
●●●●○

National Trust Camp Site, Wasdale Head, GR NY181074

2–2.5 hours
3.6km
(2.2 miles)

Corridor Route SCAFELL

'Ingenious traverse' ★ ★ ★

Summary: Traverses the northwest side of the main Scafell Pike ridge from Sty Head to Lingmell Col, then skirts under Pikes Crag to Hollow Stones. A particularly fine route taking in some of England's finest mountain scenery.

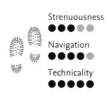 **Ascent:** Take the bridleway S to Stockley Bridge, cross it and climb the steep zigzags W, then head SE alongside Styhead Gill to Styhead Tarn. Turn E at the stretcher box and follow the bridleway to a fork. Take the R branch and descend onto the Corridor Route which is followed as it climbs steadily SSW to Lingmell Col. Cross the col and traverse S below Pikes Crags to Hollow Stones. Lord's Rake starts at the top of the scree to the S. Follow it first up a loose gully then along a narrow path over two cols to the top of Scafell Crag. Head SE up the final slopes to a col between Scafell and Symonds Knott. Turn R and make the short pull S to Scafell. Following recent rock slides there is loose rock in the rake and care should be taken to avoid dislodging it and to avoid any dislodged by other parties.

Alternatively, West Wall Traverse can be followed (Grade 1 scramble/Grade 1 winter climb). It starts just below the first col of Lord's Rake and follows a very narrow path L into Deep Gill. Once in the bed of Deep Gill climb direct to the top of Scafell Crag, then head SW across a col to Scafell.

 Descent: Descend the short distance N to the col between Scafell and Symonds Knott, then turn L and head NW skirting the edge of the crags to the head of Lord's Rake. Drop E over the two cols then down the gully and scree to Hollow Stones. Traverse N below Pikes Crags to Lingmell Col and join the Corridor Route which is taken NNE to the Sty Head bridleway (avoiding false paths beside Piers Gill). Turn W and follow the bridleway to Sty Head. From Sty Head take the bridleway NE alongside the gill, then E down to Stockley Bridge. Cross the bridge and head N to Seathwaite.

Strenuousness
● ● ● ● ○

Navigation
● ● ● ● ○

Technicality
● ● ● ● ●

 Seathwaite, Borrowdale, GR NY235121

 3–3.5 hours
8.4km
(5.2 miles)

 1020m
(3346ft)

 Valley, rocky gill, rough craggy fellside, boulder field, scree, crags and rocky summit

⚠ Can be gained from Wasdale Head (GR NY186087) by following either the bridleway to Sty Head or the path alongside Lingmell Beck, then on the east side of Piers Gill

Cam Spout Route SCAFELL

'Remote easy scramble' ★ ★ ★

Summary: An easy scramble at the side of the spectacular Cam Spout Force is reached by an approach along Upper Eskdale and a traverse across the bogs of Great Moss. Above Cam Spout Scafell can be gained by either Foxes Tarn or Broad Stand.

Ascent: Follow the lane towards the farm then take the narrow path alongside the River Esk. Head NE along Upper Eskdale to Lingcove Bridge. Cross it and climb the path N passing underneath Scar Lathing then W onto Great Moss. Head N to an old wall and follow it to where How Beck enters the River Esk. Ford the river (difficult in spate) and head NW to Cam Spout. Climb the rocks on the east side of the waterfall then follow the path up the gill. At the scree around the base of East Buttress is the Foxes Tarn Path. Follow it SW up the gully to the tarn, behind which take the pitched path NW up the scree to the col between Scafell and Symonds Knott. Turn L and make the short pull to Scafell.

Alternatively continue up the gill to Mickledore to climb Broad Stand (Grade 3 scramble/Difficult climb). Just on the east side of Mickledore climb through the cleft onto the first platform, then traverse L and climb the wall on smooth but sufficient holds onto the second platform. The wall at the back is climbed and easier ground leads across the top of Mickledore Chimney. A groove on the other side then leads to more easy scrambling to the top of the crag. Scafell is a short distance to the SW.

Descent: Descend the short distance N to the col between Scafell and Symonds Knott then turn R and drop SE down the pitched path to Foxes Tarn. At the tarn take the steep rocky path NE down the gully, then head SE down the gill to the top of Cam Spout. Scramble down the northeast side of the waterfall then follow How Beck until it joins the River Esk. Ford the river (difficult in spate) and then turn S alongside an old wall passing underneath to Scar Lathing. Follow the path E along the south side of Scar Lathing, then head S and drop down to Lingcove Bridge. Cross it and follow the path SW along Upper Eskdale to Brotherilkeld.

Strenuousness
● ● ● ● ○

Navigation
● ● ● ● ○

Technicality
● ● ● ● ●

Brotherilkeld,
Eskdale,
GR NY212011

3.5 hours
8km
(5 miles)

930m
(3051ft)

Long valley, boggy moss,
rocky gill, scree, crags and
rocky summit

Alternative path to Cam Spout on
the west side of the River Esk
via Sampson's Stones

Lingcove Bridge was originally a packhorse bridge built for the route to Esk Hause. Once across it, the path steepens and climbs to Scar Lathing and then onto Great Moss.

From Langdale via Rossett Gill SCAFELL

'One of life's big ticks!' ★★

Summary: A classic expedition. Takes a circuitous but logical route along the length of Mickleden then up Rossett Gill and over Scafell Pike via Esk Hause, Ill Crag and Broad Crag.

Ascent: Follow the bridleway at the back of the hotel W, then NW the length of Mickleden to a fork after a footbridge. Take the L branch as it climbs the zigzags alongside Rossett Gill W then NW to Angle Tarn. Pass the tarn and continue NW to the shelter near Esk Hause. Turn L and take the path W over Esk Hause turning R into Calf Cove. At the top of the cove, head SW and follow the path past Ill Crag and Broad Crag to Scafell Pike. Descend SW from the summit cairn to Mickledore – from where there are three possible routes up Scafell Crag.

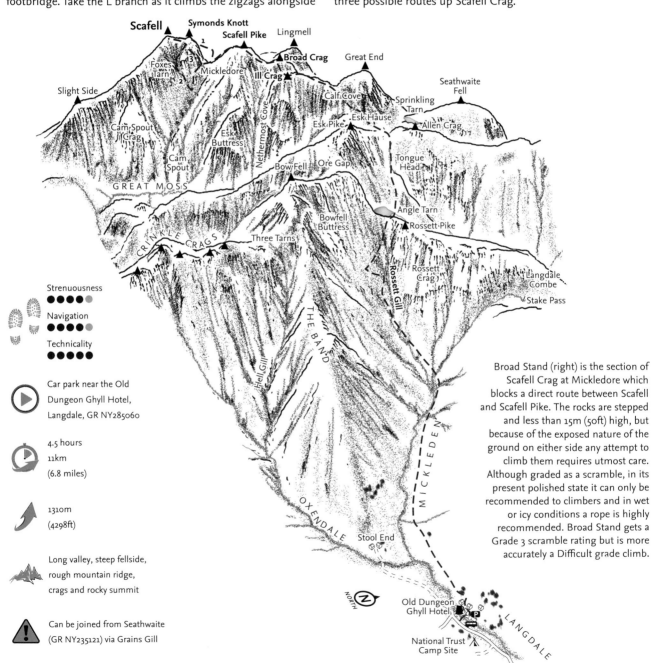

Strenuousness
●●●●○

Navigation
●●●●○

Technicality
●●●●●

Car park near the Old Dungeon Ghyll Hotel, Langdale, GR NY285060

4.5 hours
11km
(6.8 miles)

1310m
(4298ft)

Long valley, steep fellside, rough mountain ridge, crags and rocky summit

Can be joined from Seathwaite (GR NY235121) via Grains Gill

Broad Stand (right) is the section of Scafell Crag at Mickledore which blocks a direct route between Scafell and Scafell Pike. The rocks are stepped and less than 15m (50ft) high, but because of the exposed nature of the ground on either side any attempt to climb them requires utmost care. Although graded as a scramble, in its present polished state it can only be recommended to climbers and in wet or icy conditions a rope is highly recommended. Broad Stand gets a Grade 3 scramble rating but is more accurately a Difficult grade climb.

1. Lord's Rake Traverse W along the base of Scafell Crag by either Rake's Progress or the lower Walkers' Path to the start of Lord's Rake. Follow it first up a loose gully then along a narrow path over two cols to the top of Scafell Crag. Head SE up the final slopes to a col between Scafell and Symonds Knott. Turn R and make the short pull S to Scafell. Following recent rock slides there is loose rock in the rake and care should be taken to avoid dislodging it and to avoid any dislodged by other parties.

2. Foxes Tarn Path Descend the east side of Mickledore skirting around the base of East Buttress to a gully line which leads SW to Foxes Tarn. Behind the tarn take the pitched path NW up the scree to the col between Scafell and Symonds Knott. Turn L and make the short pull to Scafell.

3. Broad Stand (Grade 3 scramble/Difficult climb) On the east side of Mickledore climb through the cleft onto the first platform, then traverse L and climb the wall on smooth but sufficient holds onto the second platform. The wall at the back is climbed and easier ground leads across the top of Mickledore Chimney. A groove on the other side then leads to more easy scrambling to the top of the crag. Scafell is a short distance to the SW.

Alternatively, West Wall Traverse can be followed (Grade 1 scramble/ Grade 1 winter climb). It starts just below the first col of Lord's Rake and follows a very narrow path L into Deep Gill. Once in the bed of Deep Gill climb direct to the top of Scafell Crag, then head SW across the col to Scafell.

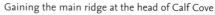
Descent: Mickledore can be gained by two routes.

1. Lord's Rake Descend the short distance N to the col between Scafell and Symonds Knott, then turn L and head NW skirting the edge of the crags to the head of Lord's Rake. Drop E over the two cols, then down the gully to join either Rake's Progress or the Walkers' Path, continuing E around the base of Scafell Crag to Mickledore.

2. Foxes Tarn Path Descend the short distance N to the col between Scafell and Symonds Knott, then turn R and drop SE down the pitched path to Foxes Tarn. At the tarn take the steep rocky path NE down the gully, then skirt the bottom of East Buttress and make the steep climb NW up to Mickledore. From Mickledore follow the path NE over Scafell Pike then past Broad Crag and III Crag to the top of Calf Cove. Drop down through the cove and follow the path to Esk Hause, then turn NE to join the bridleway by the shelter. Take the bridleway SE past Angle Tarn and follow it down the zigzags at Rossett Gill to the head of Mickleden. Follow the bridleway the length of Mickleden to the Old Dungeon Ghyll Hotel.

Gaining the main ridge at the head of Calf Cove

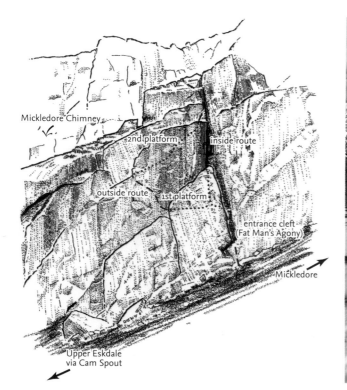

Mickledore Chimney

2nd platform — inside route

outside route — 1st platform

entrance cleft (Fat Man's Agony)

Mickledore

Upper Eskdale via Cam Spout

Helvellyn
950m (3117ft)

Lower Man 925m (3035ft)

Helvellyn is the highest peak along the long ridge of mountains, which runs north from the outskirts of Grasmere to Threlkeld Common just east of Keswick. Thirlmere marks the western boundary, while to the east long arêtes and deep coves extend towards the shores of Ullswater.

The main section of the ridge, centred around Helvellyn, consists of Dollywaggon Pike, Nethermost Pike, Lower Man, Whiteside Bank and Raise. These peaks are so closely linked in terms of both the character of terrain and proximity that any route to Helvellyn's summit inevitably crosses one or more of these satellite tops. The popularity of Helvellyn (perhaps the most climbed mountain in the Lake District) is due to the diversity of routes it offers, the convenience of access and the commanding views it affords.

The western and eastern sides of Helvellyn are as different as the proverbial chalk and cheese. To the west the slopes are generally uniform being wooded below 518m (1700ft) and very steep with few features, save for fast-flowing becks which feed Thirlmere, and the odd grassy hollow. Access is easy, from either Wythburn, Thirlspot or Stanah along the main Lakes road the A591.

The eastern side is a different story: its shaded aspect has led to it being more heavily glaciated, creating long steep-sided dales with wild rocky carries at their heads separated by fine narrow ridges. The most famous of these features are Striding Edge and Swirral Edge. Combined they make a justifiably

When you arrive

Ordnance Survey: Explorer OL4 (1:25 000); Landranger 90 (1:50 000).

Harvey Mountain Maps: Lakeland Central (1:25 000)

British Mountain Maps: Lake District (1:40 000)

Tourist Information Centres: Windermere: *Brockhole*; Ambleside; Grasmere; Keswick; Glenridding.

Youth Hostels: Grasmere: *Butharlyp Howe*; Glenridding: *Greenside*; Patterdale: *Goldrill House.*

Hotels and B&B: Grasmere; Thirlmere: *Thirlspot, Glenridding*; Patterdale.

Camp sites: Thirlmere: *Legburthwaite*; Glenridding; Patterdale.

Helvellyn's trig point, just northwest of the true summit right at the edge of the crags.

Great Ho

Thirlspot
White Stones Path
Helvellyn Gill Path
Brown Cra
Lower Man
Helvellyn
Whelp Side
Swallow Scarth
Nethermost Pike
Wythburn
Nether Cov
East Ridge
Birk Side
Wythburn Path
Dollywaggon Pike
Ruthwaite Cove
The Tongue
Cock Cove
Falcon Crag
Ruth Lo
Tarn Crag
Grisedale Track
Raise Beck Path
Seat Sandal
Grisedale Tarn
Grisedale Hause
Grisedale Hause Track
Dunmail Raise
Little Tongue Gill
Great Tongue
Tongue Gill
Grasmere
Thirlmere

Warning
Snow and ice cover greatly increase the difficulties on Striding Edge

popular route. The other routes on this side should not be ignored though; all are interesting throughout and will provide varying degrees of adventure in summer or winter. Patterdale and Glenridding are the start points for Helvellyn's eastern routes.

Although Helvellyn's crags are mostly too broken for rock climbing they do provide excellent winter climbing. The crags around Dollywaggon Cove, Nethermost Cove and those directly below Helvellyn's summit hold some of the most consistent snow-and-ice conditions in the Lake District.

Warning
Under snow cover considerable cornice build-up occurs at the edge of Helvellyn's east face. This should be taken into account when trying to find the start of Striding Edge and Swirral Edge or when visiting the summit.

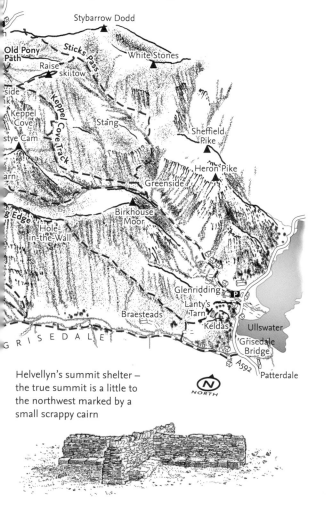

Helvellyn's summit shelter – the true summit is a little to the northwest marked by a small scrappy cairn

RIGHT
Helvellyn from Striding Edge

Grisedale Hause Track HELVELLYN

'Long but entertaining' ★★

Summary: Attains the south end of the main Helvellyn ridge via Grisedale Hause and Grisedale Tarn. The ascent from Grisedale Tarn is steep and very loose but soon gives way to a pleasant ridge path.

Ascent: Take the narrow lane from the A591 at Mill Bridge NE to the water intake at the foot of Great Tongue. The main track climbs alongside Little Tongue on the northwest side of Great Tongue. Follow this NE then E to Grisedale Hause or alternatively take the path on the southwest side of Great Tongue. From Grisedale Hause drop down to Grisedale Tarn and cross the outlet at the northeast end. After the ford turn W and join the steep zigzags which climb NW to Dollywaggon Pike, then follow the good ridge path N to Helvellyn passing Nethermost Pike en route.

Descent: Follow the main ridge path S until it forks at Swallow Scarth; take the L branch and follow it S to Dollywaggon Pike. From Dollywaggon Pike the path turns SE; continue along it and descend the steep zigzags to Grisedale Tarn. Cross the outlet at the northeast end of the tarn and climb SW to Grisedale Hause. From the top of the hause continue SW until the track forks, either take the R branch alongside Little Tongue Gill or take the path on the L alongside Tongue Gill. Both descend to the water intake from where the lane back to Mill Bridge is joined.

Strenuousness ●●●●○

Navigation ●●○○○

Technicality ●●●●○

Mill Bridge, Grasmere, GR NY335091

3–3.5 hours
8km
(5 miles)

1050m
(3445ft)

Broad open gill, bleak tarn, steep zigzags and long summit ridge

Alternative path alongside Tongue Gill

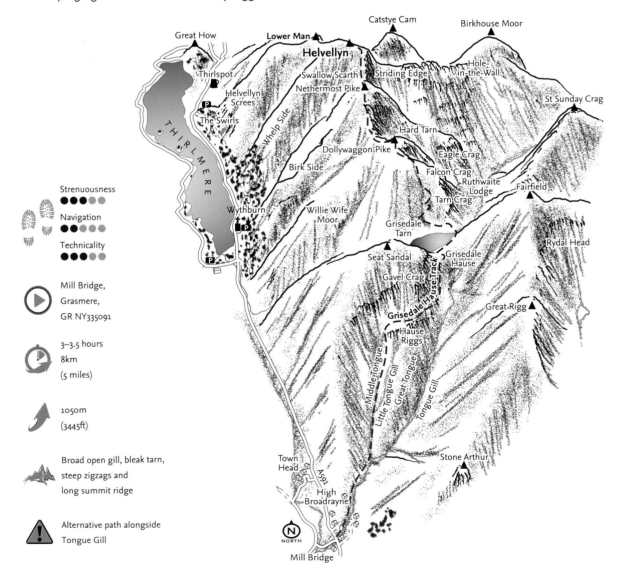

Raise Beck Path HELVELLYN

'Atmospheric and height saving' ★

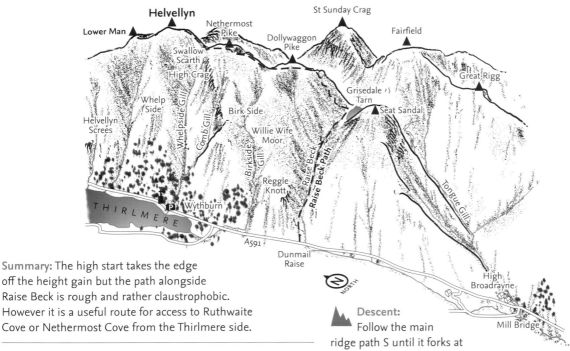

Summary: The high start takes the edge off the height gain but the path alongside Raise Beck is rough and rather claustrophobic. However it is a useful route for access to Ruthwaite Cove or Nethermost Cove from the Thirlmere side.

Ascent: From the stile at the top of Dunmail Raise head NW a short distance across the fellside to join Raise Beck. Follow the beck on the south side to a low col overlooking Grisedale Tarn. Skirt the tarn on the north side and join the steep zigzags which climb NW to Dollywaggon Pike, then follow the good ridge path N to Helvellyn.

Descent: Follow the main ridge path S until it forks at Swallow Scarth; take the L branch and follow it S to Dollywaggon Pike. From Dollywaggon Pike the path turns SE. Continue along it and descend the steep zigzags to Grisedale Tarn. At the tarn turn W and follow the path across the low col to the head of Raise Beck. Join the path on the south side of Raise Beck and follow it down to Dunmail Raise.

Helvellyn and Striding Edge from Swallow Scarth

Strenuousness
●●●●○○

Navigation
●●○○○○

Technicality
●●●○○○

Dunmail Raise
(A591)
GR NY327116

2.5–3 hours
6.2km
(3.9 miles)

850m
(2787ft)

Steep rocky gill, bleak tarn, steep zigzags and long summit ridge

Wythburn Path HELVELLYN

'Quick, with great views' ★

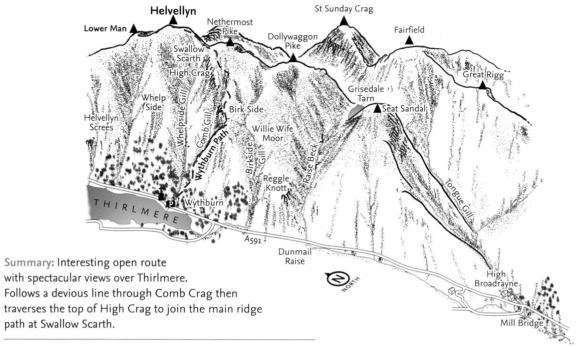

Summary: Interesting open route with spectacular views over Thirlmere. Follows a devious line through Comb Crag then traverses the top of High Crag to join the main ridge path at Swallow Scarth.

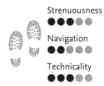 **Ascent:** From the car park follow the bridleway steeply E through the plantation to the edge of the trees; then follow it NE into Comb Gill. Before the gill is reached the bridleway turns SE – continue along it as it zigzags to the top of Comb Crag then traverses NE across the top of High Crag to Swallow Scarth. Join the main ridge path N to Helvellyn.

Descent: Follow the main ridge path S until it forks at Swallow Scarth, take the R fork and follow it SW across the top of High Crag and then NW as it zigzags down into Comb Gill. Before the beck is reached turn W and follow the bridleway down to the trees and then down to Wythburn Car Park.

Strenuousness
●●●●○

Navigation
●●●○○

Technicality
●●●●○

Car park behind the church at Wythburn, (A591) GR NY324136

2 hours
3.9km
(2.4 miles)

770m
(2526ft)

Rocky open fellside and summit ridge

Sunset at the head of the Wythburn Path

Helvellyn Gill Path HELVELLYN

'Direct and popular' ★

Summary: Continually steep, the path zigzags alongside Helvellyn Gill then climbs the scree-covered shoulder of Browncove Crags. It provides the most direct route to Helvellyn's summit and can be followed in most conditions, but because of its exposed nature, it is less easily negotiated in high winds. Browncove Crags hold a number of winter climbs in the easier grades – well worth the short diversion en route.

Ascent: Cross the footbridge over Helvellyn Gill at the back of the car park then follow the path SE alongside the gill to another footbridge. Cross the footbridge, then climb the steep zigzags to a wall. Through the gate continue climbing to the remains of another wall. From here the path ascends the steep scree-covered shoulder SE directly to Helvellyn's summit. *For access to Browncove Crags ignore the path and skirt E to the base of the climbs.*

Descent: Head NW and skirt the south side of Lower Man to a fork, take the L branch and continue NW. This section passes close by the top of Browncove Crags which can hold cornices under snow cover. Once past the crags descend the steep scree-covered shoulder and then follow the zigzags down to the footbridge over Helvellyn Gill. A short section of path leads to another footbridge and The Swirls Car Park.

The Hinkler Memorial is 229m (250yd) south from Helvellyn's summit on the main ridge path. It commemorates the successful first landing and take-off by aeroplane on Helvellyn in 1926 by John Leeming and Bert Hinkler in an Avro 585 Gosport.

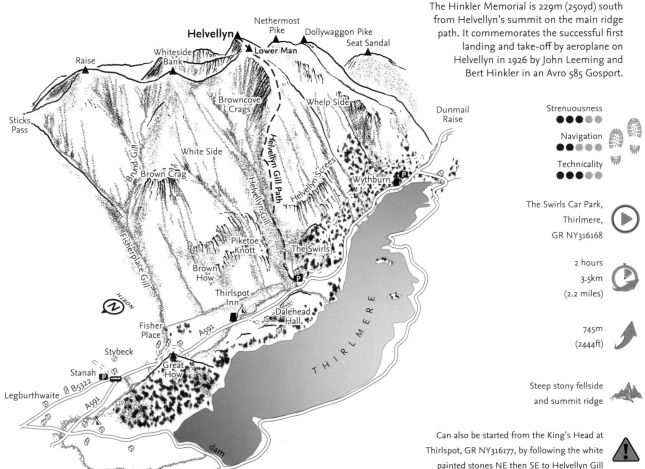

Strenuousness
●●●●○

Navigation
●●○○○

Technicality
●●●○○

The Swirls Car Park,
Thirlmere,
GR NY316168

2 hours
3.5km
(2.2 miles)

745m
(2444ft)

Steep stony fellside
and summit ridge

Can also be started from the King's Head at Thirlspot, GR NY316177, by following the white painted stones NE then SE to Helvellyn Gill

The Old Pony Route HELVELLYN

'Logical and quiet'

Summary: The original tourist route follows a pleasant meandering course via Whiteside Bank and the entertaining north ridge of Lower Man. The middle section above Brown Crag is a little indistinct and can be tricky to follow in mist.

Ascent: Take the bridleway behind the King's Head across the aqueduct and then NE to Fisherplace Gill. Ascend the south side of Fisherplace Gill then follow Brund Gill SE past Brown Crag. The bridleway continues SE to Whiteside Bank across open fellside. The going is easy but its course on the ground is vague. From Whiteside Bank join the main ridge path and follow it S to make the steep pull up the north ridge of Lower Man and then SE to Helvellyn.

Descent: Head NW then N along the summit ridge to Lower Man. Descend the rocky north ridge of Lower Man then follow the main path N to Whiteside Bank. From the summit cairn descend NW across open fellside to Brund Gill which is followed, past Brown Crag to Fisherplace Gill. At Fisherplace Gill the bridleway becomes clearer and is followed down to the King's Head at Thirlspot.

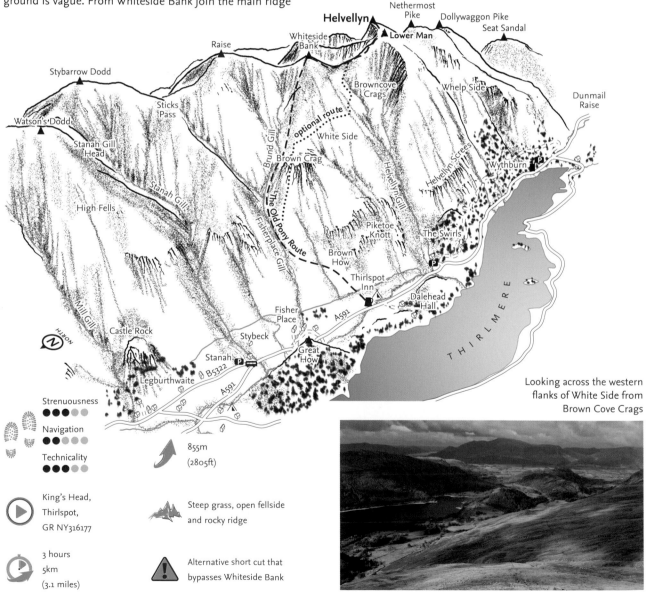

Looking across the western flanks of White Side from Brown Cove Crags

Strenuousness ●●●○○

Navigation ●●○○○

Technicality ●●●○○

855m (2805ft)

Steep grass, open fellside and rocky ridge

King's Head, Thirlspot, GR NY316177

3 hours
5km
(3.1 miles)

Alternative short cut that bypasses Whiteside Bank

Sticks Pass (from Stanah) HELVELLYN

'Adds value with extra summits' ★

Summary: Originally a packhorse route, Sticks Pass gains an altitude of 750m (2460ft) giving easy access to the northern end of the main Helvellyn ridge.

Ascent: Take the bridleway E from Stanah and follow it across the aqueduct; then cross over the footbridge onto the south side of Stanah Gill. Continue along the bridleway as it climbs alongside Stanah Gill then swing SE across a broad spur. The route then bears back to the E and climbs directly to the top of the pass. Turn R onto the main ridge path and follow it S over the rocky top of Raise, over Whiteside Bank and up the rocky north ridge of Lower Man. From Lower Man turn SE and follow the bridleway to Helvellyn's summit.

Descent: Head NW then N along the summit ridge to Lower Man. Descend the rocky north ridge of Lower Man then follow the main path N over Whiteside Bank and Raise and then down to the top of Sticks Pass. Turn L and follow the bridleway W over a broad spur then down to Stanah Gill. Continue W on the south side of Stanah Gill down to the road at Stanah.

Stanah Gill

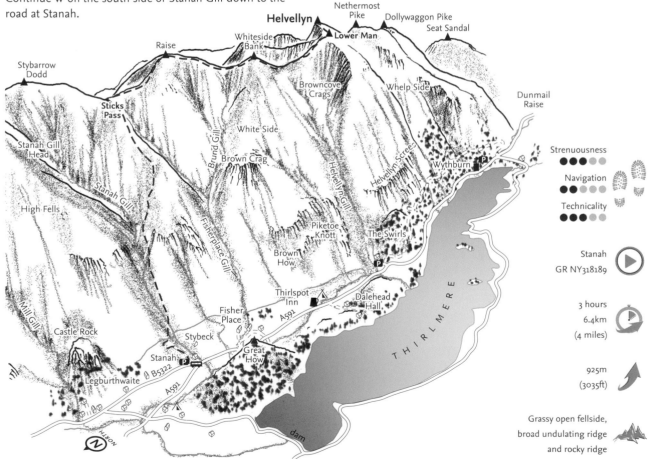

Strenuousness ●●●○○

Navigation ●●○○○

Technicality ●●●○○

Stanah
GR NY318189

3 hours
6.4km
(4 miles)

925m
(3035ft)

Grassy open fellside, broad undulating ridge and rocky ridge

Sticks Pass (from Greenside) HELVELLYN

'Fascinating industrial history' ★

Summary: Sticks Pass passes through the destruction and waste caused by the mines at Greenside and although dramatic, these workings detract from what must have been a particularly beautiful valley. Once past the workings the route greatly improves and climbs pleasantly alongside Sticks Gill onto the main Helvellyn ridge.

Ascent: From Glenridding take the Greenside Road to the old mine buildings. Pass the buildings to a fork, take the R branch and follow it as it zigzags N around Stang End to a footbridge. Cross the footbridge and follow the narrow bridleway W alongside Sticks Gill to the top of the pass. Turn L onto the main ridge path and follow it S over the rocky top of Raise, over Whiteside Bank and up the rocky north ridge of Lower Man. From Lower Man turn SE to Helvellyn.

Descent: Head NW to Lower Man. Descend the rocky north ridge of Lower Man, then follow the main path N over Whiteside Bank and Raise and then down to the top of Sticks Pass. Turn R and follow the narrow bridleway E alongside Sticks Gill to a footbridge. Cross this and then descend the zigzags S around Stang End to Greenside Mines. Pass the buildings and join the Greenside Road which is then followed down to Glenridding.

The buildings at Greenside were once part of a busy lead-mining complex. Most are now run as outdoor pursuits centres and climbing huts.

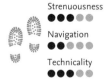

Strenuousness
●●●●○○

Navigation
●●○○○○

Technicality
●●●○○○

Glenridding Car Park, GR NY385169

960m (3150ft)

3.5 hours
9.3km
(5.8 miles)

Old mine-workings among crags, hanging valley, broad undulating ridge and rocky ridge

Keppel Cove Track HELVELLYN

'The perfect alternative to the edges' ★★

Summary: Passes beneath the impressive north face of Catstye Cam and then winds its way above Keppel Cove, joining the main Helvellyn ridge at Whiteside Bank. Easy to follow, the route offers a quieter and more remote alternative to the Red Tarn routes.

🔺 **Ascent:** From Glenridding take the Greenside Road to the old mine buildings, pass the buildings to a fork and take the L branch. Follow the track SW towards Keppel Cove then take the zigzags NW to a terrace. The terrace skirts W above Keppel Cove; follow it to Whiteside Bank. Turn L onto the main ridge path and follow it S up the rocky north ridge of Lower Man. From Lower Man turn SE to Helvellyn.

🔺 **Descent:** Head NW around the edge to Lower Man. Descend the rocky north ridge of Lower Man, then follow the main path N to Whiteside Bank. Pick up the bridleway that heads NE to a terrace. Follow the terrace E as it skirts the top of Keppel Cove then drops SE down the zigzags to join the Greenside track. Follow it E to the old mine buildings, then join Greenside Road, continuing E to Glenridding.

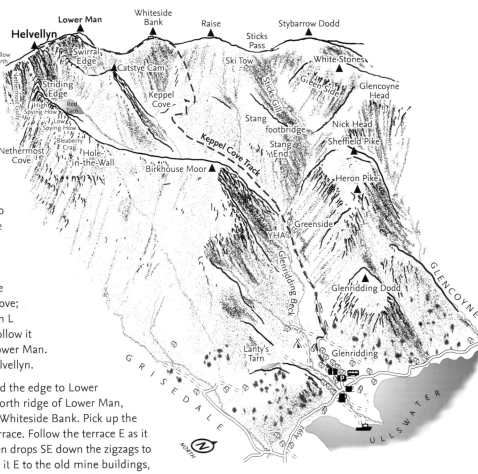

The upper reaches of Keppel Cove from Swirral Edge

Access to the Red Tarn Path is gained from Greenside via the footbridge over Glenridding Beck at the west end of the mining complex

Strenuousness
●●●●○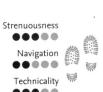

Navigation
●●○○○

Technicality
●●●○○

915m
(3002ft)

Glenridding Car Park,
GR NY385169

Old mine-workings among crags, corrie, grassy fellside and rocky ridge

3.5 hours
8.1km
(5 miles)

Swirral Edge HELVELLYN

'Exposed and exciting' ★ ★

Summary: Exposed ground on either side makes the steep rocky arête an exciting undertaking. It links Catstye Cam to Helvellyn and is easily gained by a narrow path from the side of Red Tarn. Although its difficulties are never excessive, enough people have come to grief to warrant a degree of caution – particularly under snow cover or when it is windy.

Ascent: From Glenridding take the Greenside Road to the old mine buildings. Pass the buildings to a fork and take the L branch. Continue a short distance to a footbridge on the left; cross it to the path on the other side. This is followed SW alongside Glenridding Beck to another footbridge; cross this and continue along the path first S then SW as it climbs to Red Tarn. The Swirral Edge Path traverses the steep fellside on the north side of Red Tarn. Take it to the col and then make the short, steep scramble up Swirral Edge onto the summit plateau.

Descent: Locating the correct start of Swirral Edge is critical, as the ground on either side of it is very steep and in parts loose. The top is marked by a small cairn at the lip of the crags 137m (150yd) NNW from the trig point. The initial section of Swirral Edge is quite steep (can be problematic under snow/ice), but soon eases and leads down to a narrow col from which point the path descends to Red Tarn. Catstye Cam is a short distance E along the ridge. From the outlet of Red Tarn take the path NE then N as it descends to a footbridge. Cross this and follow the path to another footbridge. After crossing this, follow the track (then road) E to Glenridding.

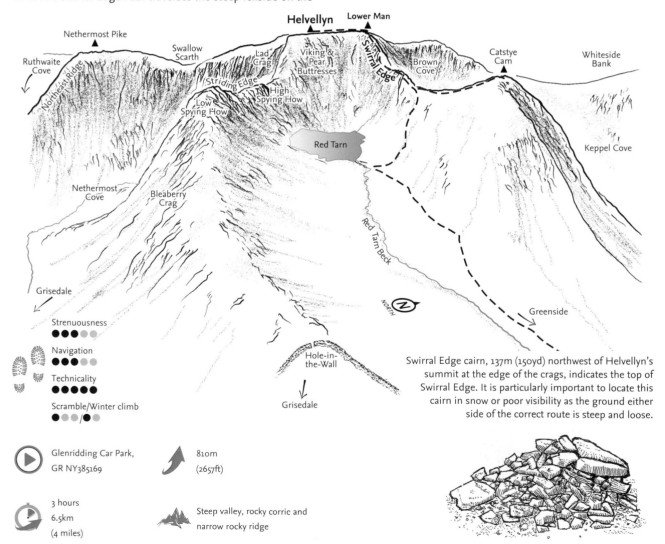

Helvellyn • Lower Man
Nethermost Pike
Swallow Scarth
Ruthwaite Cove
Northeast Ridge
Lad Crag
Striding Edge
Viking & Pear Buttresses
Swirral Edge
Brown Cove
Catstye Cam
Whiteside Bank
Low Spying How
High Spying How
Red Tarn
Keppel Cove
Nethermost Cove
Bleaberry Crag
Red Tarn Beck
NORTH
Greenside
Grisedale
Hole-in-the-Wall
Grisedale

Strenuousness
●●●○○

Navigation
●●●○○

Technicality
●●●●●

Scramble/Winter climb
●●○○ / ●○○

Swirral Edge cairn, 137m (150yd) northwest of Helvellyn's summit at the edge of the crags, indicates the top of Swirral Edge. It is particularly important to locate this cairn in snow or poor visibility as the ground either side of the correct route is steep and loose.

▶ Glenridding Car Park, GR NY385169

⬆ 810m (2657ft)

🕐 3 hours
6.5km
(4 miles)

⛰ Steep valley, rocky corrie and narrow rocky ridge

Striding Edge HELVELLYN

'The classic benchmark arête' ★ ★ ★

The Dixon Memorial. Halfway along Striding Edge on the Nethermost Cove side, a cast-iron memorial plaque commemorates Robert Dixon who fell to his death from Striding Edge while hunting in 1858.

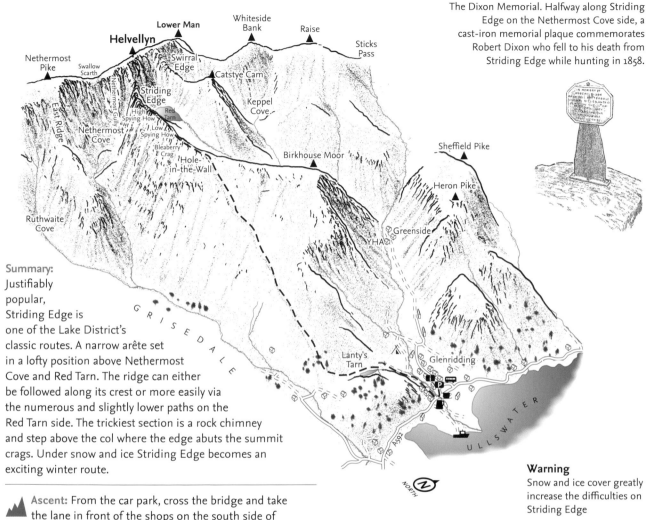

Summary:
Justifiably popular, Striding Edge is one of the Lake District's classic routes. A narrow arête set in a lofty position above Nethermost Cove and Red Tarn. The ridge can either be followed along its crest or more easily via the numerous and slightly lower paths on the Red Tarn side. The trickiest section is a rock chimney and step above the col where the edge abuts the summit crags. Under snow and ice Striding Edge becomes an exciting winter route.

Ascent: From the car park, cross the bridge and take the lane in front of the shops on the south side of Glenridding Beck W to the cottages at Westside. Then follow the path S to Lanty's Tarn. Pass the tarn and drop down towards Grisedale. At the wall turn R and follow the path W as it traverses steeply up to the Hole-in-the-Wall. Pass through the hole and head SW along the crest of Bleaberry Crag and then W along Striding Edge. At the end of the edge make the steep climb up the path onto the summit plateau.

Descent: SE from the summit shelter the Gough Memorial marks the start of the descent to Striding Edge. The descent from the summit crags crosses loose rock – avoid disturbing this as you drop E to a col. Continue E across Striding Edge then NE across Bleaberry Crag to the Hole-in-the-Wall. The path forks here, take the R branch which traverses E across the fellside down into Grisedale. At the bottom either turn R into Grisedale and then on to Patterdale or carry straight on and swing round to the N for Glenridding via Lanty's Tarn.

Warning
Snow and ice cover greatly increase the difficulties on Striding Edge

Strenuousness
● ● ● ● ○

Navigation
● ● ● ● ○

Technicality
● ● ● ● ●

Scramble/Winter climb
● ● ● /● ○

870m
(2854ft)

Woodland, steep fellside and narrow rocky ridge

From Patterdale, GR NY390161, via Grisedale

Glenridding Car Park, GR NY385169

3 hours
6km
(3.7 miles)

Nethermost Pike – East Ridge HELVELLYN

'Remote scramble' ★★

Summary: Tucked away at the head of Grisedale between Ruthwaite Cove and Nethermost Cove is the East Ridge of Nethermost Pike. It lacks the pure quality of Striding Edge but this is more than made up for by its truly wild setting. There are three possible starts to the ridge, via either Hard Tarn, Nethermostcove Beck or a scramble up Eagle Crag.

Ascent: From the A592 in Patterdale take the narrow lane SW (by the sports field) into Grisedale. Follow the track to join the bridleway. Continue SW past Crossing Plantation to the start of a vague path on the R. For access to the Nethermostcove Beck and Eagle Crag start, take this path W over Grisedale Beck. The Nethermostcove Beck route climbs the easy slopes behind

Eagle Crag onto the flat lower section of the ridge. The Eagle Crag scramble climbs the R side of the gully/vein behind the mine-ruin over slabs, then up the steps and flakes, finally working L above the gully/vein to the flat lower section of the ridge. For the Hard Tarn start ignore the path and continue along the bridleway to Ruthwaite Lodge. Behind the lodge take the vague zigzags as they climb up into Ruthwaite Cove. Hard Tarn is high on the north side of the cove (hidden by a lip). Climb to it, then traverse NE below the crags onto the East Ridge proper. All three routes climb the top section of the ridge direct onto Nethermost Pike, from which the main Helvellyn ridge path can be joined and followed N to the summit.

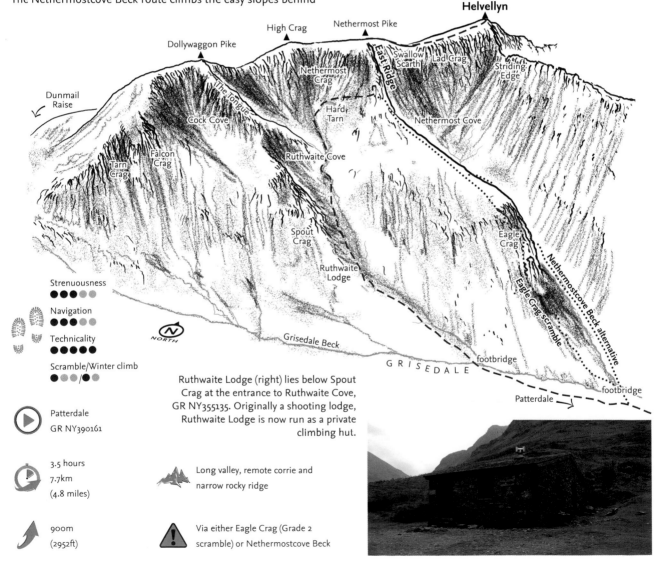

Strenuousness
● ● ● ● ○

Navigation
● ● ● ● ○

Technicality
● ● ● ● ●

Scramble/Winter climb
● ● ○ ○ / ● ● ○

⏵ Patterdale
GR NY390161

⏱ 3.5 hours
7.7km
(4.8 miles)

900m
(2952ft)

Long valley, remote corrie and narrow rocky ridge

⚠ Via either Eagle Crag (Grade 2 scramble) or Nethermostcove Beck

Ruthwaite Lodge (right) lies below Spout Crag at the entrance to Ruthwaite Cove, GR NY355135. Originally a shooting lodge, Ruthwaite Lodge is now run as a private climbing hut.

Grisedale Track HELVELLYN

'Long and easy angled' ★

Summary: Grisedale provides a convenient cross-country link between Patterdale and Grasmere via Grisedale Hause. It also gives access to the southern end of the main Helvellyn ridge. The track along it is in good order and allows short work to be made of the distance. It is a useful approach to Falcon Crag, Tarn Crag and Helvellyn's southern corries.

Ascent: From the A592 in Patterdale take the narrow lane SW (by the sports field) into Grisedale. Follow it and join the bridleway. Continue S passing Ruthwaite Lodge en route to the outlet at Grisedale Tarn. Climb the path past the outlet then turn NW and climb the steep zigzags to Dollywaggon Pike. Follow the good ridge path N to Helvellyn.

Descent: Follow the main ridge path S until it forks at Swallow Scarth, take the L branch and follow it S to Dollywaggon Pike. From Dollywaggon Pike the path turns SE; continue along it and descend the steep zigzags to Grisedale Tarn. Head NE past the outlet and follow the bridleway the length of Grisedale to join the road. Continue NE down the road to Patterdale.

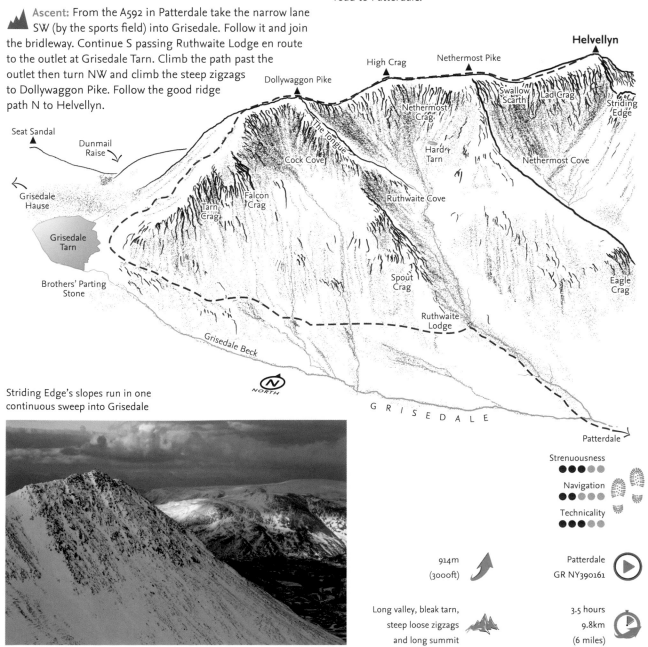

Striding Edge's slopes run in one continuous sweep into Grisedale

	Strenuousness
	●●●●○
	Navigation
	●●○○○
	Technicality
	●●●●○

914m (3000ft)

Patterdale GR NY390161

Long valley, bleak tarn, steep loose zigzags and long summit

3.5 hours 9.8km (6 miles)

Skiddaw

931m (3054ft)

Skiddaw is visually the perfect mountain. Its form is a simple combination of steep smooth flanks and deep shadowy gills; its slopes are covered with a patchwork of bracken, grass, heather and scree, which from hour to hour is in a constant state of flux displaying an infinite variety of hues and tints.

The secret to Skiddaw's symmetry lies in its rocks; they are slates and shales from the Lower Ordovician period, which tend to weather and decay in a homogeneous manner producing characteristically uniform terrain. This is of great frustration to climbers and some walkers, as it leads to few crags and gives rather monotonous walking.

However, Skiddaw's qualities are more abstract than just the pure terrain. Being in an isolated position, set apart from its neighbours, the unrestricted views from its summit and south side are arguably the best in the Lake District. Across the Vale of Derwent the peaks of the eastern, central, southern and western fells are laid out in a magnificent panorama. For those who love solitude, the northern slopes, which run down to the extensive upland valley of the River Caldew afford a wilderness comparable to corners of the Cairngorms or the northern Pennines.

The most popular route to Skiddaw's exposed and wind-blasted summit is the Jenkin Hill Path. This route was established as a pony route for Victorian tourists and still attracts the greatest number of ascensionists, partly out of habit and partly because it can be started high, from the Latrigg Car Park. In one respect this is a pity as there are far better routes to choose, most notably the crossing of Longside Edge or ascent via Sale How's lonely fells. On the other hand, it means that if you are enterprising enough to pick an alternative route you will quite probably have it to yourself.

Skiddaw from Brown Crag on the Helvellyn Range

When you arrive

Ordnance Survey: Explorer OL4 (1:25 000); Landranger 90 & 89 (1:50 000).
Harvey Mountain Maps: Northern Lakeland (1:25 000)
British Mountain Maps: Lake District (1:40 000)

Tourist Information Centres: Keswick; visit www.golakes.co.uk

Youth Hostels: Keswick: *Station Road*; Skiddaw: *Skiddaw House*.
Hotels and B&B: Keswick; Underscar; Ormathwaite; Millbeck; Braithwaite; Ravenstone; High Side; Threlkeld.
Camp sites: Keswick; Braithwaite; Chapel; Bassenthwaite; Threlkeld.

Warning
Skiddaw summit is an exposed
spot. The crescent shelters which
litter the summit afford meagre
protection, particularly if the
wind is in the north.

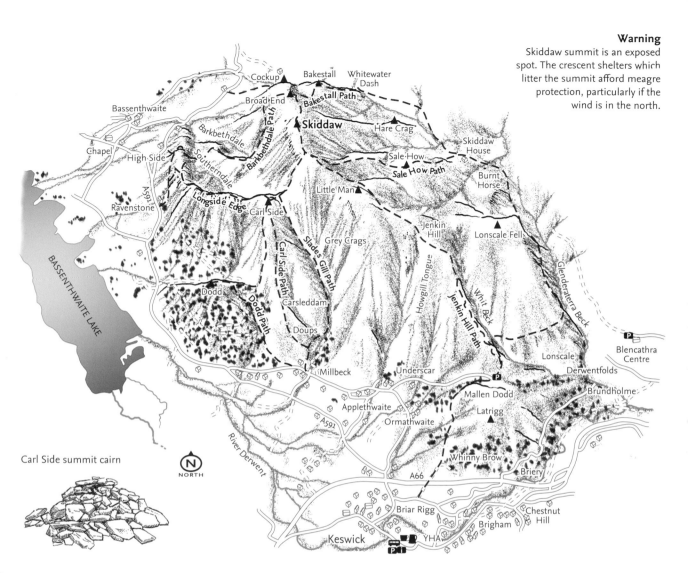

Cockup
Bakestall
Whitewater
Dash
Bassenthwaite
Broad End
Bakestall Path
Chapel
Barkbethdale
Barkbethdale Path
Skiddaw
Hare Crag
High Side
Southerndale
Skiddaw
House
Ravenstone
A591
Sale How
Sale How Path
Burnt
Horse
Longside Edge
Carl Side
Little Man
Carl Side Path
Slades Gill Path
Grey Crags
Jenkin
Hill
Lonscale Fell
Glenderaterra Beck
Dodd
Dodd Path
Carsleddam
Howgill Tongue
Jenkin Hill Path
Whit Beck
P
Blencathra
Centre
Doups
Lonscale
Derwentfolds
Millbeck
Underscar
P
Brundholme
Mallen Dodd
Applethwaite
Latrigg
River Derwent
A591
Ormathwaite
A66
Whinny Brow
Briery
N NORTH
Briar Rigg
Chestnut
Hill
Keswick
YHA
Brigham
P i

Carl Side summit cairn

Bassenthwaite Lake

Barkbethdale Path SKIDDAW

'A sneaky approach' ★

Summary: Contrived route, which climbs by crossing the mouth of Southerndale then traverses around the head of Barkbethdale, finally reaching the North Top of Skiddaw via Broad End.

Ascent: Join the bridleway which leaves the road and zigzags SE to a fork at the lower end of Southerndale. Take the L branch and follow it SE across Southerndale Beck then E as it winds up the fellside and over the ridge into Barkbethdale. The path then turns SE again; follow it right around the head of Barkbethdale until it climbs N onto Broad End. Among the scree the path becomes narrow and vague in places but generally climbs SE to the North Top of Skiddaw from which Skiddaw lies due S.

Descent: Head N to the North Top of Skiddaw then descend NW over scree to pick up the more distinct path on the west side of Broad End. Follow the path N then NW around the head of Barkbethdale then drop SW over the ridge and into Southerndale. Cross Southerndale Beck and head NW down the zigzags to the road.

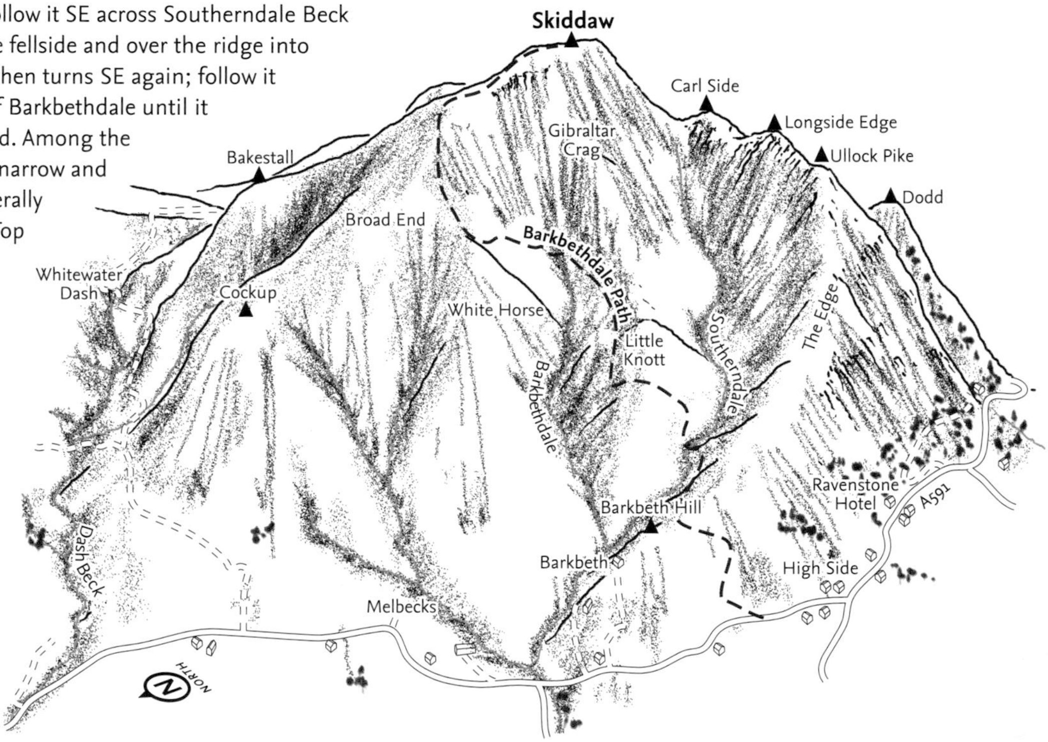

The Barkbethdale flank of Skiddaw from Bassenthwaite Lake

Strenuousness
●●●●○○

Navigation
●●○○○○

Technicality
●●●○○○

Near High Side,
GR NY236310

2.5 hours
5.7km
(3.5 miles)

790m
(2592ft)

Steep grassy valleys,
scree and stony summit

Jenkin Hill Path SKIDDAW

'Well trodden motorway'

The Hawell Monument – a stone cross inscribed with an epitaph to three shepherds from the same family – marks the start of the Jenkin Hill Path.

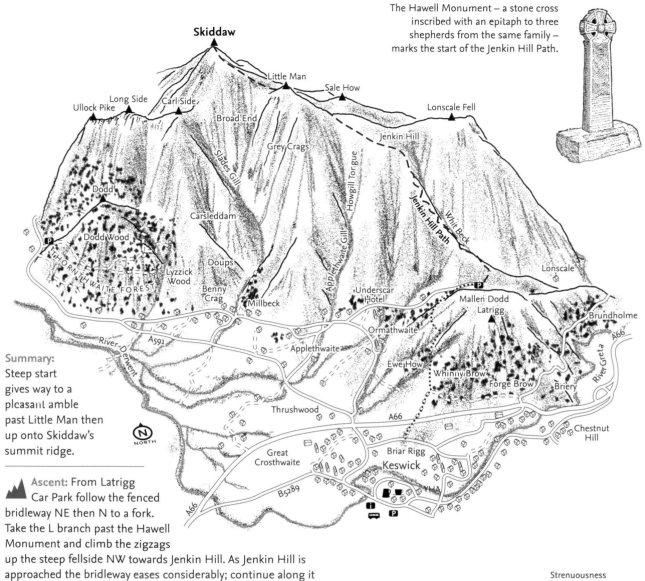

Summary:
Steep start gives way to a pleasant amble past Little Man then up onto Skiddaw's summit ridge.

Ascent: From Latrigg Car Park follow the fenced bridleway NE then N to a fork. Take the L branch past the Hawell Monument and climb the zigzags up the steep fellside NW towards Jenkin Hill. As Jenkin Hill is approached the bridleway eases considerably; continue along it to a gate. At the gate either pass through it or turn W then NW and make the short diversion to Little Man. The bridleway skirts the northeast side of Little Man and is followed to another gate and up a final climb onto the summit ridge. Turn N and follow the crest to Skiddaw's summit.

Descent: Head S along the summit ridge then turn SE and descend to a fence and gate. Continue SE around the northeast flank of Little Man to another gate. Pass through this gate and follow the bridleway as it descends the steep fellside through a series of zigzags to the Hawell Monument and onto the intake wall. Join the fenced bridleway and follow this SW back to the car park.

650m
(2133ft)

Steep grassy fellside and stony summit ridge

Alternative route can be accessed direct from Keswick via the Latrigg Bridleway starting at Briar Rigg GR NY267241.

Strenuousness
●●○○○

Navigation
●●●○○

Technicality
●●○○○

Latrigg Car Park,
GR NY281253

2 hours
5km
(3.1 miles)

Carl Side Path SKIDDAW

'Steep and adventurous' ★★

Summary: Climbs over the subsidiary peak of Carl Side and then onto Skiddaw's South Top. Views from this route are particularly good from and towards Skiddaw.

Ascent: Starts along a narrow lane at Benny Crag. Follow the path N then NW straight up the steep fellside. The path works its way up a series of rock steps then continues up the steep rounded ridge towards the summit of Carl Side. Near the top the path splits; the traverse line on the east side is the easier of the two paths. From Carl Side drop NE down to a col and either climb directly up the scree onto the summit ridge (South Top) or follow the zigzags. On the ridge follow it N to Skiddaw's summit.

Descent: Head S along the summit ridge; the zigzag starts at the second saddle (cairn). The steep direct descent starts at the South Top (cairn and low shelter). Descend SW to the flat col, then continuing SW and ascend the other side to Carl Side. Turn S and follow the steep broad ridge down to Benny Crag continuing onto the lane at Millbeck.

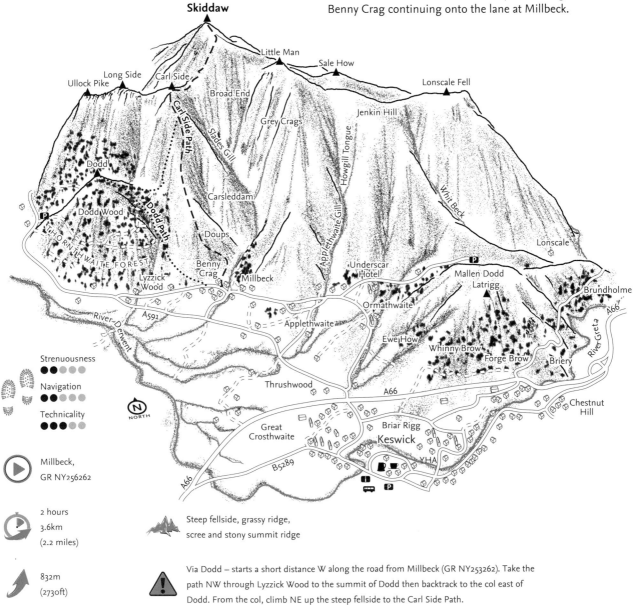

Strenuousness
●●○○○

Navigation
●●○○○

Technicality
●●●○○

Millbeck,
GR NY256262

2 hours
3.6km
(2.2 miles)

832m
(2730ft)

Steep fellside, grassy ridge, scree and stony summit ridge

Via Dodd – starts a short distance W along the road from Millbeck (GR NY253262). Take the path NW through Lyzzick Wood to the summit of Dodd then backtrack to the col east of Dodd. From the col, climb NE up the steep fellside to the Carl Side Path.

Longside Edge SKIDDAW

'High and narrow crest' ★ ★ ★

Summary: A fine shapely ridge extends north from Carl Side, separated from Skiddaw by Southerndale. From a distance the crest of Longside Edge looks deceptively narrow suggesting that there may be some scrambling involved. Closer inspection reveals otherwise; nevertheless still an excellent route.

Ascent: Join the bridleway which leaves the road and zigzags SE to a fork at the lower end of Southerndale. Take the R branch and follow it S up Ullock Pike then SE across Longside Edge and finally E up Carl Side. From Carl Side drop NE down to the col and either climb direct up the scree onto the summit ridge (South Top) or follow the zigzag. On the ridge follow it N to Skiddaw's summit.

Descent: Head S along the summit ridge; the zigzag starts at the second saddle (cairn). The steep direct descent starts at the South Top (cairn and low shelter). Descend SW to the flat col then climb the other side SW to Carl Side. Head NW and follow the crest of Longside Edge to Ullock Pike. Drop down the north ridge of Ullock Pike and follow the zigzags NW to the road near High Side.

Direction indicator near Skiddaw's trig point

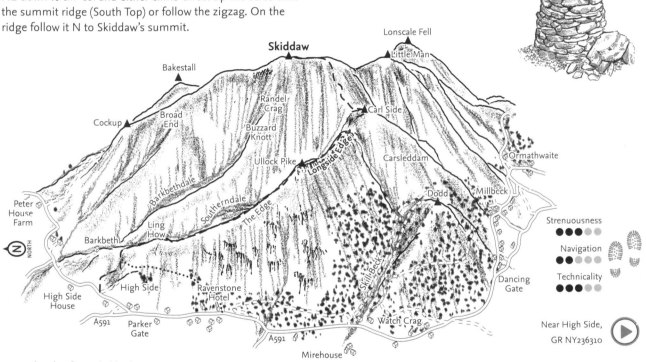

Strenuousness ●●●○○

Navigation ●●○○○

Technicality ●●●○○

Near High Side, GR NY236310

2.5–3 hours
5.9km
(3.7 miles)

862m
(2828ft)

Long narrow ridge, scree and stony summit ridge

Instead of crossing Longside Edge, Southerndale can be followed to the col between Carl Side and Skiddaw. Can also be started from Ravenstone, GR NY235296.

Longside Edge from Skiddaw's summit

Slades Gill Path SKIDDAW

'Dramatic landscape' ★

Summary: Follows Slades Beck in a deep gill between Carl Side and Skiddaw. The initial section through woodland is particularly pleasant but in misty conditions the gill is oppressive; best left for clear weather when the impressive southern slopes of Skiddaw can be viewed at close quarters.

Ascent: Starts along a narrow lane at Benny Crag. Follow the path N then NW around woodland to the side of Slades Beck. First on the west side of the beck then on the east side, follow it N then NW to the flat col between Carl Side and Skiddaw. Turn NE and either climb direct up the scree onto the summit ridge (South Top) or follow the zigzag. On the ridge follow it N to Skiddaw's summit.

Descent: Head S along the summit ridge; the zigzag starts at the second saddle (cairn). The steep direct descent starts at the South Top (cairn and low shelter). Descend SW to a flat col between Carl Side and Skiddaw, then turn L at the small cairn and drop down the gill alongside Slades Beck. At the bottom follow the path on the northwest side of the beck past woodland and down to Millbeck.

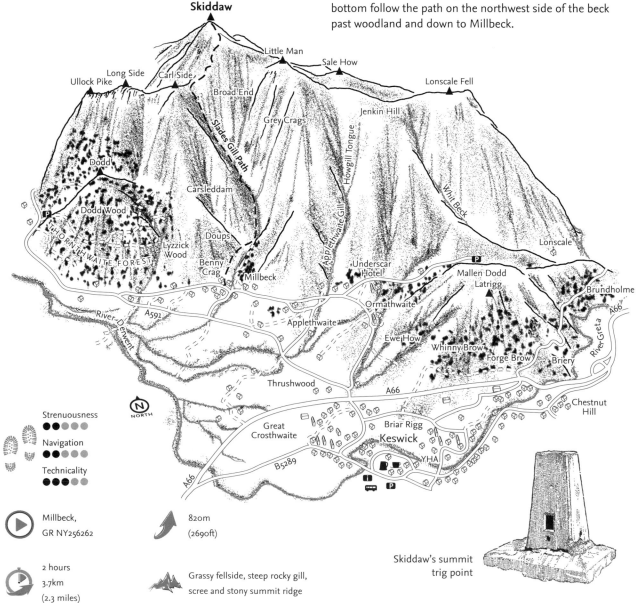

Strenuousness
●●○○○

Navigation
●●○○○

Technicality
●●●○○

Millbeck,
GR NY256262

2 hours
3.7km
(2.3 miles)

820m
(2690ft)

Grassy fellside, steep rocky gill, scree and stony summit ridge

Skiddaw's summit trig point

RIGHT
Skiddaw from Lodore

Bakestall Path SKIDDAW

'Remote with a bonus peak' ★

Summary: Dead Crags form the impressive northeast face of Bakestall and although steep, they are rough and very broken and hold no safe routes. The only alternative is the steep grassy ridge at the southern edge. This climbs directly from Whitewater Dash to the summit of Bakestall from which Skiddaw can be easily gained.

 Ascent: Head SE along the Skiddaw House access track to the gate near the top of Whitewater Dash. Turn R and climb SW directly up the steep grassy ridge (Birkett Edge) alongside the fence to the summit of Bakestall. Head S then SE and climb the final slopes to the North Top of Skiddaw from which Skiddaw lies due S.

 Descent: Head N to the North Top of Skiddaw then descend NE to Bakestall. Start descending from Bakestall by heading a short distance E to avoid the top of Dead Crags then descend NE alongside the fence to the Skiddaw House access track. Turn L onto the track and follow it NW to the road near Peter House Farm.

Skiddaw House (above) lies east of Skiddaw on the flanks of Sale How (GR NY287291) and provides basic hostel-type accommodation. Formerly a row of shepherds' cottages, Skiddaw House is now run as a private hostel bookable through the YHA. It's in a very lonely setting, although it has good access from Latrigg Car Park or Melbecks.

The approach to the Bakestall path is a popular mountain bike route

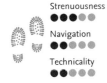

Strenuousness
●●●●○

Navigation
●●●○○

Technicality
●●○○○

751m
(2464ft)

Near Peter House Farm, GR NY249323

2.5 hours
5.6km
(3.5 miles)

Steep-sided valley, steep grassy ridge and stony summit

Via the long bridleway that starts at Latrigg Car Park (GR NY281253) and skirts around the back of Skiddaw

Sale How Path SKIDDAW

'Long with easy gradients' ★

Summary: Climbs to Skiddaw directly over the easy northeastern slopes of Sale How from Skiddaw House. Sale How itself is a little uninteresting but the surrounding hills, collectively known as the Back o' Skidda, display a magnificent wild backdrop more reminiscent of the lonely parts of the Cairngorms than the Lake District.

Ascent: From Latrigg Car Park follow the fenced bridleway NE then N to a fork. Take the R branch and follow it N to Whit Beck; ford the beck and turn E along the bridleway. The bridleway then turns N and makes an airy traverse underneath Lonscale Crags to the broad ridge of Burnt Horse. Skirt NW around the ridge to Skiddaw House. From the back of the plantation climb the path WSW over Sale How to the fence on the east side of Skiddaw. At the fence join the main

bridleway and follow it through the gate as it heads NW then N along the summit crest to Skiddaw.

Descent: Head S along the summit ridge then turn SE and descend to a fence and gate. Through the gate turn L and follow the broad ridge generally ENE over Sale How and then down the path to Skiddaw House. Join the bridleway and follow it SE to Burnt Horse then S across the steep slopes of Lonscale Fell. Once past the crags the bridleway turns W around the ridge and then S again at Whit Beck and is followed to the car park at Latrigg.

	Strenuousness
	●●●●○
	Navigation
	●●○○○
	Technicality
	●●○○○

745m
(2444ft)

Steep-sided valley, open moorland and steep grassy fellside

Latrigg Car Park, GR NY281253

Via the Skiddaw House access road from the road near Peter House Farm (GR NY249323). Alternative route can also be accessed direct from Keswick via the Latrigg Bridleway starting at Briar Rigg GR NY267241.

3 hours
9.1km
(5.7 miles)

Scotland's 4000ft Mountains

Scotland has eight 4000ft (1219m) peaks which can clearly be defined as separate mountains. They lie within two groupings. Ben Nevis, Aonach Beag, Aonach Mòr and Carn Mòr Dearg are found in the central highlands east of Fort William. Ben Macdui, Braeriach, Cairn Toul and Cairn Gorm lie in the Cairngorm Mountains between the River Spey and the River Dee.

Of a far greater altitude and lying at a more northerly latitude, Scotland's highest peaks experience more severe weather conditions than their English and Welsh counterparts. In most years each of these giants will hold snow cover into the summer months and in some corries and gullies right through the year.

The routes, which pass over these eight peaks, are generally long and testing, and require a high degree of experience in anything other than ideal conditions. For those confronting them the reward is some of Europe's finest mountain environment.

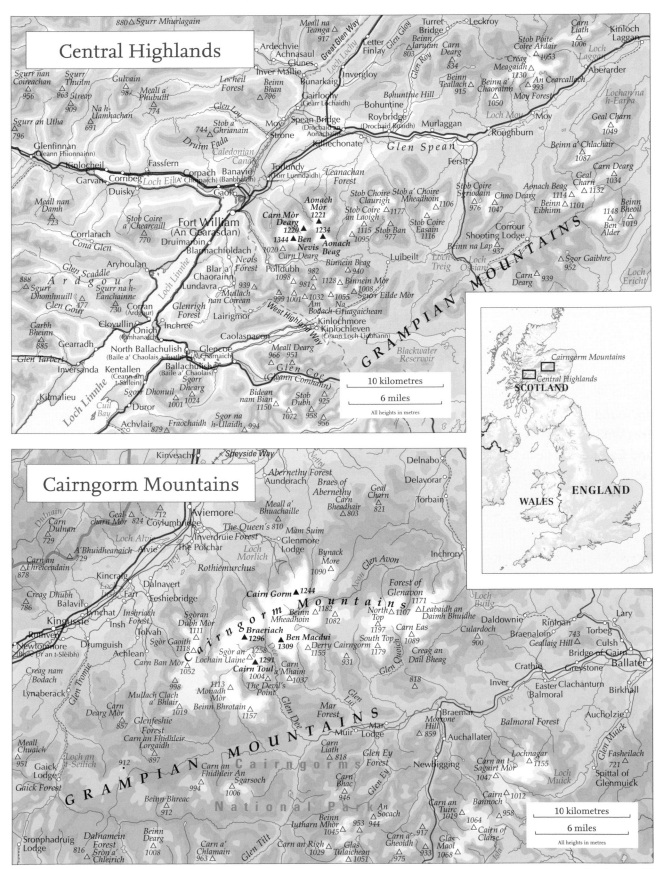

Central Highlands

880 △ Sgurr Mhurlagain

Meall na Teanga 917 △

Great Glen Way

Glen Gloy

Turret Bridge

Leckroy

Carn Liath 1006 △

Kinloch Laggan

Loch Laggan

Sgurr nan Coireachan 956

Sgurr Thuilm 963

Streap 909

Gulvain 987 △

Meall a' Phubuill 774

Lochiel Forest

Ardechvie

Achnasaul

Clunes

Inver Mallie

Bunarkaig

Gairlochy (Gearr Lochaidh)

Letter Finlay

Invergloy

Loch Lochy

Glen Roy

Beinn Iaruinn 803 △

Carn Dearg 834 △

Creag Meagaidh 1130 △

Beinn Teallach 915 △

Beinn a' Chaorainn 1050 △

An Cearcallach 993 △

Moy Forest

Aberarder

Lochan na h-Earba

Na h-Uamhachan 691

Sgurr an Utha 796

Beinn Bhan 796

Bohuntine Hill

Roybridge (Drochaid Ruaidh)

Murlaggan

Moy

Geal Charn 1049 △

Glenfinnan (Gleann Fhionnainn)

Kinlocheil

Fassfern

Corpach

Banavie (Banbhaidh)

Beinn a' Chlachair 1087 △

Carn Dearg 1034 △

Garvan

Corribeg

Duisky

Loch Eil (A' Chorpaich)

Gaoth

Torlundy (Torr Lunndaidh)

Leanachan Forest

Fersit

Stob Coire Sgriodain 976

Chno Dearg 1047

Aonach Beag 1114 △

Geal Charn 1132 △

Beinn Eibhinn 1101 △

Beinn Bheoil 1019 △

Ben Alder 1148 △

Meall nan Damh 723

Corrlarach

Cona Glen

Stob Coire a' Chearcaill 770

Aonach Mòr 1221 ▲

Carn Mòr Dearg 1220 ▲ 1234 ▲

Stob Choire Claurigh Stob a' Choire Mheadhoin 1106

Stob Coire an Laoigh 1177

Stob Coire Easain 1116

Corrour Shooting Lodge

Carn Dearg 939 △

Sgor Gaibhre 952 △

Loch Ericht

Sgurr Dhomhnuill 888

Sgurr na h-Eanchainne 730

Ardgour

Corran (Ardgour)

Fort William (An Gearasdan)

Druimarbin

Blarmachfoldach

Ben Nevis 1344 ▲

Aonach Beug

1020 Carn Dearg

Stob Ban 1115 977

Stob Choire Claurigh 1095

Beinn na Lap 937 △

Loch Ossian

Garbh Bheinn 885

Glen Gour 477

Cloyullin (Comhanach)

Gearradh

Aryhoulan

Glen Scaddle

Lundavra 939

Nevis Forest

Mullach nan Coirean

Polldubh 1098

Binnein Beag 982 940

Binnein Mòr 1128 1008

Sgor Eilde Mòr

Loch Treig

Inchree

Glenrigh Forest

Lairigmor

999 1001 1032

Am Bodach

1055

Na Gruagaichean

Onich

North Ballachulish (Baile a' Chaolais a Tuath)

Glencoe (Baile a' Chaolais)

Caolasnacon

Kinlochmore

Kinlochleven (Ceann Loch Liobhann)

West Highland Way

Inversanda

Kentallen (Ceann an t-Sailein)

Ballachulish (Baile a' Chaolais)

Sgorr Dhearg

Meall Dearg 966 951

Blackwater Reservoir

Kilmalieu

Duror

Sgor a' Chaorainn

Sgorr Dhonuil 1001 1024

Glen Coe (Gleann Comhann)

Bidean nam Bian 1150

Stob Dubh 1072 958

925

Achvlair

Fraochaidh 879

Sgor na h-Ulaidh 994

956

Loch Linnhe

Cuil Bay

GRAMPIAN MOUNTAINS

10 kilometres

6 miles

All heights in metres

Cairngorm Mountains

Kinveachy

Speyside Way

Abernethy Forest

Aundorach

Braes of Abernethy

Carn Bheadhair 803 △

Geal Charn 821

Delnabo

Delavorar

Torbain

Inchrory

Dulnain

Carn Dulnan 729

Geal-charn Mòr 824

712

Coylumbridge

Aviemore

Inverdruie Forest

The Queen's 810

Meall a' Bhuachaille

Mam Suim

Glenmore Lodge

Bynack More 1090

Glen Avon

Forest of Glenavon

A'Bhuidheanaich 729

Alvie

The Polchar

Loch Morlich

Rothiemurchus

Loch Builg

Carn an Fhreiceadain 878

Kincraig

Dalnavert

Feshiebridge

Cairn Gorm 1244 ▲

Beinn Mheadhoin 1182 1082

North Top 1171 1107

Leabaidh an Daimh Bhuidhe

Daldownie

Rinloan

Lary

Creag Dhubh 786

Balavil

Lynchat

Insh

Insfriach Forest

Sgòran Dubh Mòr 1111

Braeriach 1296 ▲

Ben Macdui 1309 ▲

Derry Cairngorm 1155

South Top 1197

Carn Eas 1089

Creag an Dail Bheag

Culardoch 900

Geallaig Hill 743

Torbeg

Bridge of Gairn

Ballater

Kingussie

Ruthven

Newtonmore (Baile Ùr an t-Slèibh)

Drumguish

Tolvah

Achlean

Sgòr Gaoith 1118

Sgòr an Lochain Uaine 1258

Cairn Toul 1291 ▲

Carn a' Mhaim 1037

Derry Cairngorm 931

Creag nam Bodach

Lynaberack

Carn Dearg Mòr 857

Carn Ban Mòr 1052

1004

Lochan Uaine

998

Glen Lui

Glen Quoich

818

Crathie

Inver

Easter Balmoral

Clachanturn

Birkhall

Aucholzie

Glen Muick

Meall Chuaich 951

Loch an t-Seilich

Mullach Clach a' Bhlair 1019

Monadh Mòr 1113

The Devil's Point

Beinn Bhrotain 1157

Glen Dee

Mar Forest

Muir

Mar Lodge

Braemar

Morrone Hill 859

Auchallater

Balmoral Forest

Greystone

Lochnagar 1155

Loch Muick

Fasheilach 721

Spittal of Glenmuick

Gaick Lodge

Gaick Forest

912

Glenfeshie Forest

Carn an Fhidhleir Lorgaidh 897

Carn Liath 818

Glen Ey Forest

Carn an t-Sagairt Mòr 1047

Cairn Bannoch 1012

1064

Cairn of Claise

958

Sronphadruig Lodge

Dalnamein Forest

816

Sròn a' Chleirich

Carn an Fhidhleir (An Sgarsoch) 994 1006

Beinn Bhreac 912

Cairngorms

National Park

Beinn Iutharn Mhòr 1045

953 944

An Socach

Glen Ey

Carn Bhac 946

Carn an Righ 1029

Glas Tulaichean 1051

Carn a' Gheoidh 917

Glas Maol 1068

Carn an Tuirc 1019

Beinn Dearg 1008

Carn a' Chlamain 963

Glen Tilt

GRAMPIAN MOUNTAINS

10 kilometres

6 miles

All heights in metres

Cairngorm Mountains

Central Highlands

SCOTLAND

WALES

ENGLAND

Ben Nevis
1344m (4409ft)

Carn Dearg Northwest
1221m (4006ft)

The most striking feature of Ben Nevis, Britain's highest peak, is the steepness of its slopes. They climb directly from sea level to its lofty summit and are not reduced by the height of the surrounding land. The south and east flanks are craggy and cut into by deep gullies and steep-sided corries. The most dramatic side though is the northeast face. It extends for over 3km (1.9 miles) in a complex series of buttresses, gullies and ridges. At its highest point it towers more than 610m (2000ft) above the waters of the Allt a' Mhuilinn.

With its great height and exposure to the full fury of Atlantic weather systems Ben Nevis receives considerable and long-lasting snow cover. This provides climbers with reliable conditions for winter climbing. Its northeast face is Scotland's (and Britain's) premier crag and an internationally renowned forcing ground for snow and ice standards.

Surrounded by precipitous terrain there are few opportunities on Ben Nevis for walking or scrambling;

Water trough at Wragg's Well, 100m (109yd) south from the observatory. Now in disrepair the trough was originally put in place to serve the observatory. The spring which feeds it can be found above it among the rocks, providing a handy water supply in summer.

Warning
The northeast face of Ben Nevis carries huge cornices well into summer

When you arrive

Ordnance Survey: Explorer 392 (1:25 000) No 32; Landranger (1:50 000) No 41.

Harvey Mountain Maps: Ben Nevis (1:25 000)

British Mountain Maps: Ben Nevis and Glen Coe (1:40 000)

Tourist Information Centres: Fort William

Youth Hostels: Glen Nevis

Hotels and B&B: Fort William; Glen Nevis.

Camp sites: Glen Nevis; Camaghael.

Bothies and Howffs: There is shelter on the summit of Ben Nevis (GR NN167712) but this is strictly for emergencies and should not be used for planned overnight stays. The CIC Hut (GR NN167722) alongside the Allt a' Mhuilinn and the Steall Hut (GR NN177683) in Glen Nevis are locked private huts and need to be booked through either the Scottish Mountaineering Club or the British Mountaineering Council.

The CIC Hut. Built by the Scottish Mountaineering Club in 1928 and dedicated to the memory of Charles Inglis Clark, a prominent club member who was killed in the First World War, the hut is private and locked. On the northwest wall of the hut a small annexe holds rescue kit and a radio telephone. The radio provides a direct link to the police and mountain rescue team to summon help in emergencies.

however, those that exist are challenging and in winter potentially hazardous. Of the five main possible routes up Ben Nevis, the Pony Track, which climbs by the easier-angled northwest flank gets the majority of the traffic. The track was constructed to service the summit meteorological observatory which operated between 1883 and 1904, the remains of which are still visible at the summit when not buried by snow, and it provides a long but well-graded route. In its time it has seen a wide variety of objects ridden, driven, carried and walked up it – mostly in aid of charity. By contrast the other routes see very little traffic and you can expect to have them to yourself on most occasions.

Warning
The eastern shoulder of Ben Nevis forms a steep convex slope which steepens abruptly to the crags of the Brenva Face, which is also prone to severe icing

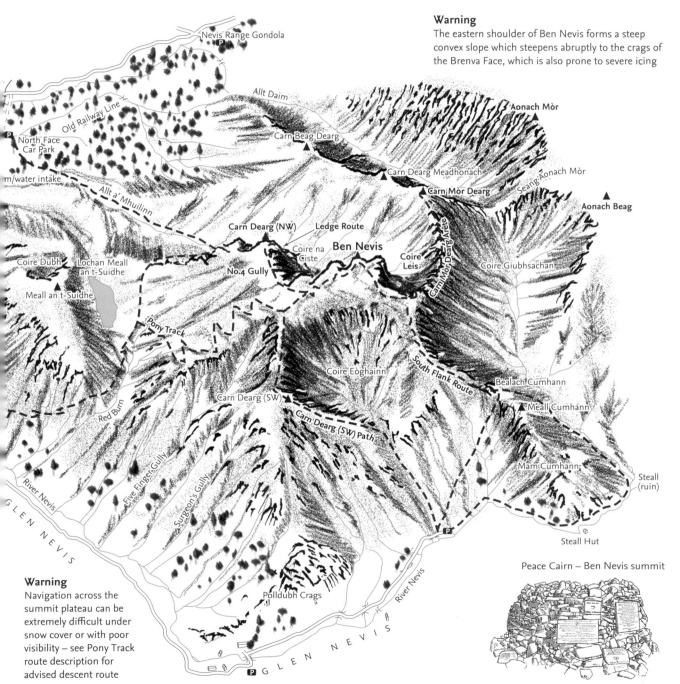

Warning
Navigation across the summit plateau can be extremely difficult under snow cover or with poor visibility – see Pony Track route description for advised descent route

Peace Cairn – Ben Nevis summit

South Flank Route BEN NEVIS

'Steep but short approach' ★

Summary: The South Flank of Ben Nevis is very steep and a little monotonous but it does provide the shortest approach.

Ascent: From the car park traverse NE up to the Bealach Cumhann. From the Bealach climb the ridge NW then NNE past the top of Sloc nan Uan to the shoulder where the Carn Mòr Dearg Arête abuts Ben Nevis (2m [6.5ft] cairn for navigation). Turn L and climb the steep path which swings NW onto the summit plateau.

Descent: Descend the southeastern ridge around the top of the Little Brenva Face (Coire Leis) to the shoulder where the Carn Mòr Dearg Arête abuts Ben Nevis (2m [6.5ft] cairn for navigation). From here descend steeply SSW to the head of Sloc nan Uan then SE down the steep ridge to Bealach Cumhann. The southeastern ridge suffers from severe icing in winter and the slopes fall away in a convex shape. A fall in these conditions would be difficult to arrest so unless you have prior experience of the terrain a descent in winter or under snow cover cannot be recommended.

The remains of the meteorological observatory with emergency shelter in position on top of the tower. The shelter contains rescue kit and is strictly for emergency use only – no overnight stays in it should be planned. In winter, snow usually covers the remains of the observatory to the top of the tower.

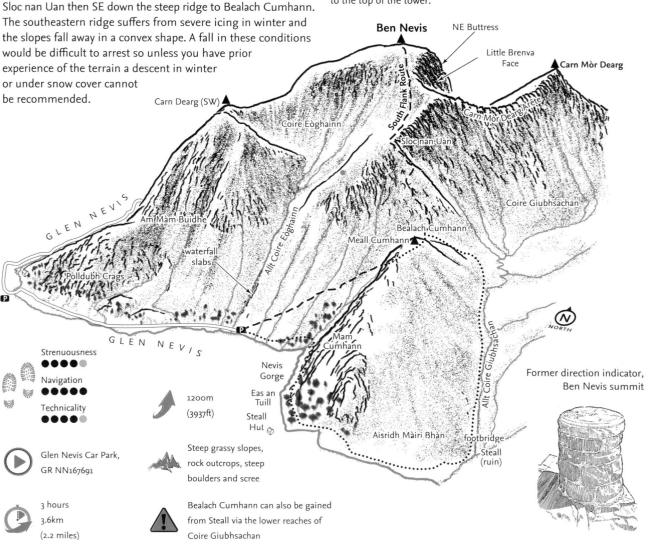

Former direction indicator, Ben Nevis summit

Strenuousness ●●●●○

Navigation ●●●●●

Technicality ●●●●○

1200m (3937ft)

Glen Nevis Car Park, GR NN167691

3 hours
3.6km
(2.2 miles)

Steep grassy slopes, rock outcrops, steep boulders and scree

Bealach Cumhann can also be gained from Steall via the lower reaches of Coire Giubhsachan

Carn Dearg (Southwest) Path BEN NEVIS

'Steep but rewarding' ★★

Summary: Coire Eòghainn on the south side of Ben Nevis is bounded by the minor peak Carn Dearg (Southwest). Its east ridge and the ridge linking it with Ben Nevis, set high above Glen Nevis with expansive Southwest (Ben Nevis) views, makes it a superb route.

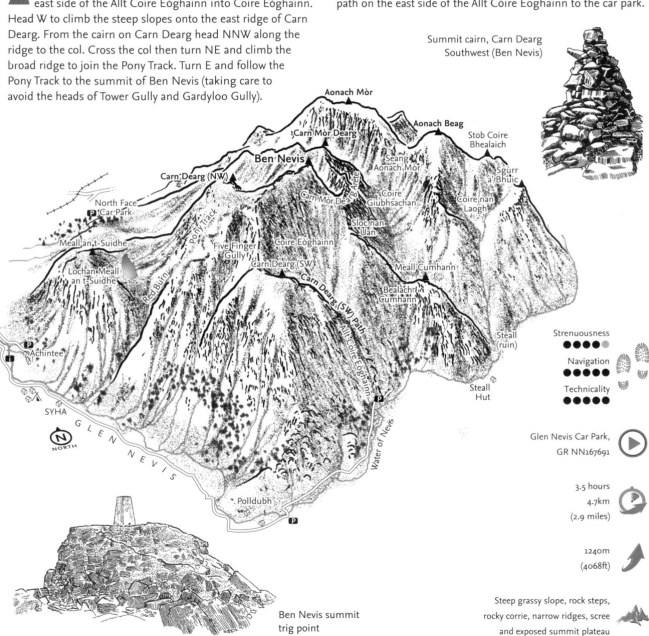

Ascent: From the car park climb the steep path on the east side of the Allt Coire Eòghainn into Coire Eòghainn. Head W to climb the steep slopes onto the east ridge of Carn Dearg. From the cairn on Carn Dearg head NNW along the ridge to the col. Cross the col then turn NE and climb the broad ridge to join the Pony Track. Turn E and follow the Pony Track to the summit of Ben Nevis (taking care to avoid the heads of Tower Gully and Gardyloo Gully).

Descent: Descend the Pony Track W (taking care to avoid the heads of Gardyloo Gully and Tower Gully) to the big bend just before the head of Five Finger Gully. Descend the broad ridge first S then SW to the col on the north side of Carn Dearg. Cross the col and climb easily SSE to Carn Dearg. From the summit cairn descend the narrow ridge E then the steep slopes NE into Coire Eòghainn. From the corrie descend the path on the east side of the Allt Còire Eoghainn to the car park.

Summit cairn, Carn Dearg Southwest (Ben Nevis)

Aonach Mòr

Aonach Beag

Carn Mòr Dearg

Stob Coire Bhealaich

Ben Nevis

Seang Aonach Mòr

Sgurr a'Bhuic

Carn Dearg (NW)

Carn Mòr De

Coire Giubhsachan

Coire nan Laogh

North Face Car Park

Sloc nan Uan

Meall an t-Suidhe

Coire Eòghainn

Five Finger Gully

Carn Dearg (SW)

Meall Cumhann

Lochan Meall an t-Suidhe

Red Burn

Pony Track

Carn Dearg (SW) Path

Bealach Cumhann

Achintee

Allt Coire Eòghainn

Steall (ruin)

SYHA

Steall Hut

G L E N   N E V I S

N
NORTH

Water of Nevis

Polldubh

Ben Nevis summit trig point

Strenuousness
●●●●○

Navigation
●●●●●

Technicality
●●●●●

Glen Nevis Car Park,
GR NN167691

3.5 hours
4.7km
(2.9 miles)

1240m
(4068ft)

Steep grassy slope, rock steps, rocky corrie, narrow ridges, scree and exposed summit plateau

Pony Track BEN NEVIS

'Well graded but dull' ★

Summary: Constructed to service the summit meteorological observatory, which opened in 1883, the Pony Track remains almost wholly intact. It traverses the southwest side of Meall an t-Suidhe, then zigzags the broad west slopes of Ben Nevis to the summit plateau. In summer its course is easy to follow but when the winter snow arrives much of it is obliterated. The hazards in winter on the Pony Track are not as obvious as on Ben Nevis's other routes; for this reason walkers and climbers regularly get into difficulty on it. The problems encountered en route include the cornices at the head of Gardyloo Gully and Tower Gully, mistaken descent into Five Finger Gully and crossing the top of the Red Burn. Despite all these problems, the Pony Track is still the safest route to take in winter.

Ascent: Exit the car park through the gate then climb the Pony Track as it climbs along the terrace first SE then NE to the moorland at the south end of Lochan Meall an t-Suidhe. At the cairn, head S and cross the top of Red Burn (in winter this can involve a short section of steep snow). Once past the Red Burn the Pony Track zigzags ESE between Coire na h-Urchaire and the top of Five Finger Gully onto the summit plateau. Turn E across the plateau to the summit taking care to avoid the edge of the northeast face and the heads of Tower and Gardyloo Gullies. Navigation cairns mark the final approach to the summit; these are positioned for winter navigation.

Descent: Head W from the summit avoiding the heads of Gardyloo and Tower Gullies then descend the zigzags down the broad slopes between Five Finger Gully and Coire na h-Urchaire. Cross the Red Burn and head N to the cairn overlooking Lochan Meall an t-Suidhe. Turn L and head SW then NW down the terrace to the car park at Achintee.

Clearing the summit plateau in winter or in poor visibility is particularly hazardous. A series of navigation cairns starting close to the summit trig point have been constructed to help avoid the worst hazards. However, even at 1.8m (6ft) high some have been buried during very snowy winters so it is imperative that you are prepared and able to navigate without the assistance of the cairns. The recommended route when snow is lying or in poor visibility is:

1. From the summit trig point follow a bearing of 231° (grid) for 150m (164yd).

2. Then turn to a bearing of 282° (grid). This will take you to the Pony Track 100m (109yd) N of the top of Five Finger Gully. (Note: you will need to make allowance for magnetic variation).

Strenuousness
● ● ● ● ○

Navigation
● ● ● ● ○

Technicality
● ● ● ○ ○

Achintee,
Glen Nevis,
GR NN126729

4 hours
7.8km
(4.8 miles)

1335m
(4380ft)

Rocky slopes, moorland, steep expansive slopes, boulder fields and exposed summit plateau

Direct start from the Glen Nevis SYHA GR NN128718

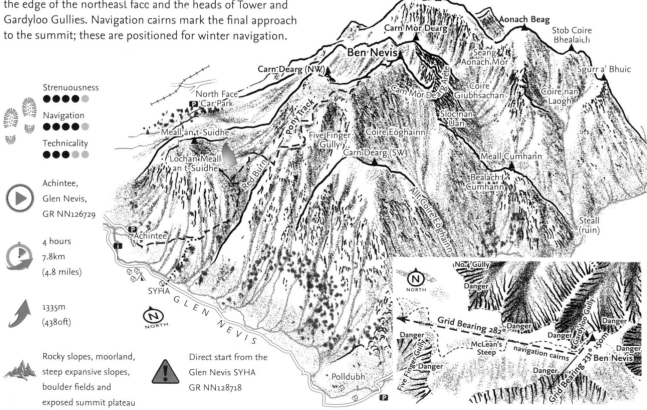

Ledge Route BEN NEVIS

'A mountaineering classic' ★ ★ ★

Summary: The northeast face of Ben Nevis extends for 3km (1.9 miles) in a complex series of corries and ridges high above the Allt a' Mhuilinn. The first most striking feature is the Great Buttress of Carn Dearg. The Ledge Route climbs a devious meandering line up its south side (No. 5 Gully Buttress) to the top of the Great Buttress, then follows the crest of the superb connecting ridge to Carn Dearg (Northwest). Snow regularly lies through summer in No. 5 Gully (the approach route), in which circumstances an ice axe is recommended.

Ascent: From the North Face Car Park follow the Ben Nevis approach path up through the trees to the side of the Allt a' Mhuilinn. Head up the Allt a' Mhuilinn on the northeast side to the CIC Hut. Cross the Allt a' Mhuilinn and climb WSW up the slabs and scree to the foot of the Great Buttress of Carn Dearg. Continue WSW up the south side of the buttress into No. 5 Gully. Climb the gully to the ramp (third from the entrance of the gully) on the R. Ascend it across a slab then around the ledge to a gully/groove system. Climb this as it trends L to gain another ledge. Turn R along this ledge and follow it to a platform (large perched boulder). From here gain the crest of the ridge and follow it as it winds its way W to Carn Dearg. From Carn Dearg skirt S around the edge of the crags to join the Pony Track which is then followed E to the summit of Ben Nevis.

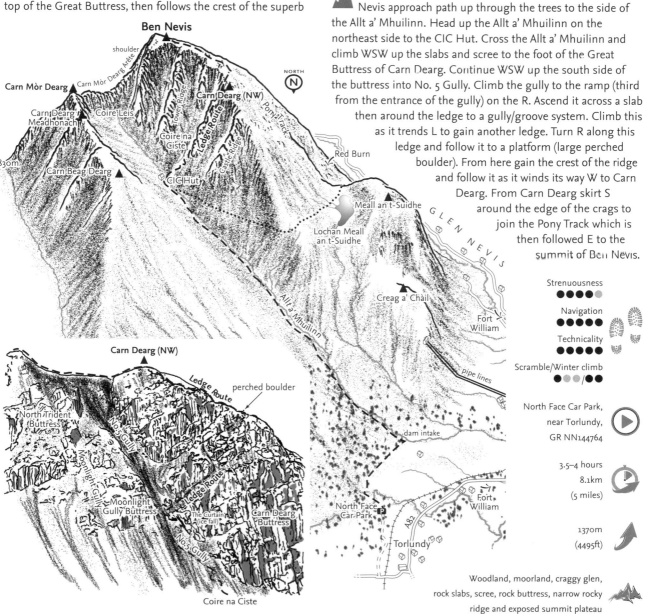

Coire na Ciste

Strenuousness
● ● ● ● ○

Navigation
● ● ● ● ●

Technicality
● ● ● ● ●

Scramble/Winter climb
● ● ○ / ● ●

North Face Car Park,
near Torlundy,
GR NN144764

3.5–4 hours
8.1km
(5 miles)

1370m
(4495ft)

Woodland, moorland, craggy glen,
rock slabs, scree, rock buttress, narrow rocky
ridge and exposed summit plateau

No. 4 Gully (see illustration on page 63) provides a slightly easier (but loose) alternative out of Coire na Ciste although it is not often snow free – under full snow cover it is a Grade 1 winter climb and usually carries a cornice. The Allt a' Mhuilinn can also be gained from Glen Nevis, first along the Pony Track then via the path along the east side of Lochan Meall an t-Suidhe.

Coire Leis Route BEN NEVIS

'Dramatic and revealing' ★

Summary: Follows the course of the Allt a' Mhuilinn then climbs the headwall of Coire Leis onto the southeast shoulder of Ben Nevis. An ideal route to view the entire northeast face at close quarters. The headwall of Coire Leis holds a considerable quantity of snow into the summer months, and in winter it is prone to avalanche and very severe icing.

Ascent: From the North Face Car Park follow the Ben Nevis approach path up through the trees to the side of the Allt a' Mhuilinn. Head up the Allt a' Mhuilinn on the northeast side to the CIC Hut then cross it and follow it up into Coire Leis. Head SW through the corrie then turn S and ascend the headwall. The best line is slightly W of the scree line from the col at the start of the Carn Mòr Dearg Arête. At the navigation cairn on the col turn R and climb the steep path which swings NW onto the summit plateau.

Descent: Descend the southeastern ridge around the top of the Little Brenva Face (Coire Leis) to the shoulder where the Carn Mòr Dearg Arête abuts Ben Nevis (2m [6.5ft] navigation cairn). From the navigation cairn descend steeply N into Coire Leis (best line lies slightly W), then follow the southwest side of the Allt a' Mhuilinn NW down to the CIC Hut. Once past the hut join the path on the northeast side and follow it down to the North Face Car Park. In poor visibility or under snow cover this descent route cannot be recommended.

Strenuousness ●●●●○

Navigation ●●●●●

Technicality ●●●●●

Scramble/Winter climb ●●●/●●

NORTH (N)

1320m (4331ft)

North Face Car Park, near Torlundy, GR NN144764

Woodland, moorland, craggy glen, rough scree-filled corrie, steep headwall, boulder-strewn ridge and exposed summit plateau

4 hours 7.4km (4.6 miles)

The Allt a' Mhuilinn can also be gained from Glen Nevis, first along the Pony Track then via the path along the east side of Lochan Meall an t-Suidhe

Carn Mòr Dearg Arête BEN NEVIS

'One of Britain's best ridges' ★★★

Summary: One of the finest ridges in Britain though more for the setting than the actual terrain.

Route: Descend the southeastern ridge around the top of the Little Brenva Face (Coire Leis) to the shoulder where the Carn Mòr Dearg Arête abuts Ben Nevis (2m [6.5ft] navigation cairn).

Join the Carn Mòr Dearg Arête and follow its crest NE then climb it N directly to the summit of Carn Mòr Dearg. In poor visibility or with snow cover, locating the correct line of descent down the southeast shoulder of Ben Nevis is very difficult.

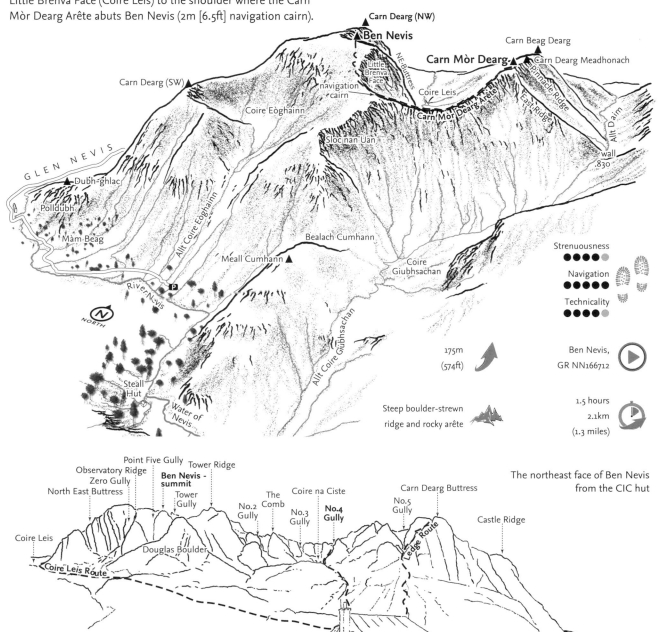

Strenuousness ●●●●○

Navigation ●●●●●

Technicality ●●●●○

175m
(574ft)

Steep boulder-strewn
ridge and rocky arête

Ben Nevis,
GR NN166712

1.5 hours
2.1km
(1.3 miles)

The northeast face of Ben Nevis
from the CIC hut

Ben Macdui
1309m (4296ft)

North Top 1295m (4247ft)
Stob Coire Sputan Dearg
1249m (4098ft)

Until the Ordnance Survey finally settled the matter in 1847 many people believed that Ben Macdui was the highest peak in Scotland (and Britain). It may now be relegated to second place, but it is, nevertheless, a big mountain in all respects. Its bulk dominates the east side of the Lairig Ghru with its outlying ridges extending north to Creag an Leth-choin and south to Carn a' Mhaim. To the east its influence is cast over the Loch Avon Basin, the broad corrie occupied by Loch Etchachan and the shapely upper reaches of Glen Luibeg.

Ben Macdui has an ill-defined shape. It looks impressive from most viewpoints, but its attractiveness lies in its detail rather than in the mountain as a whole. Lost among the clutter of subsidiary tops, ridges and corries it is a mountain better explored than viewed.

Lying at the centre of a subarctic plateau Ben Macdui experiences atrociously bad weather. All routes to its summit involve either traversing precipitous ground or passing close by it, and although they may not be very demanding technically they are notoriously difficult to retreat from.

Direction indicator, near Ben Macdui's trig point

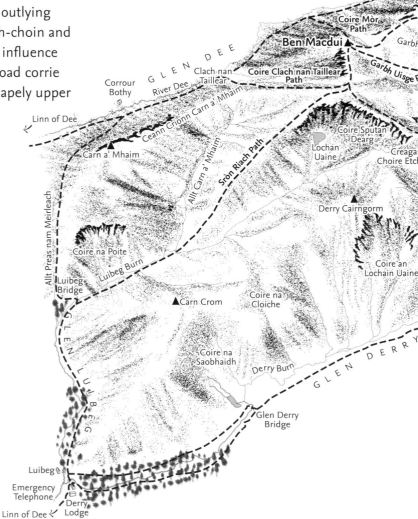

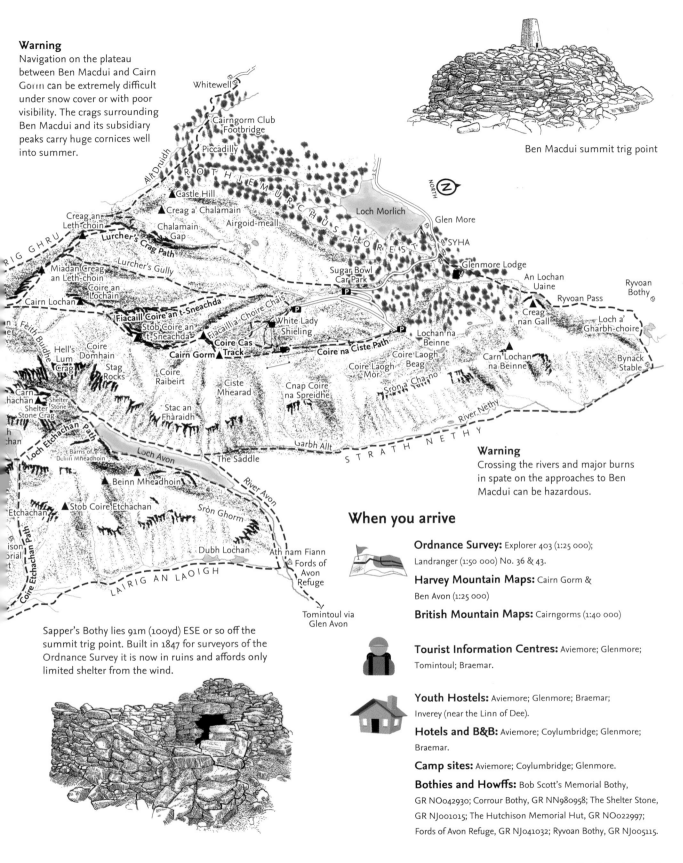

Warning
Navigation on the plateau between Ben Macdui and Cairn Gorm can be extremely difficult under snow cover or with poor visibility. The crags surrounding Ben Macdui and its subsidiary peaks carry huge cornices well into summer.

Ben Macdui summit trig point

Whitewell

Cairngorm Club Footbridge

Piccadilly

Alt Druidh

R O T H I E M U R C H U S F O R E S T

Castle Hill

Creag a' Chalamain

Creag an Leth-choin

Chalamain Gap

Airgoid-meall

Loch Morlich

NORTH

Glen More

SYHA

Glenmore Lodge

An Lochan Uaine

Ryvoan Bothy

LAIRIG GHRU

Lurcher's Crag Path

Lurcher's Gully

Miadan Creag an Leth-choin

Coire an Lochain

Cairn Lochan

Feith Buidhe

Fiacaill Coire an t-Sneachda

Stob Coire an t-Sneachda

Fiacaill a' Choire Chais

Fiacaill a' Choire Chais

Coire Cas Track

Cairn Gorm

Sugar Bowl Car Park

White Lady Shieling

Coire na Ciste Path

Lochan na Beinne

Coire Laogh Beag

Creag nan Gall

Ryvoan Pass

Loch a' Gharbh-choire

Carn Lochan na Beinne

Bynack Stable

Hell's Lum Crag

Coire Domhain

Stag Rocks

Coire Raibeirt

Ciste Mhearad

Coire Laogh Mòr

Sròn a' Cha-no

Carn Etchachan

Shelter Stone

Shelter Stone Crag

Stac an Fhàraidh

Cnap Coire na Spreidhe

Garbh Allt

S T R A T H N E T H Y

River Nethy

Loch Etchachan Path

Barns of Bynack Mheadhoin

Loch Avon

The Saddle

Beinn Mheadhoin

River Avon

Sròn Ghorm

Warning
Crossing the rivers and major burns in spate on the approaches to Ben Macdui can be hazardous.

Loch Etchachan

Stob Coire Etchachan

Dubh Lochan

Ath nam Fiann Fords of Avon Refuge

Jean's Memorial

Coire Etchachan Path

L A I R I G A N L A O I G H

Tomintoul via Glen Avon

When you arrive

Ordnance Survey: Explorer 403 (1:25 000); Landranger (1:50 000) No. 36 & 43.

Harvey Mountain Maps: Cairn Gorm & Ben Avon (1:25 000)

British Mountain Maps: Cairngorms (1:40 000)

Tourist Information Centres: Aviemore; Glenmore; Tomintoul; Braemar.

Youth Hostels: Aviemore; Glenmore; Braemar; Inverey (near the Linn of Dee).

Hotels and B&B: Aviemore; Coylumbridge; Glenmore; Braemar.

Camp sites: Aviemore; Coylumbridge; Glenmore.

Bothies and Howffs: Bob Scott's Memorial Bothy, GR NO042930; Corrour Bothy, GR NN980958; The Shelter Stone, GR NJ001015; The Hutchison Memorial Hut, GR NO022997; Fords of Avon Refuge, GR NJ041032; Ryvoan Bothy, GR NJ005115.

Sapper's Bothy lies 91m (100yd) ESE or so off the summit trig point. Built in 1847 for surveyors of the Ordnance Survey it is now in ruins and affords only limited shelter from the wind.

Sròn Riach Path BEN MACDUI

'Well graded with dramatic views' ★★

Summary: A long, straightforward route via the rounded ridge of Sròn Riach. The most direct route to Ben Macdui from Deeside.

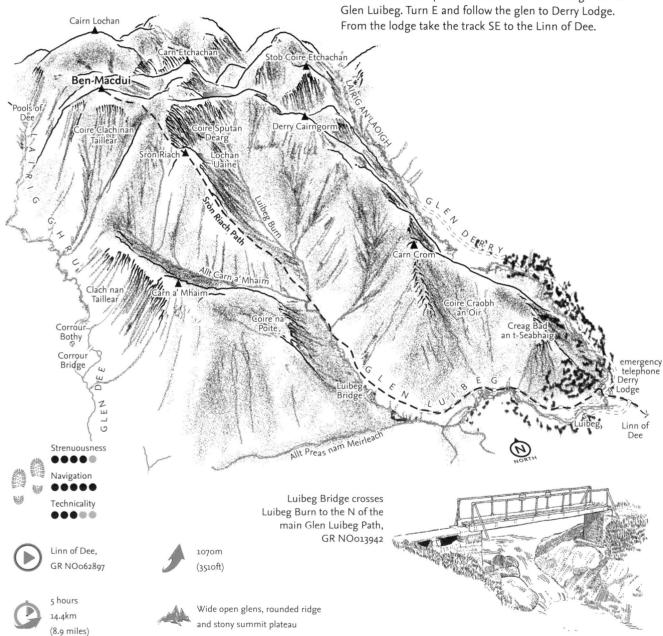 **Ascent:** From the Linn of Dee head N then NW to Derry Lodge (emergency telephone), pass the lodge and continue along Glen Luibeg to Luibeg Bridge. Pass the bridge and head N alongside Luibeg Burn to the foot of the Sròn Riach. Climb NW up the Sròn Riach past the tor at the top and onto the broad col at the head of Coire Clach nan Taillear. Turn WNW and climb directly to the summit of Ben Macdui.

Descent: Drop down to the broad col on the east-southeast side of Ben Macdui then skirt the head of Coire Clach nan Taillear to the top of the Sròn Riach. Descend SE then follow the path on the east side of Luibeg Burn to Glen Luibeg. Turn E and follow the glen to Derry Lodge. From the lodge take the track SE to the Linn of Dee.

Cairn Lochan

Carn Etchachan

Stob Coire Etchachan

Ben Macdui

Pools of Dee

LAIRIG GHRU

LAIRIG AN LAOIGH

Coire Clach nan Taillear

Coire Sputan Dearg

Derry Cairngorm

Sròn Riach

Lochan Uaine

Luibeg Burn

Sròn Riach Path

GLEN DERRY

Carn Crom

Allt Carn a' Mhaim

Clach nan Taillear

Carn a' Mhaim

Coire Craobh an Oir

Coire na Poite

Corrour Bothy

Creag Bad an t-Seabhaig

Corrour Bridge

GLEN DEE

GLEN LUIBEG

emergency telephone Derry Lodge

Luibeg Bridge

Luibeg

Linn of Dee

Allt Preas nam Meirleach

N
NORTH

Strenuousness
●●●●○

Navigation
●●●●●

Technicality
●●●○○

Luibeg Bridge crosses Luibeg Burn to the N of the main Glen Luibeg Path, GR NO013942

Linn of Dee, GR NO062897

1070m (3510ft)

5 hours
14.4km
(8.9 miles)

Wide open glens, rounded ridge and stony summit plateau

Coire Clach nan Taillear Path BEN MACDUI

'Good Lairig Ghru link'

Summary: On the south side of Ben Macdui, directly below the summit dome, Coire Clach nan Taillear falls away steeply into Glen Dee. It derives its name from the ribbed boulders (Clach nan Taillear) further S down the glen where tradition has it that three tailors died in a snow storm on New Year's Eve as they traversed the Lairig Ghru between Speyside and Deeside. It is particularly useful as an approach from Corrour Bothy. The corrie is steep and loose in parts and under snow cover it is prone to avalanche.

Ascent: From the Linn of Dee head N then NW to Derry Lodge (emergency telephone), pass the lodge and continue along Glen Luibeg to Luibeg Bridge. Cross the bridge then swing W over the col into Glen Dee. Join the Lairig Ghru Path and follow it N up Glen Dee to the Allt Clach nan Taillear. Turn NE and follow the burn steeply up Coire Clach nan Taillear. Continue NE to the crest of the col then turn W to the summit of Ben Macdui.

Descent: Head E down onto the broad col at the head of Coire Clach nan Taillear. From the col descend steeply SW down the corrie, first on the left bank then on the right, until the Lairig Ghru Path is reached. Take it S down Glen Dee until the start of the Glen Luibeg Path. Follow it SE then E over the col and over Luibeg Bridge to Derry Lodge. From the lodge take the track SE to the Linn of Dee.

Clach nan Taillear

Wide open glens, steep rocky corrie and stony summit plateau

From the Linn of Dee an alternative route is to take the Glen Dee track past White Bridge then on to the Lairig Ghru Path. Can also be started from Speyside from either Whitewell, GR NH915086, or Loch Morlich, GR NH956097.

1120m (3674ft)

Strenuousness
●●●●●

Navigation
●●●●●

Technicality
●●●○○

Linn of Dee, GR NO062897

5.5 hours
17.8km
(11 miles)

Coire Mòr Path BEN MACDUI

'Handy but very steep'

Summary: Boulder strewn and fairly steep, the Coire Mòr Path is not the most obvious route on Ben Macdui. It does provide a direct link with An Garbh Choire though, across the Lairig Ghru, and for that purpose is useful as a through route.

Ascent: From the Linn of Dee head N then NW to Derry Lodge (emergency telephone), pass the lodge and continue along Glen Luibeg to Luibeg Bridge. Cross the bridge then swing W over the col into Glen Dee. Join the Lairig Ghru Path and follow it N up Glen Dee to the Allt a' Choire Mhòir. Turn E and climb the steep broad ridge on the south side of Coire Mòr. As the angle eases (near the aircraft wreckage and memorial) turn SE to the summit of Ben Macdui.

Descent: Head NW across the summit dome as the slope steepens (near the aircraft wreckage and memorial) turn W and follow the broad ridge steeply down the south side of Coire Mòr. At the bottom join the Lairig Ghru Path and follow it S down Glen Dee until the start of the Glen Luibeg Path. Take it and follow it SE then E over the col and over Luibeg Bridge to Derry Lodge. From the lodge take the track SE to the Linn of Dee.

Strenuousness ●●●●●

Navigation ●●●●●

Technicality ●●●●○

1140m
(3740ft)

Linn of Dee,
GR NO062897

Wide open glens, steep rocky
corrie and stony summit plateau

6 hours
18.4km
(11.4 miles)

From the Linn of Dee an alternative is to take the Glen Dee track past White Bridge then on to the Lairig Ghru Path. Can also be started from Speyside from either Whitewell, GR NH915086, or Loch Morlich, GR NH956097.

Lurcher's Crag Path BEN MACDUI

'High-level approach' ★ ★ ★

Summary: Forming the impressive east wall of the Lairig Ghru, the long ridge of Creag an Leth-choin can be easily gained from Rothiemurchus via the easy slopes of the Chalamain Gap. It gives a fine high-level approach to Ben Macdui via the western shoulder of Cairn Lochan.

Ascent: Take the Gleann Eanaich track S to Lochan Deò then turn E and follow the path over the Cairngorm Club Footbridge to the junction at Piccadilly. Take the Lairig Ghru Path SE to the junction with the Chalamain Gap Path. Join it and follow it N, then turn SE and climb the steep slopes to Creag an Leth-choin. Continue SE past the head of Lurcher's Gully to the col on the west side of Cairn Lochan. From the col, head SSE past Lochan Buidhe to Ben Macdui.

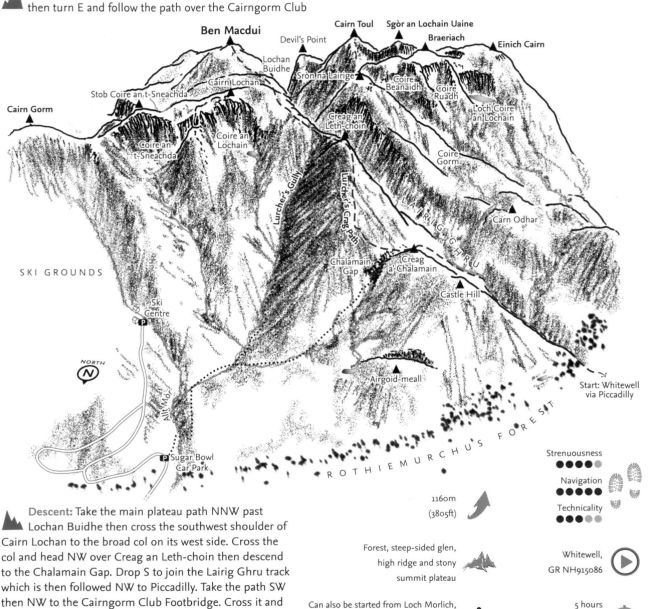

Descent: Take the main plateau path NNW past Lochan Buidhe then cross the southwest shoulder of Cairn Lochan to the broad col on its west side. Cross the col and head NW over Creag an Leth-choin then descend to the Chalamain Gap. Drop S to join the Lairig Ghru track which is then followed NW to Piccadilly. Take the path SW then NW to the Cairngorm Club Footbridge. Cross it and head W along the path to join the Gleann Eanaich track which is then followed N to Whitewell.

1160m
(3805ft)

Forest, steep-sided glen, high ridge and stony summit plateau

Can also be started from Loch Morlich, GR NH956097, or the Sugar Bowl Car Park, GR NN984073. If starting at the Sugar Bowl, Lurcher's Gully provides an easier alternative line.

Strenuousness ●●●●○

Navigation ●●●●●

Technicality ●●●○○

Whitewell, GR NH915086

5 hours
14.4km
(8.9 miles)

Fiacaill Coire an t-Sneachda BEN MACDUI

'Exciting scramble' ★ ★ ★

Summary: The Fiacaill Coire an t-Sneachda extends north between the steep crags of Coire an Lochain and Coire an t-Sneachda. An entertaining scramble, it gives an adventurous approach to Ben Macdui via the slopes of Cairn Lochan.

Ascent: From the car park cross the Allt a' Choire Chais and follow the constructed path SW across the mouth of Coire an t-Sneachda. After crossing the Allt Coire an t-Sneachda turn S and climb the broad ridge to the Fiacaill Coire an t-Sneachda. Continue S up the Fiacaill onto the slopes east of Cairn Lochan. Descend S to join the main plateau path. Take it and head SSE past Lochan Buidhe to Ben Macdui.

Descent: Take the main plateau path NNW past Lochan Buidhe to the col at the top of Coire Domhain. Climb W to the top of the Fiacaill Coire an t-Sneachda (there is a cairn, but in winter it is usually obliterated by snow – under such conditions the Fiacaill cannot be recommended as a descent). Descend N and continue down the broad ridge to join the main corries path. Follow it NE to Coire Cas Car Park.

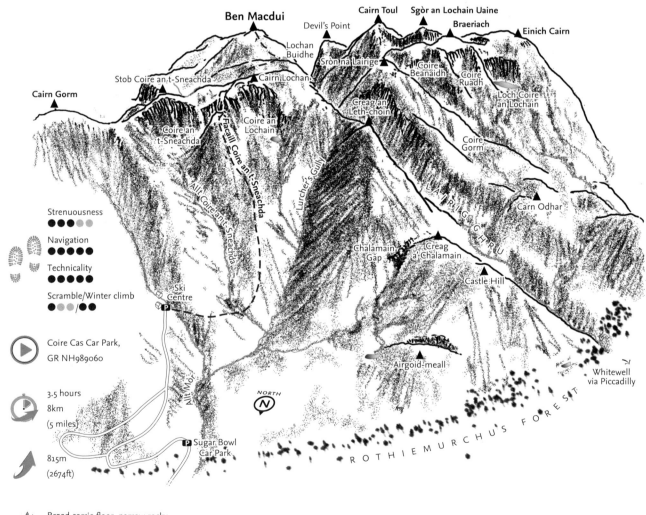

Strenuousness
● ● ● ● ○

Navigation
● ● ● ● ●

Technicality
● ● ● ● ●

Scramble/Winter climb
● ● ○ / ● ●

▶ Coire Cas Car Park,
GR NH989060

3.5 hours
8km
(5 miles)

815m
(2674ft)

Broad corrie floor, narrow rocky
ridge and high mountain plateau

RIGHT
Ben Macdui from Braeriach

Coire Cas Track BEN MACDUI

'Spoilt by the ski grounds'

Summary: A broad constructed track that winds its way through the ski grounds to the summit of Cairn Gorm. From Cairn Gorm, a well-trodden path meanders south across the plateau to Ben Macdui. In good conditions an easy walk; in a blizzard near-impossible.

Ascent: From the car park follow the track SE up through Coire Cas then traverse NE to the funicular top station. Turn S and follow the waymarked track to Cairn Gorm. Descend W from the radio relay station and follow the main plateau path as it skirts the top of Coire Raibeirt and Coire an t-Sneachda to the head of Coire Domhain. Turn S then SW and traverse the southeast side of Cairn Lochan to Lochan Buidhe. The path then swings to the SSE; follow it as it winds its way up the summit slopes of Ben Macdui.

Descent: Take the main plateau path NNW past Lochan Buidhe to the col at the top of Coire Domhain then skirt the heads of Coire an t-Sneachda and Coire Raibeirt NE to Cairn Gorm. Descend N from the radio relay station and follow the waymarked path to the funicular top station. Turn W and follow the track as it traverses around to the S and into Coire Cas. Continue along the track and follow it NW through Coire Cas to the car park.

Strenuousness
●●●○○

Navigation
●●●●●

Technicality
●●●●○

Coire Cas Car Park,
GR NH989060

950m
(3084ft)

3.5 hours
10km
(6.2 miles)

Broad open corrie, stony summit slopes and high mountain plateau

Garbh Uisge Path BEN MACDUI

'Entertaining scramble' ★ ★ ★

Summary: Garbh Uisge tumbles into the Loch Avon Basin in a series of dashes and cascades. The scramble up its east side makes a magnificent route to Ben Macdui. The surrounding rock architecture is superb and the views over Loch Avon are simply stunning. This route is considerably more difficult under snow cover, which can extend well into summer.

Ascent: Take the Glenmore Lodge road and follow it E past the lodge, then NE and take the Ryvoan Pass Track. After An Lochan Uaine the track splits. Take the right-hand branch and follow it E then SE to the footbridge. Cross the River Nethy and follow the narrow path S down Strath Nethy to The Saddle. Cross over the broad col and follow the path SW above Loch Avon to the head of the loch. Follow the Feith Buidhe to its junction with the Garbh Uisge. Then scramble S up the east side of Garbh Uisge. At the top, head SW across the huge open corrie and make the final ascent up the broad ridge to Ben Macdui's summit.

Descent: Head NE down the broad ridge then across the huge open corrie to the confluence of the Garbh Uisge Beag and the Garbh Uisge Mòr. Follow the east side of the Garbh Uisge and scramble down alongside it into the Loch Avon Basin. At the bottom join the path on the north side of the loch to The Saddle. Cross the broad col and head N the length of Strath Nethy to the footbridge. Cross it and take the path NW then W to join the Ryvoan Pass Track. Turn L onto it and follow it to Glenmore.

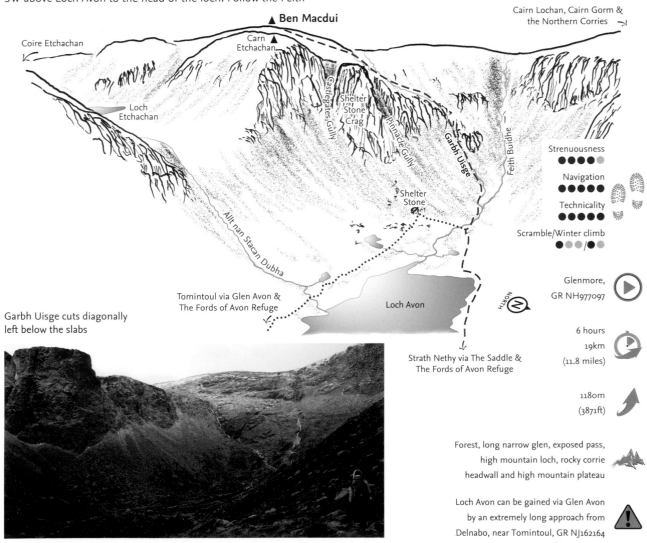

Garbh Uisge cuts diagonally left below the slabs

Strenuousness ● ● ● ● ○

Navigation ● ● ● ● ●

Technicality ● ● ● ● ●

Scramble/Winter climb ● ● ○ / ● ○

Glenmore, GR NH977097

6 hours
19km
(11.8 miles)

1180m
(3871ft)

Forest, long narrow glen, exposed pass, high mountain loch, rocky corrie headwall and high mountain plateau

Loch Avon can be gained via Glen Avon by an extremely long approach from Delnabo, near Tomintoul, GR NJ162164

Loch Etchachan Path BEN MACDUI

'Good for overnighting' ★ ★ ★

Summary: A popular path that climbs the south side of the Loch Avon Basin to Loch Etchachan from the Shelter Stone.

Ascent: Take the Glenmore Lodge road and follow it E past the lodge then NE and take the Ryvoan Pass Track. After An Lochan Uaine the track splits. Take the right-hand branch and follow it E then SE to the footbridge. Cross the River Nethy and follow the narrow path S down Strath Nethy to The Saddle. Cross over the broad col and follow the path SW above Loch Avon to the Shelter Stone at the head of the loch. Climb the path that traverses ESE to the col on the east side of Carn Etchachan then cross the open ground SSE to the outlet of Loch Etchachan. Cross the burn and join the path on the other side which is taken SW then W to Ben Macdui.

Descent: Take the path E down to the broad col then follow the path as it swings NE and steadily descends to Loch Etchachan. Cross the outlet burn and head NNW across open ground to the col on the east side of Carn Etchachan. Turn WNW and traverse down to the Shelter Stone. Join the path on the north side of the loch and follow it to The Saddle. Cross the broad col and head N the length of Strath Nethy to the footbridge. Cross it and take the path NW then W to join the Ryvoan Pass Track. Turn L onto it and follow it to Glenmore.

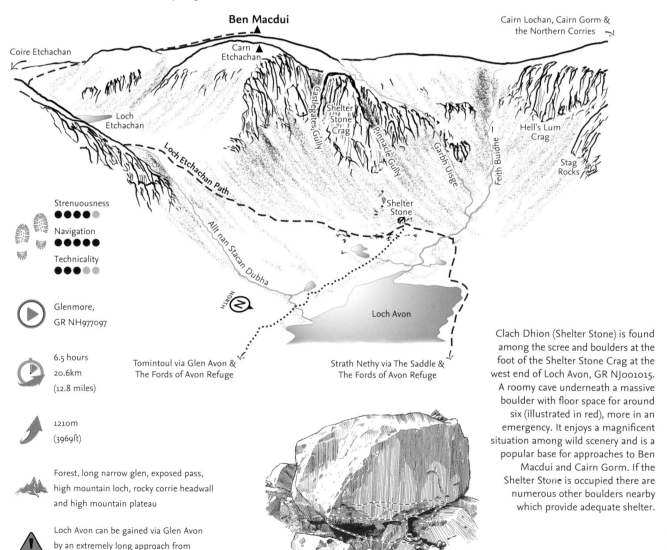

Strenuousness
● ● ● ● ○

Navigation
● ● ● ● ●

Technicality
● ● ● ○ ○

Glenmore,
GR NH977097

6.5 hours
20.6km
(12.8 miles)

1210m
(3969ft)

Forest, long narrow glen, exposed pass, high mountain loch, rocky corrie headwall and high mountain plateau

Loch Avon can be gained via Glen Avon by an extremely long approach from Delnabo, near Tomintoul, GR NJ162164

Clach Dhion (Shelter Stone) is found among the scree and boulders at the foot of the Shelter Stone Crag at the west end of Loch Avon, GR NJ001015. A roomy cave underneath a massive boulder with floor space for around six (illustrated in red), more in an emergency. It enjoys a magnificent situation among wild scenery and is a popular base for approaches to Ben Macdui and Cairn Gorm. If the Shelter Stone is occupied there are numerous other boulders nearby which provide adequate shelter.

Coire Etchachan Path BEN MACDUI

'Long and dramatic' ★ ★ ★

Summary: The route up Glen Derry and then through Coire Etchachan is a pleasant undertaking. Although the approach is long the gradients are never particularly steep and the scenery is particularly beautiful – less harsh than the normal Cairngorm terrain.

Ascent: From the Linn of Dee head N then NW to Derry Lodge (emergency telephone), pass the lodge and head N into Glen Derry. Continue N the length of Glen Derry then fork L and take the Coire Etchachan Path over the footbridge and W up through the corrie. At the Loch Etchachan outlet turn L and follow the path SW then W to Ben Macdui.

Descent: Take the path E down to the broad col then follow it as it swings NE and steadily descends to Loch Etchachan. From the outlet descend SE into Coire Etchachan. Follow the path across the corrie floor E then SE to the footbridge. Cross it and continue SE and join the Glen Derry Path. Head S down Glen Derry to Derry Lodge. From the lodge take the track SE to the Linn of Dee.

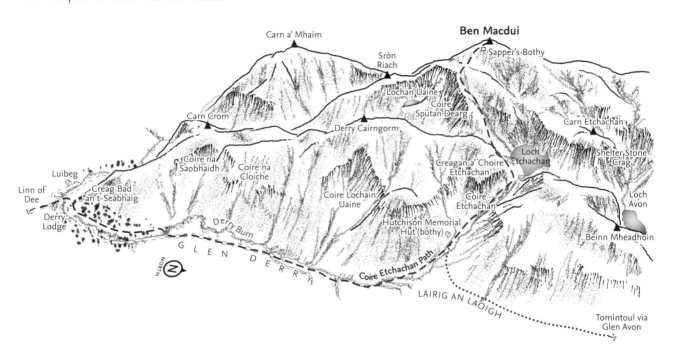

The Hutchison Memorial Hut sits at the heart of Coire Etchachan

Strenuousness
● ● ● ● ○

Navigation
● ● ● ● ●

Technicality
● ● ● ○ ○

1050m
(3445ft)

Long open glen, steep craggy corrie, high mountain loch and high summit plateau

Linn of Dee,
GR NO062897

Coire Etchachan can be gained via Lairig an Laoigh and Glen Avon by an extremely long approach from Delnabo, near Tomintoul, GR NJ162164

5.5 hours
17.1km
(10.6 miles)

Braeriach

1296m (4252ft)

Carn na Criche 1265m (4150ft)
Einich Cairn 1237m (4058ft)
North Plateau 1235m (4052ft)

Ringed by a complex system of corries the high plateau on the west side of the Lairig Ghru is the most extensive area of land above 1219m (4000ft) in Britain. The highest point on this arctic-like plateau is the rounded dome of Braeriach. Set among gravel beds and boulder fields this rather bland-looking summit has a wonderful variety of routes to it.

In the broad hollow between Braeriach and the subsidiary top Einich Cairn, the source of the River Dee percolates from a series of springs, and tumbles over the plateau edge into Garbh Choire Dhàidh which, along with Coire Bhrochain, Garbh Choire

When you arrive

Ordnance Survey: Explorer 403 (1:25 000); Landranger (1:50 000) No. 36 & 43.

Harvey Mountain Maps: Cairn Gorm (1:25 000)

British Mountain Maps: Cairngorms (1:40 000)

Tourist Information Centres: Aviemore; Glenmore; Tomintoul; Braemar.

Youth Hostels: Aviemore; Glenmore; Braemar; Inverey (near the Linn of Dee).

Hotels and B&B: Aviemore; Coylumbridge; Glenmore; Braemar.

Camp sites: Aviemore; Coylumbridge; Glenmore.

Bothies and Howffs: Bob Scott's Memorial Bothy, GR NO042930; Corrour Bothy, GR NN980958; Garbh Choire Bothy, GR NN959986 (on the south side of the Allt a' Gharbh-chorie below the Lochan Uaine Waterfall); the Dey-Smith Bivouac, GR NN946985 (a built-up cave which can just about hold two – too uncomfortable to use for a planned stay).

Mòr and Coire an Lochain, makes up the inner recesses of the huge An Garbh Choire. This remote complex of corries holds the longest-lying snow beds in Britain – they amount to the nearest thing Britain has to a glacier. Most years, they survive from winter to winter and display bergschrunds and even small crevasses. The snow that feeds these snowfields is blown off the plateau and from the barren expanse of Moine Mhòr. By mid-winter the whole corrie

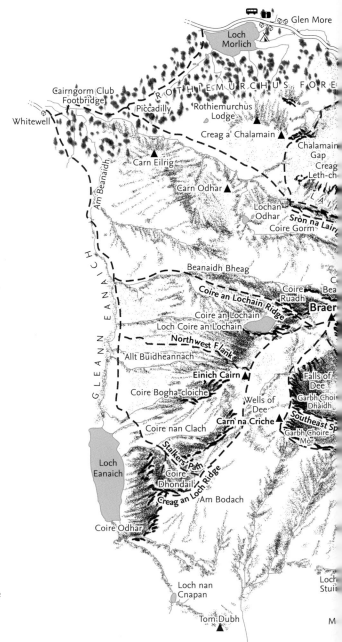

system is ringed by an almost continuous cornice, and, until they decay, routes to Braeriach from the corrie floors are the domain of climbers. Mid-summer usually sees most routes clear of snow, at which time the remote depths of An Garbh Choire provide a magnificent place to explore.

With the exception of the Creag an Loch Ridge and the Coire an Lochain Ridge, the corries and their separating ridges on the north and west sides of the Braeriach plateau tend to be less dramatic than their eastern counterparts. Gleann Einich with its access track gives a long but easy approach to the west, while to the north the traverse over the top of the Sròn na Lairige gives a fine walk, high above the Lairig Ghru.

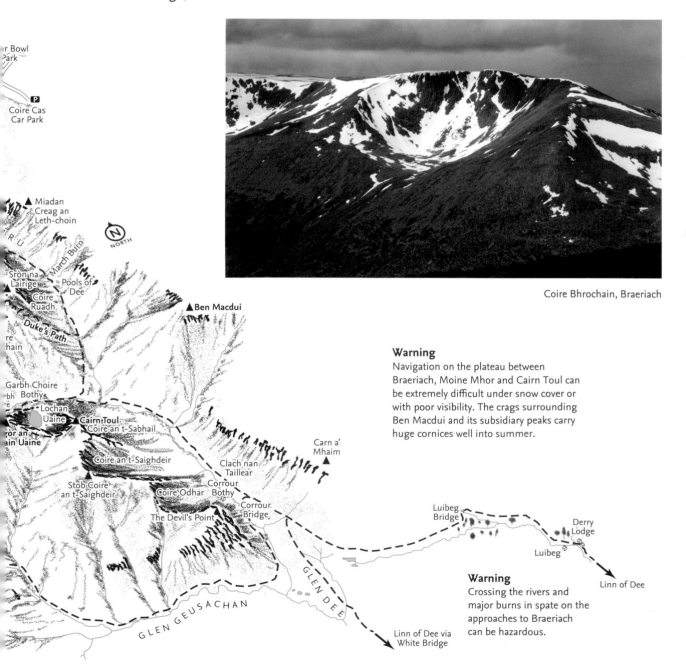

Coire Bhrochain, Braeriach

Warning
Navigation on the plateau between Braeriach, Moine Mhor and Cairn Toul can be extremely difficult under snow cover or with poor visibility. The crags surrounding Ben Macdui and its subsidiary peaks carry huge cornices well into summer.

Warning
Crossing the rivers and major burns in spate on the approaches to Braeriach can be hazardous.

Southwest Ridge BRAERIACH

'Remote expedition' ★★

Summary: Approached via the lovely Glen Geusachan, this route climbs the rounded and featureless southwest ridge of Sgòr an Lochain Uaine, then skirts the crags of Garbh Choire Mòr and Garbh Choire Dhàidh.

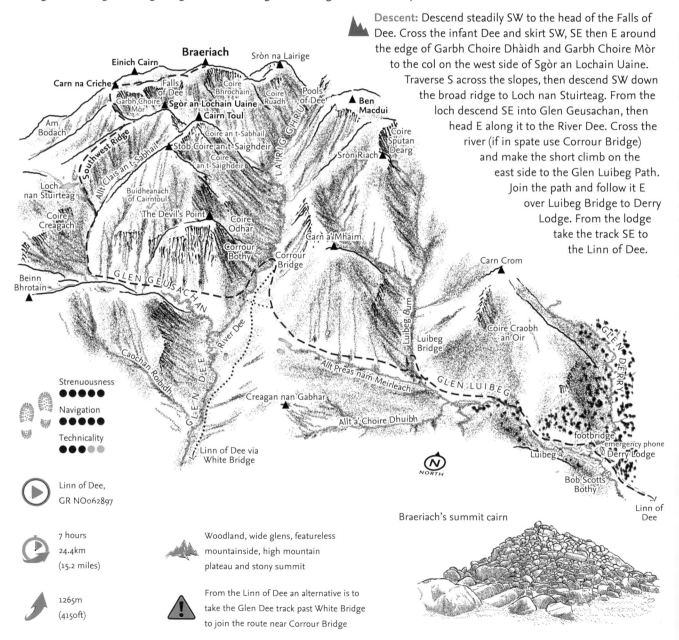

Ascent: From the Linn of Dee head N then NW to Derry Lodge (emergency telephone), pass the lodge and continue along Glen Luibeg to Luibeg Bridge. Cross the bridge then swing W over the col into Glen Dee. Cross the River Dee (if in spate use Corrour Bridge) and head W then NW up Glen Geusachan. From Loch nan Stuirteag climb the broad ridge NE towards Sgòr an Lochain Uaine. Traverse NW before the top to the col on the west side of Sgòr an Lochain Uaine. Skirt W, NW then NE around the edge of Garbh Choire Mòr and Garbh Choire Dhàidh to the head of the Falls of Dee. From the infant Dee climb steadily NE to Braeriach.

Descent: Descend steadily SW to the head of the Falls of Dee. Cross the infant Dee and skirt SW, SE then E around the edge of Garbh Choire Dhàidh and Garbh Choire Mòr to the col on the west side of Sgòr an Lochain Uaine. Traverse S across the slopes, then descend SW down the broad ridge to Loch nan Stuirteag. From the loch descend SE into Glen Geusachan, then head E along it to the River Dee. Cross the river (if in spate use Corrour Bridge) and make the short climb on the east side to the Glen Luibeg Path. Join the path and follow it E over Luibeg Bridge to Derry Lodge. From the lodge take the track SE to the Linn of Dee.

Strenuousness ●●●●●

Navigation ●●●●●

Technicality ●●●○○

Linn of Dee, GR NO062897

7 hours
24.4km
(15.2 miles)

1265m
(4150ft)

Woodland, wide glens, featureless mountainside, high mountain plateau and stony summit

From the Linn of Dee an alternative is to take the Glen Dee track past White Bridge to join the route near Corrour Bridge

Braeriach's summit cairn

Creag an Loch Ridge BRAERIACH

'Short exposed scramble' ★★★

Summary: Perched at the head of Gleann Eanaich, the fine ridge of Creag an Loch is a superb route onto the south end of the Braeriach plateau. It climbs high above the dark waters of Loch Eanaich and, although only short, gives an exciting scramble.

Ascent: Follow the access track S the full length of Gleann Eanaich. Just before Loch Eanaich take the Stalkers' Path that climbs SE then S into Coire Dhondail. Cross the corrie floor SW to the foot of Creag an Loch Ridge and climb the crest of the ridge SE to Am Bodach. Skirt the head of Coire Dhondail and climb NE onto the plateau. Continue NE across the plateau to the head of the Falls of Dee. From the infant Dee climb steadily NE to Braeriach.

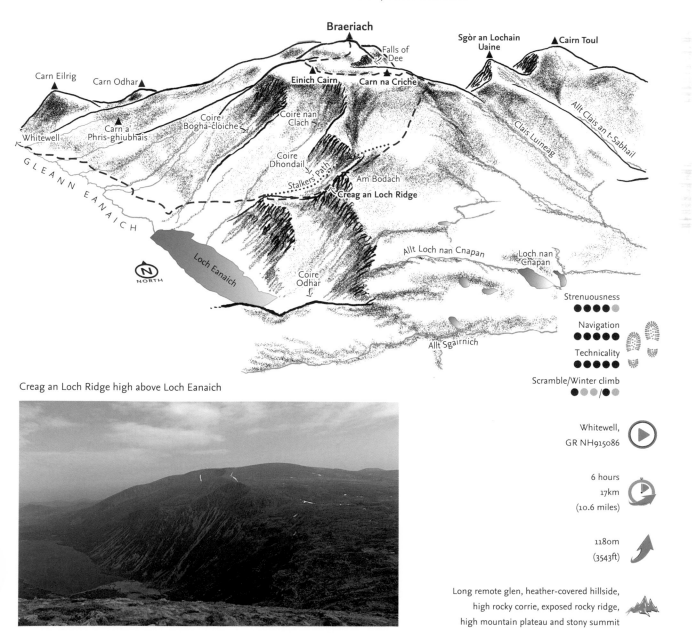

Creag an Loch Ridge high above Loch Eanaich

Strenuousness
●●●●○

Navigation
●●●●○

Technicality
●●●●●

Scramble/Winter climb
●●○○ / ●○○

Whitewell,
GR NH915086

6 hours
17km
(10.6 miles)

1180m
(3543ft)

Long remote glen, heather-covered hillside,
high rocky corrie, exposed rocky ridge,
high mountain plateau and stony summit

Stalkers' Path BRAERIACH

'Painless route on to the plateau' ★★

Summary: Follows a well-graded path which climbs through the lonely Coire Dhondail on the east side of Gleann Eanaich. Originally constructed for deerstalkers, it provides handy access onto the south end of the Braeriach plateau. In winter the corrie headwall can become icy and avalanche prone.

Ascent: Follow the access track S the full length of Gleann Eanaich. Just before Loch Eanaich take the Stalkers' Path that climbs SE then S into Coire Dhondail. Continue across the corrie floor then climb the zigzags SW up the headwall. From the head of Coire Dhondail climb NE onto the plateau. Continue NE across the plateau to the head of the Falls of Dee. From the infant Dee climb steadily NE to Braeriach.

Descent: Descend steadily SW to the head of the Falls of Dee. Cross the infant Dee then head SW across the plateau to the head of Coire Dhondail. The Stalkers' Path is marked by a small cairn; descend the zigzags NW into the corrie then turn N across the corrie floor and take the path down into Gleann Eanaich. Join the track and follow it N to Whitewell.

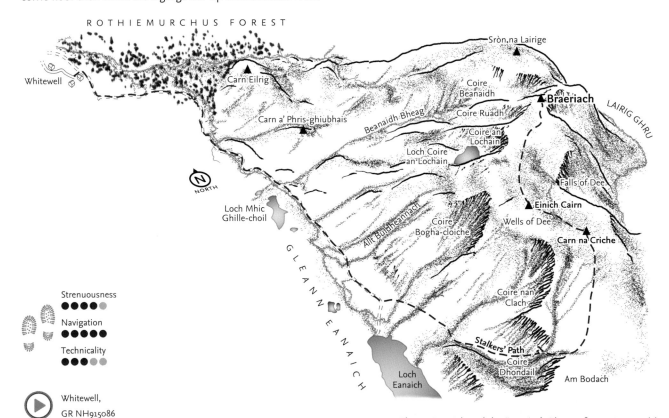

Strenuousness
●●●●○

Navigation
●●●●●

Technicality
●●●○○

Whitewell,
GR NH915086

6 hours
16.6km
(10.3 miles)

1160m
(3806ft)

Long remote glen, heather-covered hillside, high rocky corrie, high mountain plateau and stony summit

Gleann Eanaich and the Braeriach Plateau from Moine Mhòr

Northwest Flank BRAERIACH

'Reliable descent'

Summary: The featureless Northwest Flank of Braeriach provides an undramatic but relatively safe route between Gleann Eanaich and the Braeriach plateau.

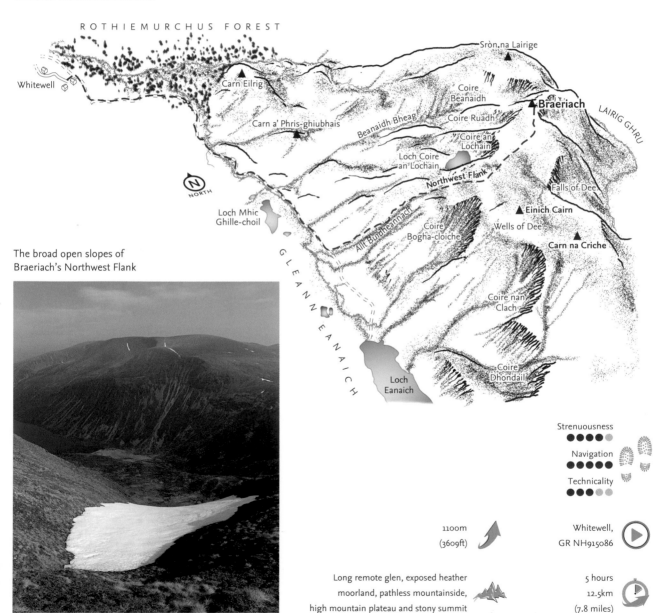

Ascent: Follow the access track S up Gleann Eanaich, then strike SE alongside Allt Buidheannach and climb the vague zigzags onto the Braeriach plateau. Once on the plateau head E across the flats and then make the steady climb to Braeriach's summit.

Descent: Head W from the summit cairn and make the short descent onto the plateau. Continue W across the plateau to the head of the broad slope between Coire an Lochain and Coire Bogha-cloiche. Descend NW down the slope (there is a vague zigzag path but it is difficult to locate from above) and follow the Allt Buidheannach down to Gleann Eanaich. Join the track and follow it N to Whitewell.

The broad open slopes of Braeriach's Northwest Flank

Strenuousness
●●●●○

Navigation
●●●●●

Technicality
●●●○○

1100m
(3609ft)

Whitewell,
GR NH915086

Long remote glen, exposed heather moorland, pathless mountainside, high mountain plateau and stony summit

5 hours
12.5km
(7.8 miles)

Coire an Lochain Ridge BRAERIACH

'Hidden gem' ★★★

Summary: Loch Coire an Lochain occupies the cold, craggy corrie on the north side of Braeriach. Rising above its icy waters on the east side is a steep rocky ridge. Not technically difficult, it nevertheless provides an airy and exciting route with superb views back over the Spey Valley.

Ascent: Follow the access track S up Gleann Eanaich then take the vague path SE along the north side of Beanaidh Bheag. At the junction with the Allt Coire an Lochain cross the Beanaidh Bheag and climb SE to the foot of Coire an Lochain Ridge. Climb the ridge S onto the plateau. Then turn SE and climb direct to the summit of Braeriach.

Descent: The top of Coire an Lochain Ridge is best located by descending W from the summit cairn, then turning N at the change in angle between the summit slopes and the plateau. Descend the ridge N, then turn NW at its foot and continue NW until the Beanaidh Bheag is reached. Cross it and follow it down to Gleann Eanaich. Join the track and follow it N to Whitewell.

Braeriach summit

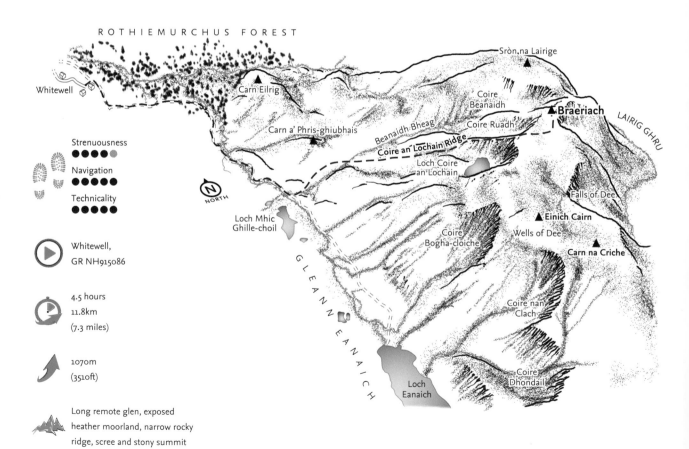

Strenuousness
●●●●○

Navigation
●●●●●

Technicality
●●●●●

▶ Whitewell,
GR NH915086

4.5 hours
11.8km
(7.3 miles)

1070m
(3510ft)

Long remote glen, exposed
heather moorland, narrow rocky
ridge, scree and stony summit

Sròn na Lairige Path BRAERIACH

'Popular approach' ★★

Summary: An excellent introductory route. It has the least arduous approach and takes in some classic Cairngorm scenery – particularly the final section to the summit with views into the wild corries of An Garbh Choire.

 Ascent: Cross the Allt Mòr at the Sugar Bowl and follow the path SW to the Chalamain Gap. Pass through the gap and follow the path S down to the Allt Druidh. Climb the hillside above SW then SE up the Sròn na Lairige. From the Sròn na Lairige head S descending slightly to a broad col. From the col swing W and make the final climb to Braeriach.

 Descent: Head E around the plateau edge then drop NE down to the col at the head of Coire Ruadh. Cross the col climbing N onto the Sròn na Lairige. From the summit continue N, then swing NW to avoid the crags on the east side of the ridge. As the slope eases turn NE and descend into the Lairig Ghru. Cross the Allt Druidh and climb N then NE to the Chalamain Gap. Once through the gap head NE to the Sugar Bowl Car Park.

Ben Macdui
Devil's Point
Cairn Toul
Sgòr an Lochain Uaine
Braeriach
Einich Cairn
Cairn Lochan
Sròn na Lairige
Coire Beanaidh
Coire Ruadh
Loch Coire an Lochain
Loch Eanaich
Coire an Lochain
Coire an t-Sneachda
Creag an Leth-choin
Coire Gorm
Sròn na Lairige Path
Lurcher's Gully
Carn Odhar
Chalamain Gap
Creag a' Chalamain
LAIRIG GHRU
Castle Hill
Allt Druidh
Ski Centre
Allt Mòr
NORTH N
Airgoid-meall
ROTHIEMURCHUS FOREST
Sugar Bowl Car Park

1055m
(3461ft)

Strenuousness
●●●●○○
Navigation
●●●●●
Technicality
●●●○○

Exposed moorland, boulder-choked valley, craggy glen, broad stony ridge and stony summit

Sugar Bowl Car Park, GR NH984073

Alternative approaches from Whitewell, GR NH915086 via the Lairig Ghru, or Loch Morlich, GR NH956097 via tracks in the Rothiemurchus Forest

4 hours
10.3km
(6.4 miles)

Duke's Path BRAERIACH

'Direct link to the Lairig Ghru' ★

Summary: Crosses the top of Lairig Ghru then climbs directly onto the plateau via Coire Ruadh. The corrie is very steep, with zigzags up the headwall – avalanche prone when snow covered.

 **Ascent:** Cross the Allt Mòr at the Sugar Bowl and follow the path SW to the Chalamain Gap. Pass through the gap and follow the path S down to the Allt Druidh. Head S through the Lairig Ghru over the top to the Pools of Dee. From the pools, skirt the slope on the west side of the Lairig Ghru to a burn issuing from Coire Ruadh. Climb NW alongside the burn and up through the corrie, then follow the zigzags onto the col. Turn W and climb the summit slopes to Braeriach.

Descent: Head E around the plateau edge, then drop NE down to the col at the head of Coire Ruadh. From the cairn on the east side of the col descend the zigzags SE into Coire Ruadh; as the angle eases continue SE alongside the burn. Before the bottom is reached traverse N towards the Pools of Dee. Continue N through the Lairig Ghru until the path forks. Take the right-hand branch N as it climbs to the Chalamain Gap. Once through the gap head NE to the Sugar Bowl Car Park.

Strenuousness
●●●●○

Navigation
●●●●●

Technicality
●●●●○

1065m
(3494ft)

Sugar Bowl Car Park, GR NH984073

4.5 hours
11.9km
(7.4 miles)

Exposed moorland, boulder-choked valley, craggy glen, boulder field, steep rocky corrie and stony summit

Can also be started from Whitewell, GR NN915086; Loch Morlich, GR NH956097; or the Linn of Dee, GR NO062897.

Scotland's longest-lying snow
The snow fields of Garbh Choire Mòr hold Scotland's longest-lying snow. They are the nearest thing Britain has to a glacier – in most years they survive through the summer and autumn. In a hard winter the crags around the corrie headwall become one continuous snow slope, with only a few features left exposed. Depths on the corrie floor in excess of 20m (65ft) are not uncommon.

South Flank BRAERIACH

'Easiest route out of An Garbh Choire' ★

Summary: Steep and boulder strewn, the South Flank of Braeriach provides access to Garbh Choire Dhàidh. In itself it is not a very exciting route; its qualities lie in views into the vast An Garbh Choire, particularly towards the Falls of Dee.

Ascent: Cross Allt Mòr at the Sugar Bowl and follow the path SW to the Chalamain Gap. Pass through the gap and follow the path down to the Allt Druidh. Head S through the Lairig Ghru over the top to the Pools of Dee. From the pools, skirt the slope on the west side of the Lairig Ghru and continue traversing into An Garbh Choire. Follow the Allt a' Gharbh-choire past Garbh Choire Bothy then turn NW climbing into the Garbh Choire Dhàidh. Head N across the corrie floor then climb steeply up the South Flank of Braeriach onto the plateau. Continue N up the easy summit slopes then E to the summit cairn.

Descent: Head W then S around the crags of Coire Bhrochain to the edge of the plateau. Descend the steep scree and boulders of the South Flank into Garbh Choire Dhàidh. Continue S across the corrie floor and drop into An Garbh Choire. Turn L and head NE, then E to Garbh Choire Bothy. Past the bothy traverse NE into the Lairig Ghru. Head N past the Pools of Dee and descend to the start of the Chalamain Gap Path. Turn R and follow it N to the gap. Once through head NE to the Sugar Bowl Car Park.

Derry Lodge at the confluence of Derry Burn and Luibeg Burn, GR NO041934. Formerly a shooting lodge, this fine building is now redundant and boarded up. Just behind it is a mountain rescue post which has an emergency telephone.

Carn Eilrig
Loch Morlich
Creag a' Chalamain
Sugar Bowl Car Park
Cairn Odhar
Chalamain Gap
Creag an Leth-choin
Cairn Lochan
GLEANN EANAICH
Sròn na Lairige
Braeriach
Einich Cairn
March Burn
Loch Eanaich
Wells of Dee
Falls of Dee
Coire Bhrochain
South Flank
Pools of Dee
NORTH
Carn na Criche
Garbh Choire Dhàidh
Garbh Choire Mòr
An Garbh Choire
Ben Macdui
Sgòr an Lochain Uaine
Lochan Uaine
LAIRIG GHRU
Cairn Toul
Coire an t-Sabhail
Linn of Dee via Derry Lodge

1205m
(3953ft)

Strenuousness ●●●●○
Navigation ●●●●●
Technicality ●●●○○

Exposed moorland, boulder-choked valley, craggy glen, boulder field, remote corries, steep scree-covered slopes and stony summit

Can also be started from Whitewell, GR NH915086; Loch Morlich, GR NH956097; or the Linn of Dee, GR NO062897.

Sugar Bowl Car Park, GR NH984073

5 hours
14km
(8.7 miles)

Southeast Spur BRAERIACH

'Remote scramble' ★★★

Summary: From below, the dramatically situated Southeast Spur at the head of An Garbh Choire seems an unlikely route. It looks very steep, and is located between two major crags. Its difficulties though are short and considerably fewer than may first appear (snow cover on this route can exist throughout summer).

Ascent: Cross Allt Mòr at the Sugar Bowl and follow the path SW to the Chalamain Gap. Pass through the gap and follow the path down to the Allt Druidh. Head S through the Lairig Ghru over the top to the Pools of Dee. From the pools, skirt the slope on the west side of the Lairig Ghru and continue traversing into An Garbh Choire. Follow the Allt a' Gharbh-choire past Garbh Choire Bothy to the mouth of Garbh Choire Mòr. Turn R and climb the steep slope NW to the foot of the Southeast Spur – the easiest way is up the left-hand side. Once on the plateau walk N to the head of the Falls of Dee. From the infant Dee climb steadily NE to Braeriach.

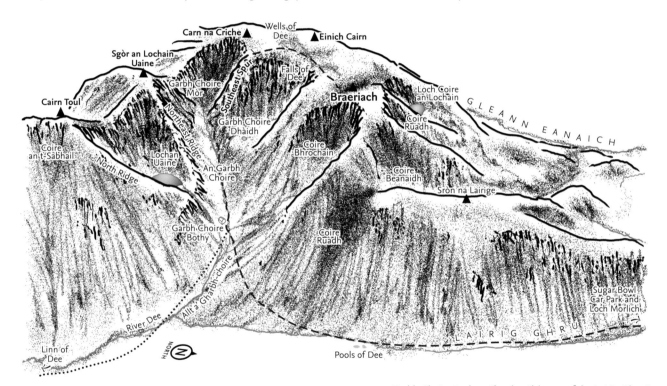

Strenuousness
●●●●●

 Navigation
●●●●●

 Technicality
●●●●●

Scramble/Winter climb
●●●/●●○

 1250m
(4101ft)

 Sugar Bowl Car Park,
GR NH984073

 5.5 hours
15.3km
(9.5 miles)

Exposed moorland, boulder-choked valley, craggy glen, boulder field, high remote corrie, steep scree, short steep ridge, high mountain plateau and stony summit

⚠ Can also be started from Speyside at Whitewell, GR NH915086; Loch Morlich, GR NH956097; or Deeside from the Linn of Dee, GR NO062897.

Garbh Choire Bothy 1.6km (1 mile) west of the Lairig Ghru in An Garbh Choire on the south bank of the Allt a' Gharbh-choire below the Lochan Uaine Waterfall, GR NN959986. A waterproofed cage within a built-up cairn, it holds six at a push. An ideal bothy, imaginatively designed, it blends beautifully into its wild surroundings – an excellent base for Braeriach and Cairn Toul or for exploring the corries of An Garbh Choire.

Cairn Toul Link BRAERIACH

'High-level traverse' ★ ★

Summary: A high-level walk around one of Scotland's most impressive corrie systems.

Route: Descend SW to the head of the Falls of Dee. Cross the infant Dee then skirt SW, SE then E around the edge of Garbh Choire Dhàidh and Garbh Choire Mòr to the col on the west side of Sgòr an Lochain Uaine. Continue E and climb Sgòr an Lochain Uaine. Descend SE to the col and make the short pull E to Cairn Toul.

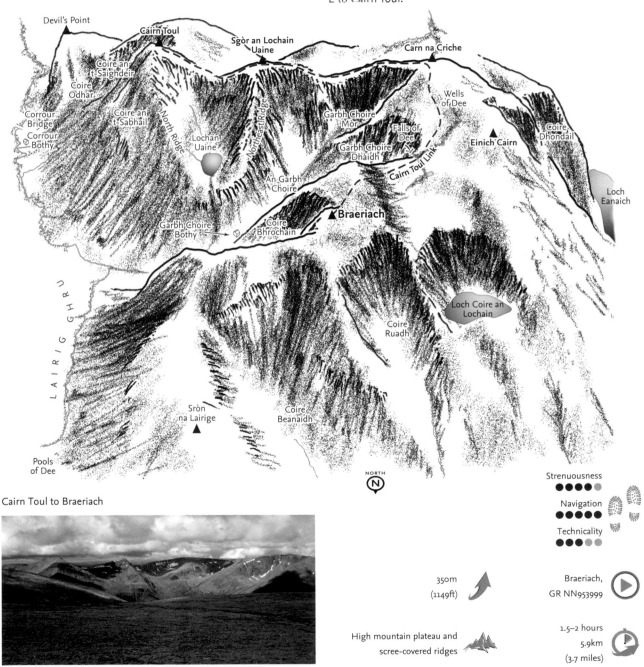

Cairn Toul to Braeriach

Strenuousness
● ● ● ● ○

Navigation
● ● ● ● ●

Technicality
● ● ● ● ○

350m
(1149ft)

High mountain plateau and scree-covered ridges

Braeriach,
GR NN953999

1.5–2 hours
5.9km
(3.7 miles)

Cairn Toul

1291m (4236ft)

Sgòr an Lochain Uaine

1258m (4127ft)

Cairn Toul is almost entirely surrounded by the headwaters of the Dee. To the north, the rushing waters of the Allt a' Gharbh-choire issue from the long-lying snow beds of Garbh Choire Mòr and Garbh Choire Dhàidh, draining east through An Garbh Choire to join the Dee in the Lairig Ghru. The River Dee in turn drains south to form the eastern boundary through the deep trench of the Lairig Ghru. Bounding the southern edge, the Geusachan Burn meanders the length of the lovely Glen Geusachan to meet the Dee at the flats below the crags of The Devil's Point. Cairn Toul's only high-level link with its neighbours is to the west

where it abuts Sgòr an Lochain Uaine and the extensive Braeriach plateau – the most extensive area of land above 1219m (4000ft) in Britain.

Arguably the most elegant of all the Cairngorm mountains, Cairn Toul's well-defined shape is instantly recognizable. Presiding over the Lairig Ghru, its steep boulder-strewn slopes are cut into

When you arrive

Ordnance Survey: Explorer 403 (1:25 000); Landranger (1:50 000) No. 36 & 43.

Harvey Mountain Maps: Cairn Gorm (1:25 000)

British Mountain Maps: Cairngorms (1:40 000)

Tourist Information Centres: Aviemore; Glenmore; Tomintoul; Braemar.

Youth Hostels: Aviemore; Glenmore; Braemar; Inverey (near the Linn of Dee).

Hotels and B&B: Aviemore; Coylumbridge; Glenmore; Braemar.

Camp sites: Aviemore; Coylumbridge; Glenmore.

Bothies and Howffs: Bob Scott's Memorial Bothy, GR NO042930; Corrour Bothy, GR NN980958; Garbh Choire Bothy, GR NN959986 (on the south side of the Allt a' Gharbh-choire below the Lochan Uaine Waterfall); the Dey-Smith Bivouac, GR NN946985 (a built-up cave which can just about hold two – too uncomfortable to use for a planned stay).

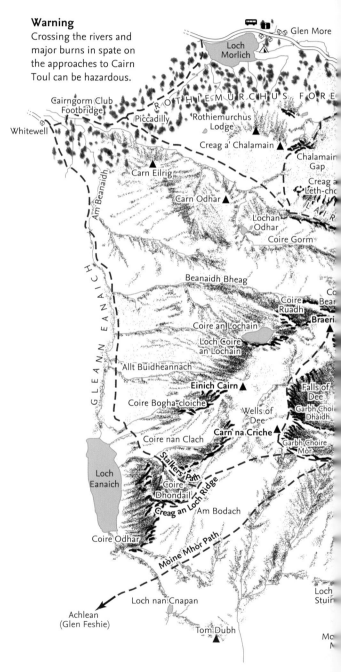

Warning
Crossing the rivers and major burns in spate on the approaches to Cairn Toul can be hazardous.

by high hanging corries which are separated by long ridges. On the Lairig Ghru side they form steep narrow arêtes, which provide easy but entertaining scrambles, while to the west they are broad and open.

Cairn Toul is most commonly approached via the Lairig Ghru either from Deeside via Glen Luibeg or Glen Dee, or from Speyside via the Rothiemurchus Forest or the Chalamain Gap. There are, however, two less obvious alternatives, one from Glen Feshie over the high exposed moorland of Mòine Mhòr, the other via Gleann Eanaich and the remote Coire Dhondail.

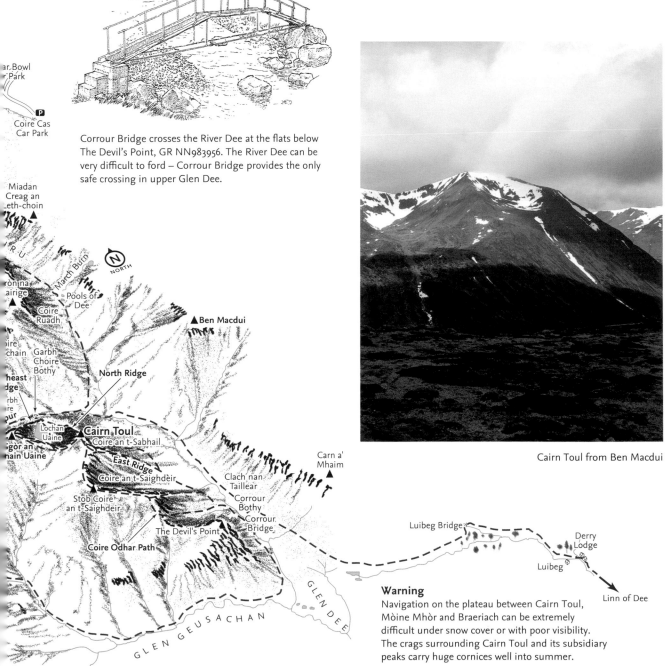

Corrour Bridge crosses the River Dee at the flats below The Devil's Point, GR NN983956. The River Dee can be very difficult to ford – Corrour Bridge provides the only safe crossing in upper Glen Dee.

Cairn Toul from Ben Macdui

Warning
Navigation on the plateau between Cairn Toul, Mòine Mhòr and Braeriach can be extremely difficult under snow cover or with poor visibility. The crags surrounding Cairn Toul and its subsidiary peaks carry huge cornices well into summer.

Southwest Ridge CAIRN TOUL

'Remote expedition' ★★

Summary: Approached via the lovely Glen Geusachan, this route climbs the rounded and featureless southwest ridge of Sgòr an Lochain Uaine. Although not the most direct line it provides a relatively easy route to follow in poor conditions.

Ascent: From the Linn of Dee head N then NW to Derry Lodge (emergency telephone), pass the lodge and continue along Glen Luibeg to Luibeg Bridge. Cross the bridge then swing W over the col into Glen Dee. Cross the River Dee (if in spate use Corrour Bridge) and head W then NW up Glen Geusachan. From Loch nan Stuirteag climb the broad ridge NE towards Sgòr an Lochain Uaine. Traverse E before the top to the col on the west side of Cairn Toul. From the col continue E and climb to Cairn Toul's summit.

Descent: Head W and drop down to the col. From the col traverse W across the slopes of Sgòr an Lochain Uaine then descend SW down the broad ridge to Loch nan Stuirteag. From the loch descend SE into Glen Geusachan then head E along it to the River Dee. Cross the river (if in spate use Corrour Bridge) and make the short climb on the east side to the Glen Luibeg path. Join the path and follow it E over Luibeg Bridge to Derry Lodge. From the lodge take the track SE to the Linn of Dee.

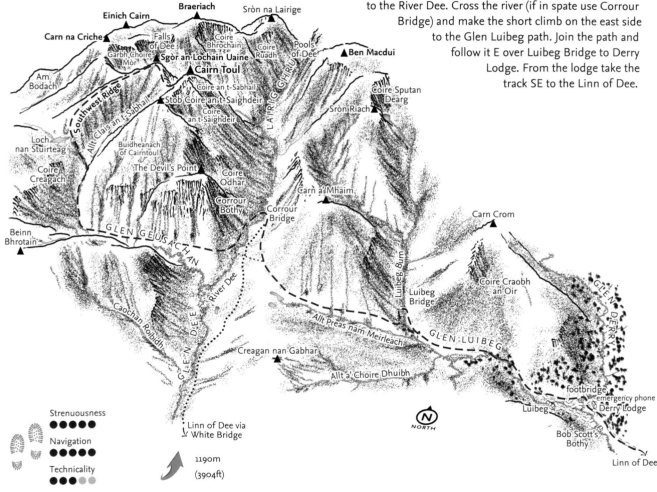

Strenuousness
●●●●●

Navigation
●●●●●

Technicality
●●●○○

 Linn of Dee,
GR NO062897

6.5 hours
21.8km
(13.5 miles)

 1190m
(3904ft)

 Woodland, wide glens, featureless mountainside, high ridge and narrow stony summit

⚠ Allt Clais an t-Sabhail provides an alternative route between the head of Glen Geusachan and the col on the west side of Cairn Toul. From the Linn of Dee another alternative is to take the Glen Dee track past White Bridge to join the route near Corrour Bridge.

Mòine Mhòr Path CAIRN TOUL

'Epic high-level approach' ★

Summary: A novel route which starts in Glen Feshie and takes advantage of the high-level link provided by Mòine Mhòr. The crossing of this high and exposed moorland is a unique experience – with a covering of soft snow or with poor visibility it can be a nightmare!

Ascent: From the car park follow the road to Auchlean, then take the path that works its way unremittingly E up the north side of the Allt Fhearnagan to Carn Bàn Mòr. From Carn Bàn Mòr descend SE to join the access track then head E to Loch nan Cnapan. From the loch swing NE then ENE and traverse the slopes to the col on the west side of Sgòr an Lochain Uaine. Climb E to Sgòr an Lochain Uaine then descend SE to the col. Finally, from the col make the short pull E to Cairn Toul.

Descent: From Cairn Toul head W then NW to Sgòr an Lochain Uaine. Descend W to the col then make a descending traverse WSW then SW to Loch nan Cnapan. From the loch continue W to the Allt Sgairnich and join the access track. Follow it to the Carn Bàn Mòr Path which is then taken NW. From Carn Bàn Mòr descend W on the north side of Allt Fhearnagan to the road at Auchlean.

Strenuousness
●●●●○

Navigation
●●●●●

Technicality
●●●○○

Car park near Auchlean, Glen Feshie, GR NN853975

5.5 hours
14.1km
(8.7 miles)

1290m
(4232ft)

Steep open corrie, high exposed moorland, featureless slope, high ridge and narrow stony summit

Sgòr an Lochain Uaine can be avoided by crossing Mòine Mhòr via Loch nan Stuirteag

Mòine Mhòr (The Great Moss)

Creag an Loch Ridge CAIRN TOUL

'Short exposed scramble' ★ ★ ★

Summary: Perched at the head of Gleann Eanaich the fine ridge of Creag an Loch is a superb route onto the Braeriach/Cairn Toul massif. It climbs high above the dark waters of Loch Eanaich and although only short, gives an exciting scramble.

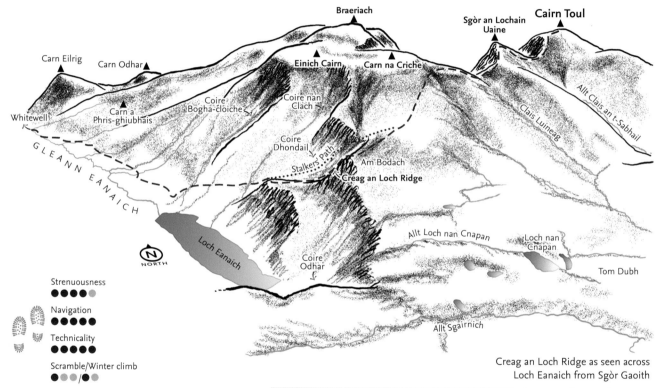

Ascent: Follow the access track S the full length of Gleann Eanaich. Just before Loch Eanaich take the Stalkers' Path which climbs SE then S into Coire Dhondail. Cross the corrie floor SW to the foot of Creag an Loch Ridge and climb the crest of the ridge SE to Am Bodach. Skirt the head of Coire Dhondail and climb E onto the plateau. Head SE then E and skirt around the crags of Garbh Choire Mòr to Sgòr an Lochain Uaine. Descend SE to the col and make the short pull E to Cairn Toul.

Strenuousness
● ● ● ● ○

Navigation
● ● ● ● ●

Technicality
● ● ● ● ●

Scramble/Winter climb
● ● ○ ○ / ● ○

Whitewell,
GR NH915086

6 hours
17.3km
(10.8 miles)

1320m
(4330ft)

Long remote glen, heather-covered hillside,
high rocky corrie, exposed rocky ridge, high
mountain ridge and narrow stony summit

Creag an Loch Ridge as seen across
Loch Eanaich from Sgòr Gaoith

Stalkers' Path CAIRN TOUL

'Painless route on to the plateau' ★★

Summary: A well-graded path, which climbs through the lonely Coire Dhondail on the east side of Gleann Eanaich. Originally constructed for deerstalkers, it provides handy access onto the Braeriach/Cairn Toul massif. In winter the corrie headwall can become icy and avalanche prone.

Ascent: Follow the access track S the full length of Gleann Eanaich. Just before Loch Eanaich take the Stalkers' Path that climbs SE then S into Coire Dhondail. Continue across the corrie floor then climb the zigzags SW up the headwall. From the head of Coire Dhondail climb E onto the plateau. Head SE then E and skirt around the crags of Garbh Choire Mòr to Sgòr an Lochain Uaine. Descend SE to the col and make the short pull E to Cairn Toul.

Descent: Head W then NW over Sgòr an Lochain Uaine, then drop W down to the col. From the col skirt W then NW around the crags of Garbh Choire Mòr, and then descend W to the head of Coire Dhondail. The Stalkers' Path is marked by a small cairn; descend the zigzags NW into the corrie then turn N across the corrie floor and take the path down into Gleann Eanaich. Join the track and follow it N to Whitewell.

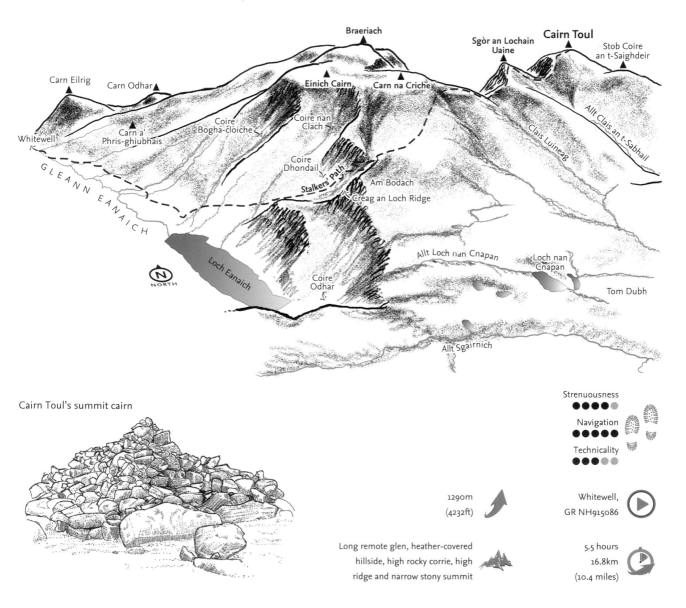

Cairn Toul's summit cairn

Strenuousness
●●●●○

Navigation
●●●●●

Technicality
●●●○○

1290m
(4232ft)

Whitewell,
GR NH915086

Long remote glen, heather-covered hillside, high rocky corrie, high ridge and narrow stony summit

5.5 hours
16.8km
(10.4 miles)

Northeast Ridge CAIRN TOUL

'Top quality scramble' ★★★

Summary: The Northeast Ridge of Sgòr an Lochain Uaine separates the picturesque hanging corrie, Coire an Lochain Uaine, from the vast super-corrie An Garbh Choire. The approach via An Garbh Choire and the steep ascent alongside the waterfall issuing from Lochan Uaine is long, but the effort is well worthwhile. This is a classic route set in an incomparable situation.

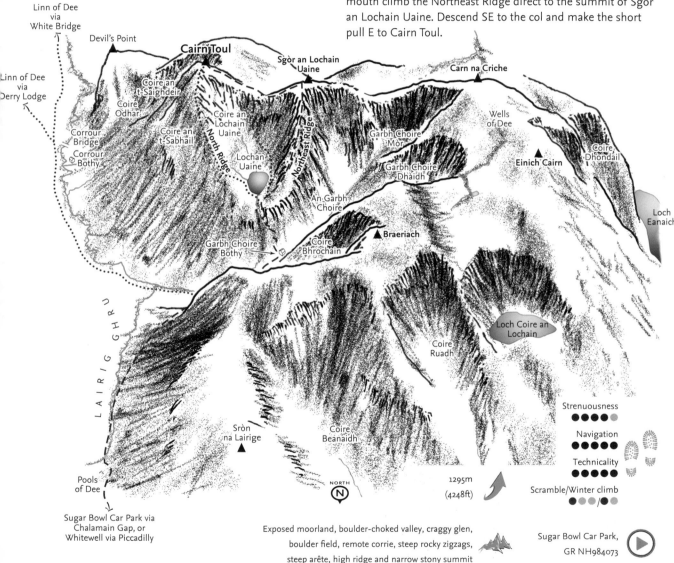

Ascent: Cross Allt Mòr at the Sugar Bowl and follow the path SW to the Chalamain Gap. Pass through the gap and follow the path down to the Allt Druidh. Head S through the Lairig Ghru over the top to the Pools of Dee. From the pools, skirt the slope on the west side of the Lairig Ghru and continue traversing into An Garbh Choire. Ascend the corrie to the Garbh Choire Bothy then turn S and climb the vague zigzags to the west of Lochan Uaine Waterfall. From the corrie mouth climb the Northeast Ridge direct to the summit of Sgòr an Lochain Uaine. Descend SE to the col and make the short pull E to Cairn Toul.

Linn of Dee via White Bridge

Devil's Point

Cairn Toul

Sgòr an Lochain Uaine

Carn na Criche

Linn of Dee via Derry Lodge

Coire an t-Saighdein

Coire Odhar

Coire an Lochain Uaine

Wells of Dee

Corrour Bridge

Coire an t-Sabhail

North Ridge

Northeast Ridge

Garbh Choire Mòr

Coire Dhondail

Corrour Bothy

Lochan Uaine

Garbh Choire Dhaidh

Einich Cairn

An Garbh Choire

Loch Eanaich

Garbh Choire Bothy

Coire Bhrochain

Braeriach

Loch Coire an Lochain

LAIRIG GHRU

Coire Ruadh

Sròn na Lairige

Coire Beanaidh

NORTH Ⓝ

1295m (4248ft)

Pools of Dee

Strenuousness
●●●●○

Navigation
●●●●●

Technicality
●●●●●

Scramble/Winter climb
●●○○/●○

Sugar Bowl Car Park via Chalamain Gap, or Whitewell via Piccadilly

Exposed moorland, boulder-choked valley, craggy glen, boulder field, remote corrie, steep rocky zigzags, steep arête, high ridge and narrow stony summit

Sugar Bowl Car Park, GR NH984073

Can also be started from Speyside at Whitewell, GR NH915086; Loch Morlich, GR NH956097; or from Deeside at the the Linn of Dee, GR NO062897. Two easier alternative routes exist to the line up the Northeast Ridge either via the back wall of Coire an Lochain Uaine or via the North Ridge of Cairn Toul.

6 hours
14.4km
(8.9 miles)

LEFT
The perfectly pitched Northeast Ridge of Sgòr an Lochain Uaine

Braeriach Link CAIRN TOUL

'High-level traverse' ★ ★ ★

Summary: A high-level walk around one of Scotland's most impressive corrie systems.

Route: Head W then NW over Sgòr an Lochain Uaine, then drop W down to the col. Skirt W, NW then NE around the edge of Garbh Choire Mòr and Garbh Choire Dhàidh to the head of the Falls of Dee. From the infant Dee climb steadily NE to Braeriach.

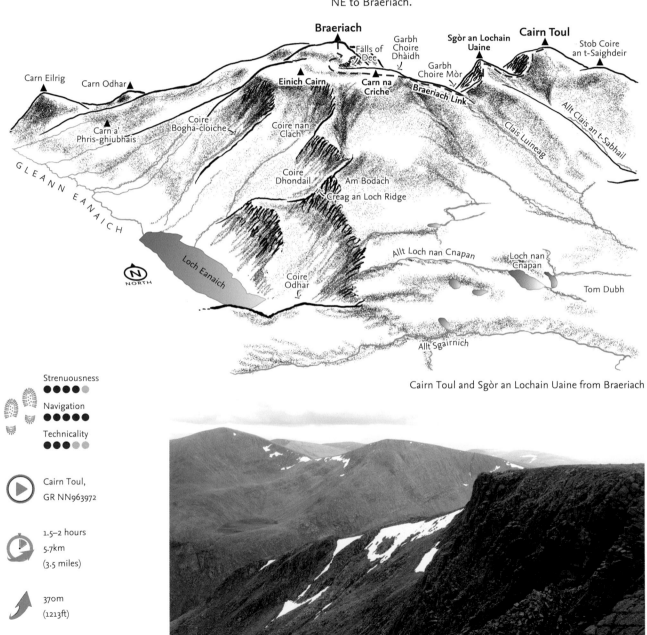

Cairn Toul and Sgòr an Lochain Uaine from Braeriach

Strenuousness
● ● ● ● ○

Navigation
● ● ● ● ●

Technicality
● ● ● ○ ○

Cairn Toul,
GR NN963972

1.5–2 hours
5.7km
(3.5 miles)

370m
(1213ft)

Scree-covered ridges and high mountain plateau

Northeast Spur CAIRN TOUL

'Challenging scramble' ★★

Summary: The ring of crags at the head of Garbh Choire Mòr have precious few lines that can be attempted by walkers. The easiest line is the spur/shelf above Crown Buttress on the south side of the corrie (this part of Garbh Choire Mòr is known as Corrie of the Chockstone Gully). In winter the top of this route is one of the few places between Cairn Toul and Braeriach that generally does not carry a cornice.

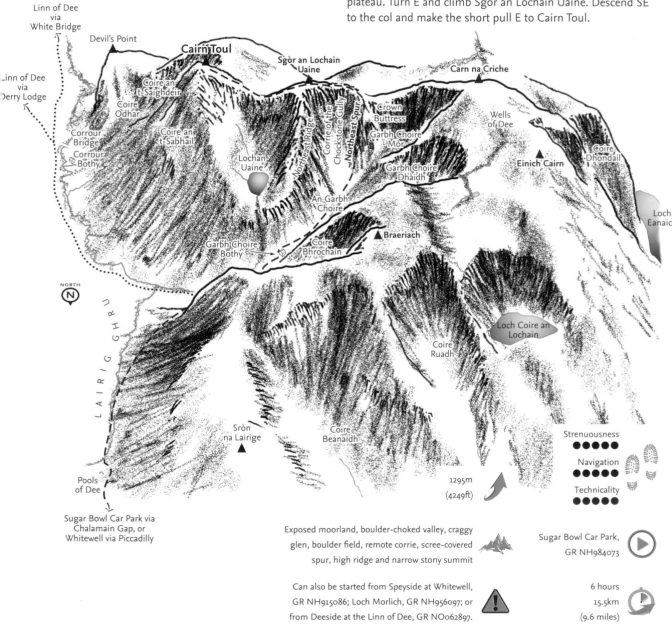

Ascent: Cross Allt Mòr at the Sugar Bowl and follow the path SW to the Chalamain Gap. Pass through the gap and follow the path down to the Allt Druidh. Head S through the Lairig Ghru over the top to the Pools of Dee. From the pools skirt the slope on the west side of the Lairig Ghru and continue traversing into An Garbh Choire. Ascend the corrie past the bothy then climb SW below the Corrie of the Chockstone Gully. At the west end of the bay ascend the shelf, then spur, onto the plateau. Turn E and climb Sgòr an Lochain Uaine. Descend SE to the col and make the short pull E to Cairn Toul.

Linn of Dee via White Bridge

Devil's Point

Cairn Toul

Sgòr an Lochain Uaine

Carn na Criche

Linn of Dee via Derry Lodge

Coire an t-Saighdein

Coire Odhar

Corrour Bridge

Corrour Bothy

Coire an t-Sabhail

Northeast Ridge

Corrie of the Chockstone Gully

Northeast Spur

Crown Buttress

Garbh Choire Mòr

Wells of Dee

Coire Dhondail

Lochan Uaine

Garbh Choire Dhaidh

Einich Cairn

An Garbh Choire

Loch Eanaich

Garbh Choire Bothy

Coire Bhrochain

Braeriach

NORTH
N

LAIRIG GHRU

Loch Coire an Lochain

Coire Ruadh

Sròn na Lairige

Coire Beanaidh

1295m (4249ft)

Strenuousness
●●●●●

Navigation
●●●●●

Technicality
●●●●●

Pools of Dee

Sugar Bowl Car Park via Chalamain Gap, or Whitewell via Piccadilly

Exposed moorland, boulder-choked valley, craggy glen, boulder field, remote corrie, scree-covered spur, high ridge and narrow stony summit

Sugar Bowl Car Park, GR NH984073

Can also be started from Speyside at Whitewell, GR NH915086; Loch Morlich, GR NH956097; or from Deeside at the Linn of Dee, GR NO062897.

6 hours
15.5km
(9.6 miles)

East Ridge CAIRN TOUL

'Bouldery scramble' ★

Summary: Climbs the fine arête between Coire an t-Saighdeir and Coire an t-Sabhail on the east side of Cairn Toul. Affords superb views of the Lairig Ghru. The most direct route to Cairn Toul from Deeside.

Ascent: From the Linn of Dee head N then NW to Derry Lodge (emergency telephone), pass the lodge and continue along Glen Luibeg to Luibeg Bridge. Cross the bridge then swing W over the col into Glen Dee. Cross the river at Corrour Bridge and head NW past Corrour Bothy up the steep slope behind, to Coire an t-Saighdeir. Head N across the mouth of the corrie to the foot of the East Ridge. Climb the ridge direct to Cairn Toul's summit.

Braeriach

Einich Cairn

Sròn na Lairige

Carn na Criche

Falls of Dee

Coire Bhrochain

Coire Ruadh

Pools of Dee

Garbh Choire Mòr

Sgòr an Lochain Uaine

Ben Macdui

Am Bodach

Cairn Toul

Coire an t-Sabhail

Coire Sputan Dearg

Stob Coire an t-Saighdeir

East Ridge

Coire an t-Saighdeir

Sròn Riach

LAIRIG GHRU

Loch nan Stuirteag

Allt Clais an t-Sabhail

Buidheanach of Cairntoul

Coire Odhar

N NORTH

Coire Creagach

The Devil's Point

Carn a' Mhaim

Corrour Bothy

Corrour Bridge

Carn Crom

Beinn Bhrotain

GLEN GEUSACHAN

Luibeg Burn

Coire Craobh an Oir

GLEN DERRY

Luibeg Bridge

Caochan Roibidh

River Dee

Allt Preas nàm Meirleach

GLEN LUIBEG

GLEN DEE

footbridge

emergency phone

Derry Lodge

Creagan nan Gabhar

Allt a' Choire Dhuibh

Luibeg

Linn of Dee via White Bridge

Bob Scott's Bothy

Linn of Dee

Corrour Bothy. Below Coire Odhar on the west side of the River Dee at the north end of Glen Dee, GR NN981958. A stone hut that formerly accommodated stalkers in the season, it is now a popular open bothy with room for ten. Composting toilet attached as a side annex.

Strenuousness
●●●●○

Navigation
●●●●●

Technicality
●●●●●

Scramble/Winter climb
●●●○○ / ○●●○

1100m
(3609ft)

Linn of Dee,
GR NO062897

5.5 hours
15.9km
(9.8 miles)

Woodland, wide open glens, steep scree-strewn slope, high remote corrie, rocky arête and narrow stony summit

An easier alternative is via Coire an t-Sabhail. Can also be started from Linn of Dee by taking the Glen Dee track past White Bridge to join the route near Corrour Bridge.

Coire Odhar Path CAIRN TOUL

'The standard approach' ★

Summary: A popular and straightforward route that climbs the steep headwall of Coire Odhar via a series of zigzags to emerge onto the verdant flats between The Devil's Point and Cairn Toul.

Ascent: From the Linn of Dee head N then NW to Derry Lodge (emergency telephone), pass the lodge and continue along Glen Luibeg to Luibeg Bridge. Cross the bridge then swing W over the col into Glen Dee. Cross the river at Corrour Bridge, pass Corrour Bothy and head NW then W up into Coire Odhar. Climb the headwall via the zigzags onto the flats at the top. Turn R and climb steadily NW then N, skirting the crags, to Cairn Toul.

Descent: Head S then SE, skirting the crags, to the flats on the northwest side of The Devil's Point. Descend E via the zigzags into Coire Odhar. Pass Corrour Bothy and turn SE to cross the River Dee at Corrour Bridge. Make the short climb on the east side to the Glen Luibeg path. Join the path and follow it E over Luibeg Bridge to Derry Lodge. From the lodge take the track SE to the Linn of Dee.

Einich Cairn
Braeriach
Sròn na Lairige
Carn na Criche
Falls of Dee
Coire Bhrochain
Coire Ruadh
Pools of Dee
Garbh Choire Mòr
Sgòr an Lochain Uaine
Ben Macdui
Am Bodach
Cairn Toul
Coire an t-Sabhail
Coire Sputan Dearg
Stob Coire an t-Saighdeir
Sròn Riach
Coire an t-Saighdeir
Loch nan Stuirteag
LAIRIG GHRU
Buidheanach of Cairntoul
Coire Creagach
Coire Odhar Path
Corrour Bothy
Carn a'Mhaim
The Devil's Point
Corrour Bridge
Beinn Bhrotain
GLEN GEUSACHAN
Carn Crom
Luibeg Burn
Coire Craobh an'Oir
GLEN DERRY
Luibeg Bridge
GLEN DEE
River Dee
Allt Clais an t-Sabhail
Caochan Roibidh
Allt Preas nam Meirleach
GLEN LUIBEG
footbridge
emergency phone
Derry Lodge
Creagan nan Gabhar
Allt a'Choire Dhuibh
Luibeg
Bob Scott's Bothy
Linn of Dee
N NORTH
Linn of Dee via White Bridge

White Bridge gives access to Glen Feshie and Glen Tilt

1150m (3773ft)

Woodland, wide open glens, remote corrie, high ridge and narrow stony summit

Strenuousness
●●●●○

Navigation
●●●●○

Technicality
●●●○○

Linn of Dee, GR NO062897

5.5 hours
16.7km
(10.3 miles)

An alternative to the zigzag path is the rocky ridge at the north side of Coire Odhar – a safer route under icy or avalanche conditions. Can also be started from Linn of Dee by taking the Glen Dee track past White Bridge to join the route near Corrour Bridge.

Cairn Gorm

1244m (4081ft)

Cairn Gorm has developed a reputation as the easiest of the 4000ft peaks to climb. Since the arrival in 1961 of the chair lift (now replaced by the Funicular Railway) and all the ski-ground paraphernalia this sentiment may well be true, but it can only be applied to the Coire Cas Track. Elsewhere on the mountain there is a wide selection of routes, some long, some short, all of which offer superb outings through some classic high mountain terrain.

Cairn Gorm shares the high plateau on the east side of the Lairig Ghru with Ben Macdui. To the south, its slopes descend steeply to the cold waters of Loch Avon, while to the north, long ridges intersected by deep corries extend towards Glen More. Two deep and long glens bind Cairn Gorm's east and west fringes. Lairig Ghru to the west is a popular and well-documented route but Strath Nethy is less well known; its high point is at The Saddle below Cairn Gorm's summit from which it runs due north to the open moorland by the Ryvoan Pass, over which it is linked to Glen More.

The popular northern corries of Cairn Gorm attract walkers and climbers as well as skiers in considerable numbers; easy access and attractive climbing have ensured this. It is altogether a different story to the south. Cairn Gorm's main ridgeline marks the start of some of Britain's wildest country. Numerous parties have set off south from Cairn Gorm only to be overtaken by vicious storms, which can arrive with frightening speed. This very difficult terrain requires a high degree of competence to navigate through and survive in.

The plateaux of the high Cairngorms are unique among the mountains of Britain, displaying many of the features associated with subarctic terrain. In early summer the high ground between Cairn Gorm and Ben Macdui and that between Cairn Toul and Braeriach are fascinating places to walk across – shrinking snow beds reveal extensive tundra covered by gravel beds and patches of mat grass, mosses, liverworts, lichens and the occasional pink flush of moss campion.

Among the boulder fields the haunting rattle of startled ptarmigan is common enough; if you are particularly lucky you may even notice the darting activity of the Arctic snow bunting – a rare and short-staying visitor.

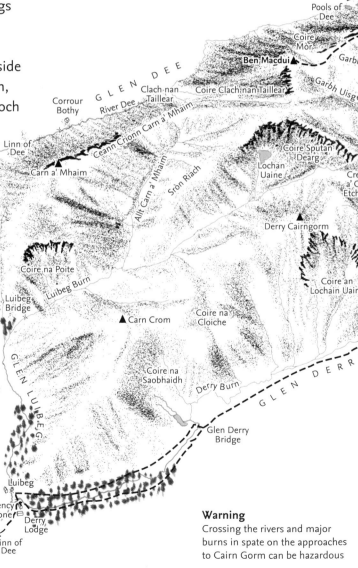

Warning
Crossing the rivers and major burns in spate on the approaches to Cairn Gorm can be hazardous

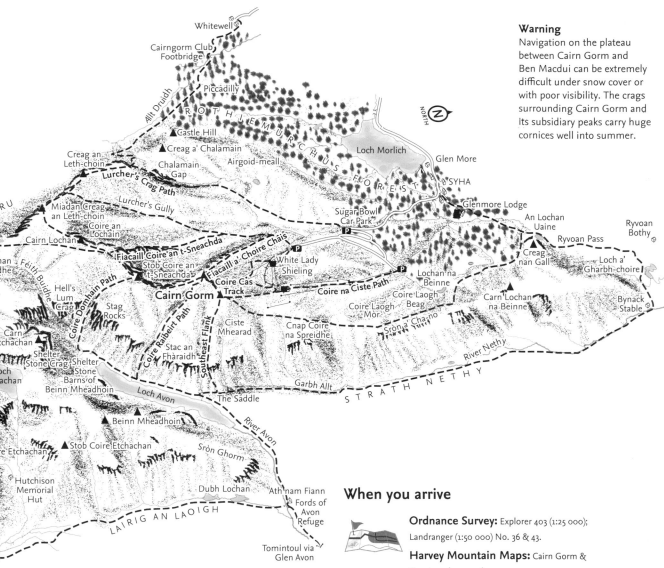

Whitewell

Cairngorm Club
Footbridge

Piccadilly

Allt Druidh

ROTHIEMURCHUS FOREST

Loch Morlich

Glen More

▲ Castle Hill

▲ Creag a' Chalamain

Creag an
Leth-choin

Airgoid-meall

Chalamain
Gap

Lurcher's Crag Path

SYHA

Lurcher's Gully

Glenmore Lodge

An Lochan
Uaine

Ryvoan
Bothy

Miadan Creag
an Leth-choin

RU

Coire an
Lochain

Sugar Bowl
Car Park

Ryvoan Pass

Cairn Lochan

Fiacaill Coire an t-Sneachda

Fiacaill a' Choire Chais

P

Creag
nan Gall

Loch a'
Gharbh-choire

Feith Buidhe

Stob Coire an
t-Sneachda

P

White Lady
Shieling

P

Lochan na
Beinne

Carn Lochan
na Beinne

Bynack
Stable

han
dhe

Coire Domhain Path

▲ Cairn Gorm

Coire Cas
Track

Coire na Ciste Path

Coire Laogh
Beag

Coire Laogh
Mòr

▲

Hell's
Lum
Crag

Stag
Rocks

Ciste
Mhearad

Cnap Coire
na Spreidhe

Sròn a' Cha-no

River Nethy

Carn
tchachan

Coire Raibeirt Path

Southeast Flank

Stac an
Fhàraidh

Garbh Allt

STRATH NETHY

Shelter
Stone Crag

Shelter
Stone

Barns of
Beinn Mheadhoin

Loch Avon

The Saddle

och
achan

▲ Beinn Mheadhoin

River Avon

▲ Stob Coire Etchachan

e Etchachan

Sròn Ghorm

Hutchison
Memorial
Hut

Dubh Lochan

Ath nam Fiann

Fords of
Avon
Refuge

LAIRIG AN LAOIGH

Tomintoul via
Glen Avon

NORTH ⊗

Warning
Navigation on the plateau between Cairn Gorm and Ben Macdui can be extremely difficult under snow cover or with poor visibility. The crags surrounding Cairn Gorm and its subsidiary peaks carry huge cornices well into summer.

Ptarmigan Restaurant adjacent to the top station of the funicular railway, GR NJ004049

When you arrive

Ordnance Survey: Explorer 403 (1:25 000); Landranger (1:50 000) No. 36 & 43.

Harvey Mountain Maps: Cairn Gorm & Ben Avon (1:25 000)

British Mountain Maps: Cairngorms (1:40 000)

Tourist Information Centres: Aviemore; Glenmore; Tomintoul; Braemar.

Youth Hostels: Aviemore; Glenmore; Braemar; Inverey (near the Linn of Dee).

Hotels and B&B: Aviemore; Coylumbridge; Glenmore; Braemar.

Camp sites: Aviemore; Coylumbridge; Glenmore.

Bothies and Howffs: Bob Scott's Memorial Bothy, GR NO042930; Corrour Bothy, GR NN980958; The Shelter Stone, GR NJ001015; The Hutchison Memorial Hut, GR NO022997; Fords of Avon Refuge, GR NJ041032; Ryvoan Bothy, GR NJ005115.

Southeast Flank CAIRN GORM

'Direct from Loch Avon' ★

Summary: The Southeast Flank of Cairn Gorm is steep and a little monotonous but provides a useful route as it can be climbed from the high start point of The Saddle. The Saddle is a broad col which separates the head of Strath Nethy from Loch Avon.

Ascent: From the Linn of Dee head N then NW to Derry Lodge (emergency telephone), pass the lodge and head N into Glen Derry. Continue N the length of Glen Derry then cross over the Lairig an Laoigh and finally descend to the Fords of Avon. Cross the ford to the Fords of Avon Refuge and follow the River Avon W to Loch Avon. Once alongside the loch continue W making a rising traverse to The Saddle. From The Saddle climb the steep slope W. As the angle eases turn NW and climb steadily to Cairn Gorm's summit.

Descent: Descend SE from the radio relay station, then E as the ground steepens to The Saddle. From The Saddle make a descending traverse E to the path at the side of Loch Avon, then follow it to the Fords of Avon Refuge. Cross the Fords of Avon and head S over the Lairig an Laoigh. Continue S down Glen Derry to Derry Lodge. From the lodge take the track SE to the Linn of Dee.

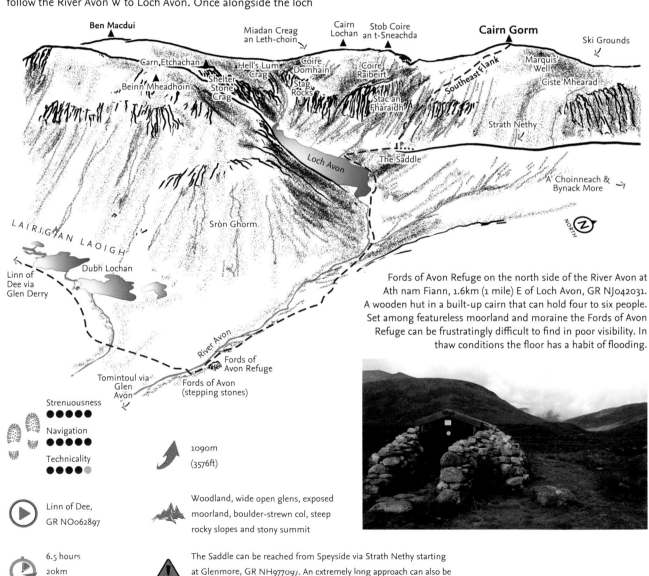

Fords of Avon Refuge on the north side of the River Avon at Ath nam Fiann, 1.6km (1 mile) E of Loch Avon, GR NJ042031. A wooden hut in a built-up cairn that can hold four to six people. Set among featureless moorland and moraine the Fords of Avon Refuge can be frustratingly difficult to find in poor visibility. In thaw conditions the floor has a habit of flooding.

Strenuousness ● ● ● ● ●

Navigation ● ● ● ● ●

Technicality ● ● ● ● ○

1090m (3576ft)

Linn of Dee, GR NO062897

Woodland, wide open glens, exposed moorland, boulder-strewn col, steep rocky slopes and stony summit

6.5 hours 20km (12.5 miles)

The Saddle can be reached from Speyside via Strath Nethy starting at Glenmore, GR NH977097. An extremely long approach can also be made via Glen Avon from Delnabo, near Tomintoul, GR NJ162164.

Coire Raibeirt Path CAIRN GORM

'Handy link route' ★★

Summary: Coire Raibeirt Path provides the most direct access to the crags at the head of Loch Avon and is popular (in descent) with climbers approaching from Speyside.

Ascent: Take the Glenmore Lodge road and follow it F past the lodge, then NE to take the Ryvoan Pass Track. After An Lochan Uaine the track splits. Take the right-hand branch and follow it E then SE to the footbridge. Cross the River Nethy and follow the narrow path S down Strath Nethy to The Saddle. Cross over the broad col and follow the path SW above Loch Avon. Continue along it until the Allt Coire Raibeirt,

then turn NW and climb the steep path into the Coire Raibeirt. At the head of the corrie turn R and follow the path E to the summit of Cairn Gorm.

Descent: Head W to the head of Coire Raibeirt and take the path SSE down through the corrie to the side of Loch Avon. Turn L and follow the path NE to The Saddle. Cross the broad col and head N the length of Strath Nethy to the footbridge. Cross it and take the path NW then W to join the Ryvoan Pass Track. Turn L onto it and follow it to Glenmore.

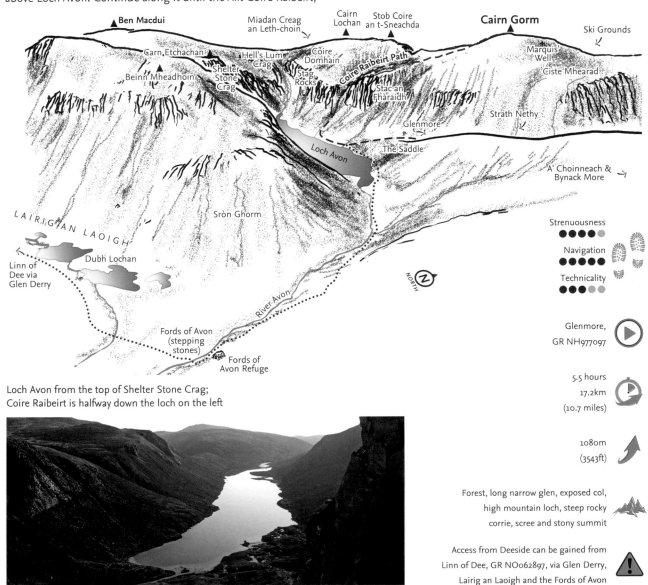

Loch Avon from the top of Shelter Stone Crag;
Coire Raibeirt is halfway down the loch on the left

Strenuousness
●●●●○

Navigation
●●●●●

Technicality
●●●○○

Glenmore,
GR NH977097

5.5 hours
17.2km
(10.7 miles)

1080m
(3543ft)

Forest, long narrow glen, exposed col,
high mountain loch, steep rocky
corrie, scree and stony summit

Access from Deeside can be gained from
Linn of Dee, GR NO062897, via Glen Derry,
Lairig an Laoigh and the Fords of Avon

Coire Domhain Path CAIRN GORM

'Dramatic corrie' ★★

Summary: The Loch Avon Basin has an impressive ring of crags; particularly striking is the towering prow of the Shelter Stone Crag. The best route past them is through Coire Domhain.

Domhain. At head of the corrie, turn R and follow the path NE around the top of Coire Raibeirt then E to the summit of Cairn Gorm.

🗻 **Ascent:** Take the Glenmore Lodge road and follow it E past the lodge then NE to take the Ryvoan Pass Track. After An Lochan Uaine the track splits. Take the right-hand branch and follow it E then SE to a footbridge. Cross the River Nethy and follow the narrow path S down Strath Nethy to The Saddle. Cross over the broad col and follow the path SW above Loch Avon to the head of the loch. Follow the Feith Buidhe to its junction with the Allt Coire Domhain. Turn NW and climb steeply between Hell's Lum Crag and Stag Rocks into Coire

🗻 **Descent:** Descend W from the radio relay station and follow the main plateau path as it skirts the top of Coire Raibeirt and Coire an t-Sneachda to the head of Coire Domhain. Drop into the corrie and follow the Allt Coire Domhain SE into the Loch Avon Basin. Turn E at the bottom and follow the path on the north side of the loch to The Saddle. Cross the broad col and head N the length of Strath Nethy to the footbridge. Cross it and take the path NW then W to join the Ryvoan Pass Track. Turn L on to it and follow it to Glenmore.

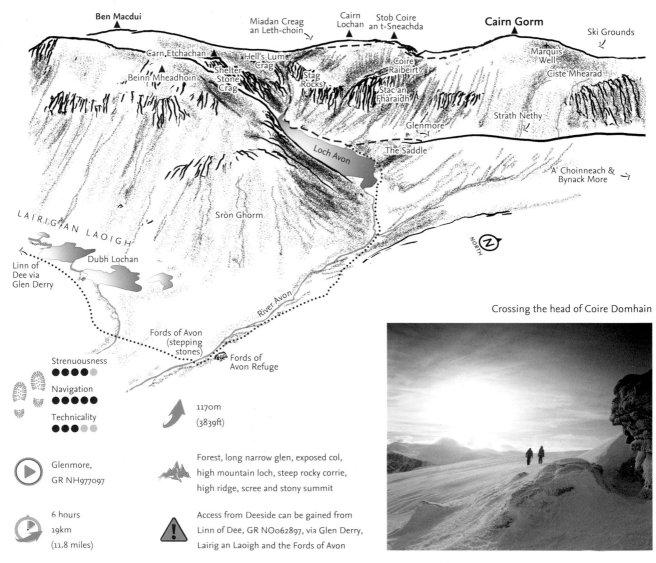

Crossing the head of Coire Domhain

Strenuousness
●●●●○

Navigation
●●●●●

Technicality
●●●○○

1170m
(3839ft)

▶ Glenmore,
GR NH977097

Forest, long narrow glen, exposed col, high mountain loch, steep rocky corrie, high ridge, scree and stony summit

⟳ 6 hours
19km
(11.8 miles)

⚠ Access from Deeside can be gained from Linn of Dee, GR NO062897, via Glen Derry, Lairig an Laoigh and the Fords of Avon

Lurcher's Crag Path CAIRN GORM

'High-level tour of the northern corries' ★ ★ ★

Summary: Forming the impressive east wall of the Lairig Ghru, the long ridge of Creag an Leth-choin can be easily gained from Rothiemurchus via the easy slopes of the Chalamain Gap. It gives a long steady approach to Cairn Gorm and passes through the complete range of terrain for which the Cairngorms are famous.

Ascent: Take the Gleann Einich track S to Lochan Deo then turn E and follow the path over the Cairngorm Club Footbridge to the junction at Piccadilly. Take the Lairig Ghru Path SE to the junction with the Chalamain Gap Path. Join it and follow it N then turn SE and climb the steep slopes to Creag an Leth-choin. Continue SE past the head of Lurcher's Gully to the col on the west side of Cairn Lochan. Climb E to Cairn Lochan and then descend ENE to join the main plateau path at the head of Coire Domhain. Take the path NE as it skirts over the top of Coire an t-Sneachda and Coire Raibeirt to Cairn Gorm.

Descent: Descend W from the radio relay station and follow the main plateau path as it skirts the top of Coire Raibeirt and Coire an t-Sneachda to the head of Coire Domhain. Turn WSW and climb over Cairn Lochan to the col on the west side. Cross the col and head NE over Creag an Leth-choin then descend to the Chalamain Gap. Drop S to join the Lairig Ghru Path which is then followed NW to Piccadilly. Take the path SW then NW to the Cairngorm Club Footbridge. Cross it and head W along the path to join the Gleann Einich track which is then followed N to Whitewell.

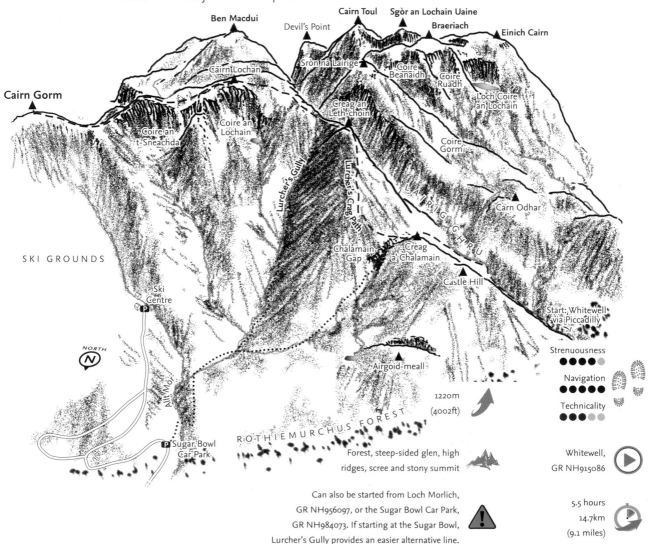

Strenuousness ● ● ● ● ○

Navigation ● ● ● ● ●

Technicality ● ● ● ○ ○

1220m (4002ft)

Forest, steep-sided glen, high ridges, scree and stony summit

Can also be started from Loch Morlich, GR NH956097, or the Sugar Bowl Car Park, GR NH984073. If starting at the Sugar Bowl, Lurcher's Gully provides an easier alternative line.

Whitewell, GR NH915086

5.5 hours
14.7km
(9.1 miles)

Ben Macdui Link CAIRN GORM

'Well trodden but worthwhile' ★★

Summary: A well-trodden path across the Cairn Gorm plateau to Britain's second-highest peak. In good conditions an easy walk; in a blizzard, near-impossible.

Route: Descend W from the radio relay station and follow the main plateau path as it skirts the top of Coire Raibeirt and Coire an t-Sneachda to the head of Coire Domhain. Turn S then SW and traverse the east side of Cairn Lochan to Lochan Buidhe. The path then swings SSE, follow it as it winds its way up to the summit slopes of Ben Macdui.

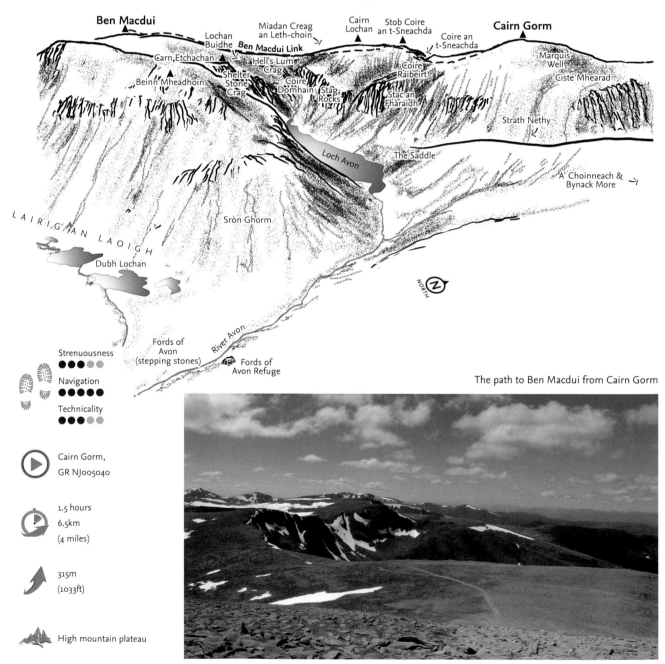

Strenuousness
●●●●○

Navigation
●●●●●

Technicality
●●●●○○

Cairn Gorm,
GR NJ005040

1.5 hours
6.5km
(4 miles)

315m
(1033ft)

High mountain plateau

The path to Ben Macdui from Cairn Gorm

Fiacaill Coire an t-Sneachda CAIRN GORM

'Classic scramble' ★ ★ ★

Summary: Easy access has ensured that the northern corries of Cairn Gorm – Coire an Lochain and Coire an t-Sneachda – are popular climbing venues. A narrow ridge projects north at an easier angle between the crags of these two steep-walled corries. The Fiacaill Coire an t-Sneachda gives an adventurous scramble to the west side of Cairn Gorm.

Ascent: From the car park cross the Allt a' Choire Chais and follow the constructed path SW across the mouth of Coire an t-Sneachda. After crossing the Allt Coire an t-Sneachda, turn S and climb the broad ridge to the Fiacaill Coire an t-Sneachda. Continue S up the Fiacaill onto the slopes east of Cairn Lochan. Descend E to the col at the head of Coire Domhain, then skirt the heads of Coire an t-Sneachda and Coire Raibeirt NE to Cairn Gorm.

Descent: Descend W from the radio relay station and follow the main plateau path as it skirts the top of Coire Raibeirt and Coire an t-Sneachda to the head of Coire Domhain. Climb W to the top of the Fiacaill Coire an t-Sneachda (there is a cairn, but in winter it is usually covered by snow; under such conditions the Fiacaill cannot be recommended as a descent). Descend N onto the ridge dropping down to meet up with the main corries' path. Follow it NE to Coire Cas Car Park.

Strenuousness
●●●●○

Navigation
●●●●●

Technicality
●●●●●

Scramble/Winter climb
●●●○/●●

805m
(2641ft)

Broad corrie floors, narrow rocky ridge, high ridge, scree and stony summit

Coire Cas Car Park,
GR NH989060

2.5 hours
6.1km
(3.8 miles)

The col on the east side of Cairn Lochan can be gained from Coire an t-Sneachda by the Goat Track. This steep series of zigzags is, however, rather unattractive, being loose in summer and avalanche prone in winter.

Fiacaill a' Choire Chais CAIRN GORM

'Avoids the worst of the ski grounds'

Summary: The west edge of Coire Cas is bounded by a slender ridge, which climbs directly to the west shoulder of Cairn Gorm. It provides a pleasant route with fine views into Coire an t-Sneachda.

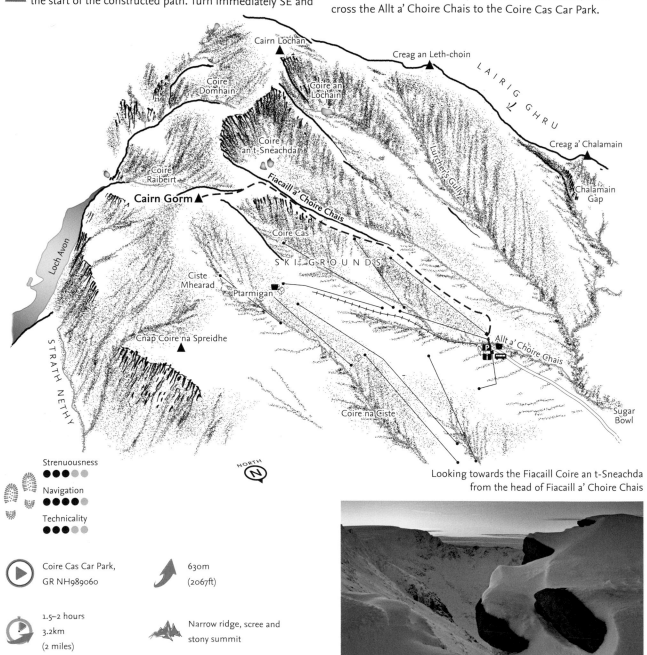

Ascent: From the car park cross the Allt a' Choire Chais to the start of the constructed path. Turn immediately SE and climb the Fiacaill a' Choire Chais to the shoulder on the west side of Cairn Gorm's summit slopes. Turn E and climb directly to the summit.

Descent: Descend W from the radio relay station and follow the main plateau path to the cairn at the top of Fiacaill a' Choire Chais. Drop NW down the Fiacaill, then cross the Allt a' Choire Chais to the Coire Cas Car Park.

Strenuousness
●●●●○○

Navigation
●●●●○

Technicality
●●●●○○

Coire Cas Car Park,
GR NH989060

630m
(2067ft)

1.5–2 hours
3.2km
(2 miles)

Narrow ridge, scree and
stony summit

Looking towards the Fiacaill Coire an t-Sneachda
from the head of Fiacaill a' Choire Chais

Coire Cas Track CAIRN GORM

'Cluttered with ski tows – best avoided'

Summary: A broad constructed track that winds its way through the ski ground paraphernalia to the top station of the funicular railway. A pitched path leads from here to Cairn Gorm's summit.

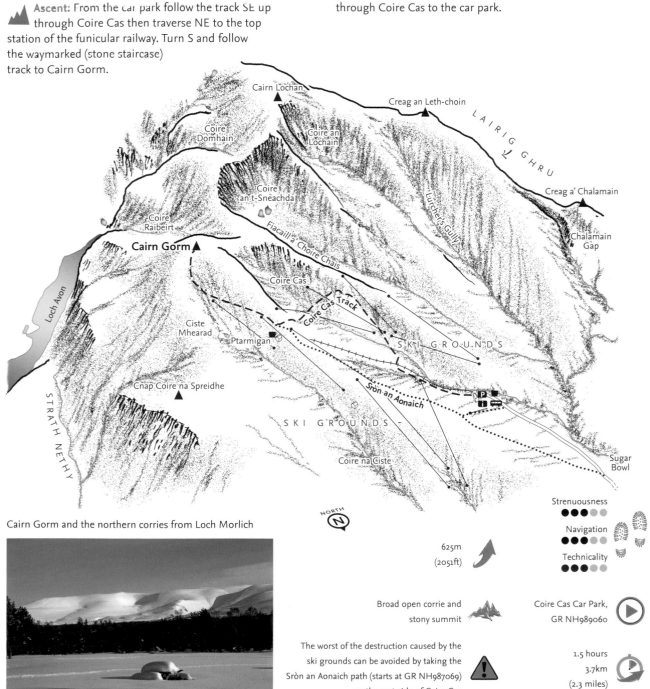

Ascent: From the car park follow the track SE up through Coire Cas then traverse NE to the top station of the funicular railway. Turn S and follow the waymarked (stone staircase) track to Cairn Gorm.

Descent: Descend N from the radio relay station and follow the waymarked path to the top station of the funicular railway. Turn W and follow the track as it traverses S into Coire Cas. Continue along the track and follow it NW through Coire Cas to the car park.

Cairn Gorm and the northern corries from Loch Morlich

Strenuousness
●●●○○

Navigation
●●●○○

Technicality
●●●○○

625m
(2051ft)

Broad open corrie and stony summit

Coire Cas Car Park, GR NH989060

The worst of the destruction caused by the ski grounds can be avoided by taking the Sròn an Aonaich path (starts at GR NH987069) up the east side of Coire Cas

1.5 hours
3.7km
(2.3 miles)

Coire na Ciste Path CAIRN GORM

'Quiet in summer'

Summary: Coire na Ciste extends directly north from the summit dome of Cairn Gorm. It shares the same fate as Coire Cas as a very popular ski ground. In winter it is generally busy with skiers but in summer it provides a quiet and pleasant walk alongside the Allt na Ciste.

Ascent: From the Coire na Ciste Car Park follow the Allt na Ciste SSE up through the narrow confines of Coire na Ciste to the old path on the east side of Cairn Gorm. Join the path and ascend it SSW to Cairn Gorm.

Descent: Take the old path NNE from the radio relay station to the head of Coire na Ciste. Descend NNW through the corrie to the car park at the bottom chair lift station.

Strenuousness

●●●●○

Navigation

●●●●○

Technicality

●●●○○

▶ Coire na Ciste Car Park, GR NH998074

2 hours
3.8km
(2.4 miles)

705m
(2313ft)

Steep narrow corrie, open upper corrie and stony summit

The Ptarmigan buildings at the junction between Coire na Ciste and Coire Cas

North Ridge CAIRN GORM

'Best walk to the top' ★★

Summary: The long North Ridge of Cairn Gorm runs the length of Strath Nethy. A superb route, it climbs the narrow ridge of Sròn a' Cha-no and takes in the fine little top of Cnap Coire na Spreidhe.

Ascent: Take the Glenmore Lodge road and follow it E past the lodge, then NE and take the Ryvoan Pass Track.

Before An Lochan Uaine turn R and climb the vague path SE below Creag nan Gall. Once through the woodland turn S and follow the vague path to Lochan na Beinne. Before the loch, swing SE and climb past the woodland enclosure to the shallow col at the foot of the Sròn a' Cha-no. Follow the ridge S then SW past Cnap Coire na Spreidhe to join the old path on the east side of Cairn Gorm. Join the path and ascend it SSW to Cairn Gorm.

Descent: Take the old path NNE from the radio relay station to the head of Coire na Ciste. Head NE across the broad col towards Cnap Coire na Spreidhe then swing N and follow the ridge as it descends steadily to the shallow col at the foot of the Sròn a' Cha-no. From the col descend past the woodland to the north end of Lochan na Beinne and join the vague path which is followed N then NW to join the Ryvoan Pass Track. Turn L and follow the track to Glenmore.

Radio relay station, Cairn Gorm summit

Strenuousness
● ● ● ● ○

Navigation
● ● ● ● ○

Technicality
● ● ● ○ ○

Glenmore,
GR NH977097

4 hours
10.2km
(6.3 miles)

1000m
(3280ft)

Long undulating ridge and stony summit

The main ridge can also be gained via Coire Laogh Mòr, starting either at Coire na Ciste Car Park, GR NH998074, or Glenmore, NH977097

Aonach Beag

1234m (4049ft)

Aonach Beag sits between the main Ben Nevis range and the peaks of The Grey Corries. Close by to the north is Aonach Mòr and to the south is the deep trough of Glen Nevis. Set in such a commanding position among such fine peaks and glens, Aonach Beag affords superb panoramic views.

The massive and complex An Aghaidh Gharbh forms the northeast face of Aonach Beag. From its base extending northeast towards Glen Spean and the Leanachan Forest is An Coire Calma, which in turn runs down into Coire an Eòin. Aonach Beag cannot be ascended directly up An Aghaidh Gharbh, instead the cols at either end of the crag have to be gained. The combined approach via either of the cols and along the length of the corries is a fine but arduous expedition across terrain which is trackless, rough and unbelievably beautiful.

The southwest side of Aonach Beag is easily accessible from Glen Nevis. Its slopes form a horseshoe around the high hanging corrie of Coire nan Laogh. The northernmost arm (Southwest Ridge) is a high, truncated spur which ends abruptly above Coire Giubhsachan. The southern arm is formed by the sharp, scree-covered peak Sgùrr a' Bhuic.

Aonach Beag's summit cairn

When you arrive

Ordnance Survey: Explorer 392 (1:25 000) No 32; Landranger (1:50 000) No 41.

Harvey Mountain Maps: Ben Nevis (1:25 000)

British Mountain Maps: Ben Nevis and Glen Coe (1:40 000)

Tourist Information Centres: Fort William; Spean Bridge.

Youth Hostels: Glen Nevis

Hotels and B&B: Fort William; Glen Nevis; Spean Bridge; Roy Bridge.

Camp sites: Glen Nevis; Camaghael.

Bothies and Howffs: Steall Hut (GR NN177683) in Glen Nevis is a locked private hut that needs to be booked through either the Scottish Mountaineering Club or the British Mountaineering Council

The eastern corries of Aonach Beag and Aonach Mòr are truly wild places: the approaches to them are long and their terrain is rough and trackless. Coire an Eòin is a particularly fine place: walking from the birch-fringed edge of Leanachan Forest and along its boggy floor you will encounter a fine range of flora from sphagnum, cotton grass, to bog myrtle and common heather. Then, as height is gained, the better drainage on steeper slopes allows heath and grass to take over. Mat grass, stiff sedge, heather, mosses and liverworts are common. Blaeberry, crowberry, bearberry and dwarf cornel occur but are more likely to be found among boulders away from the attentions of red deer. Once the snows have cleared from the crags and summits a keen eye will spot occasional dashes of colour from the tiny flowers of arctic-alpine plants; those most evident are the yellow mountain saxifrage, moss campion, alpine speedwell and arctic mouse-ear.

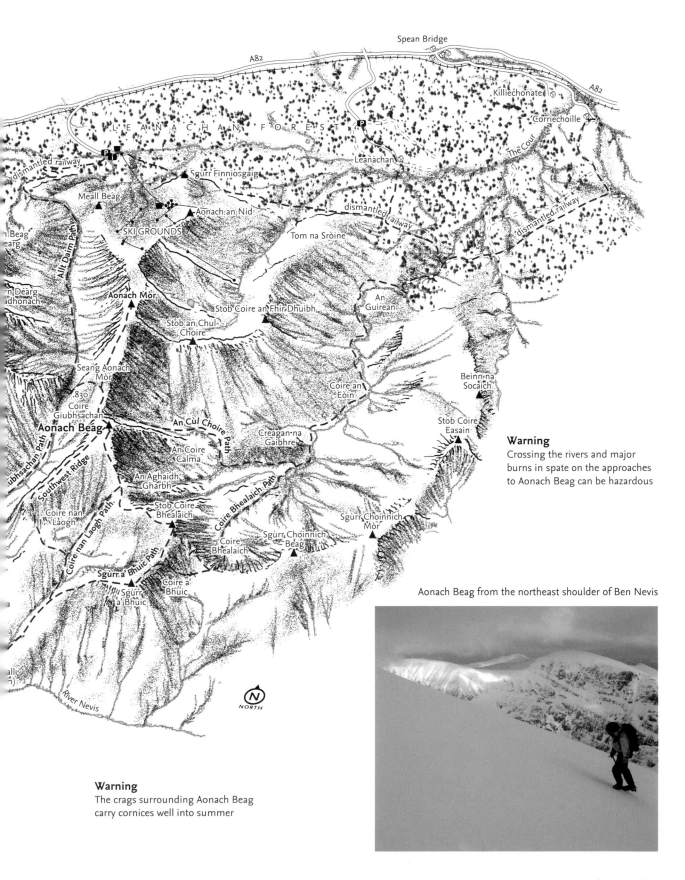

Spean Bridge

A82

Killiechonate

A82

Corriechoille

L E A N A C H A N   F O R E S T

P

dismantled railway

Leanachan

The Cour

Sgurr Finniosgaig

dismantled railway

dismantled railway

Meall Beag

Aonach an Nid

SKI GROUNDS

Tom na Sròine

Beag
earg

Allt Daim Path

n Dèarg
adhonach

Aonach Mòr

Stob Coire an Fhir Dhuibh

An
Guirean

Stob an Chul-
Choire

Seang Aonach
Mòr

Coire an
Eòin

Beinn na
Socaich

.830
Coire
Giubhsachan

Aonach Beag

An Cùl Choire Path

Creagan na
Gaibhre

Stob Coire
Easain

An Coire
Calma

Warning
Crossing the rivers and major
burns in spate on the approaches
to Aonach Beag can be hazardous

iubhsachan Path

An Aghaidh
Gharbh

Southwest Ridge

Coire nan
Laogh

Stob Coire
Bhealaich

Coire Bhealaich Path

Sgurr Choinnich
Mòr

Coire
Bhealaich

Sgùrr Choinnich
Beag

Coire nan Laogh Path

Sgurr a' Bhuic Path

Sgurr a' Bhuic

Coire a'
Bhuic

Sgùrr
a' Bhuic

River Nevis

N
NORTH

Aonach Beag from the northeast shoulder of Ben Nevis

Warning
The crags surrounding Aonach Beag
carry cornices well into summer

Coire Giubhsachan Path AONACH BEAG

'Adventurous' ★★

Summary: Climbing steadily alongside the waterslides and waterfalls of the Allt Coire Giubhsachan, the Coire Giubhsachan Path twists its way north to the col on the west side of Aonach Mòr. Access to Aonach Beag from the col involves a steep ascent up the Seang Aonach Mòr, then a walk SW along the main ridge.

the col at its head. At the col climb E up the very steep and in parts loose Seang Aonach Mòr. Turn R and descend slightly to the col on the north side of Aonach Mòr. Cross it and climb the path SE up the scree. As the angle eases turn SSE to the summit of Aonach Beag.

Ascent: From the car park follow the path as it meanders E through the gorge to the footbridge by the Steall (ruins). Turn N and follow the path up the west side of the Allt Coire Giubhsachan. Continue N up through Coire Giubhsachan to

Descent: From the summit descend NNW, then NW, following the path down the scree to the col on the north side of Aonach Beag. Cross it and climb slightly NNW to the top of the Seang Aonach Mòr (small cairn). Turn W and descend the vague path down the steep and in parts loose slope to the col. Turn S and follow the Allt Coire Giubhsachan down to the footbridge at the Steall (ruins). At the footbridge join the Glen Nevis footpath and follow it W through the gorge to the car park.

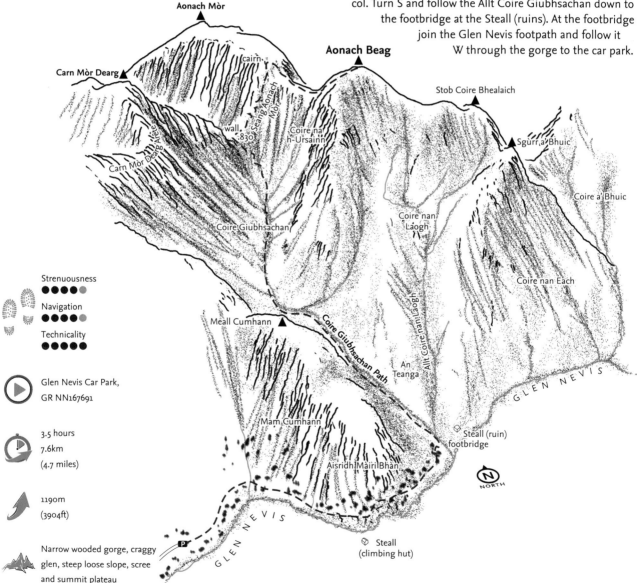

Strenuousness
●●●●○

Navigation
●●●●○

Technicality
●●●●●

Glen Nevis Car Park,
GR NN167691

3.5 hours
7.6km
(4.7 miles)

1190m
(3904ft)

Narrow wooded gorge, craggy glen, steep loose slope, scree and summit plateau

Allt Daim Path AONACH BEAG

'Confined and steep'

Summary: Climbs steadily along the wild glen occupied by the Allt Daim to the high col between Carn Mòr Dearg and the Aonachs massif. A simple, direct route although the ascent of Seang Aonach Mòr can be problematic especially with snow cover and poor visibility.

Ascent: From the car park head SW then turn S and take the zigzags up to the course of the old narrow-gauge railway. Follow it SW to the water intake, then turn SE and climb alongside the Allt Daim. Continue alongside the Allt Daim to the col, then turn E and climb the very steep and in parts loose Seang Aonach Mòr. At the top, turn R and descend to the col on the north side of Aonach Mòr. Cross it and climb the path SE up the scree. As the angle eases turn SSE to the summit of Aonach Beag.

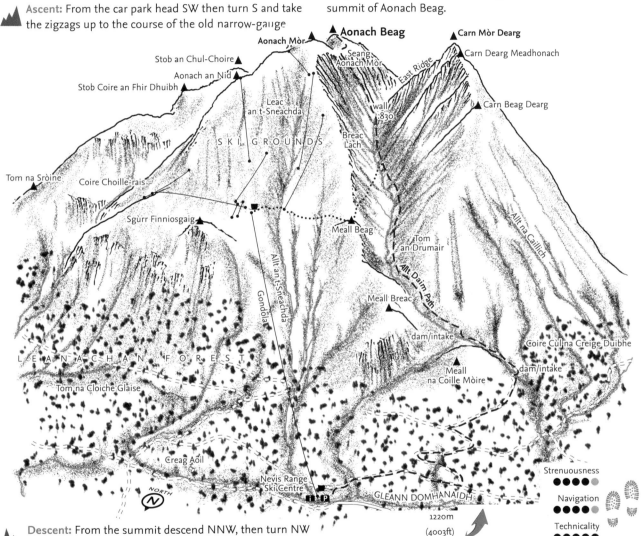

Descent: From the summit descend NNW, then turn NW following the path down the scree to the col on the north side of Aonach Beag. Cross it and climb NNW to the top of the Seang Aonach Mòr (small cairn). Turn W and descend the vague path down the steep and in parts loose slope to the col. Turn N and follow the Allt Daim on its southwest side to the water intake and join the old narrow-gauge railway. Follow its course NE, then take the zigzags N. At the bottom turn R and head NE to the Gondola Car Park.

Strenuousness
●●●●○

Navigation
●●●●○

Technicality
●●●●●

Woodland, craggy glen, steep loose slope, scree and summit plateau

Nevis Range Car Park, GR NN171773

⚠ The Allt Daim Path can be gained from the gondola top station via a steep descent from Meall Beag

4 hours
9.4km
(5.8 miles)

An Cùl Choire Path AONACH BEAG

'Long and atmospheric' ★★★

Summary: A long approach via the secretive An Cùl Choire. The route climbs through its southwest bay – tucked away behind the towering Northeast Ridge of Aonach Beag – which may contain snow even in summer.

Ascent: Follow the road then the forest track SW to a fork. Take the left branch SE over the stepping stones to the building ruins. From the ruins follow the footpath S as it climbs to the course of the old railway line. Turn E and follow its course to the Allt Coire an Eòin Bridge. Cross it and turn R onto the access track, then follow it SW to the water intake. Follow the Allt Coire an Eòin SW, S then SW through the pathless wilds of Coire an Eòin to the mouth of An Cùl Choire. Enter the corrie then climb the southwest bay to the col between Aonach Mòr and Aonach Beag. Turn L and climb the path SE up the scree. As the angle eases turn SSE onto the summit of Aonach Beag.

Descent: From the summit descend NNW, then turn NW following the path down the scree to the col on the north side of Aonach Beag. Descend the steep bay NE into An Cùl Choire. Cross the corrie floor then follow the Allt Coire an Eòin NE, N then NE through Coire an Eòin to the water intake. Take the access track NE down to the old railway line then follow its course W to the top of the Leanachan Path. Turn R and follow it past the ruins and over the stepping stones to the public road.

Water intake on the Allt Coire an Eòin, GR NN227758. Part of the Lochaber Water Power Scheme, this small dam feeds supplementary water into an underground tunnel which drains water from Loch Treig and carries it to the power station at the aluminium works at Fort William.

Strenuousness
●●●●○

Navigation
●●●●●

Technicality
●●●●●

1210m
(3970ft)

Car Park near Leanachan
GR NN211792

Forest, rough pathless glen, remote craggy corrie, scree, headwall and summit plateau

5 hours
12.9km
(8 miles)

Can also be started via the course of the old narrow-gauge railway from either the Nevis Range Car Park, GR NN171773, or Corriechoille in the Spean Valley, GR NN252807

Coire Bhealaich Path AONACH BEAG

'Long and remote' ★★

Summary: Aonach Beag drops away dramatically on its east side. The link between it and the peaks of The Grey Corries is via the big descent to the broad col above Coire Bhealaich. Approaching Coire Bhealaich along Coire an Eòin from Leanachan gives a long, diverse walk with the added spice of some exposed scrambling to finish.

Ascent: Follow the road then the forest track SW to a fork. Take the left branch SE over the stepping stones to the building ruins. From the ruins follow the footpath S as it climbs to the course of the old railway line. Turn E and follow its course to the Allt Coire an Eòin Bridge. Cross it and turn R onto the access track, then follow it SW to the water intake. Follow the Allt Coire an Eòin SW, S then SW through the pathless wilds of Coire an Eòin to the mouth of An Coire Calma. Head S up through the corrie to the col at the head of Coire Bhealaich. From the col either climb the steep, tortuous path W to Stob Coire Bhealaich or traverse SW through Coire a' Bhuic to the col then NNE to Stob Coire Bhealaich. Head W then NW along the main ridge to Aonach Beag.

Descent: Head SE then E down the main ridge to Stob Coire Bhealaich. Turn SSW and descend to the col on the north side of Sgùrr a' Bhuic. Traverse NE through Coire a' Bhuic to the broad col above Coire Bhealaich. Descend N through Coire Bhealaich then An Coire Calma to the Allt Coire an Eòin. Follow it NE, N then NE through Coire an Eòin to the water intake. Take the access track NE down to the old railway line then follow its course W to the top of the Leanachan path. Turn L and follow it past the ruins and over the stepping stones to the public road.

1124m
(3688ft)

Forest, rough pathless glen, remote rocky corrie, very steep loose slope, exposed ridge and summit plateau

Strenuousness
●●●●○

Navigation
●●●●●

Technicality
●●●●●

Car Park near Leanachan
GR NN211792

The steep slope below Stob Coire Bhealaich can be avoided by making a diagonal traverse across Coire a' Bhuic to or from the col on the northeast side of Sgùrr a' Bhuic. Can also be started via the course of the old narrow-gauge railway from either the Nevis Range Car Park, GR NN171773, or Corriechoille in the Spean Valley, GR NN252807.

4.5–5 hours
12km
(7.5 miles)

Sgùrr a' Bhuic Path AONACH BEAG

'Lofty ridge approach' ★★★

Summary: Climbs the ridge on the south side of Coire nan Laogh via the shapely peak Sgùrr a' Bhuic to join the main ridge of Aonach Beag at Stob Coire Bhealaich.

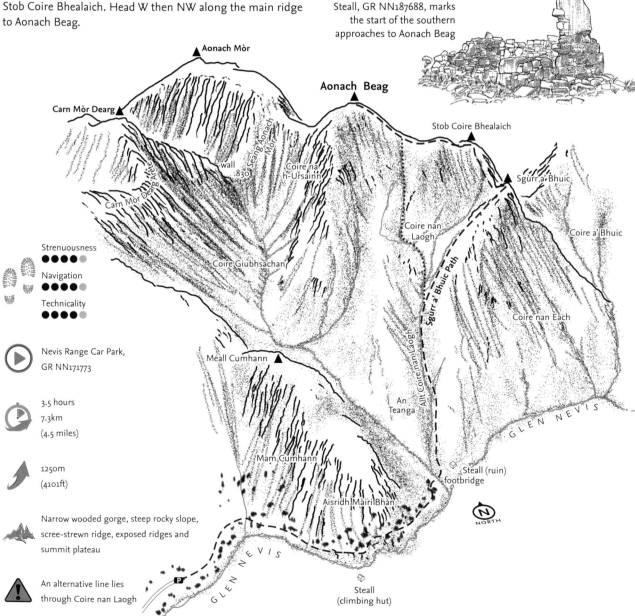

Ascent: From the car park follow the path as it meanders E through the gorge to the footbridge by the Steall (ruin). Cross it and climb NE alongside the Allt Coire nan Laogh then climb the west ridge of Sgùrr a' Bhuic. From the summit descend N to the col at the head of Coire a' Bhuic then climb NNE to Stob Coire Bhealaich. Head W then NW along the main ridge to Aonach Beag.

Descent: Head SE then E down the main ridge to Stob Coire Bhealaich. Turn SSW and descend to the col on the north side of Sgùrr a' Bhuic. Climb S to the summit of Sgùrr a' Bhuic then descend the steep ridge W to Coire nan Laogh. From the corrie head SW down the southeast side of the Allt Coire nan Laogh to the footbridge at the Steall (ruin). Cross it and follow the Glen Nevis footpath W through the gorge to the car park.

The ruined building at Steall, GR NN187688, marks the start of the southern approaches to Aonach Beag

Strenuousness
●●●●○

Navigation
●●●●○

Technicality
●●●●○

Nevis Range Car Park, GR NN171773

3.5 hours
7.3km
(4.5 miles)

1250m
(4101ft)

Narrow wooded gorge, steep rocky slope, scree-strewn ridge, exposed ridges and summit plateau

An alternative line lies through Coire nan Laogh

Aonach Mòr

Carn Mòr Dearg

Aonach Beag

Stob Coire Bhealaich

Sgùrr a' Bhuic

Carn Mòr Dearg Arête

Seang Aonach Mòr

wall
.830

Coire na h-Ursainn

Coire a' Bhuic

Coire nan Laogh

Sgùrr a' Bhuic Path

Coire Giubhsachan

Coire nan Each

Allt Coire nan Laogh

Meall Cumhann

An Teanga

GLEN NEVIS

Mam Cumhann

Steall (ruin) footbridge

Aisridh Màiri Bhan

N NORTH

P

GLEN NEVIS

Steall (climbing hut)

Southwest Ridge AONACH BEAG

'Tricky navigation' ★

Summary: Climbs the long arm of Aonach Beag's southwest ridge. With steep ground on both sides the traverse of this ridge requires careful navigation in poor weather. It is the most direct route from Glen Nevis.

Ascent: From the car park follow the path as it meanders E through the gorge to the footbridge by the Steall (ruins). Cross it and climb NE alongside the Allt Coire nan Laogh, then turn NW and cross the corrie floor to the slope on the southeast side of the southwest ridge. Climb the slope to the crest of the ridge then turn NE and follow it to the summit of Aonach Beag.

Descent: Head SW down the crest of the ridge then turn SE (taking care to avoid its steep truncated end) and descend steeply into Coire nan Laogh. Cross the corrie then head SW down the southeast side of the Allt Coire nan Laogh to the footbridge at the Steall (ruins). Cross it and follow the Glen Nevis footpath W through the gorge to the car park.

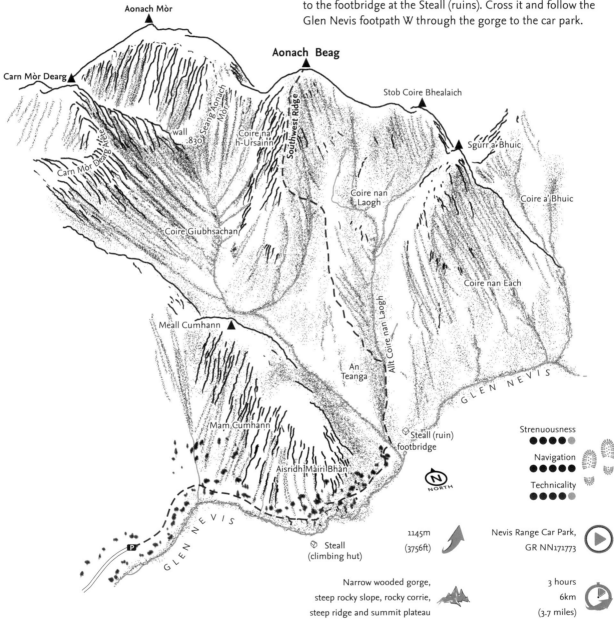

Aonach Mòr Link AONACH BEAG

'High but simple' ★

Summary: Aonach Beag is separated from Aonach Mòr by a narrow col. The walk between the two peaks is simple enough so long as the weather is clear. In mist and with snow cover it can be confusing – particularly the steep descent to the col from Aonach Beag.

Route: From the summit descend NNW, then turn NW following the path down the scree to the col on the north side of Aonach Beag. Cross it and climb the summit plateau N to Aonach Mòr.

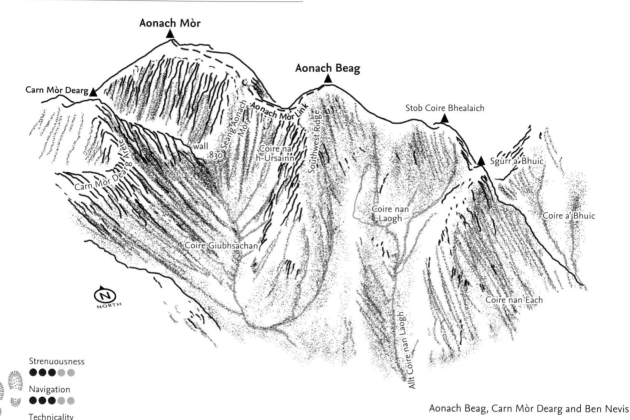

Strenuousness

 ●●●●○

Navigation

 ●●●●○

Technicality

 ●●●○○

▶ Aonach Beag, GR NN196715

⏱ 0.5 hours
1.6km
(1 mile)

↗ 150m
(492ft)

⛰ Steep scree-strewn slope, exposed col and broad summit ridge

Aonach Beag, Carn Mòr Dearg and Ben Nevis

Carn Mòr Dearg Link AONACH BEAG

'Two steep scrambles' ★

Summary: The steep descent down the loose Seang Aonach Mòr and then the climb up the sweeping East Ridge of Carn Mòr Dearg involves a considerable height loss and demands substantial leg work.

Route: From the summit descend NNW, then NW following the path down the scree to the col on the north side of Aonach Beag. Cross the col and climb NNW to the top of the Seang Aonach Mòr (small cairn). Turn W and descend the vague path down the steep and in parts loose slope to the col. Head W across the col to climb the long steep East Ridge directly to the summit of Carn Mòr Dearg.

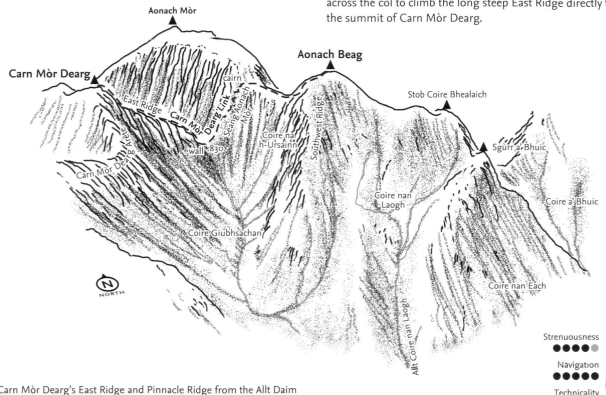

Carn Mòr Dearg's East Ridge and Pinnacle Ridge from the Allt Daim

Strenuousness
● ● ● ● ○

Navigation
● ● ● ● ●

Technicality
● ● ● ● ●

Scramble/Winter climb
● ● ● ○ / ● ○

Aonach Beag,
GR NN196715

1.5 hours
2.7km
(1.7 miles)

435m
(1427ft)

Steep loose slope and
steep rocky ridge

Aonach Mòr

1221m (4006ft)

Aonach Mòr's name could not have been more appropriately chosen, as it means big-ridged mountain, and it is just that. In profile, it has the appearance of a whale-back with a summit plateau which extends for about 1.2km (0.7 miles). To the south, the slopes end abruptly at a col adjoining Aonach Beag, while to the north the slope falls away steadily to Leanachan Forest. On the east and west are precipitous crags.

Since the completion of the Nevis Range ski grounds with gondola cable car and constructed paths, access to the northern side of Aonach Mòr has become considerably easier. The skiing area occupies almost the whole of the Coire nan Geadh (meaning corrie of the goose and not named on Ordnance Survey maps), and at either side, paths

climb the bounding ridges to the summit plateau. These two northern routes are the only easy routes on the mountain.

The western and eastern approaches pass through outstanding scenery and involve long walks and steep ascents. From the Allt Daim or Coire Giubhsachan the only feasible route onto the summit plateau is up the steep, loose slope of Seang Aonach Mòr. To the east the choice is much wider. Three superb ridges and a corrie headwall can be climbed from the rough and remote corries Coire Choille-rais and Coire an Eòin.

Water intake on the Allt Choille-rais, GR NN204767. Part of the Lochaber Water Power Scheme, this small dam feeds supplementary water into an underground tunnel which drains water from Loch Treig and carries it to the power station at the aluminium works at Fort William.

When you arrive

Ordnance Survey: Explorer 392 (1:25 000) No 32; Landranger (1:50 000) No 41.

Harvey Mountain Maps: Ben Nevis (1:25 000)

British Mountain Maps: Ben Nevis and Glen Coe (1:40 000)

Tourist Information Centres: Fort William; Spean Bridge.

Youth Hostels: Glen Nevis

Hotels and B&B: Fort William; Glen Nevis; Spean Bridge; Roy Bridge.

Camp sites: Glen Nevis; Camaghael.

Bothies and Howffs: Steall Hut (GR NN177683) in Glen Nevis is a locked private hut that needs to be booked through either the Scottish Mountaineering Club or the British Mountaineering Council

Warning
Crossing the rivers and major burns in spate on the approaches to Aonach Mòr can be hazardous

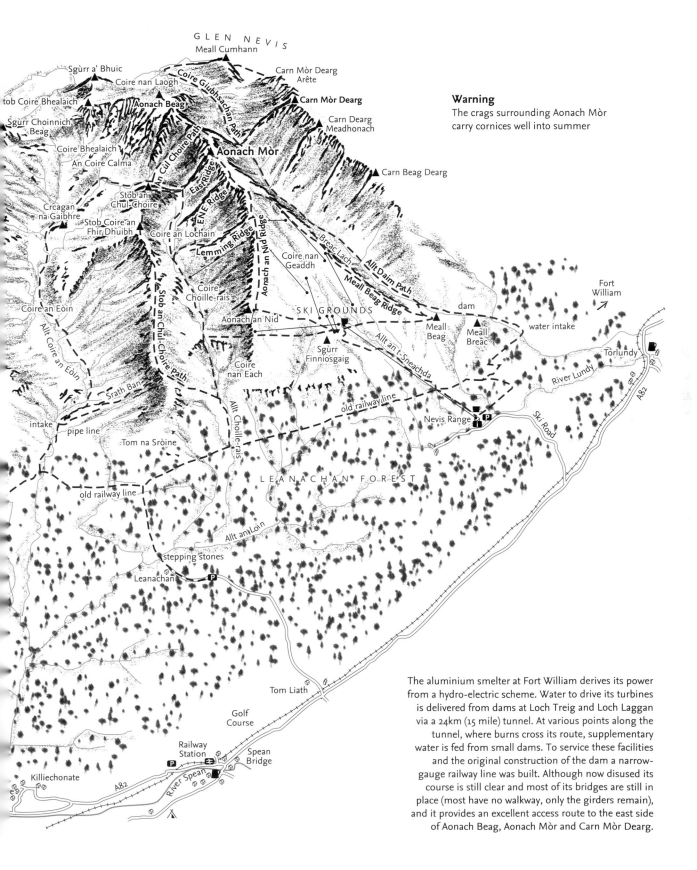

GLEN NEVIS
Meall Cumhann

Sgùrr a' Bhuic
Coire nan Laogh
Coire Giubhsachan Path
Carn Mòr Dearg Arête
Stob Coire Bhealaich
Aonach Beag
Carn Mòr Dearg
Sgùrr Choinnich Beag
Carn Dearg Meadhonach
Coire Bhealaich
An Coire Calma
Aonach Mòr
Carn Beag Dearg
Crcagan na Gaibhre
Stob an Chul-Choire
An Cùl Choire Path
East Ridge
ENE Ridge
Stob Coire an Fhir Dhuibh
Coire an Lochain
Lemming Ridge
Aonach an Nid Ridge
Coire nan Geaddh
Breac Lach
Allt Daim Path
Meall Beag Ridge

Warning
The crags surrounding Aonach Mòr
carry cornices well into summer

Fort William

Coire an Eòin
Stob an Chul-Choire Path
Coire Choille-rais
Aonach an Nid
SKI GROUNDS
Meall Beag
Meall Breac
dam
water intake

Allt Coire an Eòin
Coire nan Each
Sgùrr Finniosgaig
Allt an t-Sneachda
River Lundy
Torlundy

Srath Ban
Allt Choille-rais
old railway line
Nevis Range
Ski Road
A82

intake
pipe line
Tom na Sròine

old railway line
LEANACHAN FOREST

Allt an Lòin

stepping stones
Leanachan

Tom Liath

Golf Course

Railway Station
Spean Bridge
Killiechonate
River Spean
A82

The aluminium smelter at Fort William derives its power
from a hydro-electric scheme. Water to drive its turbines
is delivered from dams at Loch Treig and Loch Laggan
via a 24km (15 mile) tunnel. At various points along the
tunnel, where burns cross its route, supplementary
water is fed from small dams. To service these facilities
and the original construction of the dam a narrow-
gauge railway line was built. Although now disused its
course is still clear and most of its bridges are still in
place (most have no walkway, only the girders remain),
and it provides an excellent access route to the east side
of Aonach Beag, Aonach Mòr and Carn Mòr Dearg.

Coire Giubhsachan Path AONACH MÒR

'Adventurous' ★★

Summary: Climbing steadily alongside the waterslides and waterfalls of the Allt Coire Giubhsachan, the Coire Giubhsachan Path twists its way north to the col on the west side of Aonach Mòr.

Ascent: From the car park follow the path as it meanders E through the gorge to the footbridge by the Steall (ruin). Turn N and follow the path up the west side of the Allt Coire Giubhsachan. Continue N up through Coire Giubhsachan to the col at its head. At the col climb E up the very steep and in parts loose Seang Aonach Mòr. At the top, turn N and climb the summit slopes to Aonach Mòr.

Descent: Head S down the summit slopes to the top of the Seang Aonach Mòr (small cairn). Turn W and descend the vague path down the steep and in parts loose slope to the col. Turn S and follow the Allt Coire Giubhsachan down to the footbridge at the Steall (ruin). At the footbridge join the Glen Nevis footpath and follow it W through the gorge to the car park.

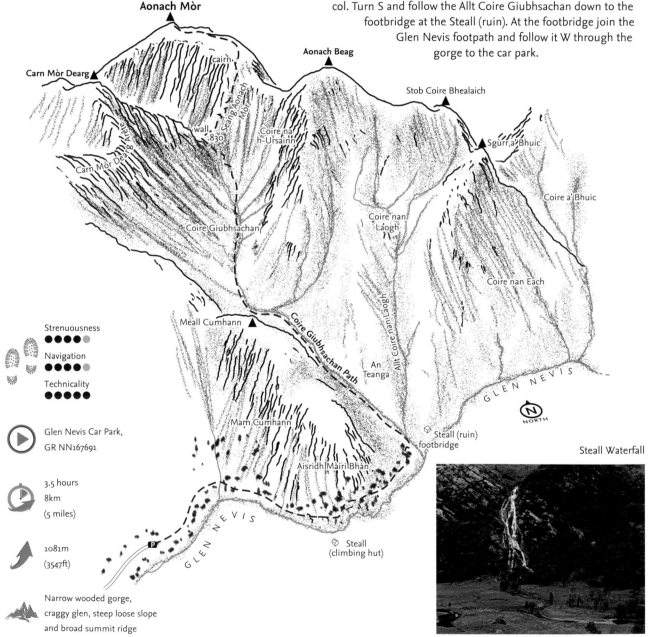

Strenuousness
●●●●○

Navigation
●●●●○

Technicality
●●●●●

Glen Nevis Car Park,
GR NN167691

3.5 hours
8km
(5 miles)

1081m
(3547ft)

Narrow wooded gorge,
craggy glen, steep loose slope
and broad summit ridge

Steall Waterfall

Allt Daim Path AONACH MÒR

'Confined and steep'

Summary: The long west wall of Aonach Mòr is a series of steep broken crags. From Allt Daim there are lines up these rocks though they would require the use of ropes. For the walker the only route is via Seang Aonach Mòr.

Aonach Mòr ▲

Aonach Beag ▲

Carn Mòr Dearg ▲

Stob an Chul-Choire ▲

Seang Aonach Mòr

Carn Dearg Meadhonach ▲

Aonach an Nid ▲

Stob Coire an Fhir Dhuibh ▲

East Ridge

Leac an t-Sneachda

Carn Beag Dearg ▲

wall :830

S K I   G R O U N D S

Breac Lach

Tom na Sròine ▲

Coire Choille-rais

Sgùrr Finniosgaig ▲

Meall Beag

Allt na Caillich

Tom an Drumair

Allt an t-Sneachda

Gondola

Allt Daim Path

Meall Breac ▲

Coire Cùl na Creige Duibhe

dam/intake

L E A N A C H A N   F O R E S T

Meall na Coille Mòire ▲

dam/intake

Tom na Cloiche Glaise

Creag Aoil

Nevis Range Ski Centre

ℹ️ P

G L E A N N D O M H A N A I D H

Ascent: From the car park head SW then turn S and take the zigzags up to the course of the old narrow-gauge railway. Follow it SW to the water intake then turn SE and climb alongside the Allt Daim. Continue alongside the Allt Daim to the col, then turn E and climb the very steep and in parts loose Seang Aonach Mòr. At the top turn N and climb the summit slopes to Aonach Mòr.

Descent: Head S down the summit slopes to the top of the Seang Aonach Mòr (small cairn). Turn W and descend the vague path down the steep and in parts loose slope to the col. Turn N and follow the Allt Daim on its southwest side to the water intake and join the old narrow-gauge railway. Follow its course NE, then take the zigzags N. At the bottom, turn R and head NE to the Gondola Car Park.

NORTH
Ⓝ

1165m
(3822ft)

Strenuousness
●●●●○

Navigation
●●●●○

Technicality
●●●●●

Woodland, craggy glen, steep loose slope and broad summit ridge

Nevis Range Car Park,
GR NN171773 ▶

The Allt Daim Path can be gained from the gondola top station via a steep descent from Meall Beag ⚠️

4 hours
9.1km
(5.7 miles) ↻

Meall Beag Ridge AONACH MÒR

'Dramatic views'

Summary: High above the Allt Daim, along the top of the steep west face of Aonach Mòr, the Meall Beag Ridge climbs steadily to the summit plateau.

Descent: Head N then descend NW down the broad ridge to the start of the constructed path at Meall Beag. Take it E to the gondola top station, then descend NW down the waymarked path to the car park.

Ascent: From the car park follow the waymarked path SE up to the gondola top station. Turn W and follow the constructed path to Meall Beag. From the end of the path climb the vague path SE up the broad ridge to the summit plateau.

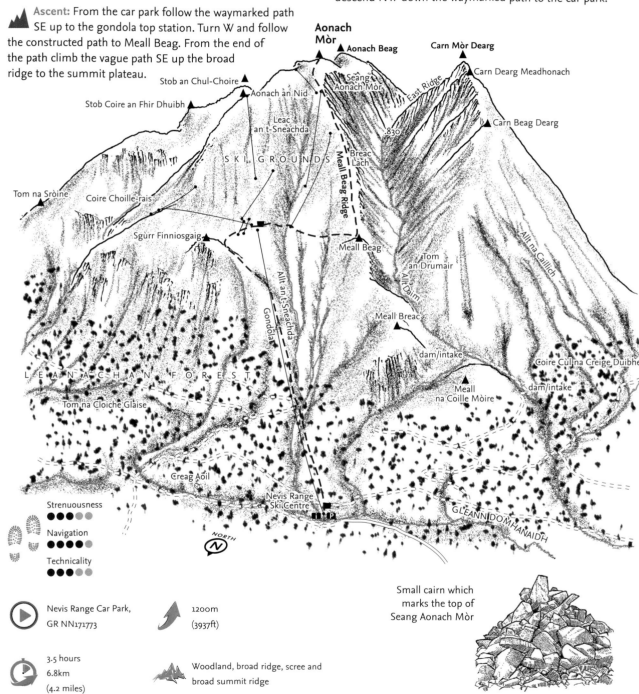

Small cairn which marks the top of Seang Aonach Mòr

Strenuousness ●●●●○

Navigation ●●●●○

Technicality ●●●○○

Nevis Range Car Park, GR NN171773

1200m (3937ft)

3.5 hours
6.8km
(4.2 miles)

Woodland, broad ridge, scree and broad summit ridge

Aonach an Nid Ridge AONACH MÒR

'Steep start with revealing views' ★

Summary: Extending north from the summit plateau of Aonach Mòr, the Aonach an Nid Ridge provides a fairly steep but easy approach. From its lofty position it affords superb views over the eastern corries into the Spean Valley.

Aonach Mòr

Aonach Beag

Carn Mòr Dearg

Carn Dearg Meadhonach

Stob an Chul-Choire

Seang Aonach Mòr

East Ridge

Aonach an Nid

Stob Coire an Fhir Dhuibh

Carn Beag Dearg

Leac an t-Sneachda

Aonach an Nid Ridge

.830

Breac Lach

SKI GROUNDS

Tom na Sròine

Coire Choille-rais

chair lift

Allt na Gaillich

Meall Beag

Sgùrr Finniosgaig

Tom an Drumair

Allt an t-Sneachda

Allt Daim

Gondola

Meall Breac

dam/intake

Coire Cul na Creige Duibhe

LEANACHAN FOREST

dam/intake

Tom na Cloiche Glaise

Meall na Coille Mòire

Creag Aoil

Nevis Range Ski Centre

GLEANN DOMHANAIDH

NORTH

Ascent: From the car park follow the waymarked path SE to the gondola top station. Turn E and skirt the ski grounds, then head SE to join the broad ridge. Climb S up the ridge to Aonach an Nid, after which it becomes more defined. Continue S up the ridge to the summit plateau.

Descent: Head N and descend the ridge to Aonach an Nid. Continue down the ridge as it becomes broader, then swing around to the NW. Skirt the ski grounds and join the constructed path W to the gondola top station. Then descend NW down the waymarked path to the car park.

3.5 hours
6km
(3.7 miles)

1216m
(3989ft)

Woodland, expansive corrie, steep ridge and broad summit ridge

Strenuousness
●●●●○○

Navigation
●●●●○○

Technicality
●●●●○○

Nevis Range Car Park, GR NN171773

Lemming Ridge AONACH MÒR

'Airy crest' ★★★

Summary: Coire an Lochain is the beautiful high corrie on the east side of Aonach Mòr; bounding its northern edge is Lemming Ridge. It provides a short simple scramble – useful as a route down into the remote Coire Choille-rais.

Ascent: Follow the road then the forest track SW to a fork. Take the left branch SE over the stepping stones to the ruined buildings. From the ruins follow the footpath S as it climbs to the course of the old railway line. Turn R onto it and follow it W over the Allt Choille-rais Bridge to a forest track on the left. Take this as it climbs round to the water intake. From the intake follow the Allt Choille-rais as it climbs steeply S then W into Coire an Lochain. Climb N from the lochan to the foot of Lemming Ridge then climb its crest W onto the summit plateau. Head S around the edge of the crags to the summit of Aonach Mòr.

Descent: Head N around the edge of the crags to the top of Lemming Ridge. Descend its steep crest E into Coire an Lochain then turn N and descend the length of Coire Choille-rais to the water intake. Take the access track down to the course of the old railway line. Join it and follow it E to the top of the Leanachan Path. Turn L onto it and follow it past the ruins and over the stepping stones to the public road.

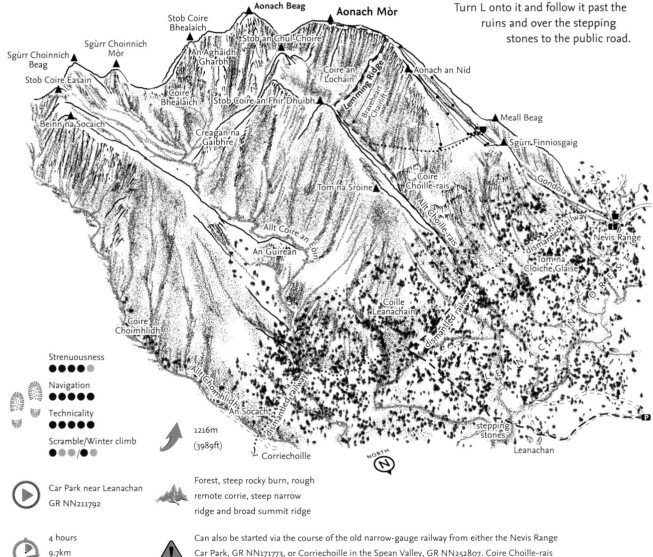

Strenuousness
●●●●○

Navigation
●●●●○

Technicality
●●●●●

Scramble/Winter climb
●●○○/●○○

Car Park near Leanachan
GR NN211792

4 hours
9.7km
(6 miles)

1216m
(3989ft)

Forest, steep rocky burn, rough remote corrie, steep narrow ridge and broad summit ridge

Can also be started via the course of the old narrow-gauge railway from either the Nevis Range Car Park, GR NN171773, or Corriechoille in the Spean Valley, GR NN252807. Coire Choille-rais can be gained from the gondola top station via a descent into Coire nan Each.

East-Northeast Ridge AONACH MÒR

'Scramble between dramatic corries' ★★

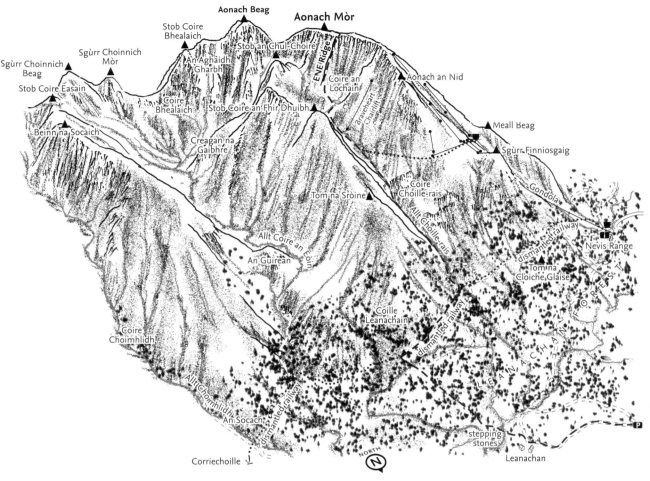

Summary: Bounding the south side of Coire an Lochain the East-Northeast Ridge of Aonach Mòr is longer and slightly harder than its near neighbour, Lemming Ridge. The ridge steepens as height is gained and the final section is poised high above the corrie floor.

the foot of the East-Northeast Ridge then climb its crest W onto the summit plateau. Head S around the edge of the crags to the summit of Aonach Mòr.

🏔 **Ascent:** Follow the road then the forest track SW to a fork. Take the left branch SE over the stepping stones to the ruined buildings. From the ruins follow the footpath S as it climbs to the course of the old railway line. Turn R onto it and follow it W over the Allt Choille-rais Bridge to a forest track on the left. Take this as it climbs round to the water intake. From the intake follow the Allt Choille-rais as it climbs steeply S then W into Coire an Lochain. Climb S from the lochan to

Strenuousness
●●●●○

Navigation
●●●●●

Technicality
●●●●●

Scramble/Winter climb
●●○○/●○○

1168m
(3832ft)

Forest, steep rocky burn, rough remote corrie, steep narrow ridge and broad summit ridge

Car Park near Leanachan
GR NN211792

Can also be started via the course of the old narrow-gauge railway from either the Nevis Range Car Park, GR NN171773, or Corriechoille in the Spean Valley, GR NN252807. Coire Choille-rais can be gained from the gondola top station via a descent into Coire nan Each.

4 hours
9.4km
(5.8 miles)

East Ridge AONACH MÒR

'Remote and rewarding scramble' ★ ★ ★

Summary: Directly below the summit of Aonach Mòr the East Ridge climbs onto the summit plateau from the exposed col at the head of An Cùl Choire. The approach to it is long up the pathless wilderness of the beautiful Coire an Eòin.

Ascent: Follow the road then the forest track SW to a fork. Take the left branch SE over the stepping stones to the building ruins. From the ruins follow the footpath S as it climbs to the course of the old railway line. Turn E and follow its course to the Allt Coire an Eòin Bridge. Cross the bridge and turn R onto the access track, and then follow it SW to the water intake. Follow the Allt Coire an Eòin SW, S then SW through the pathless wilds of Coire an Eòin to the mouth of An Cùl Choire. Climb the corrie NW to the col at its head. Then turn L and climb the East Ridge to the summit of Aonach Mòr.

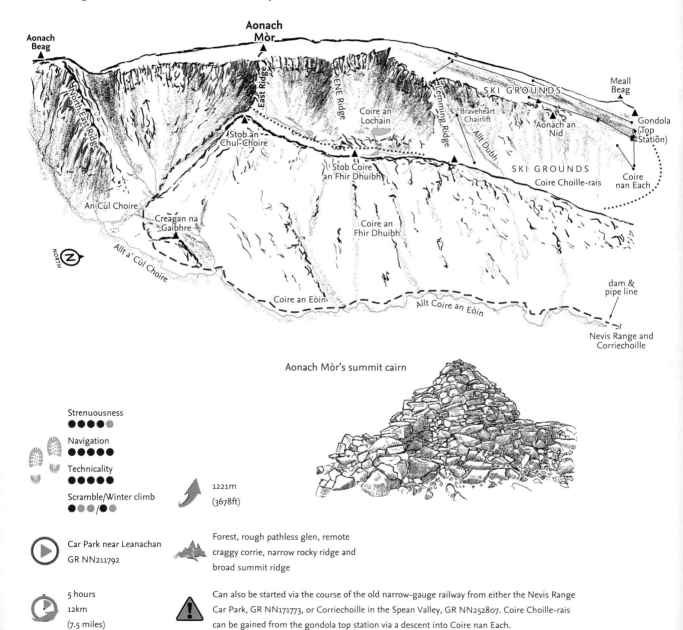

Aonach Mòr's summit cairn

Strenuousness
● ● ● ● ●

Navigation
● ● ● ● ●

Technicality
● ● ● ● ●

Scramble/Winter climb
● ● ○ ○ / ● ○ ○

1221m
(3678ft)

Car Park near Leanachan
GR NN211792

Forest, rough pathless glen, remote craggy corrie, narrow rocky ridge and broad summit ridge

5 hours
12km
(7.5 miles)

Can also be started via the course of the old narrow-gauge railway from either the Nevis Range Car Park, GR NN171773, or Corriechoille in the Spean Valley, GR NN252807. Coire Choille-rais can be gained from the gondola top station via a descent into Coire nan Each.

RIGHT
The crags between the ridges on Aonach Mòr's East Face provide a challenging and reliable range of winter climbs

Stob an Chul-Choire Path AONACH MÒR

'High and challenging' ★★

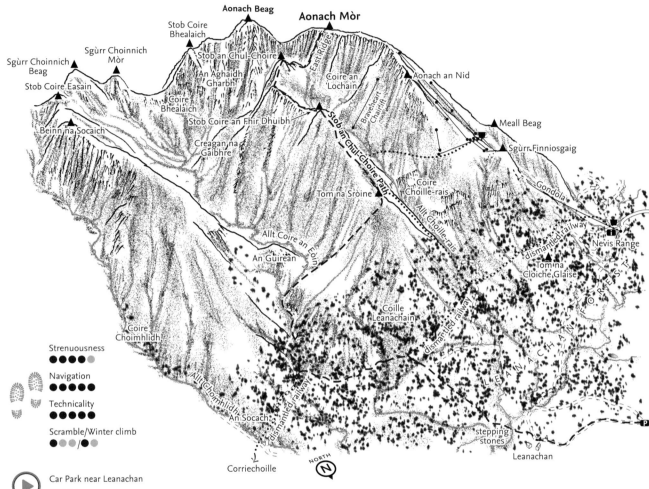

Strenuousness
●●●●○

Navigation
●●●●●

Technicality
●●●●●

Scramble/Winter climb
●●○○/●○○

Car Park near Leanachan
GR NN211792

4.5 hours
10.3km
(6.4 miles)

1298m
(4258ft)

Forest, steep rocky slope, long
narrow ridge, narrow rocky ridge
and broad summit ridge

The northern end of the main ridge can be gained from Coire
Choille-rais. Can also be started via the course of the old
narrow-gauge railway from either the Nevis Range Car Park,
GR NN171773, or Corriechoille in the Spean Valley, GR NN252807.

Summary: Situated between two of Scotland's wildest corries, the long northern ridge of Stob an Chul-Choire gives a particularly fine approach to the eastern side of Aonach Mòr.

Ascent: Follow the road then the forest track SW to a fork. Take the left branch SE over the stepping stones to the building ruins. From the ruins follow the footpath S as it climbs to the course of the old railway line. Turn E and follow its course to the Allt Coire an Eòin Bridge. Cross the bridge and turn R onto the access track, and follow it SW to the water intake. Climb the hillside E from the intake to the broad ridge at Tom na Sròine then climb S to the unnamed top. Continue S down the ridge to Stob Coire an Fhir Dhuibh, then follow it as it swings round to the SW to gain Stob an Chul-Choire. Descend W to the col, cross it, and climb the East Ridge to the summit of Aonach Mòr.

Aonach Beag Link AONACH MÒR

'High but simple' ★

Summary: Aonach Mòr is separated from Aonach Beag by a narrow col. The walk between the two peaks is simple enough so long as the weather is clear – in mist and with snow cover it can be confusing.

Route: Head S down the summit plateau to the narrow col. Cross it and climb the path SE up the scree. As the angle eases turn SSE to the summit of Aonach Beag.

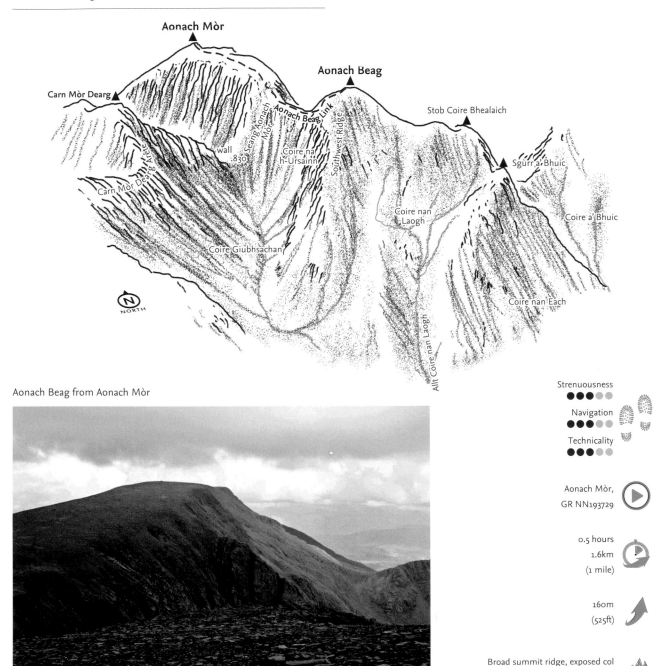

Aonach Beag from Aonach Mòr

Strenuousness
●●●●○○

Navigation
●●●●○○

Technicality
●●●●○

Aonach Mòr,
GR NN193729

0.5 hours
1.6km
(1 mile)

160m
(525ft)

Broad summit ridge, exposed col and steep scree-strewn slopes

Carn Mòr Dearg Link Aonach Mòr

'Two steep scrambles' ★

Summary: The steep descent down the loose Seang Aonach Mòr and then the climb up the sweeping East Ridge of Carn Mòr Dearg involves a considerable height loss and demands a great deal of leg work.

Route: Head S down the summit slopes to the top of the Seang Aonach Mòr (small cairn). Turn W and descend the vague path down the steep and in parts loose slope to the col. Head W across the col and climb the long steep East Ridge directly to the summit of Carn Mòr Dearg.

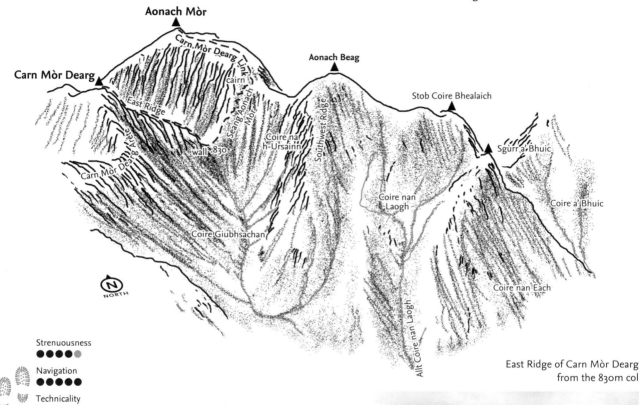

East Ridge of Carn Mòr Dearg from the 830m col

Strenuousness
●●●●○

Navigation
●●●●●

Technicality
●●●●●

Scramble/Winter climb
●●●○○/●○○

▶ Aonach Mòr,
GR NN193729

1.5 hours
2.5km
(1.6 miles)

382m
(1253ft)

Steep loose slope and
steep rocky ridge

An Cùl Choire Path AONACH MÒR

'Long and atmospheric' ★ ★ ★

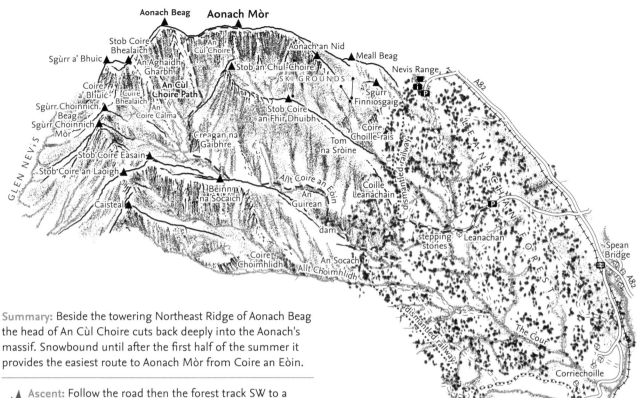

Summary: Beside the towering Northeast Ridge of Aonach Beag the head of An Cùl Choire cuts back deeply into the Aonach's massif. Snowbound until after the first half of the summer it provides the easiest route to Aonach Mòr from Coire an Eòin.

Ascent: Follow the road then the forest track SW to a fork. Take the left branch SE over the stepping stones to the building ruins. From the ruins follow the footpath S as it climbs to the course of the old railway line. Turn E and follow its course to the Allt Coire an Eòin Bridge. Cross it and turn R onto the access track which is followed SW to the water intake. Follow the Allt Coire an Eòin SW, S then SW through the pathless wilds of Coire an Eòin to the mouth of An Cùl Choire. Enter the corrie then climb the southwest bay to the col between Aonach Mòr and Aonach Beag. Turn R and climb N across the summit plateau to Aonach Mòr.

Descent: Head S across the summit plateau to the col between Aonach Mòr and Aonach Beag. Descend the steep bay NE into An Cùl Choire. Cross the corrie floor then follow the Allt Coire an Eòin NE, N then NE through Coire an Eòin to the water intake. Take the access track NE down to the old railway line then follow its course W to the top of the Leanachan path. Turn L onto it and follow it past the ruins and over the stepping stones to the public road.

1221m (4006ft)	Strenuousness ●●●●○ 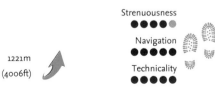
	Navigation ●●●●●
	Technicality ●●●●●
Forest, rough pathless glen, remote craggy corrie, headwall and broad summit ridge	Car Park near Leanachan GR NN211792
Can also be started via the course of the old narrow-gauge railway from either the Nevis Range Car Park, GR NN171773, or Corriechoille in the Spean Valley, GR NN252807	5 hours 12.2km (7.6 miles)

Carn Mòr Dearg

1220m (4003ft)

Carn Mòr Dearg's simple elegant lines tend to be overshadowed by the close proximity of Ben Nevis. The two peaks may share the same cirque at the head of the Allt a' Mhuilinn, around which they are linked by the magnificent knife-edge of the Carn Mòr Dearg Arête, but they are completely different. Carn Mòr Dearg is formed from a uniform granite, from which it gets its red hue, while Ben Nevis is the product of a complex series of geological events, including volcanic activity, cauldron subsidence and glacial erosion. As a result, they each have totally different shapes.

Carn Mòr Dearg forms a long high ridge running northwest between the Allt a' Mhuilinn and the Allt Daim. The Allt a' Mhuilinn side is a long, unbroken slope with few features except for drainage gullies and a liberal covering of scree. The Allt Daim side is much more interesting: cut into by steep-sided corries it has three fine ridges each of which makes an excellent route. The East Ridge is the most popular of the three as it affords direct access to Glen Giubhsachan and is a through route to Aonach Mòr and Aonach Beag. For quality though, Pinnacle Ridge is best, giving easy but exciting scrambling.

When you arrive

Ordnance Survey: Explorer 392 (1:25 000) No 32; Landranger (1:50 000) No 41.

Harvey Mountain Maps: Ben Nevis (1:25 000)

British Mountain Maps: Ben Nevis and Glen Coe (1:40 000)

Tourist Information Centres: Fort William

Youth Hostels: Glen Nevis

Hotels and B&B: Fort William; Glen Nevis.

Camp sites: Glen Nevis; Camaghael.

Bothies and Howffs: There is shelter on the summit of Ben Nevis (GR NN167712) but this is strictly for emergencies and should not be used for planned overnight stays. The CIC Hut (GR NN167722) alongside the Allt a' Mhuilinn and the Steall Hut (GR NN177683) in Glen Nevis are locked private huts and need to be booked through either the Scottish Mountaineering Club or the British Mountaineering Council.

Warning
Crossing the rivers and major
burns in spate on the approaches to
Carn Mòr Dearg can be hazardous

Carn Mòr Dearg's summit cairn

Fort William

Torlundy

A82

A82

A82

▲ Meall an t-Suidhe

Lochan
all an t-Suidhe

▲ Carn Dearg (NW)

Nevis
Range

Northwest Flank

Carn Beag Dearg ▲

North Flank

Meall Beag ▲

Gondola

Carn Dearg Meadhonach ▲

CIC Hut

Northeast Ridge

Allt Daim

Carn Mòr Dearg ▲

Pinnacle Ridge

SKI GROUNDS

Aonach
an Nid

Carn Mòr Dearg Arête

East Ridge

Aonach Mòr ▲

wall 830

Seang
Aonach Mòr

Coire Giubhsachan Path

Coire
Giubhsachan

Coire
na h-Ursainn

oire Giubhsachan

Aonach Beag ▲

anga

Carn Mòr Dearg from the Carn Mòr Dearg Arête

Warning
The east face of Carn Mòr Dearg
carries a cornice well into summer

Carn Mòr Dearg Arête CARN MÒR DEARG

'One of Britain's best ridges' ★★★

Summary: Sickle-shaped ridge around the head of Coire Leis linking Carn Mòr Dearg with Ben Nevis. A truly classic route; the crossing of the Carn Mòr Dearg is a justifiably popular undertaking that combines exciting walking with a magnificent setting. It is usual to complete it as a round but it is equally worthwhile as a direct approach to Carn Mòr Dearg.

Ascent: From the car park traverse NE up to the Bealach Cumhann. From the Bealach climb the ridge NW then NNE past the top of Sloc nan Uan to the shoulder where the Carn Mòr Dearg Arête abuts Ben Nevis (2m [6.5ft] navigation cairn). This is the start of the Carn Mòr Dearg Arête. Follow its crest NE then climb N directly to the summit of Carn Mòr Dearg.

Descent: Descend steeply S onto the Carn Mòr Dearg Arête and follow its crest around to the SW and to the shoulder where it abuts Ben Nevis (2m [6.5ft] navigation cairn). From the shoulder descend steeply SSW to the head of Sloc nan Uan then SE down the steep ridge to Bealach Cumhann. In poor visibility and under snow cover this descent cannot be recommended.

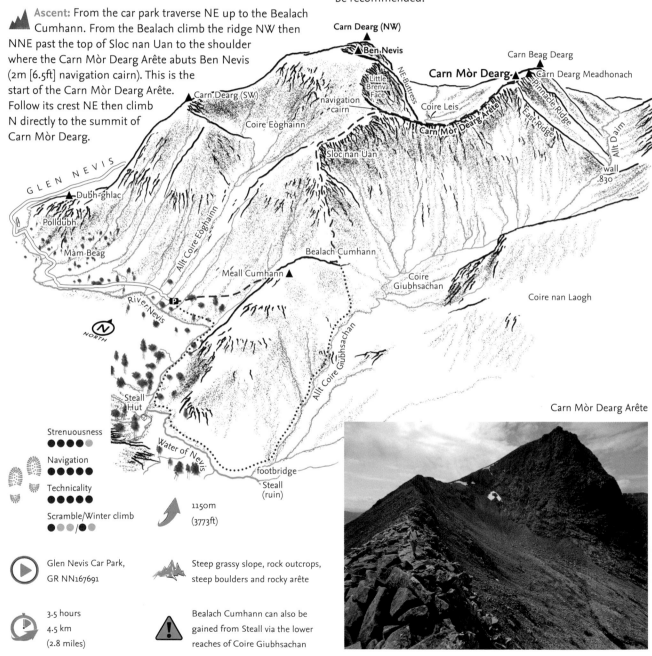

Carn Mòr Dearg Arête

Strenuousness
●●●●○

Navigation
●●●●●

Technicality
●●●●●

Scramble/Winter climb
●●○○○ / ○○

1150m
(3773ft)

Glen Nevis Car Park, GR NN167691

3.5 hours
4.5 km
(2.8 miles)

Steep grassy slope, rock outcrops, steep boulders and rocky arête

Bealach Cumhann can also be gained from Steall via the lower reaches of Coire Giubhsachan

Northwest Flank CARN MÒR DEARG

'The simplest approach' ★

Summary: A featureless rounded slope, which provides a simple and direct route. Useful as a descent to the Allt a' Mhuilinn.

Ascent: From the North Face Car Park follow the Ben Nevis approach path up through the trees to the side of the Allt a' Mhuilinn. Head up the Allt a' Mhuilinn on the northeast side then turn SE and climb the steep rounded ridge SE to Carn Beag Dearg. Turn SSE and follow the fine ridge over Carn Dearg Meadhonach to Carn Mòr Dearg.

Descent: Head NNW down the ridge over Carn Dearg Meadhonach to Carn Beag Dearg. Turn NW and descend the steep rounded ridge NW to the Allt a' Mhuilinn. Follow the path on its northeast side to the intake and then N down through the trees to the North Face Car Park.

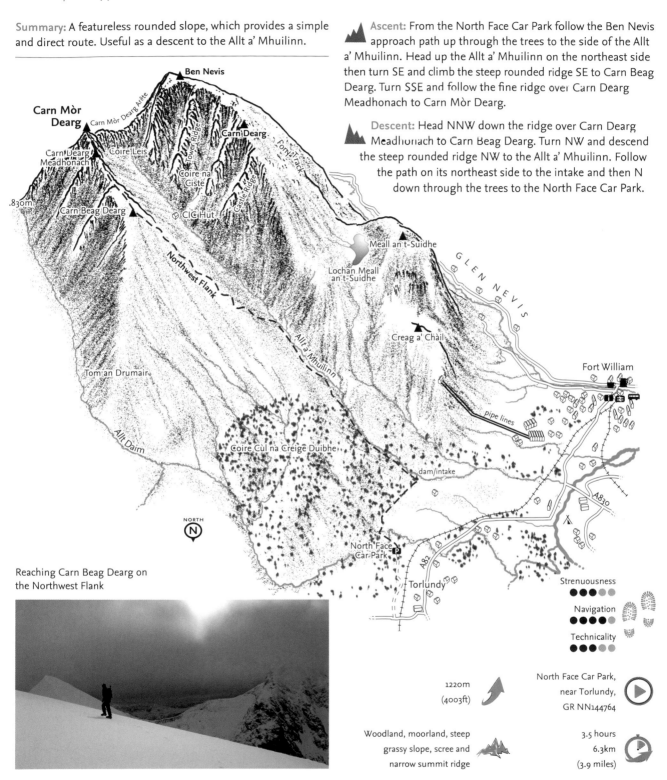

Reaching Carn Beag Dearg on the Northwest Flank

Strenuousness ●●●●○

Navigation ●●●●○

Technicality ●●●●○

1220m (4003ft)

Woodland, moorland, steep grassy slope, scree and narrow summit ridge

North Face Car Park, near Torlundy, GR NN144764

3.5 hours 6.3km (3.9 miles)

North Flank CARN MÒR DEARG

'Steep and direct'

Summary: A featureless rounded slope, which provides a simple and direct route. Useful as a descent to the Allt Daim.

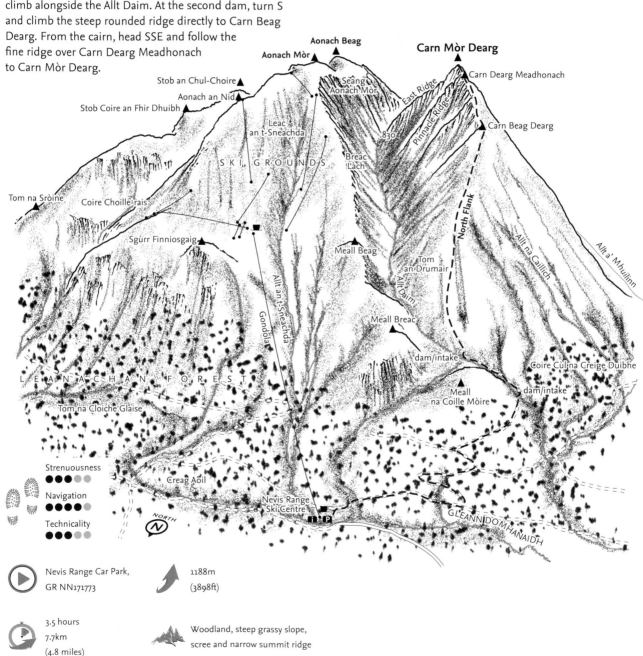 **Ascent:** From the car park, head SW then turn S and take the zigzags up to the course of the old narrow-gauge railway. Follow it SW to the water intake, then turn SE and climb alongside the Allt Daim. At the second dam, turn S and climb the steep rounded ridge directly to Carn Beag Dearg. From the cairn, head SSE and follow the fine ridge over Carn Dearg Meadhonach to Carn Mòr Dearg.

 Descent: Head NNW down the ridge over Carn Dearg Meadhonach to Carn Beag Dearg. From the cairn descend the steep rounded ridge N to the Allt Daim. Follow it on its southwest side to the water intake and join the old narrow-gauge railway. Follow its course NE then take the zigzags N. At the bottom turn R and head NE to the Gondola Car Park.

Strenuousness
●●●○○

Navigation
●●●●○

Technicality
●●●○○

Nevis Range Car Park,
GR NN171773

1188m
(3898ft)

3.5 hours
7.7km
(4.8 miles)

Woodland, steep grassy slope,
scree and narrow summit ridge

Northeast Ridge CARN MÒR DEARG

'Shapely arête' ★

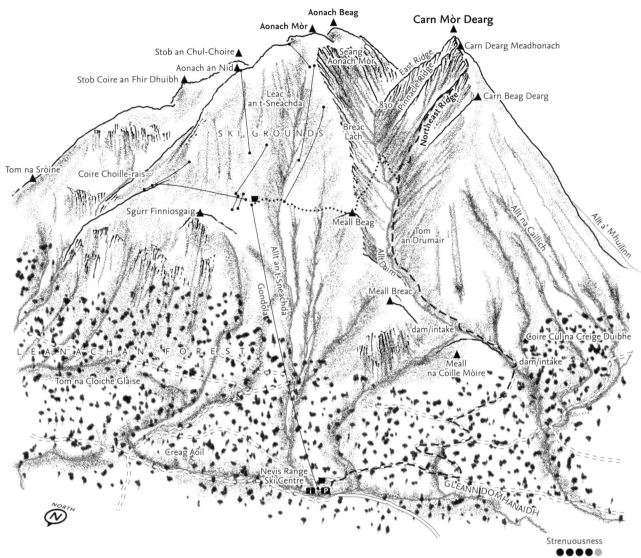

Summary: Displaying a steep and graceful line, the Northeast Ridge provides a pleasant scramble onto the main Carn Mòr Dearg Ridge.

Ascent: From the car park head SW, then turn S and take the zigzags up to the course of the old narrow-gauge railway. Follow it SW to the water intake, then turn SE and climb alongside the Allt Daim. Three significant ridges abut the northeast face of Carn Mòr Dearg; the Northeast Ridge is the first one up the glen. Turn SW and climb the scree to its base, then climb the crest of the ridge directly. At the top, turn L to head SSE along the ridge, over Carn Dearg Meadhonach to Carn Mòr Dearg.

Strenuousness
●●●●○

Navigation
●●●●○

Technicality
●●●●●

Scramble/Winter climb
●●●/●○

1195m
(3921ft)

Woodland, craggy glen, steep rocky ridge and narrow summit ridge

Nevis Range Car Park, GR NN171773

The Allt Daim Path can be gained from the gondola top station via a steep descent from Meall Beag

3.5 hours
8.3km
(5.2 miles)

Pinnacle Ridge CARN MÒR DEARG

'Exposed and dramatic' ★ ★ ★

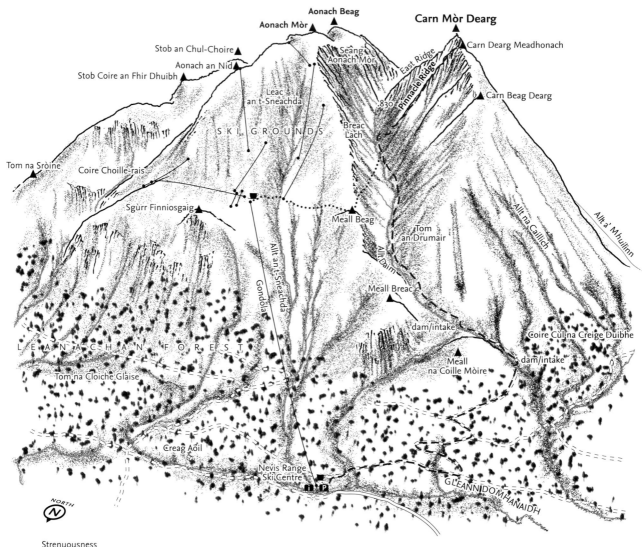

Summary: From the Allt Daim the most striking feature on the northeast face of Carn Mòr Dearg is the Pinnacle Ridge. It climbs steeply up the side of the glen to the minor peak Carn Dearg Meadhonach. From below it looks quite daunting but once established on its crest it proves to be an uncomplicated scramble. The most exciting line follows the crest throughout.

Strenuousness
● ● ● ● ●

  Navigation
● ● ● ● ●

 Technicality
● ● ● ● ●

 Scramble/Winter climb
● ● ● ● / ● ●

 1190m
(3904ft)

Nevis Range Car Park,
GR NN171773

 Woodland, craggy glen,
steep rocky ridge and
narrow summit ridge

4 hours
8.3km
(5.2 miles)

 The Allt Daim Path can be gained
from the gondola top station via
a steep descent from Meall Beag

Ascent: From the car park, head SW then turn S and take the zigzags up to the course of the old narrow-gauge railway. Follow it SW to the water intake then turn SE and climb alongside the Allt Daim. Pinnacle Ridge's distinct bump is clearly visible from the glen. Once below it turn SW and climb the scree to its base, then climb the crest of the ridge directly. At the top turn L and head SSE along the ridge to Carn Mòr Dearg.

Aonach's Link CARN MÒR DEARG

'Two steep scrambles' ★

Summary: The steep descent down the sweeping East Ridge, then the steep loose ascent up the Seang Aonach Mòr involves a considerable height loss and demands a fair amount of legwork.

Route: Descend steeply E down the narrow ridge to the col at the head of Coire Giubhsachan. Cross the col and climb E up the very steep and in parts loose Seang Aonach Mòr. At the top either head N for Aonach Mòr or head S then SE for Aonach Beag.

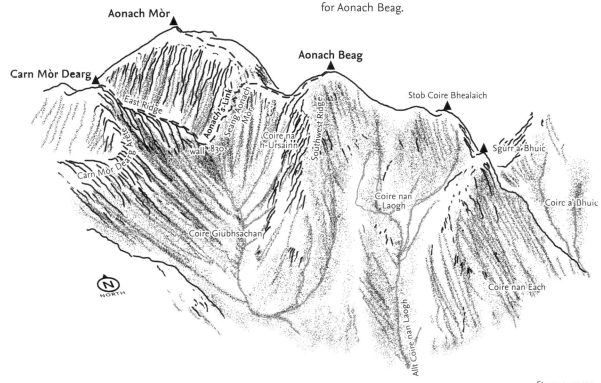

Ben Nevis and Carn Mòr Dearg with the East Ridge on the far right

Strenuousness
● ● ● ● ●

Navigation
● ● ● ● ●

Technicality
● ● ● ● ●

Carn Mòr Dearg,
GR NN177721

1.5 hours
2.6km
(1.6 miles)

395m
(1296ft)

Steep rocky ridge and
steep loose slope

East Ridge CARN MÒR DEARG

'Remote with a challenging finish' ★ ★ ★

Summary: Coire Giubhsachan and the headwaters of the Allt Daim are separated by a high col. Sweeping down to it from Carn Mòr Dearg is the beautiful curve of the East Ridge. A perfect adjunct to the Carn Mòr Dearg Arête, it makes Carn Mòr Dearg appear a true alpine-like giant when viewed from the south.

Descent: Descend steeply E down the narrow ridge to the col at the head of Coire Giubhsachan. Turn S and follow the Allt Coire Giubhsachan down to the footbridge at the Steall (ruin). At the footbridge join the Glen Nevis footpath and follow it W through the gorge to the car park.

Ascent: From the car park follow the path as it meanders E through the gorge to the footbridge by the Steall (ruin). Turn N and follow the path up the west side of the Allt Coire Giubhsachan. Continue N up through Coire Giubhsachan to the col at its head. At the col turn W and climb the long, steep East Ridge directly to the summit of Carn Mòr Dearg.

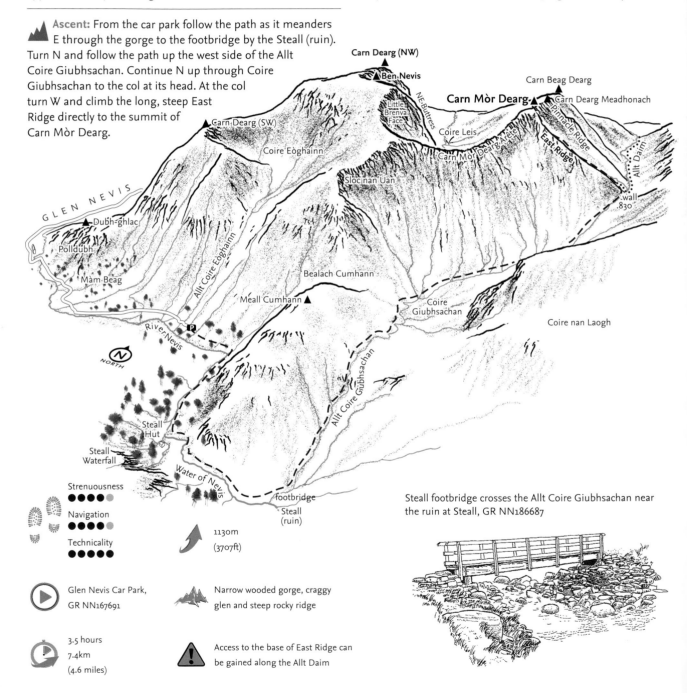

Steall footbridge crosses the Allt Coire Giubhsachan near the ruin at Steall, GR NN186687

Strenuousness ● ● ● ● ○	
Navigation ● ● ● ● ○	
Technicality ● ● ● ● ●	

1130m (3707ft)

▶ Glen Nevis Car Park, GR NN167691

🕐 3.5 hours
7.4km (4.6 miles)

Narrow wooded gorge, craggy glen and steep rocky ridge

⚠ Access to the base of East Ridge can be gained along the Allt Daim

Ben Nevis Link CARN MÒR DEARG

'Classic ridge scramble' ★ ★ ★

Summary: Follows the Carn Mòr Dearg Arête, then climbs the southeast shoulder of Ben Nevis.

Route: Descend steeply S onto the Carn Mòr Dearg Arête and follow its crest around to the SW to the shoulder where the

Carn Mòr Dearg Arête abuts Ben Nevis (2m [6.5ft] navigation cairn). From the cairn climb the steep path which swings NW onto the summit plateau.

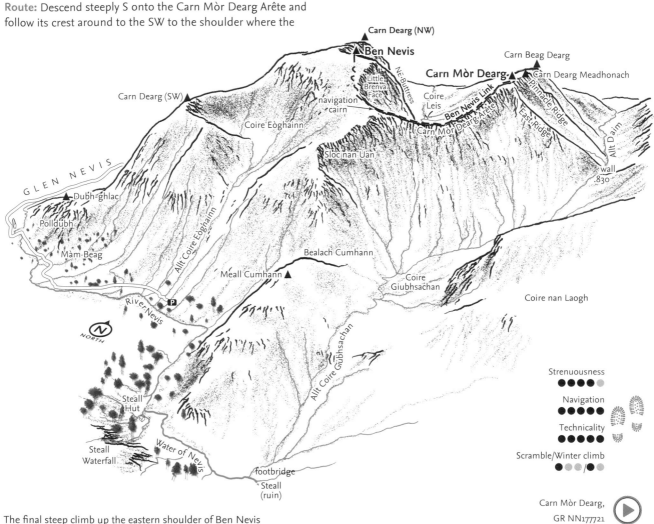

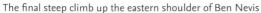

The final steep climb up the eastern shoulder of Ben Nevis

Strenuousness
● ● ● ● ○

Navigation
● ● ● ● ●

Technicality
● ● ● ● ●

Scramble/Winter climb
● ● ○ ● ○ / ● ● ○

Carn Mòr Dearg,
GR NN177721   ▶

1.5 hours
2km
(1.2 miles)

300m
(984ft)

Rocky arête and steep
boulder-strewn ridge

Wales's 3000ft Mountains

Wales has fifteen summits over 3000ft (914m), eight of which can clearly be defined as separate mountains. They lie between the Conwy Valley and the coast within the Snowdonia National Park, and are conveniently situated in three distinct but compact groups.

Each of the three groups is clearly defined geographically, being separated from its adjacent group by a major valley. To the south of the Llanberis Pass, Snowdon's sprawling bulk provides routes with a fitting mountaineering flavour. In the middle, between the Llanberis Pass and the Ogwen Valley, the four peaks of the Glyders massif – Glyder Fawr, Y Garn, Elidir Fawr and Tryfan – offer steep but short routes with a predominance of fine scrambles. The northern group containing Carnedd Llewelyn, Carnedd Dafydd and Foel-fras forms a high extensive plateau with rounded undulating ridges and impressive hidden crags.

Snowdonia

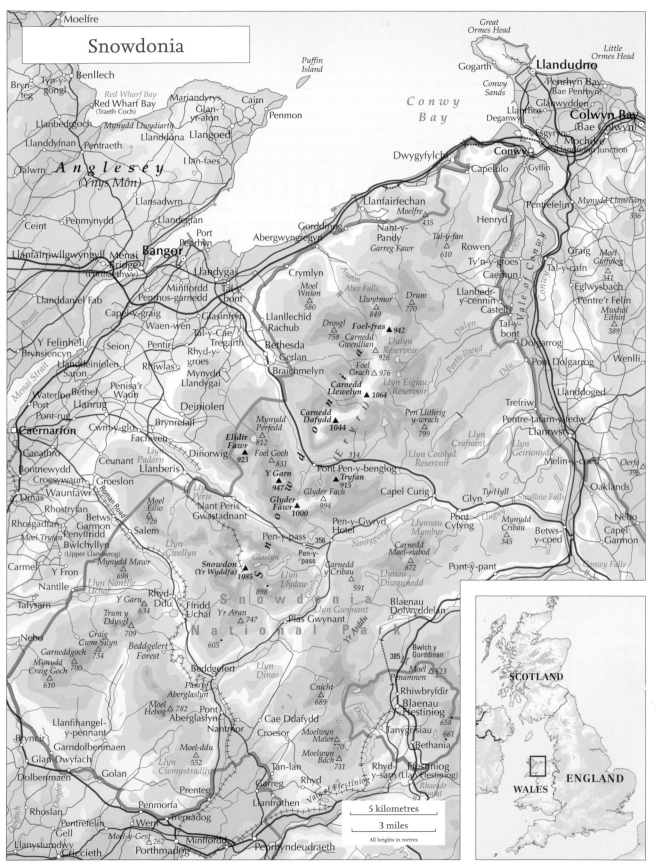

Moelfre

Benllech

Bryn-teg
Tyn-y-gongl

Llanbedrgoch
Mariandyrys
Glan-yr-afon
Caim
Penmon

Red Wharf Bay
(Traeth Coch)

Llanddona
Llangoed

Mynydd Llwydiarth

Puffin Island

Conwy Bay

Great Ormes Head

Little Ormes Head

Gogarth
Llandudno

Penrhyn Bay
(Bae Penrhyn)
Glanwydden

Conwy Sands

Llanrhos
Deganwy
Colwyn Bay
(Bae Colwyn)

Llanddyfnan
Pentraeth

Llansadwrn

Llanddona

Penmon

Anglesey
(Ynys Môn)

Esgyryog
Mochdre
Llandudno Junction

Talwrn

Penmynydd

Llandegfan

Port Penrhyn

Conwy

Dwygyfylchi
Capelulo
Gyffin

Ceint

Llanfairpwllgwyngyll
Menai Bridge
(Porthaethwy)

Bangor

Llanfairfechan

Pentrefelin
Mynydd Llanelian
336

Moelfre
435

Abergwyngregyn
Gorddinog

Nant-y-Pandy

Henryd
Rowen

Llanddaniel Fab

Penrhos-garnedd

Llandygai
Tal-y-bont

Crymlyn

Tal-y-fan
610

Garreg Fawr

Ty'n-y-groes
Caerhun

Craig
Moel Gyffylog
341

Capel-y-graig
Minffordd

Waen-wen

Glasinfryn

Moel Wnion
580

Aber Falls

Afon

Llwytmor
849

Drum
770

Llanbedr-y-cennin
Castell

Eglwysbach

Pentre'r Felin
Mwdwl Eithin
389

Y Felinheli
Brynsiencyn

Pentir

Tal-y-Cae
Tregarth
Rhyd-y-groes

Llanllechid
Rachub

Drosgl
758

Foel-fras
942

Carnedd Gwenllian
926

Dulyn Reservoir

Tal-y-bont

Dolgarrog

Wenlli

Llandudeiniolen
Saron

Rhiwlas

Bethesda
Gerlan
Braichmelyn

Foel Grach
976

Llyn Eigiau Reservoir

Pont Dolgarrog

Llanddoged

Waterloo Port
Bethel

Penisa'r Waun

Mynydd Llandygai

Foel Grach
976

Carnedd Llewelyn
1064

Pen Llithrig y-wrach
799

Trefriw

Caernarfon
Caeathro

Pont-rug

Llanrug

Deiniolen

Brynrefail

Mynydd Perfedd

Carnedd Dafydd
1044

Llyn Crafnant

Llyn Cowlyd Reservoir

Llyn Geirionydd

Pentre-tafarn-y-fedw

Llanrwst

Cwm-y-glo
Fachwen

Elidir Fawr
812

Foel Goch
831

314

Melin-y-coed

Oerfa
396

Bontnewydd
Croesywaun

Groeslon

Dinorwig

Y Garn
947

Pont Pen-y-benglog

Tryfan
915

Capel Curig

Ty Hyll

Oaklands

Dinas

Waunfawr

Nant Peris

Elidir Fawr
923

Glyder Fach
994

Swallow Falls

Rhostryfan
Rhosgadfan
Betws Garmon
Penyffridd

Llyn Padarn

Llanberis

Glyder Fawr
1000

Pen-y-Gwryd Hotel

Glyn

Pont Cyfyng

Mynydd Cribau
345

Nebo

Capel Garmon

Moel Tryfan
Bwlchyllyn
(Upper Llandwrog)

Moel Eilio
726

Nant Peris
Gwastadnant

Pen-y-pass
356

Nant-y-gwryd

Carnedd Moel-siabod
872

Betws-y-coed

Carmel
Y Fron

Mynydd Mawr
698

Llyn Cwellyn

Pen-y-pass

Snowdon
(Yr Wyddfa)
1085

Glaslyn

Llyn Llydaw

Carnedd y Cribau
591

Llynnau Diwaunedd

Pont-y-pant

Nantlle

Llyn Nantlle Uchaf

Y Garn
634

Rhyd-Ddu

Glaslyn
898

Carnedd y Cribau

Conwy Falls

Talysarn

Trum y Ddysgl
709

Ffridd Uchaf

Yr Aran
747

Plas Gwynant

Snowdonia National Park

Llyn Gwynant

Blaenau Dolwyddelan

Nebo

Craig Cwm Silyn
734

Beddgelert Forest

605

Yr Aran

Yr Arddu

385

Bwlch y Gorddinan

Garneddgoch
734

Mynydd Craig Goch
700
610

Beddgelert

Llyn Dinas

Moel Penamnen

Moel
623

Rhiwbryfdir

Llanfihangel-y-pennant

Pass of Aberglaslyn

Moel Hebog
782

Pont Aberglaslyn

Cnicht
689

Afon Dwyryd

Blaenau Ffestiniog

Bryncir

Garndolbenmaen

Nantmor

Cae Ddafydd
Croesor

Moelwyn Mawr
770

Tanygrisiau
658

661

Bethania

Glan Dwyfach

Golan

Moel-ddu
552

Tan-lan

Moelwyn Bach
711

Rhyd-y-sarn (Llan Ffestiniog)

Ffestiniog

Dolbenmaen

Llyn Cwmystradllyn

Carreg
Rhyd

Llanfrothen

Rhaeadr Cynfal

Rhoslan
Prenteg

Penmorfa

Vale of Ffestiniog

Pentrefelin
Gell

Wern
Tremadog

Moel-y-Gest
262

Minffordd

Penrhyndeudraeth

Llanystumdwy
Criccieth

Porthmadog

5 kilometres

3 miles

All heights in metres

SCOTLAND

WALES

ENGLAND

Snowdon (Yr Wyddfa)
1085m (3560ft)

Crib y Ddysgl 1065m (3494ft)
Crib Goch 923m (3028ft)

On viewing Snowdon there can be no doubt of its status as the highest peak in Wales. Majestic and refined, the impressive proportions of its pyramidal lines are instantly recognisable. Often described as having five ridges and five cwms in a star-like symmetry, this description is apt but only tells half the story. Its ridges have numerous spurs and crags while its corries are twisted and multi-levelled, reflecting past glacial activity. By anybody's standards Snowdon is a very complex mountain.

When you arrive

Ordnance Survey: Explorer OL17 (1:25 000); Landranger 115 (1:50 000).

Harvey Mountain Maps: Snowdonia Snowdon (1:25 000)

British Mountain Maps: Snowdonia (1:40 000)

Tourist Information Centres: Caernarfon; Llanberis; Betws-y-Coed; Bangor.

Youth Hostels: Nant y Betws: *Snowdon Ranger*; Llanberis; Llanberis Pass: *Pen-y-pass*; Capel Curig; Nantgwynant: *Bryn Gwynant*.

Hotels and B&B: Beddgelert; Rhyd-Ddu; Betws Garmon; Llanberis; Nant Peris; Capel Curig; Nantgwynant.

Camp sites: Beddgelert; Rhyd-Ddu; Betws Garmon; Llanberis Pass: *Nant Peris, Gwastadnant*; Capel Curig; Nantgwynant.

Snowdon's influence is massive; it covers an area greater than the Glyders and comparable to the whole of the Carneddau. The northeast side is a continual line of crags forming a steep wall above Llanberis Pass. To the south the slopes are less dour but only marginally less steep. They extend to Beddgelert and are bounded to the southwest by Nant Colwyn and to the southeast by the lovely wooded Nantgwynant.

The roll call of names of Snowdon's crags and ridges is intertwined with the history of Welsh mountaineering. From the early days of rock climbing on Y Lliwedd's alpine-like north face to the modern-day test pieces on Clogwyn Du'r Arddu's blank walls, and from the highway-like Llanberis Path to the teetering exposure of the scramble over Crib Goch's fine pinnacles, Snowdon provides adventure for all who venture onto it.

Sadly for such a fine mountain, Snowdon has not remained inviolate to less altruistic human activities. In the depths of Cwm Glaslyn are the remains of copper mines and a series of constructed paths; blighting Cwm Dyli are the bold lines of hydro-electric water pipes, and climbing the Northwest Ridge is the Snowdon Mountain Railway. All of these projects have, or have had, their supporters to present a strong case for their existence – but most people must surely feel that Snowdon would be better without them.

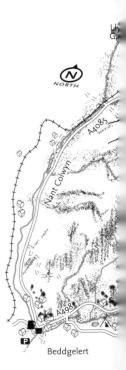

Beddgelert

North Ridge of Crib Goch and Snowdon

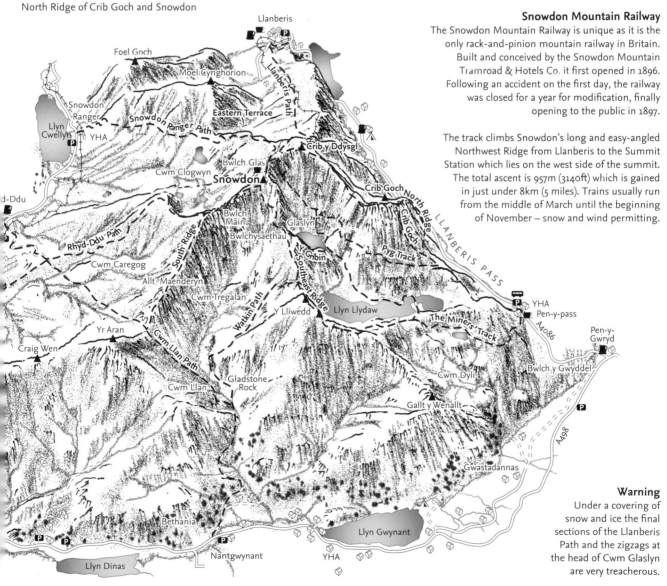

Snowdon Mountain Railway

The Snowdon Mountain Railway is unique as it is the only rack-and-pinion mountain railway in Britain. Built and conceived by the Snowdon Mountain Tramroad & Hotels Co. it first opened in 1896. Following an accident on the first day, the railway was closed for a year for modification, finally opening to the public in 1897.

The track climbs Snowdon's long and easy-angled Northwest Ridge from Llanberis to the Summit Station which lies on the west side of the summit. The total ascent is 957m (3140ft) which is gained in just under 8km (5 miles). Trains usually run from the middle of March until the beginning of November – snow and wind permitting.

Warning

Under a covering of snow and ice the final sections of the Llanberis Path and the zigzags at the head of Cwm Glaslyn are very treacherous.

South Ridge SNOWDON

'Entertaining crest' ★

Summary: An enjoyable and straightforward approach along a fine airy ridge. Strangely, the South Ridge does not see as much traffic as the other routes on the south side of Snowdon despite the fact that it is more entertaining.

Ascent: From Rhyd-Ddu take the bridleway E to the junction at Pen ar Lôn. Continue E straight across the junction and climb to Bwlch Cwm Llan. Turn N at the col and climb straight up the crest of the South Ridge. At Bwlch Main the path meets the Rhyd-Ddu bridleway. Join it and follow it NE along the narrow ridge over the exposed Bwlch Main and up to Snowdon's summit.

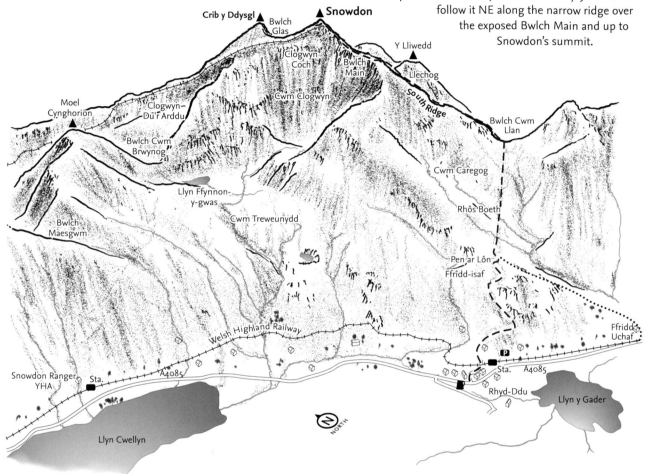

Descent: From the south end of the Summit Station drop SE down the scree then follow the narrow ridge to Bwlch Main. Cross the exposed col SE to a split in the bridleway. Take the left branch (path) and follow it S down the crest of the South Ridge to Bwlch Cwm Llan. At the col turn R and make the steady descent W to Rhyd-Dhu.

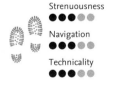

Strenuousness
●●●●○

Navigation
●●●●○

Technicality
●●●●○

925m
(3035ft)

Rhyd-Ddu,
GR SH569527

Moorland, exposed col
and long narrow ridge

3 hours
6.5km
(4 miles)

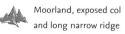
Can also be started from Nantgwynant,
GR SH626506, via Cwm Llan and from
the A4085 near Ffridd Uchaf, GR SH576514

Rhyd-Ddu Path SNOWDON

'Classic finishing crest' ★ ★

Summary: Climbs an easy course across the mouth of the featureless Cwm Caregog then circles the impressive cliffs of Cwm Clogwyn.

Ascent: From Rhyd-Ddu take the bridleway E to the junction at Pen ar Lôn. Take the left turn and follow the Rhyd-Ddu Path (bridleway) NE up the rounded slopes of Llechog. On Llechog the bridleway swings SE then NE around the head of Cwm Clogwyn to Bwlch Main. Continue NE over Bwlch Main and climb the crest of the ridge to Snowdon's summit.

Descent: From the south end of the Summit Station drop SE down the scree then follow the narrow ridge to Bwlch Main. Cross the exposed col SE to a split in the bridleway. Take the right branch, the Rhyd-Ddu Path, and follow it SW then NW around the head of Cwm Clogwyn. Once past Llechog the bridleway swings SW and descends to the junction at Pen ar Lôn. At the junction turn R and follow the bridleway down to Rhyd-Ddu.

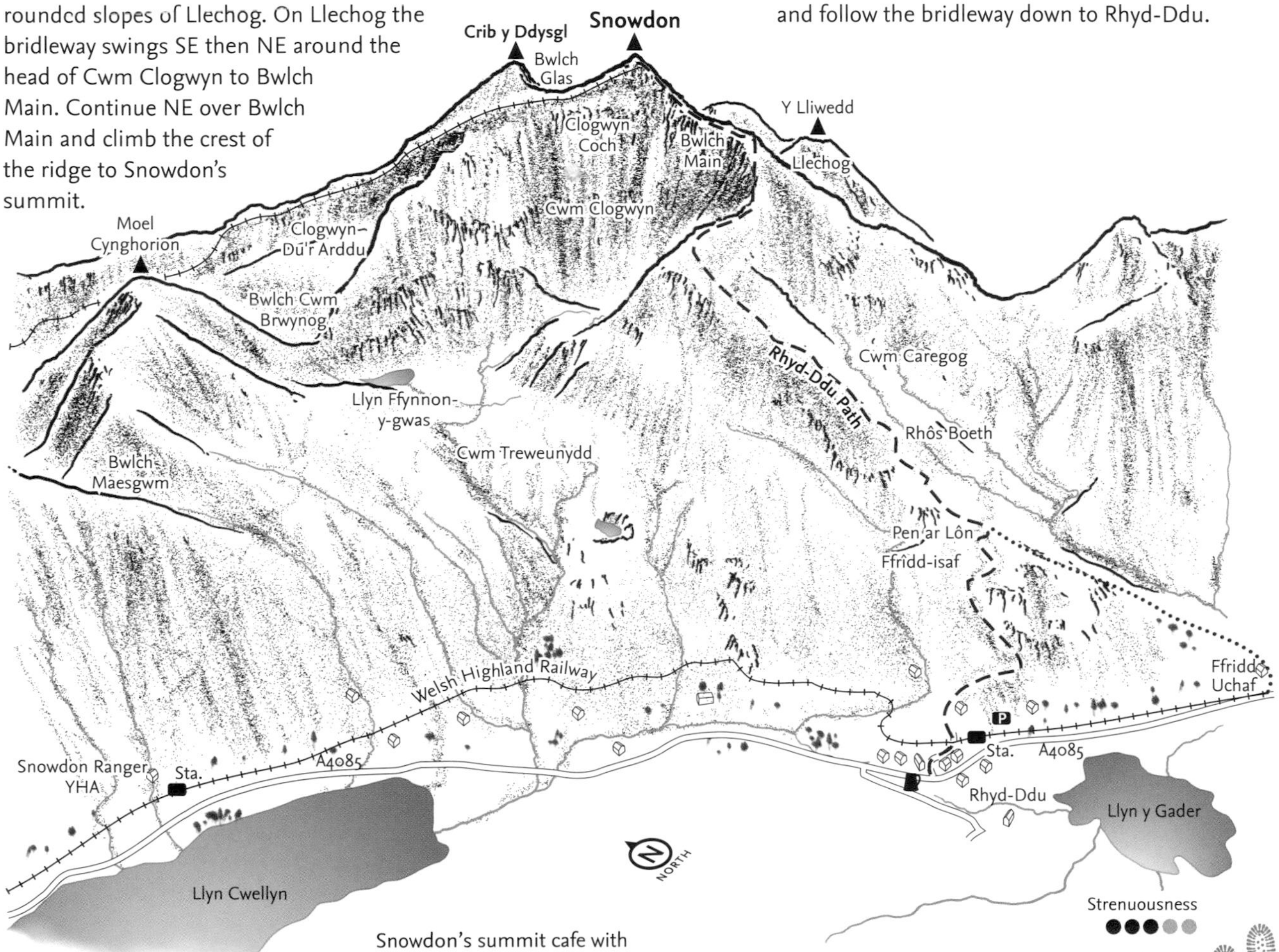

Snowdon's summit cafe with Lechog in the distance

935m
(3067ft)

Moorland, steep rocky slopes and long narrow ridge

Can also be started from the A4085 near Ffridd Uchaf, GR SH576514

Strenuousness
● ● ● ○ ○

Navigation
● ● ● ○ ○

Technicality
● ● ● ○ ○

Rhyd-Ddu, GR SH569527

3 hours
6km
(3.7 miles)

Snowdon Ranger Path SNOWDON

'The perfect walking route' ★ ★ ★

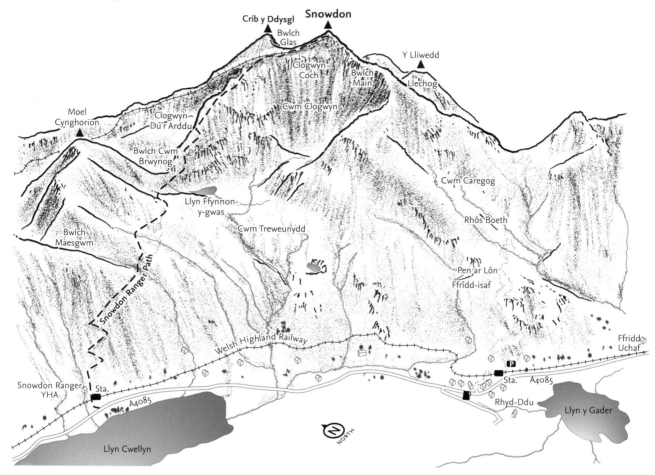

Summary: The Snowdon Ranger path derives its name from the old inn at its start (now a youth hostel) which was run by the mountain guide, John Morton. He used to take clients up Snowdon along the course of the present-day bridleway, which is generally regarded as the oldest route to the summit.

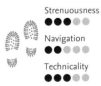
Strenuousness
● ● ● ○ ○

Navigation
● ● ○ ○ ○

Technicality
● ● ● ○ ○

940m
(3084ft)

Alongside the Snowdon Ranger Youth Hostel, GR SH564551

Steep pasture, huge open corrie, exposed col, narrow ridge and broad summit ridge

3 hours
6.2km
(3.9 miles)

The lower section of the Snowdon Ranger Path can be accessed from Llanberis via the long Maesgwm bridleway

Originally used as a pony route, its course zigzags steadily up the featureless west side of Snowdon.

Ascent: From the A4085 take the bridleway on the northwest side of the youth hostel and follow it as it zigzags NE up the steep pasture. At the top of the zigzags the bridleway turns E; continue along it as it traverses the slopes of Cwm Treweunydd to Bwlch Cwm Brwynog. From the col the bridleway steepens and continues ESE up the side of Snowdon's west-northwest ridge. At the top of the ridge the gradient eases and the bridleway turns SE to join the Llanberis Path (bridleway) alongside the mountain railway. At the junction turn S and follow the course of the railway to the summit.

Descent: Follow the course of the railway line N to the fork in the bridleway at Bwlch Glas. Take the L fork and follow it WNW to Bwlch Cwm Brwynog. From the south side of the col the bridleway swings W; continue along it across the slopes of Cwm Treweunydd to the top of the zigzags. Descend the zigzags SW to the A4085 at the side of the youth hostel.

Eastern Terrace (Clogwyn Du'r Arddu)

SNOWDON

'A sheep among wolves' ★★

Summary: One of the most impressive pieces of rock in Wales, the steep cliffs of Clogwyn Du'r Arddu have been a major forcing ground for rock-climbing standards. The Eastern Terrace follows a diagonal weakness between East and West Buttresses and is used as a descent route by climbers. As a scrambling route its course offers an exciting way of taking a close look at these awe-inspiring cliffs.

Ascent: Take the minor road SW out of Llanberis up to Cader Ellyll. Join the Llanberis Path (bridleway) and follow it SE to the Halfway House. Leave the bridleway and contour the slopes S to Llyn Du'r Arddu. Walk around the lake, and once on the south side climb up to the base of the East Buttress. To the left of the base of the crags gain the ramp which is

followed R onto the Eastern Terrace proper. Ascend the ramp turning the difficult section by the zigzags to the upper scree slope (avoiding dislodging stones) which is climbed to the top of the cliffs. Head S across the grass to join the Snowdon Ranger Path (bridleway). Turn L onto it and follow it ESE up the side of Snowdon's west-northwest ridge. At the top of the ridge the gradient eases and the bridleway turns SE to join the Llanberis Path (bridleway) alongside the mountain railway. At the junction turn S and follow the course of the railway to the summit.

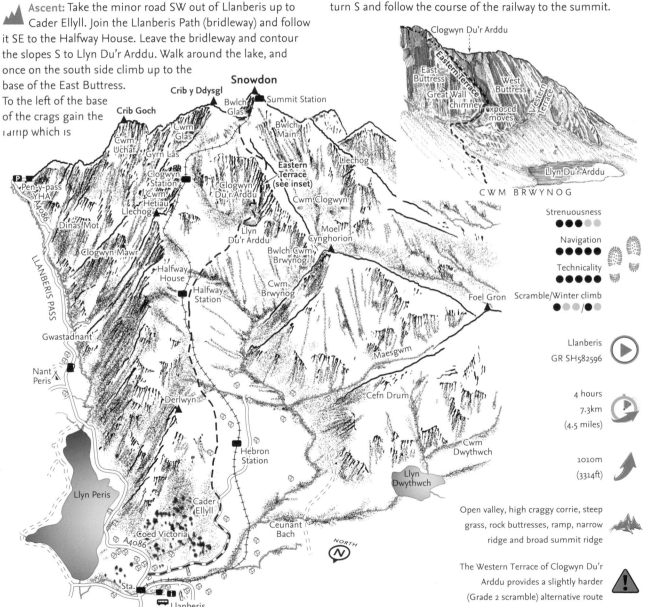

Strenuousness
●●●○○

Navigation
●●●●●

Technicality
●●●●●

Scramble/Winter climb
●●●○○/●●○○

Llanberis
GR SH582596

4 hours
7.3km
(4.5 miles)

1010m
(3314ft)

Open valley, high craggy corrie, steep grass, rock buttresses, ramp, narrow ridge and broad summit ridge

The Western Terrace of Clogwyn Du'r Arddu provides a slightly harder (Grade 2 scramble) alternative route

Llanberis Path SNOWDON

'Great out of season'

Summary: Gains height steadily along the west side of Snowdon's long Northwest Ridge roughly following the course of the Snowdon Mountain Railway. In summer the distracting presence of trains and the throngs of tourists greatly detract from the quality of the otherwise pleasant route – best left until the winter months when a little of its former tranquillity returns.

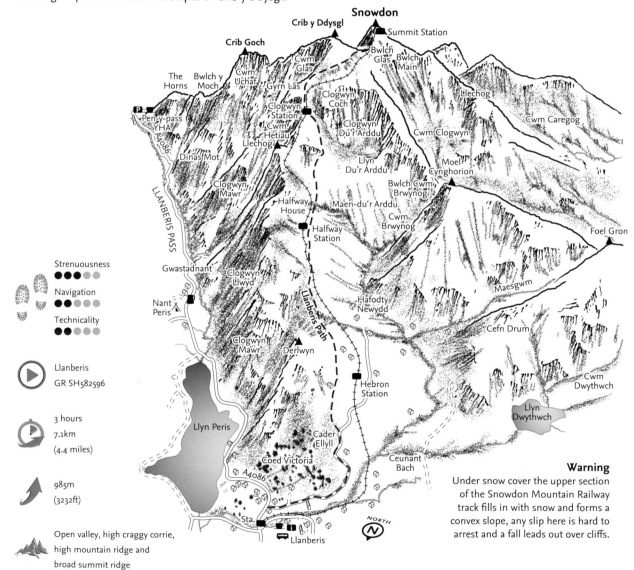

Ascent: Take the minor road SW out of Llanberis up to Cader Ellyll. Join the Llanberis Path (bridleway) and follow it SE past the Halfway House and on towards Clogwyn Station. After the bridleway has passed beneath the railway line it starts to swing S up onto the summit slopes of Crib y Ddysgl.

Continue generally S across the slopes of Crib y Ddysgl to Bwlch Glas, then make the final ascent SSE to the summit of Snowdon.

Descent: From the Summit Station take the bridleway NNW to Bwlch Glas. From Bwlch Glas the bridleway descends N then NNE and finally NNW across the summit slopes of Crib y Ddysgl to the bridge beneath the railway line. Once past the bridge the bridleway swings NW and is followed down the side of the Northwest Ridge to the minor road at Cader Ellyll. Turn R and follow the road down into Llanberis.

Strenuousness
●●●●○

Navigation
●●○○○

Technicality
●●○○○

Llanberis
GR SH582596

3 hours
7.1km
(4.4 miles)

985m
(3232ft)

Open valley, high craggy corrie, high mountain ridge and broad summit ridge

Warning
Under snow cover the upper section of the Snowdon Mountain Railway track fills in with snow and forms a convex slope, any slip here is hard to arrest and a fall leads out over cliffs.

RIGHT
Snowdon from Plas y Brenin

Crib Goch SNOWDON

'Exposed and popular' ★ ★ ★

Summary: A fine undulating arête high above magnificent mountain scenery, the passage through which involves exciting scrambling. Arguably the best mountain route in Wales.

Ascent: From Pen-y-pass take the Pyg Track WSW to Bwlch y Moch. Cross Bwlch y Moch and climb the well-worn East Ridge to the exposed summit of Crib Goch. From the summit of Crib Goch follow the crest of the ridge WSW then weave a route through the pinnacles to make the descent to Bwlch Coch. Cross the col and climb directly W up the steepening ridge to the summit of Crib y Ddysgl. From the summit trig point make the slight descent SW to join the Llanberis Path (bridleway) which is then taken S and SSE to the summit of Snowdon.

Descent: From the Summit Station take the bridleway NNW to Bwlch Glas. Head N across Bwlch Glas then immediately swing R and take the path NE to the summit of Crib y Ddysgl. From the trig point descend E and make the steep scramble down the crest of the ridge to Bwlch Coch. From the col follow the path E that weaves its way through the pinnacles and heads ENE onto the summit of Crib Goch. From the summit scramble E down the very steep ridge to the easier ground of Bwlch y Moch. From Bwlch y Moch join the Pyg Track and take it ENE to Pen-y-pass.

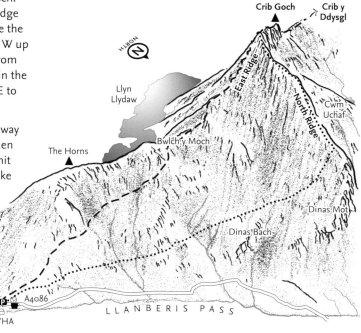

Strenuousness
●●●○○

Navigation
●●●●●

Technicality
●●●●●

Scramble/Winter climb
●○○○/●○

Pen-y-pass,
GR SH647555

3.5 hours
5.2km
(3.3 miles)

915m
(3002ft)

Rocky slopes, craggy mountainside, rocky arête, pinnacles, exposed col, high mountain ridge and broad summit ridge

⚠ Crib Goch can also be gained by the North Ridge (Grade 1 scramble; Grade 1 winter climb) which offers a quieter alternative to the usual East Ridge approach. To gain the North Ridge start from Pen-y-pass (GR SH647555) and follow the Pyg Track W before leaving it to contour NE around Cwm Beudy Mawr to the shoulder above Dinas Mot. From the shoulder climb the crest of the ridge S to Crib Goch.

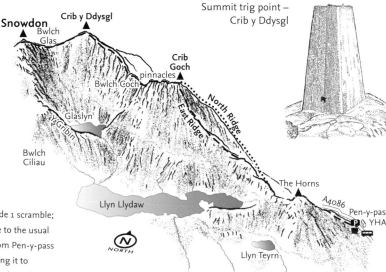

Summit trig point –
Crib y Ddysgl

Pyg Track SNOWDON

'Very popular' ★

Summary: Skirts the southern slopes of Crib Goch high above the beautiful waters of Llyn Llydaw and Glaslyn. The over-zealous techniques used to reconstruct the zigzag path below Bwlch Glas tend to detract from the wild setting through which the Pyg Track passes.

Ascent: From Pen-y-pass take the Pyg Track WSW to Bwlch y Moch. Cross Bwlch y Moch and continue WSW then W as the path skirts across the southern slopes of Crib Goch to a junction with the Miners' Track high above Glaslyn. From the junction climb the steep zigzags W up the headwall to Bwlch Glas. At Bwlch Glas the path joins the Llanberis Path (bridleway) which is taken S then SSE to Snowdon's summit.

Descent: From the Summit Station take the bridleway NNW to Bwlch Glas. At the stone marker turn E and descend the zigzags towards Glaslyn. Midway down the corrie headwall, the path splits. Take the left fork (the right-hand fork is the Miners' Track) and follow it E then ENE across the southern slopes of Crib Goch to Bwlch y Moch. Continue generally ENE across Bwlch y Moch and then make the final descent to Pen-y-pass.

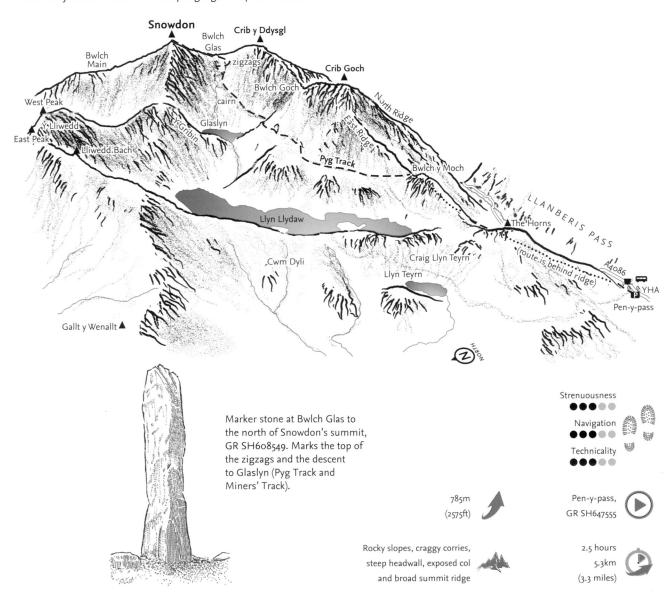

Marker stone at Bwlch Glas to the north of Snowdon's summit, GR SH608549. Marks the top of the zigzags and the descent to Glaslyn (Pyg Track and Miners' Track).

Strenuousness
●●●○○

Navigation
●●●○○

Technicality
●●●○○

785m
(2575ft)

Pen-y-pass,
GR SH647555

Rocky slopes, craggy corries, steep headwall, exposed col and broad summit ridge

2.5 hours
5.3km
(3.3 miles)

The Miners' Track SNOWDON

'Fascinating views' ★

Summary: Originally an access track to the mines, the Miners' Track climbs an easy gradient to Llyn Llydaw and then on to Glaslyn after which it joins the Pyg Track and climbs the constructed zigzags to Bwlch Glas. As with the Pyg Track it suffers from over-zealous path construction techniques, but these are more than compensated for by the fine views of Y Lliwedd and the crags of Clogwyn y Garnedd.

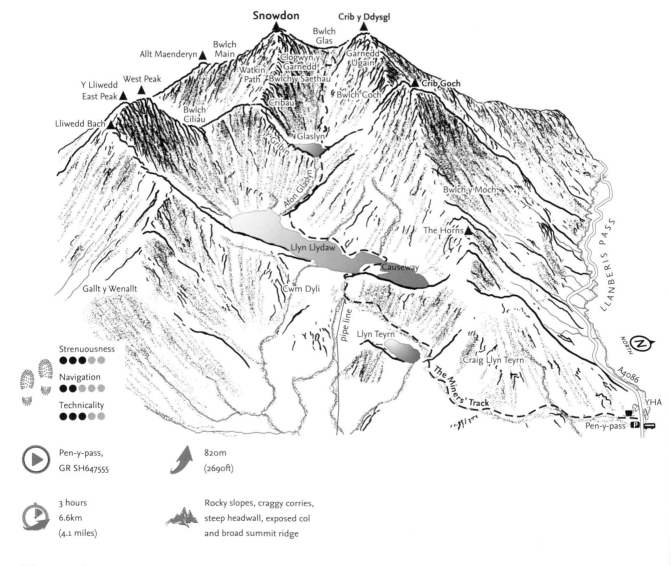

Ascent: From Pen-y-pass take the Miners' Track (access track) S, W, then SW to Llyn Llydaw. Cross Llyn Llydaw NW via the Causeway, then follow the track SW around the lake, then W up to Glaslyn. Head NW around the lake and then make the steep ascent to the junction with the Pyg Track.

From the junction climb the steep zigzags W up the headwall to Bwlch Glas. At Bwlch Glas the path joins the Llanberis Path (bridleway) which is taken S then SSE to Snowdon's summit.

Descent: From the Summit Station take the bridleway NNW to Bwlch Glas. At the stone marker turn E and descend the zigzags towards Glaslyn. Midway down the corrie headwall the path splits. Take the right-hand fork (the left fork is the Pyg Track) and follow it SE down the steep slope to Glaslyn. From Glaslyn follow the good track E to Llyn Llydaw, then NE around the lake to the Causeway. Cross it and follow the track generally NE to Pen-y-pass.

Strenuousness ●●●○○

Navigation ●●○○○

Technicality ●●●○○

Pen-y-pass, GR SH647555

820m (2690ft)

3 hours
6.6km
(4.1 miles)

Rocky slopes, craggy corries, steep headwall, exposed col and broad summit ridge

Y Gribin SNOWDON

'Broken but exciting scrambling' ★

Summary: Y Gribin is the pronounced spur that extends NE from Snowdon's Southeast Ridge. It climbs high above Glaslyn and offers a short but exciting scramble.

🏔 **Ascent:** From Pen-y-pass take the Miners' Track (access track) S, W, then SW to Llyn Llydaw. Cross Llyn Llydaw NW via the Causeway, then follow the track SW around the lake, then W up to Glaslyn. Cross the Afon Glaslyn and climb the grass-and-rocks slope SW on the shallow col. From the col climb the crest of the ridge SW onto the levelling on the Southeast Ridge of Snowdon. Once on the Southeast Ridge either descend slightly SW to join the Watkin Path W then NE to the summit, or scramble directly (NW) up the more exciting crest of the Southeast Ridge.

Y Lliwedd, Llyn Llydaw and Y Gribin from the Pyg Track

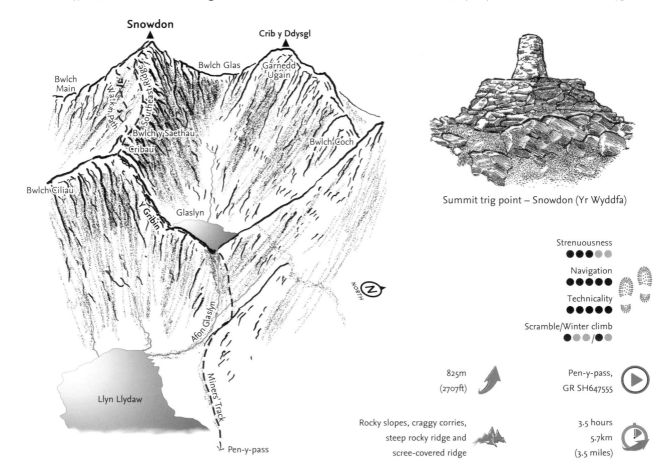

Summit trig point – Snowdon (Yr Wyddfa)

Strenuousness
●●●●○

Navigation
●●●●●

Technicality
●●●●●

Scramble/Winter climb
●●●○○/●○○

825m
(2707ft)

Pen-y-pass,
GR SH647555

Rocky slopes, craggy corries, steep rocky ridge and scree-covered ridge

3.5 hours
5.7km
(3.5 miles)

Southeast Ridge SNOWDON

'Snowdon's grandest views' ★★

Summary: Snowdon's Southeast Ridge, although a little broken in parts, provides a superb high-level link with Y Lliwedd. Most people complete a traverse of its length as part of the classic 'Snowdon Horseshoe' usually in descent. As an ascent route its qualities are equally good, particularly for the views of Snowdon's summit pyramid.

Ascent: From Pen-y-pass take the Miners' Track (access track) S, W, then SW to Llyn Llydaw. Before the Causeway turn L off the track and follow the path which climbs the steep rounded ridge SSW towards Lliwedd Bach. Climb onto the Northeast Ridge of Y Lliwedd and follow it SW over Lliwedd Bach, then W to Y Lliwedd. From the summit descend NW down the steep ridge (this involves some simple scrambling)

to Bwlch Ciliau. Cross the col then follow the Watkin Path NW to a levelling. As the Southeast Ridge starts to rear up, leave the Watkin Path and scramble up the crest of the ridge NW to Snowdon's summit.

Descent: From the trig point scramble down the crest of the Southeast Ridge to a levelling and then join the Watkin Path for a short distance to Bwlch Ciliau. Cross the col and climb SE up the rocky ridge to Y Lliwedd. Head E then NE from the summit of Y Lliwedd to Lliwedd Bach. Continue NE a short distance down the ridge until it is possible to take the narrow path NNE down the steep rounded ridge to Llyn Llydaw. At the side of the lake join the Miners' Track and follow it generally NE to Pen-y-pass.

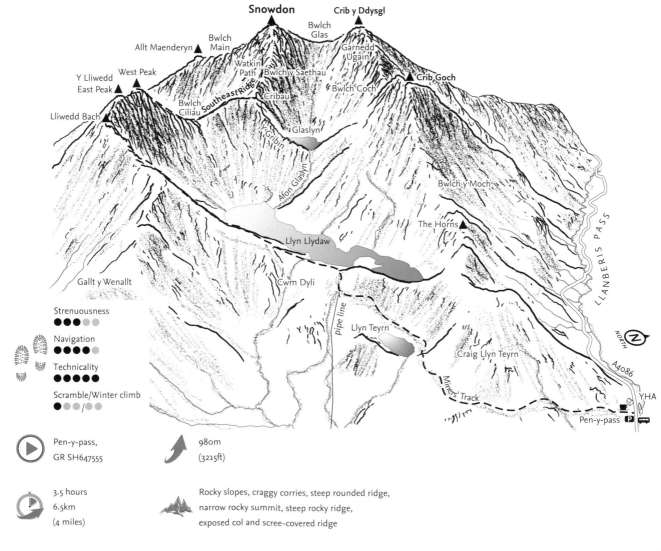

Strenuousness ●●●○○

Navigation ●●●●○

Technicality ●●●●●

Scramble/Winter climb ●●○○/○○○

Pen-y-pass, GR SH647555

980m (3215ft)

3.5 hours
6.5km
(4 miles)

Rocky slopes, craggy corries, steep rounded ridge, narrow rocky summit, steep rocky ridge, exposed col and scree-covered ridge

Watkin Path SNOWDON

'Historic and adventurous' ★

Summary: The product of a dedication by Sir Edward Watkin and opened by Gladstone on 13 September 1892, the Watkin Path climbs a logical route up the headwall of the wild and lovely Cwm Llan. The upper section has collapsed in parts and there are many false trails onto exposed and loose ground. Careful attention to route finding is essential particularly in descent.

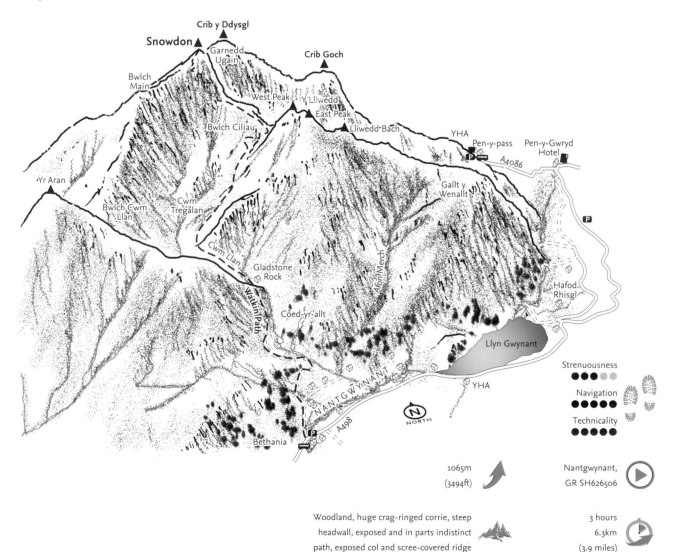

Ascent: From the A498 at Nantgwynant take the lane N to the start of the Watkin Path on the left. Join the path and follow it as it weaves its way NW over a bridge and past the Gladstone Rock into Cwm Llan. Through the spoil heaps at the abandoned quarries the path turns NE then N and climbs the steep headwall to Bwlch Ciliau. Once on the col turn NW and follow the Watkin Path NW then W across the south side of Snowdon's summit pyramid. As the Southwest Ridge is gained turn NE and make the final short ascent to the Summit Station.

Descent: From the Summit Station descend the Southwest Ridge a short distance, then turn sharp L and descend E down the zigzags of the Watkin Path. Past the zigzags continue E to the levelling at the base of the Southeast Ridge, then head SE to Bwlch Ciliau. At the col turn SW then S down the steep headwall of Cwm Llan. Follow the path through the old workings, then turn SE along the Watkin Path down through Cwm Llan to join the access lane which is followed the short distance S to the A498 at Nantgwynant.

Strenuousness ●●●●○

Navigation ●●●●●

Technicality ●●●●●

1065m (3494ft)

Nantgwynant, GR SH626506

Woodland, huge crag-ringed corrie, steep headwall, exposed and in parts indistinct path, exposed col and scree-covered ridge

3 hours
6.3km
(3.9 miles)

Carnedd Llewelyn
1064m (3491ft)

Foel Grach 976m (3202ft)
Yr Elen 962m (3156ft)
Carnedd Gwenllian/
Carnedd Uchaf 926m (3038ft)

Carnedd Llewelyn, the second-highest peak in
Wales, lies at the very heart of the Carneddau.
It acts as a hub for the whole massif, radiating
a series of complex ridges and subsidiary tops.
Characterised by rounded summit ridges, which
form an extensive plateau, and by steep crags
hidden on the surrounding flanks, Carnedd
Llewelyn has the added edge of being remote.
Whether approaching from the Conwy Valley,
the Ogwen Valley, Bethesda or Aber, your route
will involve either crossing a subsidiary top or
a complex valley approach.

When you arrive

Ordnance Survey: Explorer OL17 (1:25 000);
Landranger 115 (1:50 000).

Harvey Mountain Maps: Snowdonia North (1:25 000)

British Mountain Maps: Snowdonia (1:40 000)

Tourist Information Centres: Llanberis; Bangor;
Llanfairfechan; Betws-y-Coed.

Youth Hostels: Ogwen Valley: *Idwal Cottage*;
Rowen: *Rhiw Farm*; Capel Curig.

Hotels and B&B: Capel Curig; Bethesda; Ogwen Valley;
Aber; Llanfairfechan; Tal-y-Bont; Betws-y-Coed; Capel Curig.

Camp sites: Capel Curig; Ogwen Valley: *Gwern Gof Uchaf*;
Bethesda: *Ogwen Bank*; Betws-y-Coed.

To the northwest of Carnedd Llewelyn's summit
dome along a narrow ridge lies the shapely Yr Elen.
Three of the four Bethesda approaches climb this
subsidiary top first; the other follows the steep
course of the Nant Fach out of Cwm Llafar. Of the
three routes up Yr Elen the Northeast Ridge is the
most exciting, as it climbs a very steep line high
above the remote waters of Ffynnon Caseg.

Carnedd Llewelyn has a wealth of long meandering
routes, which are excellent for long days when time
is not a problem and plenty of diversions
can be made to explore quiet corners.
Fitting the bill perfectly are
the Cwm Eigiau Path
and the Cwm
Goch Path;

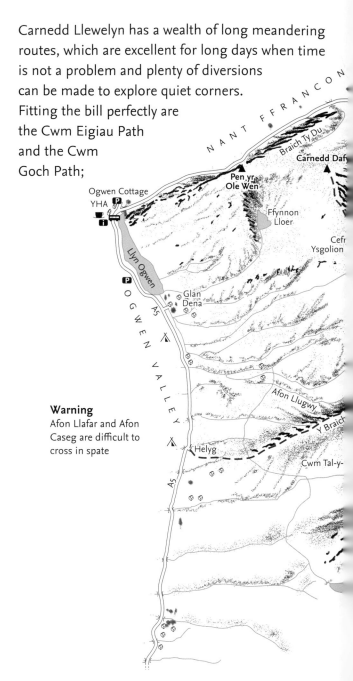

Warning
Afon Llafar and Afon
Caseg are difficult to
cross in spate

each has its own hidden secrets which reward those who are prepared to spend time searching them out. As could be expected with such a major peak Carnedd Llewelyn has its fair share of cliffs – these in the main occur on the Conwy Valley side. The cliffs of Craig y Dulyn and Craig-fawr lie to the east of the subsidiary top Foel Grach; between them a steep spur provides an adventurous route which is worth climbing after exploring their dark corries. Further south on the southeast side of Carnedd Llewelyn itself is Craig yr Ysfa. This extensive crag always seems dark and forbidding but in its time has produced some classic rock climbs. The most notable feature on it is the wide gully at its centre, Amphitheatre Gully, which, surprisingly for such an intimidating line, produces a scramble.

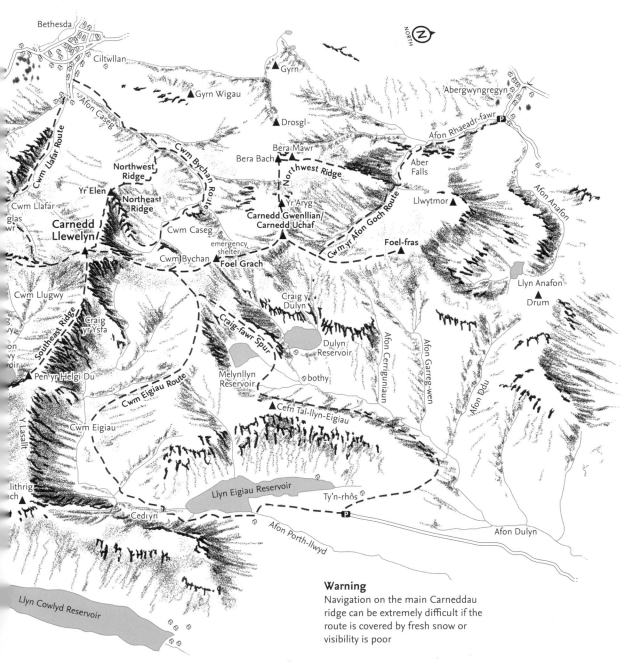

Warning
Navigation on the main Carneddau ridge can be extremely difficult if the route is covered by fresh snow or visibility is poor

Southeast Ridge CARNEDD LLEWELYN

'Narrow and airy' ★ ★

Summary: The long Southeast Ridge of Carnedd Llewelyn extends to the satellite peak, Pen yr Helgi Du. An enjoyable way of gaining it from the Ogwen Valley is along the rounded grassy ridge Y Braich.

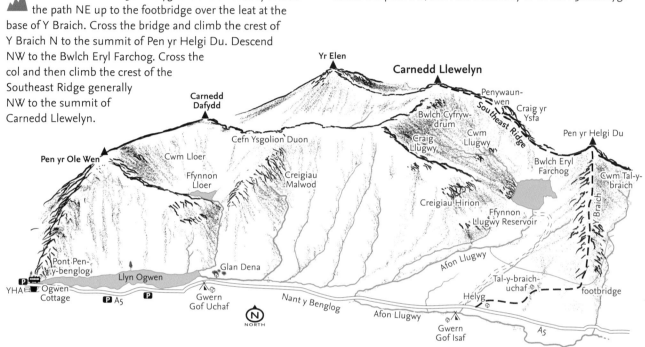

Ascent: From the A5 at Helyg take the bridleway E then the path NE up to the footbridge over the leat at the base of Y Braich. Cross the bridge and climb the crest of Y Braich N to the summit of Pen yr Helgi Du. Descend NW to the Bwlch Eryl Farchog. Cross the col and then climb the crest of the Southeast Ridge generally NW to the summit of Carnedd Llewelyn.

Descent: Head ESE to start then descend SE down the crest of the Southeast Ridge to Bwlch Eryl Farchog. Cross the narrow col and make the ascent SE to the summit of Pen yr Helgi Du. From the summit descend S down the crest of Y Braich to the footbridge over the leat. Cross it and follow the path SW, then the bridleway W to the A5 at Helyg.

Strenuousness
● ● ● ○ ○

Navigation
● ● ● ○ ○

Technicality
● ● ● ● ○

A5 near Helyg,
GR SH690602

3 hours
5.6km
(3.5 miles)

870m
(2854ft)

Major valley, steep ridge, narrow col,
high mountain ridge and exposed summit

⚠ The col on the northwest side of Pen yr Helgi Du can also be gained by taking the access road to Ffynnon Llugwy Reservoir (a popular approach), then climbing the steep headwall of the corrie – start at the side of the A5, GR SH687602

Looking down the Southeast Ridge from
Carnedd Llewelyn towards Pen yr Helgi Du

Northwest Ridge (Yr Elen) CARNEDD LLEWELYN

'A slog with an exciting finish' ★ ★

Summary: A simple ridge line to the fine subsidiary top Yr Elen. Set between two beautiful corries, this route is best left for a descent at the end of the day when low-angled sunlight will show the surrounding scenery at its most magnificent.

Ascent: Take the access track E then NW as it winds its way round to the pumping station. Pass the pumping station and turn E along the track. Follow it to the intake gate then take the vague path SE to the Afon Caseg. Cross the Afon Caseg (difficult in spate) and then climb steadily SSE to the broad shoulder at the base of the Northwest Ridge. Turn ESE and climb the crest of the ridge to Foel Ganol. Pass Foel Ganol then turn SE up the ridge proper and climb the crest to Yr Elen. From the summit skirt SE down to a narrow col. Cross it and climb SE up the crest of the ridge to Carnedd Llewelyn.

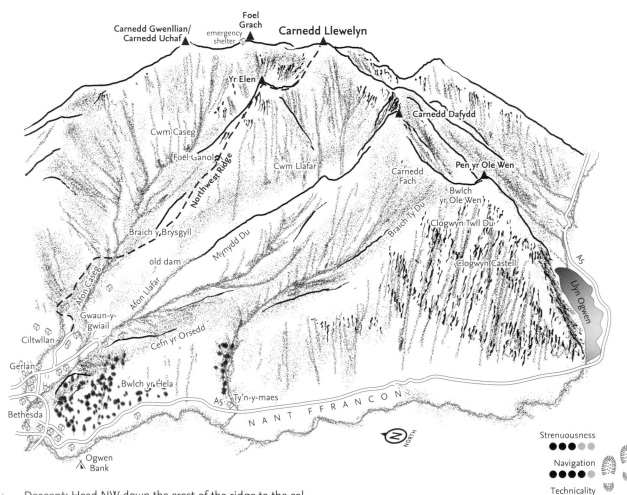

Descent: Head NW down the crest of the ridge to the col on the southeast side of Yr Elen. Skirt NW from the col to the summit of Yr Elen. Continue NW over the summit and descend the crest of the steep ridge to Foel Ganol. Descend WNW past Foel Ganol and down the crest of the ridge until the gradient eases at its base. Turn NNE and follow the vague path to the Afon Caseg. Cross the Afon Caseg (difficult in spate) then head NW to join the access track. Follow the track W to the pumping station, then turn SE and then W to Ciltwllan.

Strenuousness ●●●○○

Navigation ●●●●○

Technicality ●●●●○

875m
(2871ft)

Ciltwllan on the east side of Bethesda, GR SH637663

Pasture, moorland, long grassy ridge, exposed summit, exposed col and rounded summit ridge

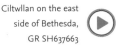

3 hours
6.2km
(3.9 miles)

Carnedd Dafydd Link CARNEDD LLEWELYN

'Easy' ★★

Summary: Simple high-level ridge walk around the edge of Cwm Llafar.

Route: Descend SE down the rounded ridge to Bwlch Cyfryw-drum. Cross the col and continue along the main ridge path as it swings SW then W skirting the top of Ysgolion Duon to the summit of Carnedd Dafydd.

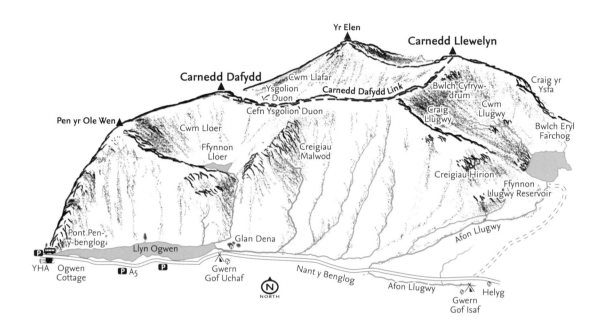

Strenuousness
●●●○○

Navigation
●●●○○

Technicality
●●●○○

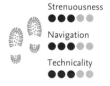

▶ Carnedd Llewelyn,
GR SH683644

1 hour
3.1km
(1.9 miles)

145m
(476ft)

High mountain ridge and exposed summit

Ysgolion Duon (also known as The Black Ladders)

Northeast Ridge (Yr Elen) CARNEDD LLEWELYN

'Alpine' ★ ★ ★

Summary: Tucked away on the north side of Yr Elen the Northeast Ridge climbs a steep, uncompromising route above the wild Cwm Caseg. A real hidden gem, this route is one of the finest approaches to Carnedd Llewelyn.

Ascent: Take the access track E then NW as it winds its way round to the pumping station. Pass the pumping station and turn E along the track. After the settlement remains the track becomes less distinct. Roughly follow the course of the Afon Caseg E then SE to the mouth of Cwm Caseg. Turn SW and climb the very steep slope then the narrow ridge directly to the summit of Yr Elen. From the summit skirt SE down to a narrow col. Cross it and climb SE up the crest of the ridge to Carnedd Llewelyn.

Descent: Head NW down the crest of the ridge to the col on the southeast side of Yr Elen. Skirt NW from the col to the summit of Yr Elen. Descend the very steep narrow ridge and slope NE to the mouth of Cwm Caseg. Cross the Afon Caseg and roughly follow its north side NW then W to pick up the access track at the settlement remains. Take it W to the pumping station, then turn SE along it and finally W to Ciltwllan.

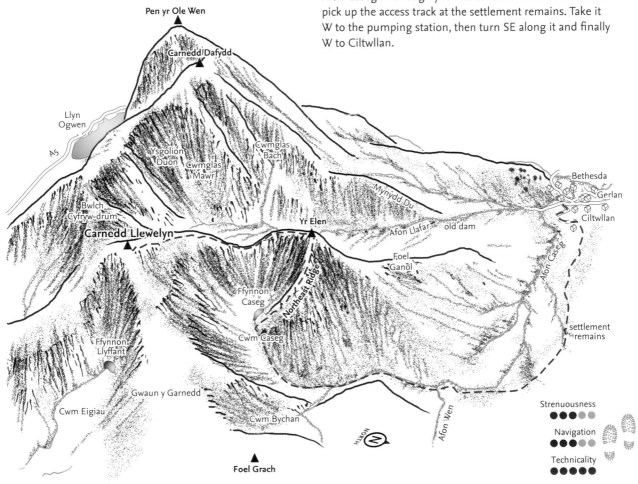

Summit cairn – Carnedd Llewelyn

Strenuousness
● ● ● ● ○

Navigation
● ● ● ● ○

Technicality
● ● ● ● ●

870m
(2854ft)

Pasture, moorland, steep-sided valley, high remote corrie, steep narrow ridge, exposed summit, exposed col and rounded summit ridge

Ciltwllan on the east side of Bethesda, GR SH637663

3.5 hours
7.6km
(4.7 miles)

Cwm Llafar Route CARNEDD LLEWELYN

'Reliable descent'

Summary: Gains the southern side of Carnedd Llewelyn along the length of Cwm Llafar and up the course of the fast-flowing Nant Fach. The lower half of this lonely valley is open and quite pleasant but the upper half is of a completely different nature – ringed by the dark cliffs of Ysgolion Duon it is an intimidating place.

Ascent: Cross the Afon Llafar then follow the path S then SE past the waterworks. Continue SE along the path past the old dam and along the side of the Afon Llafar to the entrance to Cwmglas Bach. Continue SE a short distance, then at the mouth of Cwmglas Mawr turn ENE and climb the steepening slopes alongside Nant Fach to Bwlch Cyfryw-drum. On the col turn L and climb N up the rounded ridge to the summit of Carnedd Llewelyn.

Descent: Descend S down the rounded ridge to Bwlch Cyfryw-drum. At the col turn and descend the steep slope alongside Nant Fach SW, W then WSW to the mouth of Cwmglas Mawr. Head NW and pick up the Cwm Llafar Path which is followed NW past the old dam, past the waterworks then over the Afon Llafar to the road head.

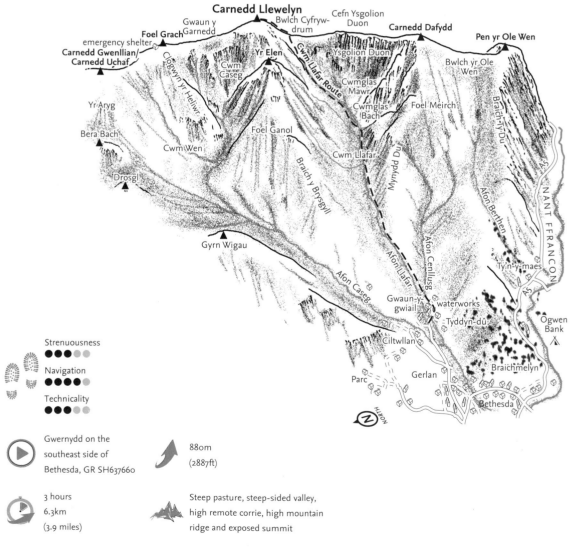

Strenuousness
●●●●○

Navigation
●●●●○

Technicality
●●●○○

Gwernydd on the southeast side of Bethesda, GR SH637660

880m (2887ft)

3 hours
6.3km
(3.9 miles)

Steep pasture, steep-sided valley, high remote corrie, high mountain ridge and exposed summit

RIGHT
The final few metres to Carnedd Llewelyn with Carnedd Dafydd and Ysgolion Duon behind

Northwest Ridge (Carnedd Gwenllian/Carnedd Uchaf) CARNEDD LLEWELYN

'Long expedition' ★★

Summary: A long, meandering route over moorland and up a gentle, grassy ridge to gain the subsidiary top, Carnedd Uchaf, on the north side of Carnedd Llewelyn.

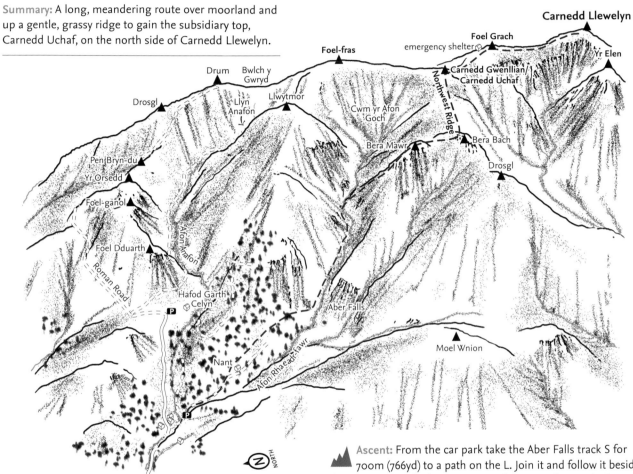

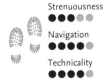

Strenuousness
●●●●○○

Navigation
●●●●●○

Technicality
●●●●○

 Aber Falls car park,
GR SH663719

 1105m
(3625ft)

 4 hours
9.3km
(5.8 miles)

 Pasture, moorland,
long rounded ridge and
high mountain ridge

Ascent: From the car park take the Aber Falls track S for 700m (766yd) to a path on the L. Join it and follow it beside the trees to gain the lower section of Cwm yr Afon Goch. Once in the corrie cross the stream and make the climb S to the summit of Bera Mawr. Cross the rocky summit then swing SW to gain Bera Bach. From here climb the rounded crest of the ridge SE to Carnedd Gwenllian/Carnedd Uchaf. Head S along the main ridge path over Foel Grach then SSW to Carnedd Llewelyn.

Descent: Head NNE along the main ridge path then trend N over Foel Grach and continue to Carnedd Gwenllian/Carnedd Uchaf. From the summit turn L and make the steady descent NW along the rounded crest of the ridge then trend W to Bera Bach. Turn NW and make for the rocky summit of Bera Mawr. Descend N and pick your way down the blunt rocky ridge to gain the Afon Goch. Cross the Afon Goch and then follow the path on the other side N past Aber Falls and down to the road at the falls car park.

Foel-fras Link CARNEDD LLEWELYN

'High-level promenade' ★

Summary: In good conditions a pleasant stroll along an undulating ridge with fine panoramic views. In poor visibility and with snow cover it can be a nightmare as the featureless terrain makes navigation difficult.

Route: Head NNE along the main ridge path then trend N over Foel Grach and continue to Carnedd Gwenllian/Carnedd Uchaf. From the summit descend NE to the col at the head of Cwm yr Afon Goch. From the col continue NE climbing the rounded ridge to Foel-fras.

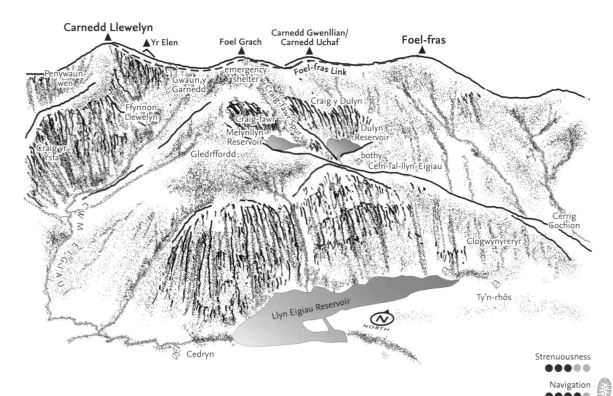

Yr Elen from Gwaun y Garnedd

Strenuousness
●●●○○

Navigation
●●●●○

Technicality
●●●○○

Carnedd Llewelyn,
GR SH683644

1 hour
4.2km
(2.6 miles)

130m
(427ft)

High mountain ridge

Cwm Bychan Route CARNEDD LLEWELYN

'Peace and quiet' ★

Summary: Follows the course of the Afon Caseg then gains the north side of Carnedd Llewelyn via the lonely Cwm Bychan.

Ascent: Take the access track E then NW as it winds its way round to the pumping station. Pass the pumping station and turn E along the track. After the settlement remains, the track becomes less distinct. Roughly follow the course of the Afon Caseg E then SE to the mouth of Cwm Bychan. Climb E up through the corrie, then on the final slopes trend SE to join the main ridge path at the broad col on the northeast side of Carnedd Llewelyn. Head SW up the path to the summit.

Descent: Head NE along the main ridge path then NW across the broad col and descend into Cwm Bychan. Trend W down through the corrie to gain the north side of the Afon Caseg. Roughly follow its north side NW then W to pick up the access track at the settlement remains. Follow the track W to the pumping station, then turn SE and then W to Ciltwllan.

Strenuousness
●●●●○

Navigation
●●●●●

Technicality
●●●○○

▶ Gwernydd on the southeast side of Bethesda, GR SH637660

810m (1017ft)

3 hours
7.2km
(4.5 miles)

Pasture, moorland, steep-sided valley, high remote corrie and rounded summit ridge

Hitting the main ridge at the head of Cwm Bychan

Cwm yr Afon Goch Route CARNEDD LLEWELYN

'Isolated and atmospheric' ★

Summary: An interesting route; it samples classic Carneddau scenery. It starts with the delights of the Aber Falls then the remoteness of Cwm yr Afon Goch and finishes with the high exposed slopes of the main ridge.

Ascent: From the car park take the Aber Falls track S for 700m (766yd) to a path on the L. Join it and follow it beside the trees to gain the lower section of Cwm yr Afon Goch. Follow the Afon Goch generally SE into Cwm yr Afon Goch. Continue SE up the corrie headwall to the col on the southwest side of Foel-fras. Join the main ridge path and take it SW up onto Carnedd Gwenllian/Carnedd Uchaf. From the summit turn S along the main ridge path over Foel Grach then SSW to Carnedd Llewelyn.

Descent: Head NNE along the main ridge path then trend N over Foel Grach and continue to Carnedd Uchaf. From the summit descend NE to the col at the head of Cwm yr Afon Goch. Descend NW down the headwall then follow the Afon Goch generally NW towards the Aber Falls. Follow the path on the other side (N) of the Afon Goch N past Aber Falls and down to the road at the falls car park.

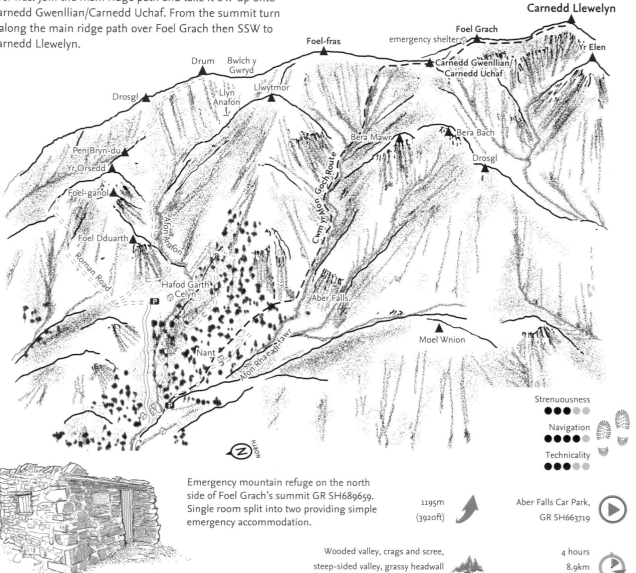

Emergency mountain refuge on the north side of Foel Grach's summit GR SH689659. Single room split into two providing simple emergency accommodation.

1195m (3920ft)

Aber Falls Car Park, GR SH663719

Wooded valley, crags and scree, steep-sided valley, grassy headwall and high mountain ridge

4 hours
8.9km
(5.5 miles)

Strenuousness ●●●○○

Navigation ●●●●○

Technicality ●●●○○

Craig-fawr Spur CARNEDD LLEWELYN

'Dramatic crags' ★

Summary: The north side of the subsidiary top Foel Grach is occupied by two secluded corries. Between their steep craggy headwalls a steep spur extends east – this is the Craig-fawr Spur. Its base can be reached easily via the Melynllyn Reservoir access track which gives a steep but exciting route onto the main ridge.

Ascent: At the northeast end of the car park take the Melynllyn Reservoir access track NW. It climbs around the flanks of Clogwynyreryr and is then followed SW then NW to the outlet stream. Cross the Afon Melynllyn then climb the steep slope NW onto the Craig-fawr Spur. Follow the crest of the spur SW then climb the headwall to join the Cwm Eigiau Path on the east side of Foel Grach. Trend SW and gain the main ridge path which is followed to the summit of Carnedd Llewelyn.

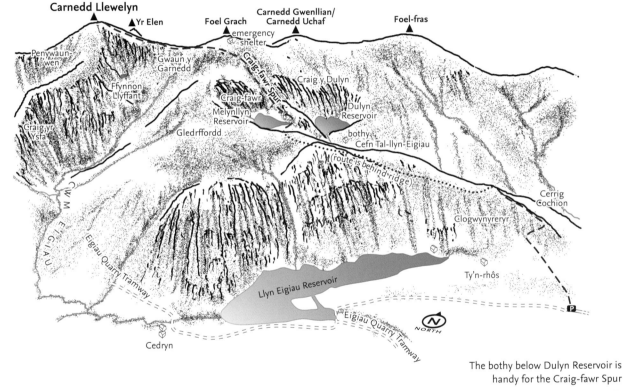

The bothy below Dulyn Reservoir is handy for the Craig-fawr Spur

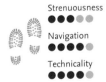

Strenuousness
●●●●○

Navigation
●●●●○

Technicality
●●●●○

 Cwm Eigiau Car Park, GR SH731663

 725m (2378ft)

 3 hours 6.8km (4.2 miles)

 Moorland, open valley, craggy corrie, steep spur, craggy headwall and high mountain ridge

Cwm Eigiau Path CARNEDD LLEWELYN

'Hauntingly wild'

Summary: Long, steady approach from the Conwy Valley side of the Carneddau via the cold depths of Cwm Eigiau. At the head of Cwm Eigiau the impressive cliffs of Craig yr Ysfa can be viewed in all their glory.

Ascent: From the car park follow the access track SW to the old dam. Cross the Afon Porth-llwyd then follow the rough track SSW then SW up into Cwm Eigiau. At the old quarry tips and buildings take the vague path NW, N then NW as it climbs up onto the east flank of Foel Grach. Turn SW and climb to the col on the south side of Foel Grach. From the col join the main ridge path and take it SSW to Carnedd Llewelyn.

Descent: Head NNE along the main ridge path to the col on the north side of Carnedd Llewelyn. From the col descend NE to join the Cwm Eigiau Path on the east flank of Foel Grach (the path is vague and can be difficult to locate in poor visibility). Once on it, take it SE, S and then SE to the old quarry tips and buildings in Cwm Eigiau. Join the access track and take it E then NE around Cwm Eigiau to the old dam. Cross the Afon Porth-llwyd and head NE along the access track to the car park at the road head.

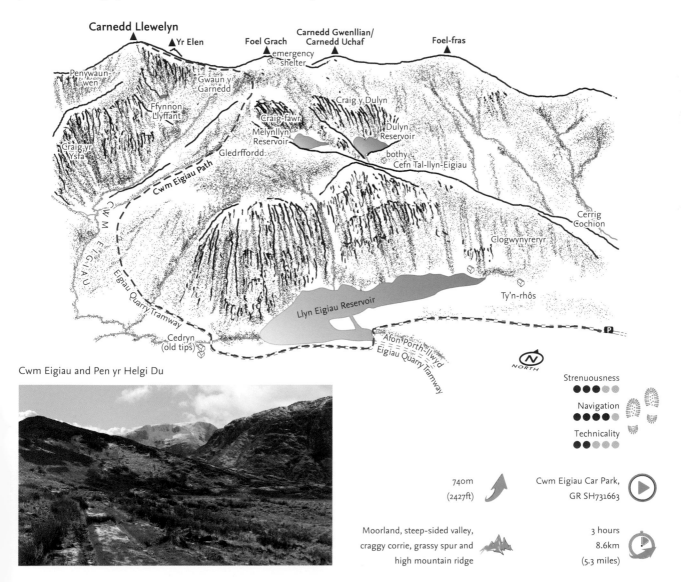

Cwm Eigiau and Pen yr Helgi Du

Strenuousness
●●●○○○

Navigation
●●●●○

Technicality
●●○○○○

740m
(2427ft)

Cwm Eigiau Car Park,
GR SH731663

Moorland, steep-sided valley,
craggy corrie, grassy spur and
high mountain ridge

3 hours
8.6km
(5.3 miles)

Carnedd Dafydd

1044m (3425ft)

Pen yr Ole Wen 978m (3209ft)

Carnedd Dafydd's presence is big and dramatic. Rearing up from the shores of Llyn Ogwen its south face dominates the entire length of the north side of the Ogwen Valley. To the west it extends two long ridges which cast their influence for over three miles to the outskirts of Bethesda. Most dramatic of all are the formidable cliffs of

Ysgolion Duon, presenting a long north wall which in aspect and character has more in common with the great cliffs of the Scottish Highlands than its more moderate neighbours.

The plateau-like ridge which links the peaks and tops of the Carneddau can be very misleading. Its undulating form tends to give the impression of rounded rolling mountains, and while this is true for the ridge lines the vast amount of rock to be found on the flanks is often overlooked.

The most direct route to the ravaged summit of Carnedd Dafydd is from Pen y Benglog (Ogwen Cottage) via the very steep South Ridge of the subsidiary top Pen yr Ole Wen. This popular

When you arrive

Ordnance Survey: Explorer OL17 (1:25 000); Landranger 115 (1:50 000).

Harvey Mountain Maps: Snowdonia North (1:25 000)

British Mountain Maps: Snowdonia (1:40 000)

Tourist Information Centres: Caernarfon; Llanberis; Betws-y-Coed; Bangor.

Youth Hostels: Ogwen Valley: *Idwal Cottage*; Capel Curig.

Hotels and B&B: Nantgwryd: *Pen-y-Gwryd Hotel*; Nant Peris; Llanberis; Bethesda; Ogwen Valley; Capel Curig.

Camp sites: Ogwen Bank; Ogwen Valley: *Gwern Gof Uchaf*; Capel Curig.

Warning

Navigation on the main Carneddau ridge can be extremely difficult if the route is obliterated with fresh snow or visibility is poor

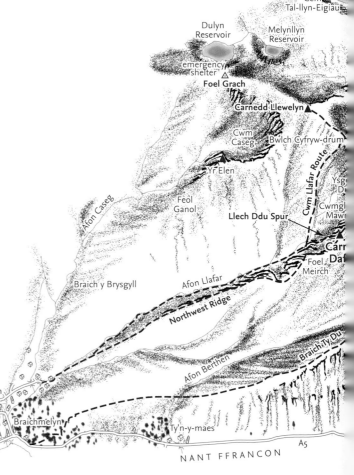

and rather joyless approach can only really be recommended for its views along the Ogwen Valley and towards the Glyders massif. The East Ridge of Pen yr Ole Wen and the Craig Llugwy Spur are far more interesting and do not involve as much hard work. From Bethesda either the Northwest Ridge or the Braich Ty Du follow pleasant courses, which have the distinct advantage of being quiet.

The classic route to Carnedd Dafydd has to be the Llech Ddu Spur. Climbing from the depths of Cwmglas Bach this steep truncated spur feels very alpine. It offers a fine scramble in the shadow of the huge towering cliffs of Ysgolion Duon – ground which is the preserve of roped parties.

Warning
Afon Llafar is difficult to cross in spate

RIGHT
Carnedd Dafydd from Carnedd Llewelyn

South Ridge CARNEDD DAFYDD

'Unrelentingly steep'

Summary: A steep approach to Carnedd Dafydd from the Ogwen Valley via the subsidiary top Pen yr Ole Wen.

Ascent: Cross the Afon Ogwen via the A5 road bridge and take the vague path E to the base of the ridge. Make the short scramble onto the ridge proper. Follow the crest NNE as it climbs unremittingly to the summit of Pen yr Ole Wen. From the summit cairn continue NNE then trend NE around the head of Cwm Lloer and climb the summit slopes to Carnedd Dafydd.

Descent: Head SW then SSW around the head of Cwm Lloer to the summit of Pen yr Ole Wen. From the summit cairn descend the steep rocky ridge SSW to the Afon Ogwen. Head W and cross the river via the A5 road bridge.

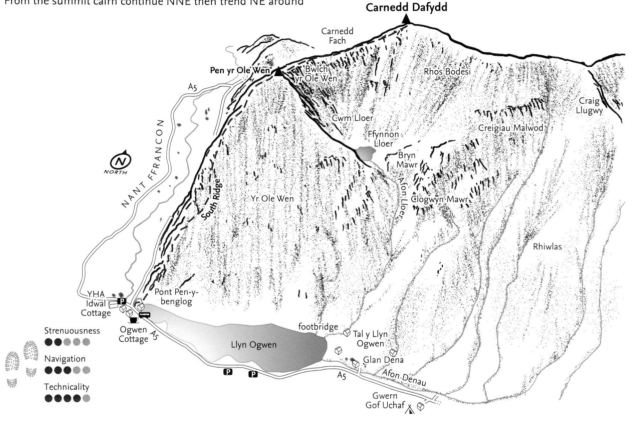

Strenuousness
● ● ● ○ ○

Navigation
● ● ● ○ ○

Technicality
● ● ● ● ○

Ogwen Cottage
(Pen y Benglog),
GR SH649603

2 hours
3.5km
(2.2 miles)

790m
(2592ft)

Steep rocky ridge, high mountain ridge and exposed summit

Pen yr Ole Wen and Carnedd Dafydd from the Glyders

Braich Ty Du CARNEDD DAFYDD

'Quiet and easy angled' ★

Summary: A long steady approach up the featureless northwest limb of the subsidiary top Pen yr Ole Wen. Useful as a descent route to Bethesda.

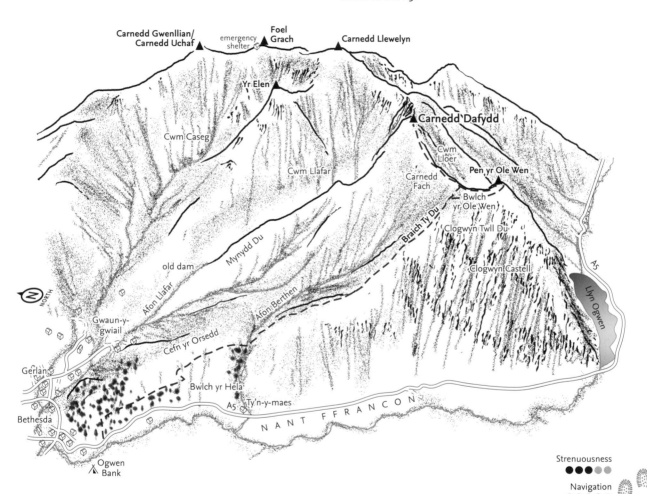

Descent: Head SW then SSW around the head of Cwm Lloer to the summit of Pen yr Ole Wen. From the summit cairn descend NW along the Braich Ty Du, trending N at the bottom to cross the Afon Berthen. Once across, contour NNW to join the footpath that descends W to the trees. Follow the path W then SW through the trees and down to the A5.

Ascent: From the side of the A5 take the path NE then E up through the trees. Once onto open mountainside, trend SSE and cross the Afon Berthen to gain the Braich Ty Du proper. Ascend it S then SE to the summit of Pen yr Ole Wen. From the summit cairn continue NNE, then trend NE around the head of Cwm Lloer and climb the summit slopes to Carnedd Dafydd.

Strenuousness
● ● ● ○ ○

Navigation
● ● ● ● ○

Technicality
● ● ● ○ ○

880m (2887ft)

Opposite Ogwen Bank on the A5, GR SH627654

Steep woodland, long rounded ridge, high mountain ridge and exposed summit

3 hours 6km (3.7 miles)

Northwest Ridge CARNEDD DAFYDD

'Dramatic views' ★

Summary: A direct approach to Carnedd Dafydd from Bethesda. Mostly across featureless and uninteresting ground – the only distraction being the views down into Cwm Llafar. Better saved as a descent route.

Ascent: Cross the Afon Llafar, then follow the path S then SE past the waterworks. Continue SE along the path until the old dam is reached. Leave the side of the Afon Llafar and climb SE up Mynydd Du onto the Northwest Ridge, which is followed around the edge of Cwmglas Bach to the summit of Carnedd Dafydd.

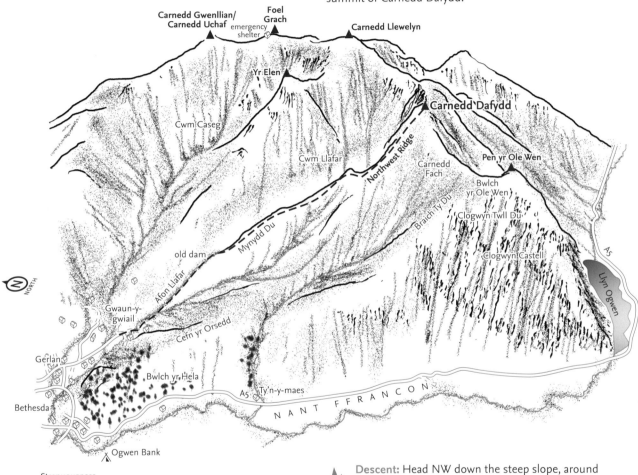

Descent: Head NW down the steep slope, around the edge of Cwmglas Bach and down the crest of Mynydd Du. At the old dam join the Cwm Llafar Path and take it NW down past the waterworks, then over the Afon Llafar to the road head.

Strenuousness
●●●●○○

Navigation
●●●○○○

Technicality
●●●○○○

▶ Gwernydd on the southeast side of Bethesda, GR SH637660

810m (2657ft)

2.5 hours
4.4km (2.7 miles)

Steep pasture, moorland, rounded ridge, steep grassy slopes and exposed summit

Llech Ddu Spur CARNEDD DAFYDD

'Remote scramble' ★ ★ ★

Summary: The Llech Ddu Spur provides a superb scrambling route to the summit dome of Carnedd Dafydd between the complex corrie system of Cwmglas Bach and the dark forbidding cliffs of Ysgolion Duon. For a route set among such awesome surroundings, the scrambling encountered on the Llech Ddu Spur is surprisingly easy.

Bivi Boulder, Cwmglas Bach GR SH664636. Builtup cave beneath boulder – not very appealing as it is very popular with sheep.

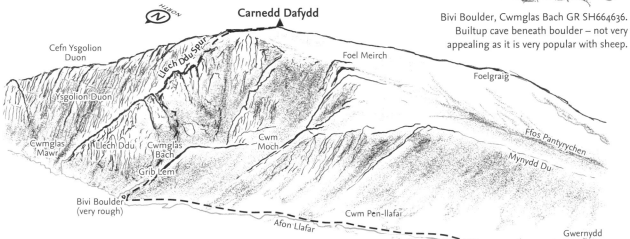

Ascent: Cross the Afon Llafar, then follow the path S then SE past the waterworks. Continue SE along the path past the old dam and along the side of the Afon Llafar to the Bivi Boulder at the entrance to Cwmglas Bach. From the boulders, head S into the corrie then turn E and climb up the west flank of the Llech Ddu Spur. On reaching the crest turn S and follow it as it steepens to abut the summit slopes. Climb these SW to Carnedd Dafydd's summit.

The sunlight picks out the Llech Ddu Spur's narrow crest

Strenuousness
● ● ● ○ ○

Navigation
● ● ● ● ●

Technicality
● ● ● ● ●

Scramble/Winter climb
● ● ○ ○ / ● ○

Gwernydd on the southeast side of Bethesda, GR SH637660

3.5 hours
4.8km
(3 miles)

840m
(2756ft)

Steep pasture, steep-sided valley, complex corrie system, truncated spur and boulder-strewn summit slope

Carnedd Llewelyn Link CARNEDD DAFYDD

'Easy' ★★

Summary: Simple high-level ridge walk around the edge of Cwm Llafar.

Route: Take the main ridge path E, then NE to Bwlch Cyfryw-drum. Cross the col and continue NE up the rounded ridge to the summit of Carnedd Llewelyn.

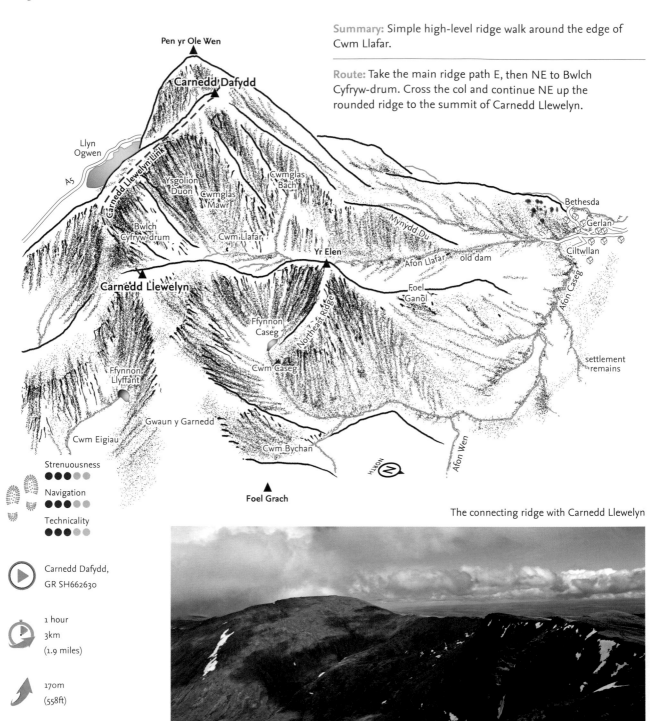

Pen yr Ole Wen

Carnedd Dafydd

Llyn Ogwen

A5

Carnedd Llewelyn Link

Ysgolion Duon

Cwmglas Mawr

Cwmglas Bach

Bwlch Cyfryw-drum

Cwm Llafar

Mynydd Du

Bethesda

Gerlan

Ciltwllan

Carnedd Llewelyn

Yr Elen

Afon Llafar

old dam

Foel Ganol

Afon Caseg

Ffynnon Caseg

North-east Ridge

settlement remains

Ffynnon Llyffant

Cwm Caseg

Cwm Eigiau

Gwaun y Garnedd

Cwm Bychan

Afon Wen

NORTH

Foel Grach

Strenuousness
●●●●○

Navigation
●●●●○

Technicality
●●●●○

Carnedd Dafydd,
GR SH662630

1 hour
3km
(1.9 miles)

170m
(558ft)

High mountain ridge and exposed summit

The connecting ridge with Carnedd Llewelyn

Cwm Llafar Route CARNEDD DAFYDD

'Useful escape route'

Summit cairn – Carnedd Dafydd

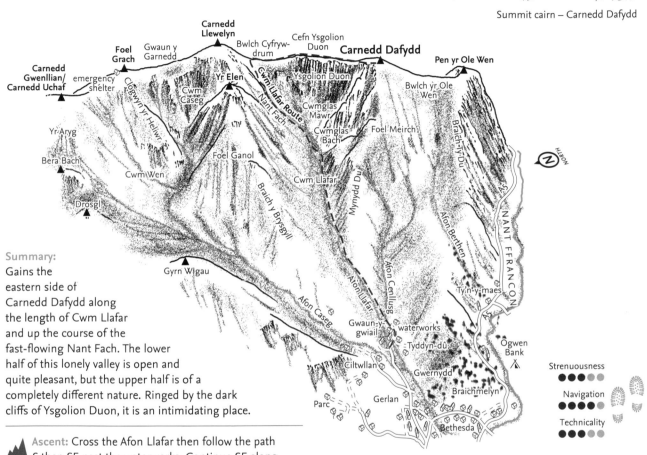

Summary:
Gains the
eastern side of
Carnedd Dafydd along
the length of Cwm Llafar
and up the course of the
fast-flowing Nant Fach. The lower
half of this lonely valley is open and
quite pleasant, but the upper half is of a
completely different nature. Ringed by the dark
cliffs of Ysgolion Duon, it is an intimidating place.

Ascent: Cross the Afon Llafar then follow the path
S then SE past the waterworks. Continue SE along
the path past the old dam and along the side of the Afon
Llafar to the entrance of Cwmglas Bach. Continue SE a
short distance, then at the mouth of Cwmglas Mawr
turn ENE and climb the steepening slopes alongside
Nant Fach to Bwlch Cyfryw-drum. On the col, turn R and
follow the main ridge path SW then W to the summit of
Carnedd Dafydd.

Descent: Take the main ridge path E then NE to
Bwlch Cyfryw-drum. At the col, turn L and descend the
steep slope alongside Nant Fach NW, W then WNW to the
mouth of Cwmglas Mawr. Head NW and pick up the Cwm
Llafar Path which is followed NW past the old dam, past the
waterworks, then over the Afon Llafar to the road head.

Gwernydd on the southeast
side of Bethesda,
GR SH637660

3 hours
7.7km
(4.8 miles)

880m
(2887ft)

Strenuousness
●●●●○○

Navigation
●●●●●○

Technicality
●●●●○○

Steep pasture, steep-sided valley,
high remote corrie, high mountain
ridge and exposed summit

East Ridge CARNEDD DAFYDD

'Elevated crest' ★

Summary: The East Ridge of Pen yr Ole Wen separates the wild craggy Cwm Lloer from the Ogwen Valley. It climbs a logical and pleasing line, which gains height quickly, and as most people tend to head for its more prominent neighbour, the South Ridge, you are likely to have it to yourself.

 Ascent: Take the path N past Glan Dena and follow it as it meanders up the hillside along the course of the Afon Lloer. As the path starts to turn into Cwm Lloer, turn W and climb the crest of the East Ridge to the summit of Pen yr Ole Wen. From the summit cairn turn NNE, then trend NE around the head of Cwm Lloer and climb the summit slopes to Carnedd Dafydd.

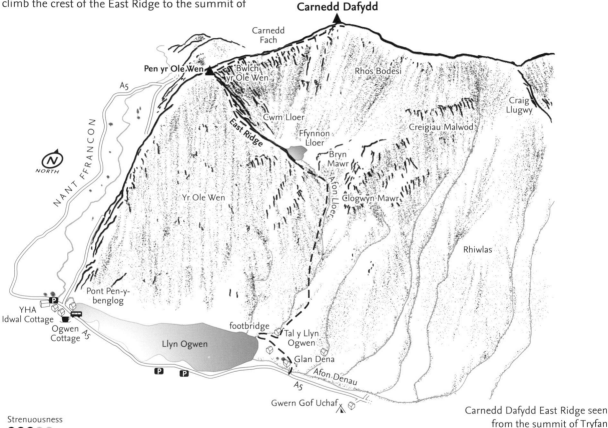 **Descent:** Head SW then SSW around the head of Cwm Lloer to the summit of Pen yr Ole Wen. From the summit cairn descend E down the crest of the steep rocky ridge. At the bottom pick up the Cwm Lloer Path and follow it down alongside the Afon Lloer to the A5 at Glan Dena.

Carnedd Dafydd East Ridge seen from the summit of Tryfan

Strenuousness
 ●●●●○

Navigation
●●●●○

Technicality
●●●○○

A5 at Glan Dena,
GR SH668605

785m
(2575ft)

2.5 hours
4.2km
(2.6 miles)

Major valley, steep ridge,
high mountain ridge and
exposed summit

Craig Llugwy Spur CARNEDD DAFYDD

'Lofty and quiet' ★

Summary: The Craig Llugwy Spur provides an adventurous and quiet route onto the eastern side of Carnedd Dafydd. Above the Ffynnon Llugwy Reservoir the views south to Tryfan and the Glyders are truly magnificent.

Ascent: Follow the access road NE then NW to the reservoir. Cross the Afon Llugwy then climb NW up the crest of the Craig Llugwy Spur. At the top join the main ridge path and take it W as it skirts around the top of Ysgolion Duon to the summit of Carnedd Dafydd.

Descent: Skirt E around the top of Ysgolion Duon, then at the head of Cwm Llugwy turn SE then ESE and descend the crest of the Craig Llugwy Spur. At the bottom, cross the Afon Llugwy and join the reservoir access road which is followed SE then SW down to the A5.

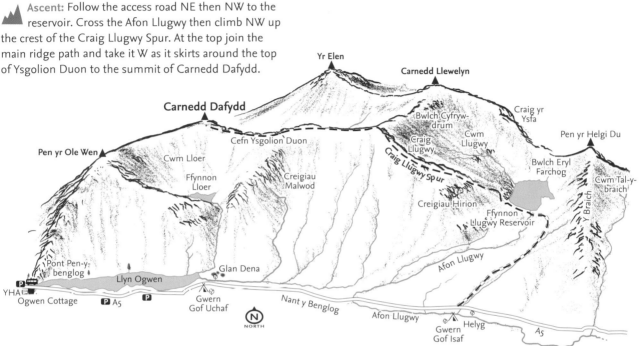

Ffynnon Llugwy Reservoir with the Craig Llugwy Spur on the right

Strenuousness
●●●○○

Navigation
●●●○○

Technicality
●●●○○

A5 at the start of the reservoir access road, GR SH687602

3 hours
6km
(3.7 miles)

780m
(2556ft)

Major valley, high corrie, steep ridge, high mountain ridge and exposed summit

Glyder Fawr

1000m (3281ft)

Glyder Fach 994m (3261ft)

Glyder Fawr is the major peak of the Glyders massif. It occupies a central position between the Ogwen Valley to the north and the Llanberis Pass to the south. Falling into the Llanberis Pass, its slopes for the most part are convex and featureless, the only significant crags lying at their base. To the north the story is reversed; the slopes are concave with deeply indented corries, ringed by crags and ridges, forming a significant wall at the top.

The north-facing crags and ridges of the Glyders are justifiably famous. They run the entire length of the Ogwen Valley in a complex series of hanging corries at varying levels. The crags, in particular those of Cwm Idwal, give a good selection of middle-grade climbs – a walk past the base of Idwal Slabs in the summer months will usually see climbers queueing to get onto climbs. Walkers, with good reason, head for Bristly Ridge and Y Gribin Ridge.

When you arrive

Ordnance Survey: Explorer OL17 (1:25 000); Landranger 115 (1:50 000).
Harvey Mountain Maps: Snowdonia North (1:25 000)
British Mountain Maps: Snowdonia (1:40 000)

Tourist Information Centres: Caernarfon; Llanberis; Betws-y-Coed; Bangor.

Youth Hostels: Llanberis Pass: *Pen-y-pass*; Llanberis; Ogwen Valley: *Idwal Cottage*; Capel Curig.
Hotels and B&B: Nantgwryd: *Pen-y-Gwryd Hotel*; Nant Peris; Llanberis; Bethesda; Ogwen Valley; Capel Curig.
Camp sites: Llanberis Pass: *Nant Peris, Gwastadnant*; Llanberis: *Deiniolen*; Bethesda: *Ogwen Bank*; Ogwen Valley: *Gwern Gof Uchaf*; Capel Curig.

The best way to tackle these two fine ridges is by ascending Bristly Ridge, the harder of the two, then descending Y Gribin Ridge. This fine circuit can be completed without too much effort, and takes in some superb scrambling set against a backdrop of ever-changing scenery.

Surprisingly for such a popular mountain with easy access, it is not difficult to find solitude on Glyder Fawr. Once away from the wide paths of Cwm Idwal and Cwm Bochlwyd you can usually avoid other people until the main ridge is gained, particularly if you aim for the more secluded corries such as Cwm Cneifio or Cwm Tryfan.

Having been less affected by glaciation, the southern slopes of the Glyders look rather bland; only from Pont y Gromlech in the Llanberis Pass do they display any dramatic features – in the shape of the crags of Dinas y Gromlech, Garreg Wastad and Clogwyn y Grochan. Above this line of crags most features are lost by the effect of perspective foreshortening. The routes on this side of the Glyders require a certain amount of foresight to embark upon, because not until you are established on them do their qualities become apparent. They each provide interesting going at some point, but their real value lies in their unrivalled views of Snowdon.

Carned Filias

The highest peaks of Wales support numerous arctic-alpine plants. These remnants of the ice age survive in some of the most exposed locations on summits and along high ridges. Most common are purple mountain saxifrage, moss campion, woolly-hair moss and dwarf willow. Not so common is the Snowdon lily: this only occurs in Snowdonia, most notably among the cliffs and rocks of Twll Du (the Devil's Kitchen).

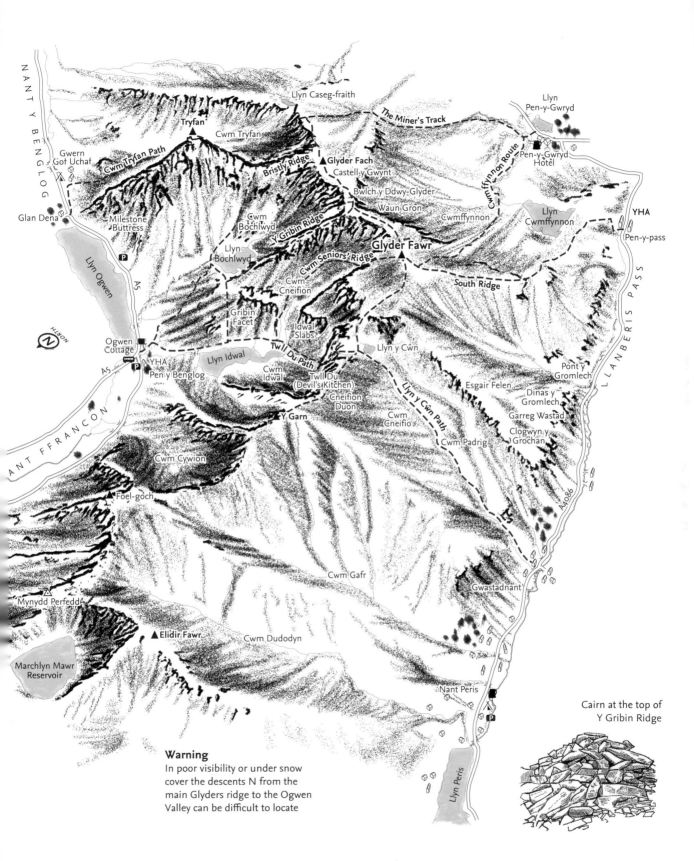

NANT Y BENGLOG

Llyn Caseg-fraith

Llyn Pen-y-Gwryd

The Miner's Track

▲ Tryfan

Cwm Tryfan

Gwern Gof Uchaf

Cwm Tryfan Path

Bristly Ridge

▲ Glyder Fach
Castell y Gwynt

Pen-y-Gwryd Hotel

Cwmffynnon Route

Glan Dena

Milestone Buttress

Cwm Bochlwyd

Y Gribin Ridge

Bwlch y Ddwy-Glyder

Waun Gron

Cwmffynnon

Llyn Cwmffynnon

YHA

Pen-y-pass

Llyn Ogwen

P

A5

Llyn Bochlwyd

Cwm Seniors' Ridge

Glyder Fawr ▲

South Ridge

LLANBERIS PASS

NORTH

Ogwen Cottage

Cwm Cneifion

Gribin Facet

Idwal Slabs

Llyn y Cwn

YHA
Pen y Benglog

P

A5

Llyn Idwal

Twll Du Path

Cwm Idwal

Twll Du (Devil's Kitchen)
Cneifion Duon

Llyn y Cwn Path

Pont y Gromlech

Esgair Felen

Dinas y Gromlech

▲ Y Garn

Cwm Cneifio

Garreg Wastad

Clogwyn y Grochan

NANT FFRANCON

Cwm Padrig

Cwm Cywion

▲ Foel-goch

A4086

Cwm Gafr

Gwastadnant

Mynydd Perfedd

▲ Elidir Fawr

Cwm Dudodyn

Marchlyn Mawr Reservoir

Nant Peris

P

Warning

In poor visibility or under snow cover the descents N from the main Glyders ridge to the Ogwen Valley can be difficult to locate

Llyn Peris

Cairn at the top of Y Gribin Ridge

South Ridge GLYDER FAWR

'Direct but steep'

Summary: Viewed from Pen-y-pass, the South Ridge of Glyder Fawr looks like a bit of a slog and a little unappealing. However, this view is misleading for although it is steep, the walking is always interesting and the views are magnificent – particularly looking down Llanberis Pass.

Ascent: Leave the A4086 on the left side of the youth hostel and climb the path as it zigzags NE onto the low spur. On the spur turn R and climb the South Ridge first NW then N, and finally NE onto the summit slopes of Glyder Fawr.

Descent: From the summit rocks head SW down to the top of the South Ridge (this can be difficult in poor visibility as the ridge is rounded and difficult to identify) then turn S to descend the ridge. Midway down the ridge, crags fringe its west side; these are avoided by turning SE and heading straight down towards the low spur on the north side of Pen-y-pass. From the crest of the spur turn R and zigzag SW down to the A4086.

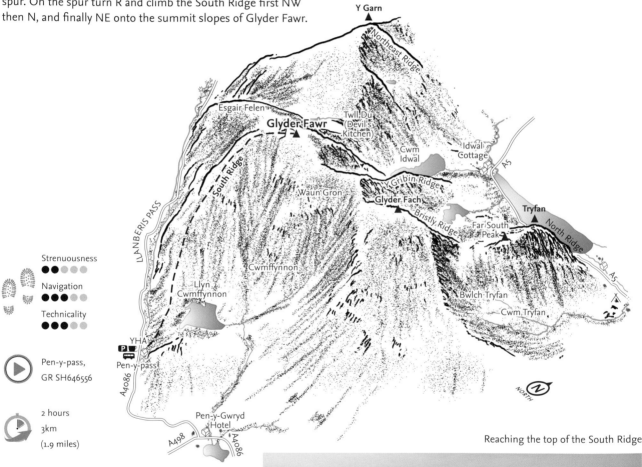

Strenuousness
●●○○○

Navigation
●●●○○

Technicality
●●●○○

Pen-y-pass,
GR SH646556

2 hours
3km
(1.9 miles)

660m
(2165ft)

Low rocky ridge, shallow col, broad steep ridge, rock outcrops and rocky summit

The main ridge can also be gained from Cwmffynnon

Reaching the top of the South Ridge

Y Garn Link GLYDER FAWR

'Dramatic' ★ ★

Summary: The ridge between Glyder Fawr and Y Garn involves a fair amount of height loss with the dip down to the broad col occupied by Llyn y Cŵn. The paths are good though, and the views excellent – particularly down into Cwm Clyd from the final ascent to Y Garn.

Route: Head NW then N down the steep slopes to Llyn y Cŵn. At the north end of the lake cross the outlet stream and take the path that forks R (not the Twll Du Path – that descends NE) and climbs N up the broad stony slopes of Y Garn. The path climbs to the lip of the crags of Cwm Clyd then turns NW to make the final ascent to Y Garn's distinct summit. There are two paths above the lip of Cwm Clyd: under snow cover, or for those who do not appreciate exposure, the higher of the two would be a better choice.

Llyn y Cŵn and Y Garn from Glyder Fawr

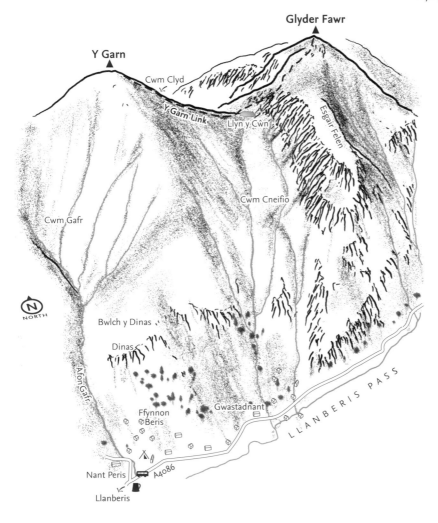

Strenuousness
●●○○○

Navigation
●●●○○

Technicality
●●○○○

Glyder Fawr,
GR SH642579

1 hour
2.5km
(1.6 miles)

230m
(755ft)

High mountain ridge and
mountain lake

Llyn y Cŵn Path GLYDER FAWR

'Relaxed approach with a fine finish' ★

Summary: A pleasant approach via the beautifully situated Llyn y Cŵn on the northwest side of Glyder Fawr. The path up through Cwm Padrig is fairly steep but easy to follow.

Ascent: From the A4086 take the track then path NE to the side of the Afon Las. Continue NE up the path as it climbs alongside the course of the Afon Las, detouring slightly E to avoid the crags by the waterfalls, to arrive at the broad col occupied by Llyn y Cŵn. Walk around the north end of Llyn y Cŵn to the main Glyders ridge path. Join it, and follow it S then SE as it ascends the steep slopes of Glyder Fawr's summit dome.

Descent: Head NW then N down the steep slopes to Llyn y Cŵn. At the north end of the lake cross the outlet stream and take the path that forks L then descends SW alongside the Afon Las into Cwm Padrig. In Cwm Padrig the path detours slightly S then W to avoid the crags adjacent to the waterfalls. Once past the waterfalls continue SW on the good path alongside the Afon Las to join the track to the A4086.

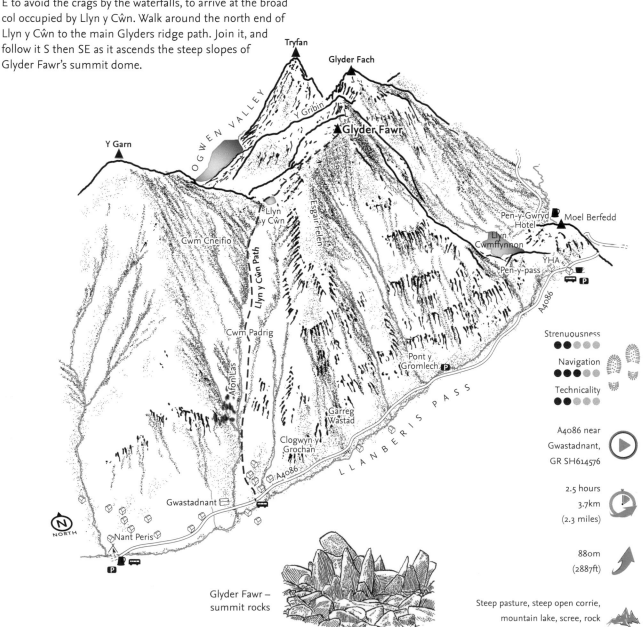

Strenuousness
●●○○○

Navigation
●●●○○

Technicality
●●○○○

A4086 near Gwastadnant, GR SH614576

2.5 hours
3.7km
(2.3 miles)

880m
(2887ft)

Steep pasture, steep open corrie, mountain lake, scree, rock outcrops and rocky summit

Glyder Fawr – summit rocks

LEFT
Castell y Gwynt and Glyder Fawr from Glyder Fach

Twll Du (Devil's Kitchen) Path GLYDER FAWR

'Stunning rock architecture' ★★

Summary: The head of Cwm Idwal is ringed by a series of high towering crags. The likelihood of a walkers' route ascending these great buttresses seems remote, but across the flank of the darkest of these cliffs, Twll Du, is a narrow winding path. It is a handy route to the west side of the main Glyders ridge and passes some awesome rock architecture.

Ascent: From Ogwen Cottage take the Cwm Idwal Path SE then SW to Llyn Idwal. Take the path on the east side of the lake and follow it S past the base of Idwal Slabs then W up the scree path towards Twll Du. At the base of Twll Du, among the boulders, the path swings S and climbs a vague ramp line before turning SW up an open groove. Ascend the groove to reach the broad col occupied by Lyn y Cŵn and join the main Glyders ridge path. Turn L onto it and follow it S, then SE, as it ascends the steep slopes of Glyder Fawr's summit dome.

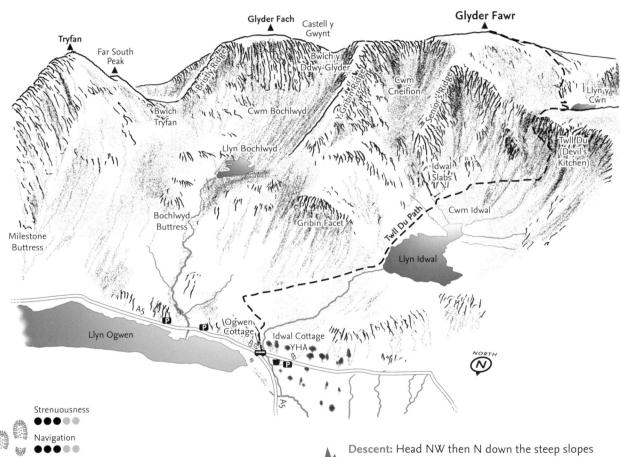

Strenuousness
●●●○○

Navigation
●●●○○

Technicality
●●●●○

▶ Ogwen Cottage (Pen y Benglog), GR SH649603

◆ 705m (2313ft)

⏱ 2.5 hours 3.9km (2.4 miles)

⛰ Broad craggy corrie, mountain lake, scree, crags, stony col, rock outcrops and rocky summit

Descent: Head NW then N down the steep slopes towards Llyn y Cŵn. At the east end of the lake descend NE down the Twll Du Path. It enters an open groove and is followed to the top of a vague ramp line. Descend N down the ramp then at the base of Twll Du follow the scree path as it swings around to the E past Idwal Slabs. Head N and make the steady descent to the north end of Llyn Idwal. Join the Ogwen Cottage Path and follow it NE, then NW, to the buildings and car park at Ogwen Cottage.

Cwm Seniors' Ridge GLYDER FAWR

'Mountaineering challenge' ★★

Summary: Seniors' Ridge divides the remote hanging corrie of Cwm Cneifion from Cwm Idwal. Its broad rocky crest offers a wonderfully remote route up on to the north slopes of Glyder Fawr. The going is adventurous and involves some simple scrambling – the terrain can be confusing so for a first ascent this route is best attempted when visibility is good.

 Ascent: From Ogwen Cottage take the Cwm Idwal Path SE then SW to Llyn Idwal. Take the path on the east side of the lake and follow it S for about 500m (547yd) towards the base of Idwal Slabs until you reach a 'Matterhorn'-shaped boulder. Turn L off the path and climb the steep slopes SE up into Cwm Cneifion. Head SSW across the floor of the corrie then swing SW and gain the ridge on the right-hand side of the corrie. Ascend the ridge's rounded crest (all difficulties can be avoided by short by-passes), which leads to Glyder Fawr's summit slopes. Continue SSW across them to the summit rocks.

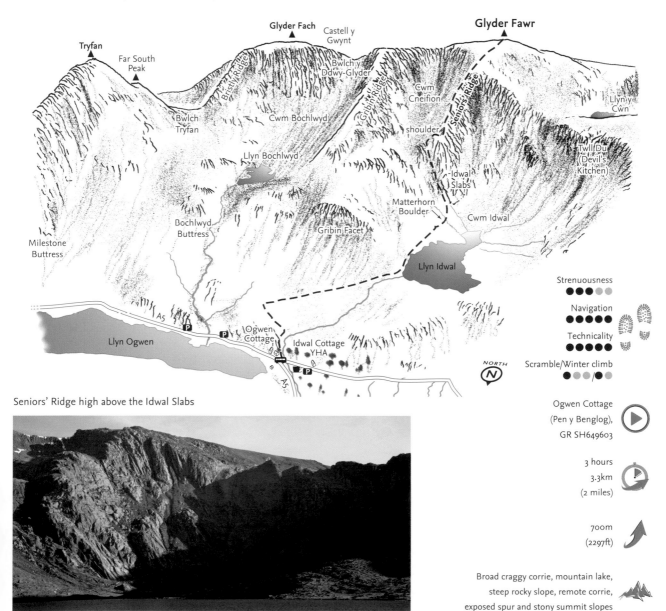

Seniors' Ridge high above the Idwal Slabs

Strenuousness
●●●○○

Navigation
●●●●●

Technicality
●●●●●

Scramble/Winter climb
●●○/●○

Ogwen Cottage
(Pen y Benglog),
GR SH649603

3 hours
3.3km
(2 miles)

700m
(2297ft)

Broad craggy corrie, mountain lake, steep rocky slope, remote corrie, exposed spur and stony summit slopes

Y Gribin Ridge GLYDER FAWR

'Perfect arête' ★ ★ ★

Summary: The elegant Y Gribin Ridge attains the main Glyders ridge midway between Glyder Fawr and Glyder Fach. Poised high above the Ogwen Valley between Cwm Cneifion and Cwm Bochlwyd, it gains height steadily and finishes suitably with a simple scramble – a classic route.

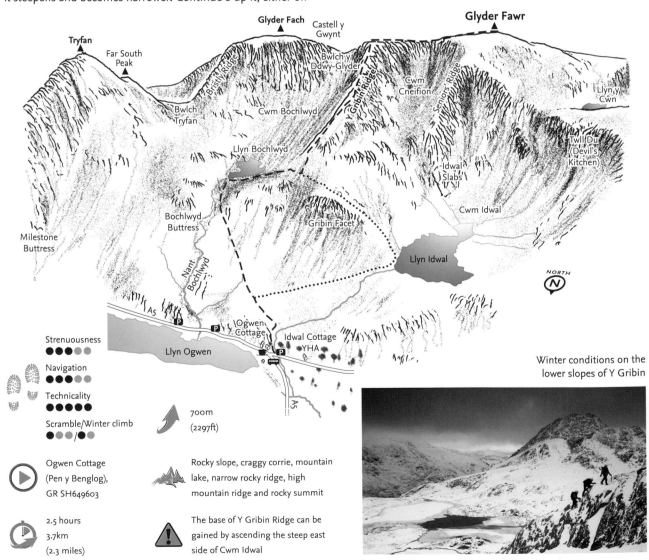

Ascent: From Ogwen Cottage take the Cwm Idwal Path SE to a fork at the first bend. Take the left branch and continue SE to Cwm Bochlwyd. At the north end of Llyn Bochlwyd turn R and climb the path W onto the base of Y Gribin. On the rounded crest turn S and climb directly up the ridge. The ridge climbs steadily to a shoulder after which it steepens and becomes narrower. Continue S up it, either on the crest or more easily on the west (Cwm Cneifion) side to the main Glyders ridge. Turn R and skirt the top of the Cwm Cneifion crags first SW, then WSW, to Glyder Fawr's summit rocks.

Descent: Take the main ridge path ENE then leave it and skirt NE around the top of Cwm Cneifion's crags to the top of Y Gribin Ridge. Scramble N down the ridge, either along its crest or more easily on its west (Cwm Cneifion) side. The gradient of the ridge soon eases; continue N down its crest then turn R and descend E to the north end of Llyn Bochlwyd. At the outlet of Nant Bochlwyd turn L and follow the path N, then NW, down to Ogwen Cottage.

Strenuousness ● ● ● ● ○

Navigation ● ● ● ○ ○

Technicality ● ● ● ● ●

Scramble/Winter climb ● ● ○ ○ / ● ●

700m (2297ft)

Ogwen Cottage (Pen y Benglog), GR SH649603

2.5 hours
3.7km
(2.3 miles)

Rocky slope, craggy corrie, mountain lake, narrow rocky ridge, high mountain ridge and rocky summit

The base of Y Gribin Ridge can be gained by ascending the steep east side of Cwm Idwal

Winter conditions on the lower slopes of Y Gribin

Bristly Ridge GLYDER FAWR

'Challenging scramble' ★★★

Summary: Steep and imposing, the pinnacled crest of Bristly Ridge presents a daunting sight. It is justifiably popular, as it provides an adventurous scramble and serves as a convenient route onto the east end of the main Glyders ridge. Although it is only a Grade 1 scramble its difficulties should not be underestimated as there are a number of harder alternative lines which are easy to wander on to.

Ascent: From Ogwen Cottage take the Cwm Idwal path SE to a fork at the first bend. Take the left branch and continue SE to Cwm Bochlwyd. Cross the Nant Bochlwyd and climb SE to Bwlch Tryfan. At the col, turn R and ascend the scree SW to the mouth of a gully system at the base of Bristly Ridge. Follow the gully, avoiding the difficult sections on the L, to gain the crest of the ridge via a short traverse R (when wet the gully system can be particularly difficult). Follow the crest over the undulations of the pinnacles (all the steep sections can be avoided) to join the main Glyders ridge on the east side of Glyder Fach. Turn R and follow the main ridge path WSW over Glyder Fach and over Bwlch y Ddwy-Glyder to Glyder Fawr.

Descent: The descent of Bristly Ridge is possible, but is best left until experience has been gained with an ascent. An easier descent to Bwlch Tryfan is via the scree path on the east side of Bristly Ridge. From Glyder Fawr take the main ridge ENE over Glyder Fach. As the main path starts its descent E it splits at a fork. Take the left branch which descends the scree NNE around the east side of Bristly Ridge to Bwlch Tryfan. From the col, descend NW and follow the path down to Llyn Bochlwyd. Cross the Nant Bochlwyd and continue NW down to Ogwen Cottage.

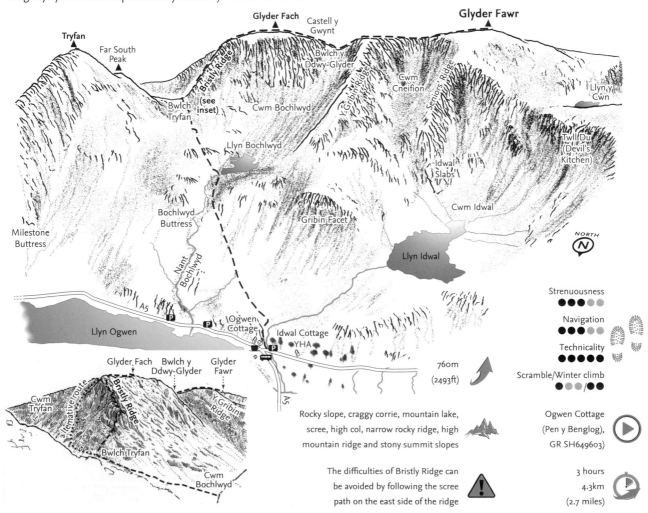

Strenuousness
●●●○○

Navigation
●●●○○

Technicality
●●●●●

Scramble/Winter climb
●●●○○ / ●●

Rocky slope, craggy corrie, mountain lake, scree, high col, narrow rocky ridge, high mountain ridge and stony summit slopes

The difficulties of Bristly Ridge can be avoided by following the scree path on the east side of the ridge

Ogwen Cottage (Pen y Benglog), GR SH649603)

3 hours
4.3km
(2.7 miles)

760m (2493ft)

Tryfan Link GLYDER FAWR

'Illogically entertaining' ★

Summary: It is usual to climb Tryfan first and then continue on to the main Glyders ridge. Doing it in reverse goes slightly against the grain, particularly in relation to the best of the scrambling, but nevertheless it provides an entertaining outing.

Route: From Glyder Fawr take the main ridge ENE over Glyder Fach. As the main path starts its descent E, it splits at a fork. Take the left branch which descends the scree NNE around the east side of Bristly Ridge to Bwlch Tryfan. From the col, take the path N up the South Ridge of Tryfan (avoiding the Far South Peak on its west side) and scramble up Tryfan's crest to the summit blocks.

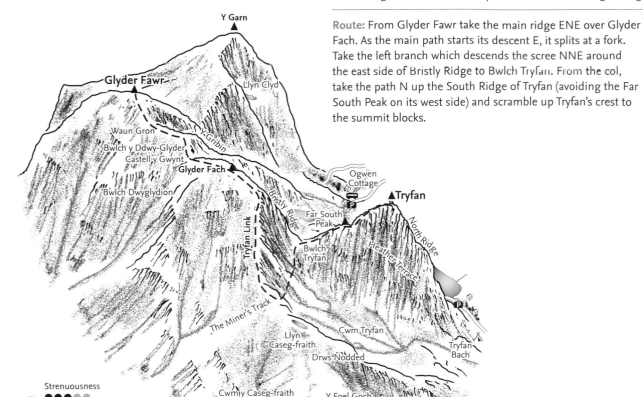

Strenuousness
●●●○○

Navigation
●●●●○

Technicality
●●●●○

▶ Glyder Fawr
GR SH642579

🕐 1.5 hours
3km
(1.9 miles)

260m
(853ft)

High mountain ridge, steep scree,
high col and rocky ridge

Tryfan from The Miner's Track

Cwm Tryfan Path GLYDER FAWR

'Best way to view Tryfan' ★ ★

Summary: A rough corrie in the shadow of Tryfan's impressive east face provides a lonely route to the eastern end of the main Glyders ridge.

Ascent: From the A5 take the track E towards Gwern Gof Uchaf. Before the farm, turn R and head SW towards Tryfan Bach. Pass below the slabs of Tryfan Bach and continue generally SW to enter the rough bounds of Cwm Tryfan. Follow the narrow path as it works its way to the corrie head to join The Miner's Track. Once on it, take it ESE as it climbs to the bleak col at the east side of Glyder Fach. Turn R, off The Miner's Track, and climb W up the moderate grassy slopes to Glyder Fach. Head WSW over the summit of Glyder Fach and over Bwlch y Ddwy-Glyder to Glyder Fawr.

Descent: From Glyder Fawr take the main ridge ENE over Bwlch y Ddwy-Glyder to Glyder Fach then descend E to the bleak col at the head of Cwm Tryfan. Turn L and descend WNW along The Miner's Track into the head of Cwm Tryfan. As The Miner's Track starts to level, it forks. Take the right-hand branch and follow it NNE and along the corrie floor to Tryfan Bach. Pass the slabs of Tryfan Bach and head NE towards Gwern Gof Uchaf. Before the farm turn L and take the track W to the A5.

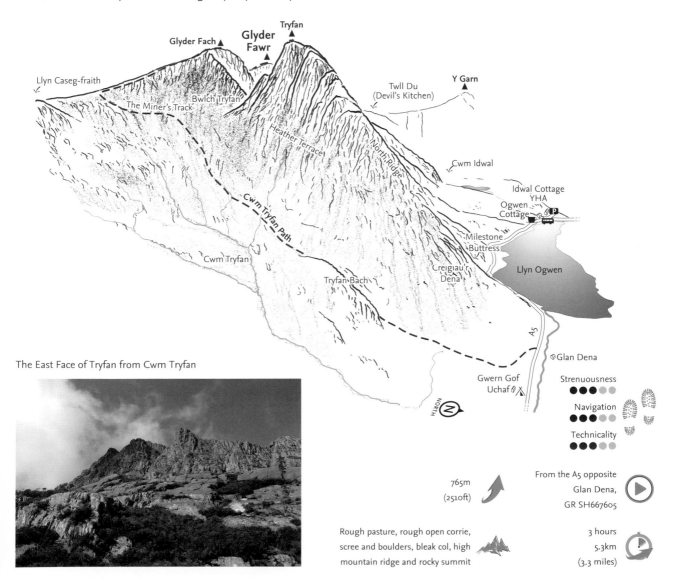

The East Face of Tryfan from Cwm Tryfan

Strenuousness ●●●●○○

Navigation ●●●●○○

Technicality ●●●●○○

765m
(2510ft)

From the A5 opposite
Glan Dena,
GR SH667605

Rough pasture, rough open corrie,
scree and boulders, bleak col, high
mountain ridge and rocky summit

3 hours
5.3km
(3.3 miles)

The Miner's Track GLYDER FAWR

'Efficient height gain' ★★

Summary: Gains the east end of the main Glyders ridge by traversing the gentle southern slopes of Glyder Fach.

Ascent: From the side of the A4086 take the footpath NW to the footbridge. Cross it and follow the path NE as it climbs steadily up the south and east flanks of Glyder Fach. As the crest of the main ridge line is reached, the path levels at a bleak col. Turn L and climb W up the moderate grassy slopes to Glyder Fach. Head WSW over the summit of Glyder Fach and over Bwlch y Ddwy-Glyder to Glyder Fawr.

Descent: From Glyder Fawr take the main ridge ENE over Bwlch y Ddwy-Glyder to Glyder Fach then descend E to the bleak col at the head of Cwm Tryfan. Turn R and descend S then SW to the footbridge across the Nant Gwryd. Once across it, head SE to the A4086.

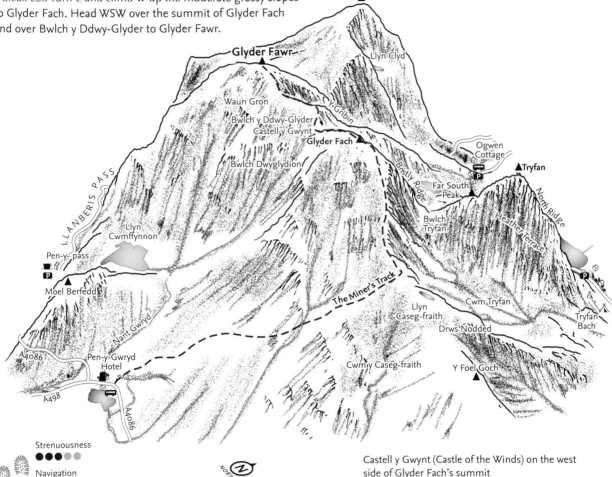

Strenuousness
●●●○○

Navigation
●●●○○

Technicality
●●●○○

 A4086 near the Pen-y-Gwryd Hotel, GR SH660559

795m (2680ft)

 3 hours 5.6km (3.5 miles)

Open rocky mountainside, bleak col, high mountain ridge and rocky summit

Castell y Gwynt (Castle of the Winds) on the west side of Glyder Fach's summit

Cwmffynnon Route GLYDER FAWR

'Steep slog'

Summary: Climbs direct to Glyder Fawr from Pen-y-Gwryd via the steep head walk of the wild Cwmffynnon.

Ascent: From the side of the A4086 take the footpath NW to the footbridge. Cross it and follow the Nant Gwryd NW then W into Cwmffynnon. From the corrie floor turn NW again and climb the headwall via the vague gully line (Heather Gully). At the top continue NW up the summit dome to Glyder Fawr.

Pen-y-Gwryd Hotel, made famous as the training base for numerous Everest expeditions

Strenuousness

Navigation

Technicality

 715m (2346ft)

A4086 near the Pen-y-Gwryd Hotel, GR SH660559

Extensive open corrie, steep grass and heather-covered headwall and stony summit

2 hours
3.1km
(1.9 miles)

Y Garn

947m (3107ft)

Although Cwm Idwal is more closely linked to Glyder Fawr, viewed from its wide corrie floor Y Garn looks by far the more prominent of the two peaks. This is due in part to Glyder Fawr's summit dome being hidden by the foreshortening effect of its steep, craggy north face but also because Y Garn has such a distinct profile. Elegant and angular with four faces its shape is an almost perfect pyramid. The two Ogwen Valley faces with their colder north and east aspects hold shallow ice-carved corries while on the Llanberis side the south and west faces fall away in long unbroken slopes.

Y Garn's most striking feature is its long Northeast Ridge. It descends towards the mouth of Cwm Idwal between the hanging corries Cwm Cywion and Cwm Clyd. Climbing the spine of this lofty arête is a fine undertaking, particularly with a covering of snow, when it is endowed with an almost alpine quality.

The most popular approaches to Y Garn are either along the main ridge or from the Ogwen Valley via the impressive but well-worn Twll Du Path. This is predictable because of the popularity of completing the main Glyders ridge and because of the honey-pot attraction of Ogwen Cottage. However, this is rather unfortunate as these two approaches neglect some of Y Garn's finer aspects.

The southern approaches from Nant Peris and the Llanberis Pass provide moderately steep walks, first through pasture and woodland, then through pleasant open corries. Once on the cols, expansive views of starkly contrasting terrain open out on either side of Y Garn. The other northern option apart from the Northeast Ridge is the remote and lonely Cwm Cywion. Considering its close proximity to the crowds of Cwm Idwal its pleasant solitude will come as a welcome surprise.

When you arrive

Ordnance Survey: Explorer OL17 (1:25 000); Landranger 115 (1:50 000).

Harvey Mountain Maps: Snowdonia North (1:25 000)

British Mountain Maps: Snowdonia (1:40 000)

Tourist Information Centres: Caernarfon; Llanberis; Betws-y-Coed; Bangor.

Youth Hostels: Llanberis Pass: *Pen-y-pass*; Llanberis; Ogwen Valley: *Idwal Cottage*; Capel Curig.

Hotels and B&B: Nantgwryd: *Pen-y-Gwryd Hotel*; Nant Peris; Llanberis; Bethesda; Ogwen Valley; Capel Curig.

Camp sites: Llanberis Pass: *Nant Peris, Gwastadnant*; Llanberis: *Deiniolen*; Bethesda: *Ogwen Bank*; Ogwen Valley: *Gwern Gof Uchaf*; Capel Curig.

Y Garn from Glyder Fawr

Warning
In poor visibility or under snow cover the descents N from Y Garn to the Ogwen Valley can be difficult to locate

Carnedd y Filiast

Mynydd Perfedd

Marchlyn Mawr Reservoir

Bwlch y Brecan

Bwlch y Marchlyn

Elidir Fawr

Elidir Fawr Link

NANT FFRANCON

N NORTH

Afon Ogwen

OGWEN VALLEY

Pont Pen-y-benglog

YHA

Llyn Ogwen

Tryfan

Cwm Cywion

Cwm Cywion Route

Cwm Gwion

Northeast Ridge

Idwal Cottage

Llyn Bochlwyd

Y Garn

Cwm Clyd

Cwm Dudodyn

Cwm Gafr

Esgair y Ceunant

Cwm Gafr Path

Southwest Ridge

Llyn Idwal

Twll Du Path

Glyder Fach

Twll Du (Devil's Kitchen)

Llyn y Cwn

Glyder Fawr Link

Glyder Fawr

Afon Dudodyn

Afon Gafr

Cwm Cneifio

Llyn y Cwn Path

Waun Gron

Esgair Felen

Cwm Padrig

Bryn Du

Cwmffynnon

Nant Peris

Llyn Cwmffynnon

Gwastadnant

Dinas y Gromlech

Pont y Gromlech

YHA

Pen-y-pass

Afon Nant Peris

LLANBERIS PASS

Llyn y Cŵn Path Y GARN

'Pleasant and direct' ★

Summary: A pleasant approach via the beautifully situated Llyn y Cŵn on the southeast side of Y Garn. The path up through Cwm Padrig is fairly steep but easy to follow.

Ascent: From the A4086 take the track then the path NE to the side of the Afon Las. Continue NE up the path as it climbs alongside the course of the Afon Las, detouring slightly E to avoid the crags by the waterfalls to arrive at a broad col occupied by Llyn y Cŵn. Walk to the north end of Llyn y Cŵn, then as the path splits take the left fork and follow it N up the broad stony slopes of Y Garn. The path climbs to the lip of the crags of Cwm Clyd then turns NW to make the final ascent to Y Garn's distinct summit. There are two paths above the lip of Cwm Clyd: under snow cover, or for those who do not appreciate exposure, the higher of the two would be a better choice.

Descent: Take the path which descends SE and follow it as it skirts the crags then turns SSE down the broad stony slopes to Llyn y Cŵn. At the north end of the lake turn R and follow the path which descends SW alongside the Afon Las into Cwm Padrig. In Cwm Padrig the path detours slightly S then W to avoid the crags adjacent to the waterfalls. Once past the waterfalls continue SW on the good path alongside the Afon Las to join the track to the A4086.

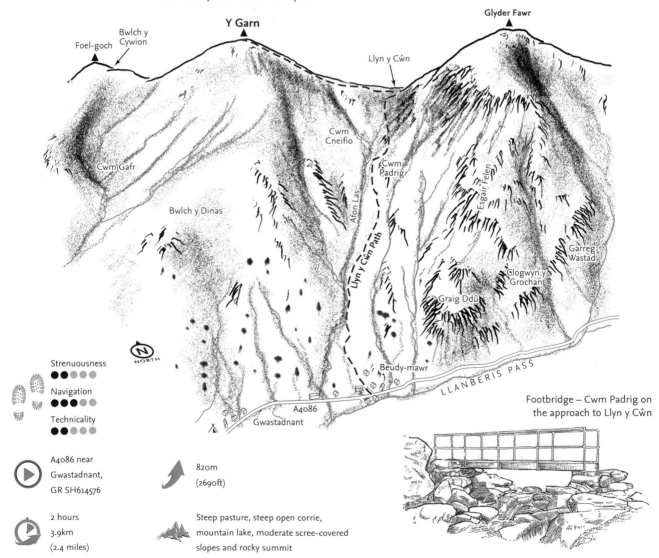

Footbridge – Cwm Padrig on the approach to Llyn y Cŵn

Strenuousness ●●○○○

Navigation ●●●○○

Technicality ●●○○○

A4086 near Gwastadnant, GR SH614576

820m (2690ft)

2 hours
3.9km
(2.4 miles)

Steep pasture, steep open corrie, mountain lake, moderate scree-covered slopes and rocky summit

Cwm Gafr Path Y GARN

'Best in descent'

Summary: Cwm Gafr is the steep open corrie high above Nant Peris on the west side of Y Garn. The path through it provides the most direct route to Y Garn from Nant Peris.

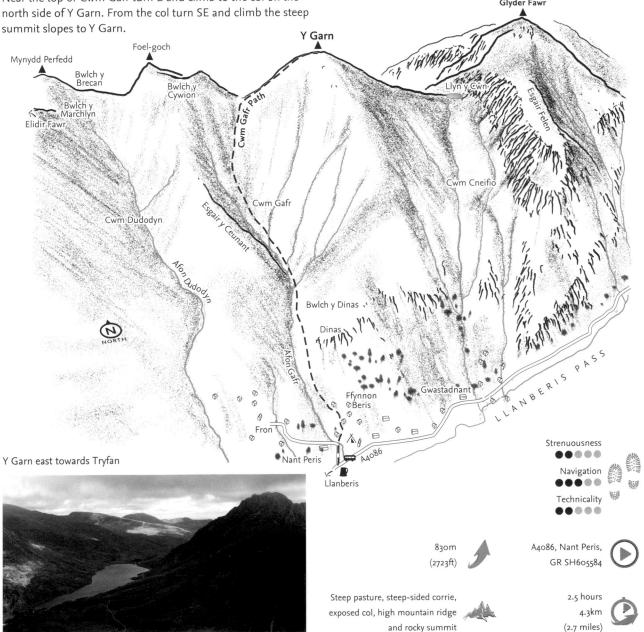

Ascent: From Nant Peris take the lane NE. At the sharp left-hand bend join the Cwm Gafr Path and follow it as it winds E through the buildings then NE up through Cwm Gafr. Near the top of Cwm Gafr turn E and climb to the col on the north side of Y Garn. From the col turn SE and climb the steep summit slopes to Y Garn.

Descent: Head NW from the summit rocks skirting the crags of Cwm Cywion down to the col on the northwest side of Y Garn. From the col descend the steep grassland W to join the vague path on the southeast side of Afon Gafr. Follow the path SE the length of Cwm Gafr, then W as it winds its way through the buildings to the lane. Join the lane and follow it SW a short distance to the A4086 in Nant Peris.

Glyder Fawr

Y Garn

Foel-goch

Mynydd Perfedd

Bwlch y Brecan

Bwlch y Cywion

Llyn y Cwn

Esgair Felen

Bwlch y Marchlyn

Elidir Fawr

Cwm Gafr Path

Cwm Cneifio

Cwm Dudodyn

Esgair y Ceunant

Cwm Gafr

Afon Dudodyn

NORTH

Bwlch y Dinas

Dinas

Afon Gafr

LLANBERIS PASS

Gwastadnant

Ffynnon Beris

Fron

Nant Peris

A4086

Llanberis

Y Garn east towards Tryfan

Strenuousness ●●○○○

Navigation ●●●●○

Technicality ●●○○○

830m
(2723ft)

A4086, Nant Peris,
GR SH605584

Steep pasture, steep-sided corrie,
exposed col, high mountain ridge
and rocky summit

2.5 hours
4.3km
(2.7 miles)

Elidir Fawr Link Y GARN

'Exciting ridge walk' ★★

Summary: Pleasant high-level walk between two fine mountains. The classic approach to Elidir Fawr when completing the 'Welsh 3000-ers'.

Route: Head NW from the summit rocks skirting the crags of Cwm Cywion down to the col on the northwest side of Y Garn. From the col, head generally N along the main ridge path then W around the head of Cwm Dudodyn to Bwlch y Marchlyn. From the col climb the steep narrow ridge WSW to the summit of Elidir Fawr.

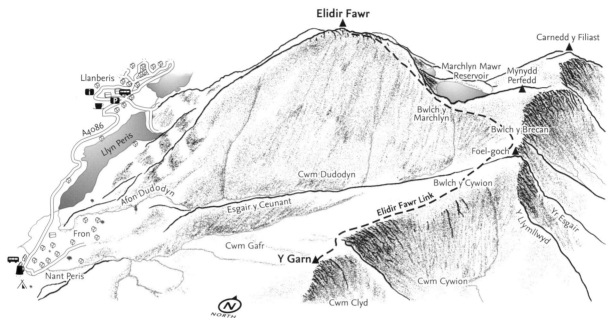

Strenuousness
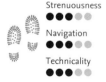
●●●○○

Navigation
●●●○○

Technicality
●●●○○

Y Garn,
GR SH631596

1 hour
3.7km
(2.3 miles)

240m
(787ft)

High mountain ridge, exposed col and narrow summit ridge

Foel-goch and Y Garn from Mynydd Perfedd

Southwest Ridge Y GARN

'Great views in descent'

Summary: Useful as a descent, the Southwest Ridge offers a direct route down to the Llanberis side of Y Garn.

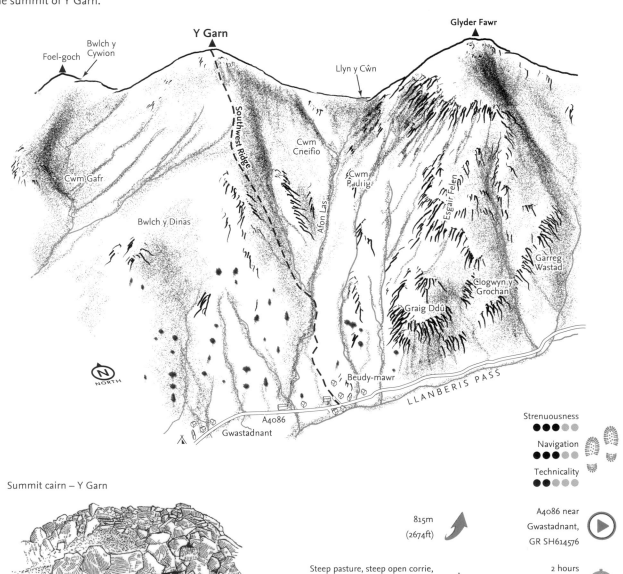

Ascent: From the A4086 take the track then path NE to the side of the Afon Las. Continue NE up the path as it climbs alongside the course of the Afon Las, detouring slightly E to avoid the crags by the waterfalls. Once above the waterfalls cross the Afon Las and climb N up the steep slopes onto the rounded crest of the Southwest Ridge. On the ridge climb NW to the summit of Y Garn.

Descent: Head SW from the summit rocks down the rounded ridge, then turn S and descend the steep slopes into Cwm Padrig. Cross the Afon Las and join the path on the southeast side. Descend the path as it detours slightly S then W to avoid the crags adjacent to the waterfalls. Once past the waterfalls continue SW on the good path alongside the Afon Las to join the track to the A4086.

Summit cairn – Y Garn

Strenuousness

Navigation

Technicality

815m
(2674ft)

A4086 near
Gwastadnant,
GR SH614576

Steep pasture, steep open corrie,
mountain lake, scree, rock
outcrops and rocky summit

2 hours
2.9km
(1.8 miles)

Cwm Cywion Route Y GARN

'Wild corrie' ★★

Summary: The remote and little-visited Cwm Cywion, perched high on the north side of Y Garn, provides a quiet alternative approach away from the crowds found on the more popular Ogwen Valley routes.

Ascent: From Ogwen Cottage take the Cwm Idwal Path SE then SW to Llyn Idwal. Cross the footbridge at the northeast end of the lake and follow the vague path that snakes up to the base of the Northeast Ridge of Y Garn. Before the base of the ridge is reached leave the path and contour round the steep slopes NW into Cwm Cywion. Continue NW up through Cwm Cywion to Llyn Cywion then ascend the headwall, still generally NW, to Bwlch y Cywion. Cross the col and make the short descent to join the path on the southwest side of Foel-goch. Turn L on the path and follow it S then SE to the summit rocks of Y Garn.

Descent: Head NW from the summit rocks skirting the crags of Cwm Cywion down to the col on the northwest side of Y Garn. From the col, head generally N along the main ridge path, then on the southwest side of Foel-goch make the short ascent E to Bwlch y Cywion. Cross the col and make the steep descent SE to Llyn Cywion. Continue descending SE through Cwm Cywion and contour around to the bottom of the Northeast Ridge of Y Garn. At the base of the ridge join the vague path and follow it ESE to the footbridge at the northeast end of Llyn Idwal. Cross it and join the Ogwen Cottage Path which is followed NE then NW to the buildings and car park at Ogwen Cottage.

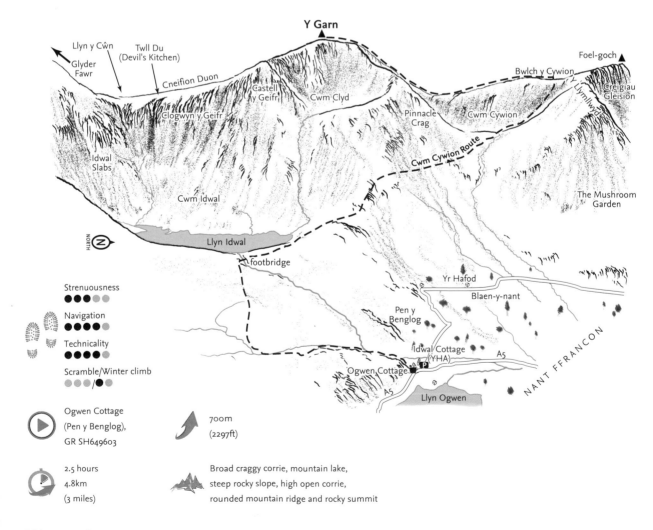

Strenuousness ●●●●○

Navigation ●●●●○

Technicality ●●●●○

Scramble/Winter climb ●●●○/●●○

▶ Ogwen Cottage (Pen y Benglog), GR SH649603

700m (2297ft)

2.5 hours
4.8km
(3 miles)

Broad craggy corrie, mountain lake, steep rocky slope, high open corrie, rounded mountain ridge and rocky summit

Northeast Ridge Y GARN

'The perfect ridge' ★ ★ ★

Summary: A superb knife-edge ridge which rears up steeply from the Ogwen Valley direct to Y Garn's summit rocks.

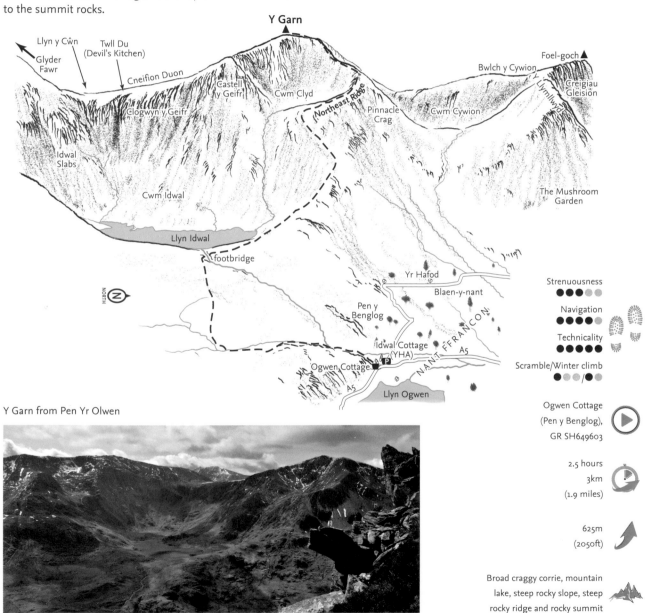

Ascent: From Ogwen Cottage take the Cwm Idwal Path SE then SW to Llyn Idwal. Cross the footbridge at the northeast end of the lake and follow the vague path which snakes W up the hillside to the base of the Northeast Ridge. Continue along the path as it climbs the crest of the ridge SW to Y Garn's summit ridge. At the top turn L and head S to the summit rocks.

Descent: Head N from the summit rocks to the top of the Northeast Ridge. Descend directly down the crest of the ridge, then at the base follow the vague path that snakes E to the footbridge at the northeast end of Llyn Idwal. Cross it and join the Ogwen Cottage Path which is followed NE then NW to the buildings and car park at Ogwen Cottage.

Y Garn from Pen Yr Olwen

Strenuousness
● ● ● ○ ○

Navigation
● ● ● ● ○

Technicality
● ● ● ● ●

Scramble/Winter climb
● ○ ○ / ● ○

Ogwen Cottage
(Pen y Benglog),
GR SH649603

2.5 hours
3km
(1.9 miles)

625m
(2050ft)

Broad craggy corrie, mountain lake, steep rocky slope, steep rocky ridge and rocky summit

Glyder Fawr Link Y GARN

'Steep but rewarding' ★★

Summary: The ridge between Y Garn and Glyder Fawr involves a fair amount of height loss with the dip down to the broad col occupied by Llyn y Cŵn. The paths are good though and the views excellent – particularly of the main Glyders massif and across Llanberis Pass towards Snowdon.

Route: Take the path which descends SE and follow it as it skirts the crags then turns SSE down the broad stony slopes to Llyn y Cŵn. At the north end of the lake cross the outlet stream and follow the path ESE then S and finally SE as it ascends the steep slopes of Glyder Fawr's summit dome.

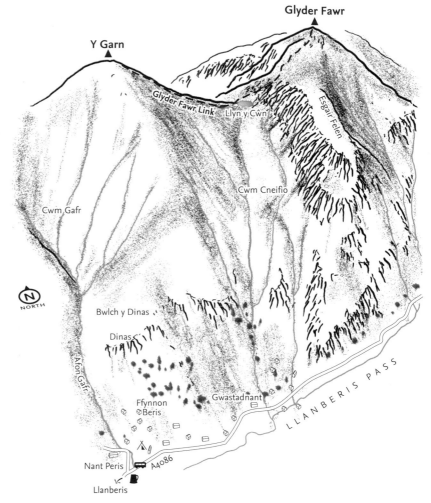

Strenuousness
●●○○○

Navigation
●●●○○

Technicality
●●○○○

Y Garn,
GR SH631596

1 hour
2.4km
(1.5 miles)

280m
(918ft)

High mountain ridge and mountain lake

Llyn y Cŵn

Twll Du (Devil's Kitchen) Path Y GARN

'Stunning rock architecture' ★★

Summary: The head of Cwm Idwal is ringed by a series of high towering crags. The likelihood of a walkers' route ascending these great buttresses seems remote but across the flank of the darkest of these cliffs, Twll Du, is a narrow winding path. It is a handy route to the broad col on the southwest side of Y Garn.

Ascent: From Ogwen Cottage take the Cwm Idwal Path SE then SW to Llyn Idwal. Take the path on the east side of the lake and follow it S past the base of Idwal Slabs then W up the scree path towards Twll Du. At the base of Twll Du, among the boulders, the path swings S and climbs a vague ramp line before turning SW up an open groove. Ascend the groove to reach the broad col occupied by Llyn y Cŵn. At the east end of Llyn y Cŵn the path splits; take the right-hand branch and follow it WNW over the outlet stream to another fork. Again take the right-hand branch and follow it N up the broad stony slopes of Y Garn. The path climbs to the lip of the crags of Cwm Clyd then turns NW to make the final ascent to Y Garn's distinct summit. There are two paths above the lip of Cwm Clyd: under snow cover, or for those who do not appreciate exposure, the higher of the two would be a better choice.

Descent: Take the path which descends SE and follow it as it skirts the crags then turns SSE down the broad stony slopes to Llyn y Cŵn. At the north end of the lake cross the outlet stream and turn ESE to a fork. Take the left branch and descend NE down the Twll Du Path. The path enters an open groove and is followed to the top of a vague ramp line. Descend N down the ramp, then at the base of Twll Du follow the scree path as it swings round to the east and passes the base of Idwal Slabs. Head N and make the steady descent to the north end of Llyn Idwal. Join the Ogwen Cottage Path and follow it NE then NW to the buildings and car park at Ogwen Cottage.

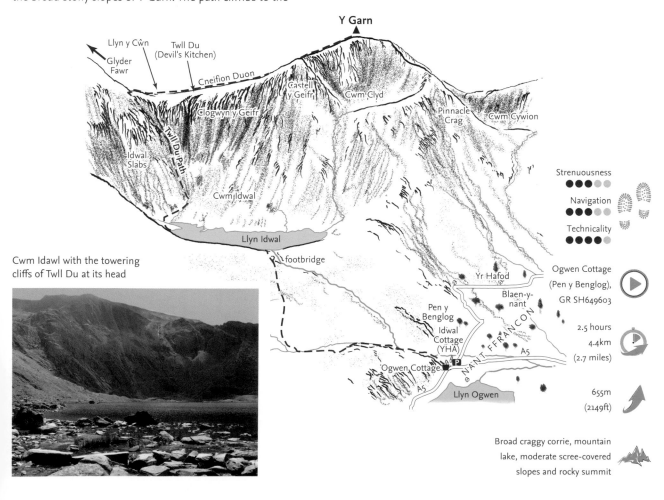

Cwm Idawl with the towering cliffs of Twll Du at its head

Strenuousness ●●●●○

Navigation ●●●○○

Technicality ●●●●○

Ogwen Cottage (Pen y Benglog), GR SH649603

2.5 hours
4.4km
(2.7 miles)

655m
(2149ft)

Broad craggy corrie, mountain lake, moderate scree-covered slopes and rocky summit

Foel-fras

942m (3091ft)

The smooth rounded form of Foel-fras at the northern end of the Carneddau is a welcome sight for walkers completing the 'Welsh 3000-ers'. Its boulder-strewn summit marks the start of the final leg of this long expedition. Any walker thinking they are in for an easy descent, though, will be in for a little shock, for like the other peaks in the Carneddau, it is a long way from anywhere.

Apart from the dark brooding cliffs of Craig y Dulyn and Craig-fawr, the terrain of Foel-fras is of a gentle nature displaying a grandeur derived from subtle changes in shape rather than from individual eye-catching features. On the northwest side, the Aber side, the valleys of the Afon Anafon and Afon Goch are separated by the long ridge of Llwytmor. To the southeast, the Conwy Valley side, grassy slopes fall away steeply, interrupted only by fast-flowing streams and the occasional minor rock outcrop, to the waters of the Afon Dulyn.

For those seeking an adventurous approach to Foel-fras there is really only one option: the spur extending east from the subsidiary top Foel Grach. It climbs high between Cwm Dulyn and Craig-fawr and involves some simple scrambling. The other routes up Foel-fras follow uncomplicated lines over ground which requires stamina, rather than agility, and the ability to navigate with few landmarks.

When you arrive

Ordnance Survey: Explorer OL17 (1:25 000); Landranger 115 (1:50 000).

Harvey Mountain Maps: Snowdonia North (1:25 000)

British Mountain Maps: Snowdonia (1:40 000)

Tourist Information Centres: Llanberis; Bangor; Llanfairfechan; Betws-y-Coed.

Youth Hostels: Ogwen Valley: *Idwal Cottage*; Rowen: *Rhiw Farm*; Capel Curig.

Hotels and B&B: Capel Curig; Bethesda; Ogwen Valley; Aber; Llanfairfechan; Tal-y-Bont; Betws-y-Coed; Capel Curig.

Camp sites: Capel Curig; Ogwen Valley: *Gwern Gof Uchaf*; Bethesda: *Ogwen Bank*; Betws-y-Coed.

The summit rocks and trig point of Foel-fras

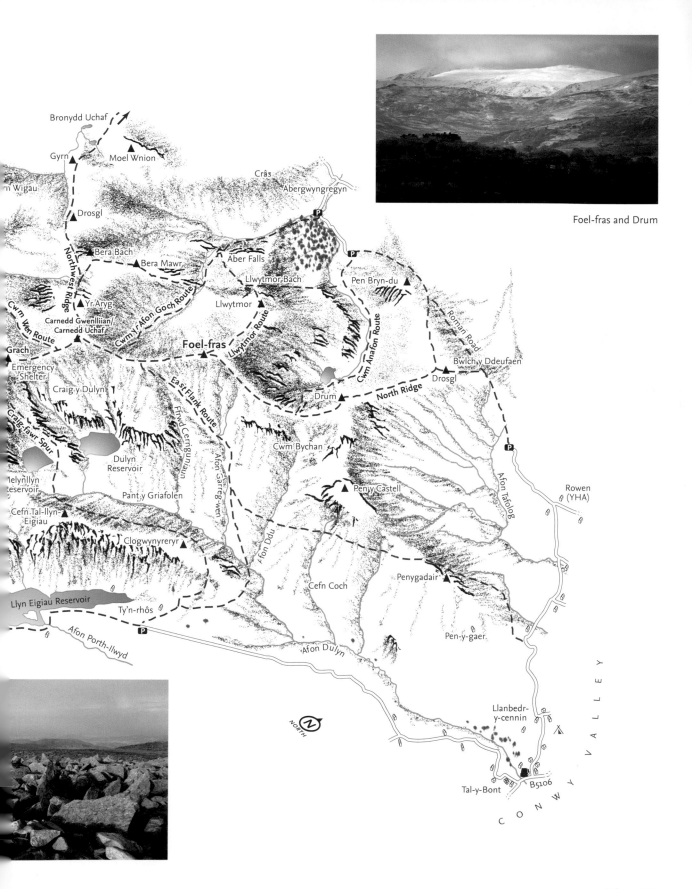

Bronydd Uchaf

Gyrn ▲
Moel Wnion ▲

n Wigau

Cràs

Abergwyngregyn

Drosgl ▲

Bera Bach ▲
Bera Mawr ▲
Aber Falls

Llwytmor Bach

Pen Bryn-du ▲

Yr Aryg ▲

Llwytmor ▲

Carnedd Gwenlliian/
Carnedd Uchaf ▲

Foel-fras ▲

Grach

Emergency
Shelter

Craig y Dulyn

Bwlch y Ddeufaen
Drosgl ▲

Drum ▲

North Ridge

Craig-fawr Spur

Dulyn
Reservoir

Cwm Bychan

Aelynllyn
reservoir

Pant y Griafolen

Cefn Tal-llyn-
Eigiau ▲

Pen y Castell ▲

Clogwynyreryr ▲

Cefn Coch

Penygadair ▲

Llyn Eigiau Reservoir

Ty'n-rhôs

Pen-y-gaer

Afon Porth-llwyd

Afon Dulyn

Rowen
(YHA)

Afon Tafolog

Llanbedr-
y-cennin

NORTH

Tal-y-Bont

B5106

C O N W Y   V A L L E Y

Foel-fras and Drum

Carnedd Llewelyn Link FOEL-FRAS

'Open and elevated' ★

Summary: In good conditions a pleasant stroll along an undulating ridge with fine panoramic views. In poor visibility and with snow cover, it can be a nightmare as the featureless terrain makes navigation difficult.

Route: Head SSW then SW along the main ridge path to Carnedd Gwenllian/Carnedd Uchaf. From the summit turn S and continue along the main ridge path over Foel Grach, then SSW to Carnedd Llewelyn.

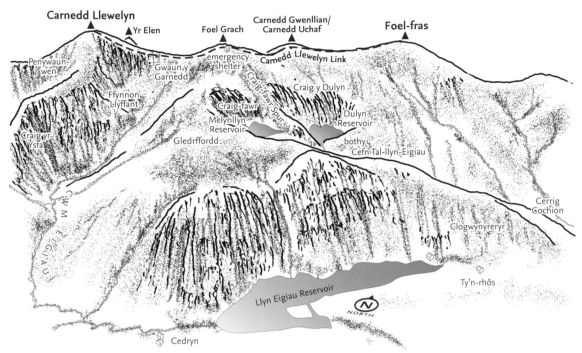

The final pull onto Carnedd Llewelyn

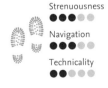

Strenuousness
●●●○○

Navigation
●●●○○

Technicality
●●○○○

Foel-fras,
GR SH696681

1.5 hours
4.25km
(2.6 miles)

255m
(835ft)

High mountain ridge

Cwm Wen Route FOEL-FRAS

'Long steady climb'

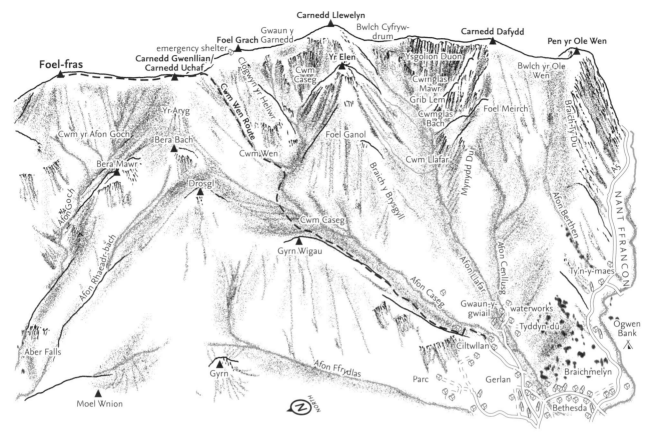

Summary: Follows the course of the Afon Caseg then gains the south side of Foel-fras via the lonely Cwm Wen and the subsidiary top Carnedd Gwenllian/Carnedd Uchaf.

Ascent: Take the access track E then NW as it winds its way round to the pumping station. Pass the pumping station and turn E along the track. After the settlement remains, the track becomes less distinct. Roughly follow the course of the Afon Caseg E, then SE to the mouth of Cwm Wen. Climb E up through the corrie to join the main ridge path at the broad col on the north side of Foel Grach. Head N along it to Carnedd Gwenllian/Carnedd Uchaf then turn NE and follow the broad ridge, finally trending NNE to the summit of Foel-fras.

Descent: Head SSW then SW along the main ridge path to Carnedd Gwenllian/Carnedd Uchaf. From the summit turn S to the broad col at the head of Cwm Wen. Turn R and descend Cwm Wen to gain the north side of the Afon Caseg. Roughly follow its north side NW then W to pick up the access track at the settlement remains. Follow it W to the pumping station, then turn SE along it and finally W to Ciltwllan.

Rock outcrop on Yr Aryg on the Northwest Ridge of Carnedd Uchaf

Strenuousness
●●●○○

Navigation
●●●●○

Technicality
●●●○○

710m
(2329ft)

Ciltwllan on the east side of Bethesda, GR SH637663

Pasture, moorland, steep-sided valley, high remote corrie, and high mountain ridge

3 hours
7.7km
(4.8 miles)

Northwest Ridge (Carnedd Gwenllian/ Carnedd Uchaf) FOEL-FRAS

'Summit collecting walk' ★

Summary: A meandering route over minor summits and up a gentle, grassy ridge to gain the subsidiary top, Carnedd Gwenllian/Carnedd Uchaf, to the southwest of Foel-fras.

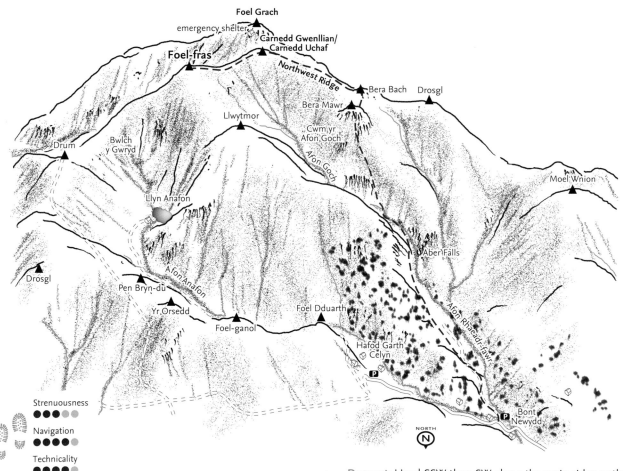

Ascent: From the car park take the Aber Falls track S for 700m (766yd) to a path on the L. Join it and follow it beside the trees to gain the lower section of Cwm yr Afon Goch. Once in the cwm cross the stream and make the climb S to the summit of Bera Mawr. Cross the rocky summit then swing SW to gain Bera Bach. From here climb the rounded crest of the ridge SE to Carnedd Gwenllian/Carnedd Uchaf. From the summit turn NE and follow the broad ridge NE, then NNE to the summit of Foel-fras.

Strenuousness ●●●●○

Navigation ●●●●●

Technicality ●●●●○

 Aber Falls Car Park, GR SH663719

 930m (3051ft)

 3.5 hours 8.1km (5 miles)

 Pasture, moorland, craggy summits, long rounded ridge and high mountain ridge

Descent: Head SSW then SW along the main ridge path to Carnedd Uchaf. From the summit turn R and make the steady descent NW along the rounded crest of the ridge, then trend W to Bera Bach. Turn NW and make for the rocky summit of Bera Mawr. Descend N and pick your way down the blunt rocky ridge to gain the Afon Goch. Cross the Afon Goch and then follow the path on the other side N past Aber Falls and down to the road at the falls car park.

Cwm yr Afon Goch Route FOEL-FRAS

'Isolated and atmospheric' ★

Summary: An interesting route; it samples classic Carneddau scenery. Starts with the delights of the Aber Falls, then the remoteness of Cwm yr Afon Goch and finishes with the high exposed slopes of the main ridge.

Ascent: From the car park take the Aber Falls track S for 700m (766yd) to a path on the L. Join it and follow it beside the trees to gain the lower section of Cwm yr Afon Goch. Follow the Afon Goch generally SE into Cwm yr Afon Goch. Continue SE up the corrie headwall to the col on the southwest side of Foel-fras. Turn L and climb the main ridge path NE then NNE to the summit of Foel-fras.

Descent: From the summit descend SSW then SW to the col at the head of Cwm yr Afon Goch. Descend NW down the headwall then follow the Afon Goch generally NW towards the Aber Falls. Follow the path on the other side (NW) of the Afon Goch, N past Aber Falls and down to the road at the falls car park.

Foel Grach
emergency shelter
Carnedd Gwenllian/
Carnedd Uchaf
Foel-fras
Yr Aryg
Cwm yr Afon Goch Route
Bera Bach
Drosgl
Bera Mawr
Llwytmor
Drum
Bwlch y Gwryd
Cwm yr Afon Goch
Moel Wnion
Llyn Anafon
Marian Rhaeadr-fawr
Aber Falls
Afon Anafon
Drosgl
Afon Rhaeadr-fawr
Pen Bryn-du
Yr Orsedd
Foel Dduarth
Foel-ganol
Hafod Garth Celyn
Bont Newydd
NORTH
N

Aber Falls at the mouth of Cwm yr Afon Goch

Strenuousness
●●●○○

Navigation
●●●●○

Technicality
●●●○○

880m
(2887ft)

Aber Falls Car Park,
GR SH663719

Wooded valley, crags and scree,
steep-sided valley, grassy headwall
and high mountain ridge

3 hours
6.8km
(4.2 miles)

Cwm Anafon Route FOEL-FRAS

'Easy tracked approach'

Summary: Straightforward approach via the reservoir access track then up the moderate headwall of Cwm Anafon to the broad col on the northeast side of Foel-fras. A useful descent route – easy to follow if conditions are bad.

Ascent: Follow the track N then climb the hairpin bend S onto the Llyn Anafon Reservoir access track. Join the track and follow it as it winds its way SE to Llyn Anafon. From the reservoir climb steadily SE to Bwlch y Gwryd. Turn R at the col and take the main ridge path as it climbs SW up the curving ridge to Foel-fras.

Descent: Head NE down the curving ridge to Bwlch y Gwryd. At the col turn L and drop down into Cwm Anafon. From the northeast side of Llyn Anafon join the reservoir access track as it winds generally NW down Cwm Anafon. As it contours the steep flanks of Foel Dduarth the track forks. Take the left branch and follow the hairpin bend round to the road head and car park.

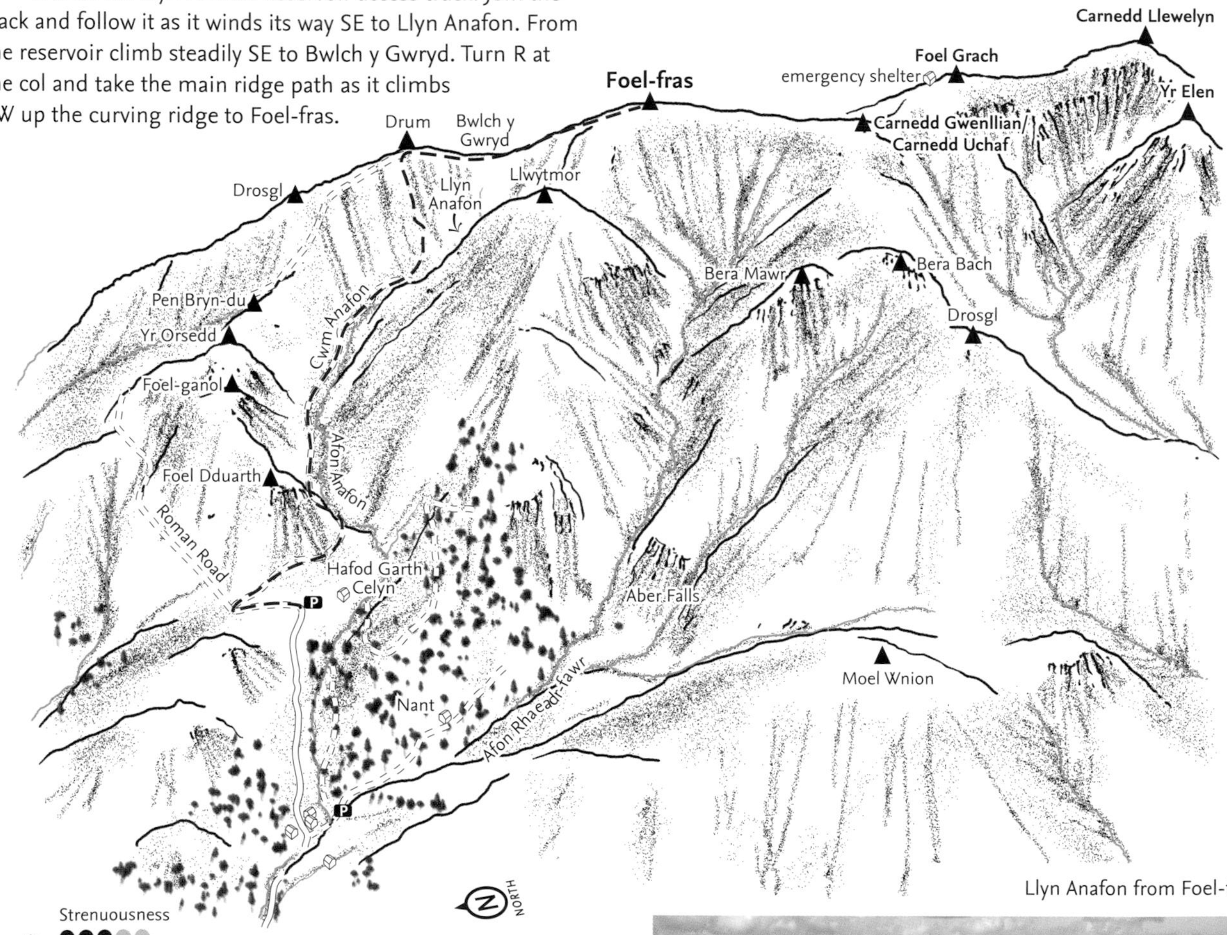

Llyn Anafon from Foel-fras

Strenuousness ●●●○○

Navigation ●●●○○

Technicality ●●○○○

Car park at the top of the minor road, GR SH675715

805m (2641ft)

3 hours
6.7km
(4.2 miles)

Wooded valley, steep-sided valley, open corrie, steep grassy ridge and exposed summit

East Flank Route FOEL-FRAS

'Long and pathless'

Summary: Ascends the east flank of Foel-fras in a long traverse to gain the main ridge at the col on the southwest side of Foel-fras's summit dome. Generally good going although the top section is a little vague and can be awkward to locate when trying to descend from the main ridge.

Ascent: Follow the track, then path, SW across the flanks of Penygadair, Pen y Castell and finally Foel-fras to the broad col on the southwest side of Foel-fras. At the col join the main ridge path and take it NE then NNE to the summit of Foel-fras.

Descent: Head SSW then SW down the main ridge path to the col on the southwest side of Foel-fras. At the col turn L (almost doubling back) and follow the vague path (difficult to locate in poor visibility) NE across the flanks of Foel-fras, Pen y Castell and Penygadair to join the minor road.

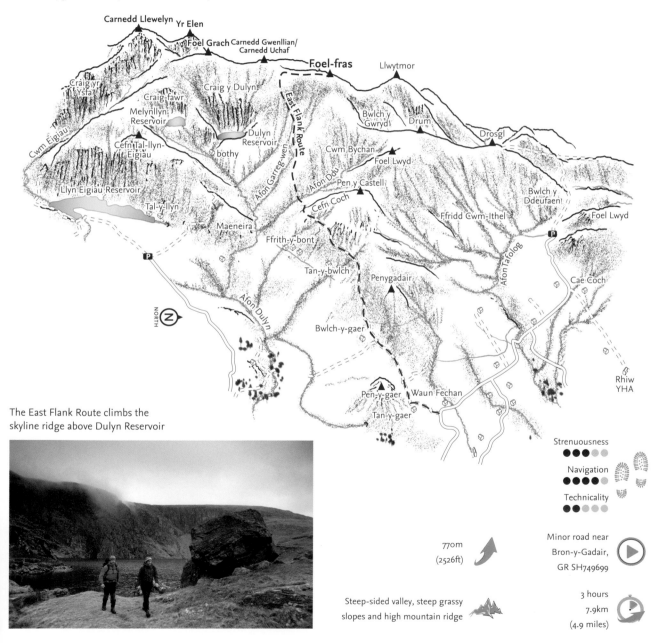

The East Flank Route climbs the skyline ridge above Dulyn Reservoir

Strenuousness ●●●●○○

Navigation ●●●●●○

Technicality ●●○○○○

770m
(2526ft)

Minor road near
Bron-y-Gadair,
GR SH749699

Steep-sided valley, steep grassy slopes and high mountain ridge

3 hours
7.9km
(4.9 miles)

North Ridge FOEL-FRAS

'Rounded crest' ★

Summary: The Carneddau are generally quieter than the other Snowdonia peaks but no area is more lonely than the northern side of Foel-fras. The route along the North Ridge samples the best of this area and provides a straightforward route with modest height gain.

Ascent: From the road head follow the track (Roman Road) NW to Bwlch y Ddeufaen. Turn L and follow the path SSW up the rounded spur. As the gradient eases head SE then S along the crest of the ridge to Drum. Continue S over Drum to Bwlch Y Gwryd. Cross the col and then climb SW up the curving ridge to Foel-fras's summit.

Descent: Head NE down the curving ridge to Bwlch y Gwryd. Cross the col and follow the main ridge to Drum. Continue N over Drum along the crest of the ridge then swing NW. As the crest of the ridge starts to steepen into a slope turn R and descend the rounded spur NE to Bwlch y Ddeufaen. From the broad col take the track (Roman Road) SE to the road head and car park.

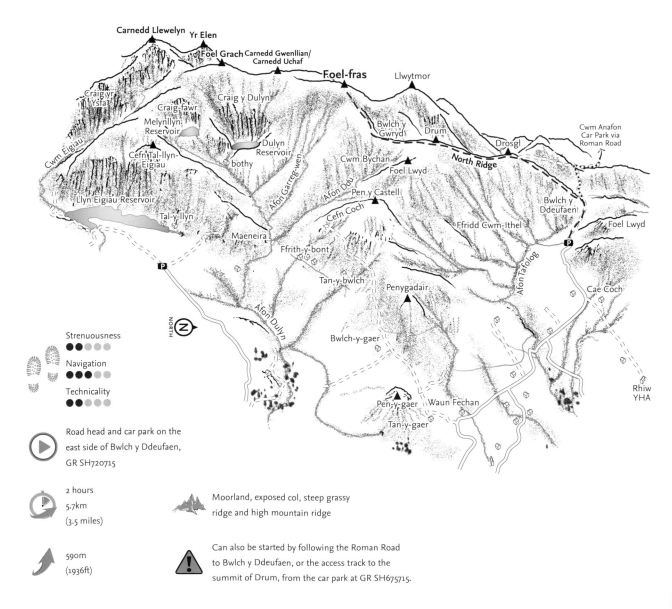

Strenuousness
● ● ○ ○ ○

Navigation
● ● ● ○ ○

Technicality
● ● ○ ○ ○

▶ Road head and car park on the east side of Bwlch y Ddeufaen, GR SH720715

2 hours
5.7km
(3.5 miles)

Moorland, exposed col, steep grassy ridge and high mountain ridge

590m
(1936ft)

⚠ Can also be started by following the Roman Road to Bwlch y Ddeufaen, or the access track to the summit of Drum, from the car park at GR SH675715.

Llwytmor Route FOEL-FRAS

'High-level ridge' ★

Summary: Llwytmor occupies a high point on the northwest arm of Foel-fras. Gaining this fine vantage point involves some hard leg-work on the steep slopes above Aber Falls but once they have been negotiated the rest of the route follows a pleasant elevated line.

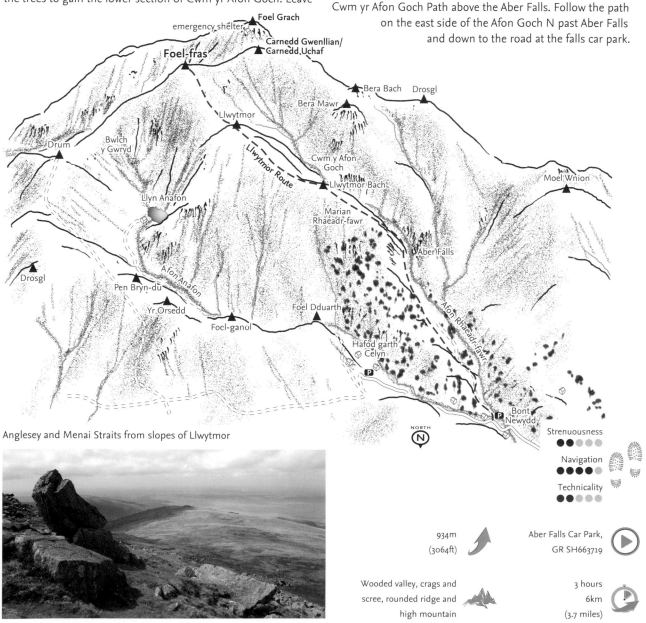

Ascent: From the car park take the Aber Falls track S for 700m (766yd) to a path on the L. Join it and follow it beside the trees to gain the lower section of Cwm yr Afon Goch. Leave the path and climb the steep slope E onto Llwytmor Bach. Turn SE and climb the steep slope to Llwytmor. Continue SE over the summit and then up the summit slopes of Foel-fras to the trig point on the top.

Descent: From the trig point head NW down the broad ridge to Llwytmor. Continue NW over the summit and descend to Llwytmor Bach. Turn W and drop down the steep slope (avoiding the crags of Marian Rhaeadr-fawr) to join the Cwm yr Afon Goch Path above the Aber Falls. Follow the path on the east side of the Afon Goch N past Aber Falls and down to the road at the falls car park.

Anglesey and Menai Straits from slopes of Llwytmor

Strenuousness ●●●○○○

Navigation ●●●●○

Technicality ●●○○○○

934m
(3064ft)

Aber Falls Car Park,
GR SH663719

Wooded valley, crags and
scree, rounded ridge and
high mountain

3 hours
6km
(3.7 miles)

Craig-fawr Spur FOEL-FRAS

'Dramatic crags' ★

Summary: The north side of the subsidiary top, Foel Grach is occupied by two secluded corries. Between their steep craggy headwalls a steep spur extends east, this is the Craig-fawr Spur. Its base can be reached easily via the Melynllyn Reservoir access track from where it gives a steep but exciting route onto the main ridge.

Ascent: At the northeast end of the car park take the Melynllyn reservoir access track NW. It climbs around the flanks of Clogwynyreryr and is then followed SW then NW to the outlet stream. Cross the Afon Melynllyn then climb the steep slope NW onto the Craig-fawr Spur. Follow the crest of the spur SW then climb the upper slopes to join the Cwm Eigiau Path on the east side of Foel Grach. Take it NW to join the main ridge path on the summit of Foel Grach. From Foel Grach head N then NE to Foel-fras.

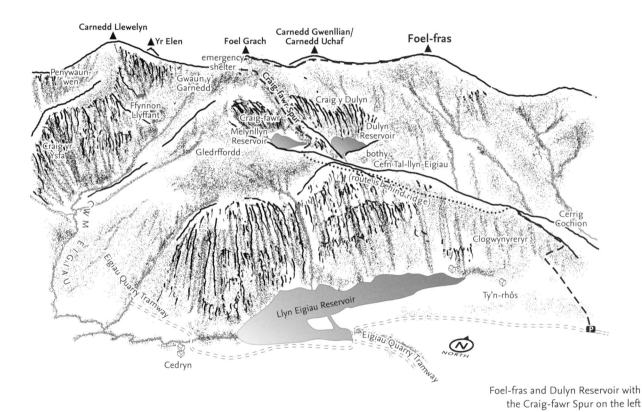

Foel-fras and Dulyn Reservoir with the Craig-fawr Spur on the left

Strenuousness
●●●○○

Navigation
●●●●○

Technicality
●●●●○

 Cwm Eigiau Car Park, GR SH731663

 700m (2297ft)

 3.5 hours 8.2km (5 miles)

 Moorland, open valley, craggy corrie, steep spur and high mountain ridge

Cwm Eigiau Path FOEL-FRAS

'Hauntingly wild'

Summary: Long steady approach from the Conwy Valley side of the Carneddau via the cold depths of Cwm Eigiau. At the head of Cwm Eigiau the impressive cliffs of Craig yr Ysfa can be viewed in all their glory.

Ascent: From the car park follow the access track SW to the old dam. Cross the Afon Porth-llwyd then follow the rough track SSW then SW up into Cwm Eigiau. At the old quarry tips and buildings, take the vague path NW, N then NW as it climbs across the east flank of Foel Grach to the col on its northeast side. From the col join the main ridge path and follow it NE then NNE to the summit of Foel-fras.

Descent: Head SSW then SW along the main ridge path to the col on the southwest side of Foel-fras. From the col join the Cwm Eigiau Path as it descends SE across the east flank of Foel Grach (the path is vague and can be difficult to locate in poor visibility) then S, and finally SE to the old quarry tips and buildings in Cwm Eigiau. Join the access track and take it E then NE around Cwm Eigiau to the old dam. Cross the Afon Porth-llwyd and head NE along the access track to the car park at the road head.

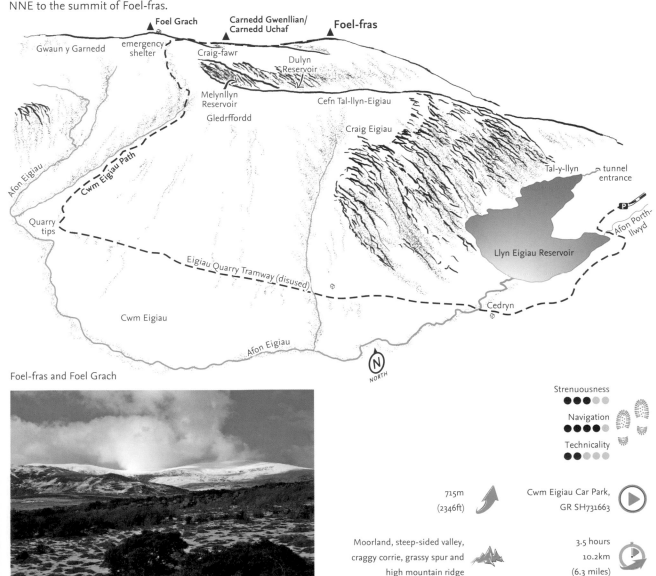

Foel-fras and Foel Grach

Strenuousness
●●●○○

Navigation
●●●●○

Technicality
●●○○○

715m
(2346ft)

Cwm Eigiau Car Park,
GR SH731663

Moorland, steep-sided valley,
craggy corrie, grassy spur and
high mountain ridge

3.5 hours
10.2km
(6.3 miles)

Elidir Fawr

923m (3028ft)

Elidir Fawr is the last major peak at the western end of the Glyders massif. From its summit there is a distinct sense of being between the sea and the mountains. This perhaps comes about because of its position; detached and somewhat out on a limb, its main axis lies at right angles to that of its nearest neighbour, Mynydd Perfedd, to which it is connected by the narrow neck of Bwlch y Marchlyn. From the rocky crest of the summit the views are starkly contrasting. To the west you can look out across the roads and towns of coastal plains towards the Menai Straits and to the east across the sharp relief of the Snowdonian mountains.

Sadly the vistas from the summit are not the only contrasts Elidir Fawr displays. The extensive slate quarrying on the west and north flanks have left ugly gaping holes and terraced tips like festering wounds – and if this were not enough of a blight, a pumped-storage hydro-electric scheme has been built in chambers in the very heart of the mountain, which takes its visual toll, from day to day, by raising and lowering the dammed Marchlyn Mawr Reservoir. In comparison the wild and lovely Cwm Dudodyn, the summit plateau and the headwall of Cwm Marchlyn, retain a little of the fastness that this once-fine mountain must have previously exhibited throughout.

The standard approach to Elidir Fawr is along the main ridge from Y Garn via Bwlch y Marchlyn, a route popular with walkers completing the 'Welsh 3000-ers'. An interesting and quiet variation to this approach, and the most direct route from the Ogwen Valley, is to gain the main ridge via Cwm Cywion. From the Nant Peris side the two routes from Cwm Dudodyn avoid the worst ravages of the quarries and provide steep but entertaining routes. The top section of the South Flank is particularly fine involving simple scrambling along the narrow rocky crest of the summit ridge. Approaches from the north are a little more problematic. Limited access from the Marchlyn Mawr Reservoir means that both the North Flank and the North Ridge have to be started from the north end of the Marchlyn Bach Reservoir. This does not greatly affect the North Ridge but it leads to a rather circuitous start to the North Flank Route.

When you arrive

Ordnance Survey: Explorer OL17 (1:25 000); Landranger 115 (1:50 000).
Harvey Mountain Maps: Snowdonia North (1:25 000)
British Mountain Maps: Snowdonia (1:40 000)

Tourist Information Centres: Caernarfon; Llanberis; Betws-y-Coed; Bangor.

Youth Hostels: Llanberis Pass: *Pen-y-pass*; Llanberis; Ogwen Valley: *Idwal Cottage*; Capel Curig.
Hotels and B&B: Nantgwryd: *Pen-y-Gwryd Hotel*; Nant Peris; Llanberis; Bethesda; Ogwen Valley; Capel Curig.
Camp sites: Llanberis Pass: *Nant Peris, Gwastadnant*; Llanberis: *Deiniolen*; Bethesda: *Ogwen Bank*; Ogwen Valley: *Gwern Gof Uchaf*; Capel Curig.

Summit cairn – Elidir Fawr

Elidir Fawr from Llyn Padarn

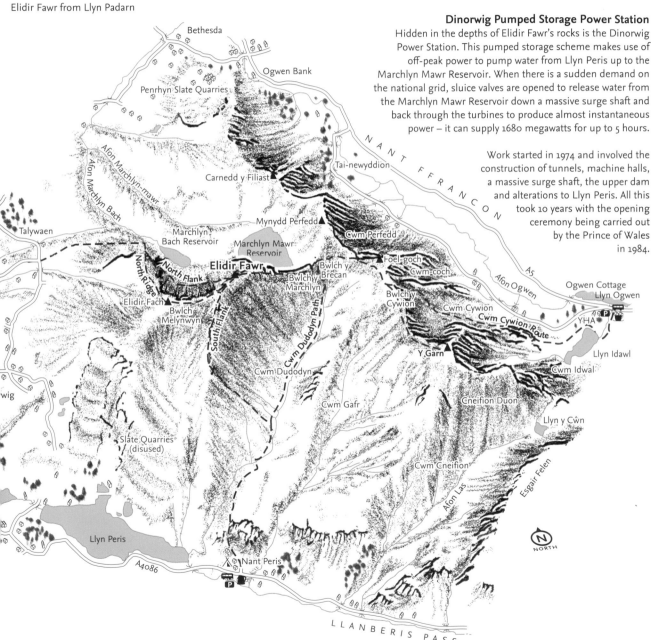

Dinorwig Pumped Storage Power Station
Hidden in the depths of Elidir Fawr's rocks is the Dinorwig Power Station. This pumped storage scheme makes use of off-peak power to pump water from Llyn Peris up to the Marchlyn Mawr Reservoir. When there is a sudden demand on the national grid, sluice valves are opened to release water from the Marchlyn Mawr Reservoir down a massive surge shaft and back through the turbines to produce almost instantaneous power – it can supply 1680 megawatts for up to 5 hours.

Work started in 1974 and involved the construction of tunnels, machine halls, a massive surge shaft, the upper dam and alterations to Llyn Peris. All this took 10 years with the opening ceremony being carried out by the Prince of Wales in 1984.

South Flank ELIDIR FAWR

'Steep and best saved for descent'

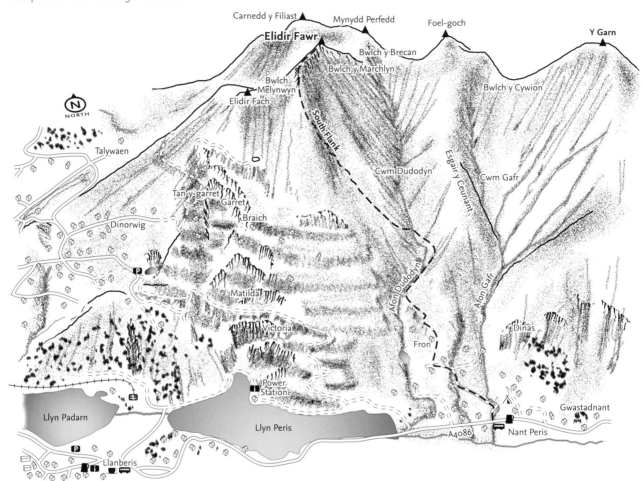

Summary:

An unremitting slog from the mouth of Cwm Dudodyn to the southwest end of Elidir Fawr's summit ridge. The final section on the summit ridge is entertaining involving some boulder hopping, but on balance this route probably best serves as a descent.

Strenuousness ●●●○○

Navigation ●●●○○

Technicality ●●●●○

Nant Peris,
GR SH605584

2.5 hours
4.2km
(2.6 miles)

825m
(2707ft)

Steep pasture, steep-sided corrie, rocky ridge and narrow rocky summit

Ascent: From Nant Peris take the lane NE then NW to join a track. Continue generally NW along it, as it climbs to the start of the Cwm Dudodyn Path. Follow the path as it zigzags up to the Afon Dudodyn. The path follows the Afon Dudodyn NE, first on the south bank then over a footbridge onto the north bank. Continue along it to the mouth of Cwm Dudodyn proper, then make the steep ascent NW up the South Flank. As the summit ridge is reached turn NE. Scramble easily up the crest to the summit cairn and shelter.

Descent: Scramble SW down the narrow crest of the summit ridge. As the angle steepens and the crest becomes less pronounced, turn S and descend the steep South Flank to join the Cwm Dudodyn Path. Follow it generally SW alongside the Afon Dudodyn to a footbridge. Cross it and head W along the path to the top of a series of zigzags. Descend the zigzags and pick up the track then lane down into Nant Peris.

North Ridge ELIDIR FAWR

'Short and interesting' ★

Summary: Climbs directly up the rounded North Ridge to the subsidiary peak Elidir Fach, then gains Elidir Fawr via the expansive col and scree slopes of Bwlch Melynwyn. Elidir Fach affords panoramic views of the coast.

Ascent: From the road take the Marchlyn Mawr access road (part of the Dinorwig hydro-electric power scheme) ESE to the junction below the Marchlyn Bach Reservoir. Leave the road and ascend the ridge S to Elidir Fach. From the summit of Elidir Fach head SE and cross Bwlch Melynwyn to make the short but steep ascent to the summit ridge of Elidir Fawr. On the ridge turn NE and scramble easily up the crest to the summit cairn and shelter.

Descent: Scramble SW down the narrow crest of the summit ridge. As the angle steepens and the crest becomes less pronounced turn NW and descend the steep slope to Bwlch Melynwyn. Continue NW across the col to Elidir Fach then turn N and descend the North Ridge to the access road junction below the Marchlyn Bach Reservoir. Once on the main access road follow it WNW to the road near Talywaen.

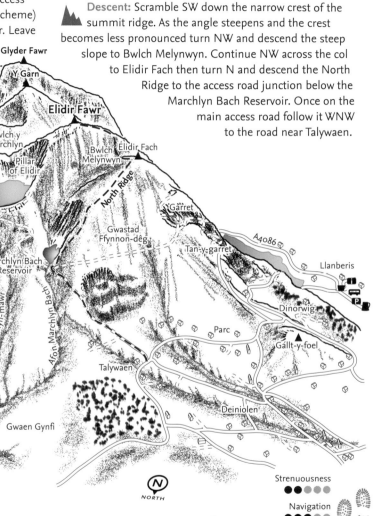

Summit cairn – Elidir Fach

595m
(1952ft)

Moorland, rocky corrie, rounded ridge, high open col, scree and narrow summit ridge

If time allows, a detour up and down the access road to Marchlyn Mawr Reservoir is worth making to view the impressive Cwm Marchlyn.

Strenuousness
●●○○○

Navigation
●●●○○

Technicality
●●●●○

Talywaen on the east side of Deiniolen
GR SH593631

2 hours
3.8km
(2.4 miles)

North Flank Route ELIDIR FAWR

'Short and direct'

Summary: Ringed by dark and secretive crags Cwm Marchlyn cuts deeply into the north side of Elidir Fawr. Skirting the top of these crags the North Flank Route works a circuitous, but interesting, line to Elidir Fawr's rocky summit.

Ascent: From the road take the Marchlyn Mawr access road (part of the Dinorwig hydro-electric power scheme) ESE to the junction below the Marchlyn Bach Reservoir. Leave the road and ascend the ridge S to Elidir Fach. As the angle of the ridge eases at a shallow shoulder, contour SE then E towards the edge of the crags of Cwm Marchlyn. Before the edge is

reached, turn S (in mist or snow this can be difficult to judge – better to err on the cautious side and turn early) and climb the steep scree-covered slopes to Elidir Fawr's summit ridge. On the ridge turn SW and follow the crest to the summit cairn and shelter.

Descent: Head NE along the summit ridge then turn N and descend the steep scree, skirting the top of Cwm Marchlyn's headwall (in mist or snow this can be difficult to judge – better to err on the cautious side and descend from Elidir Fawr's summit NW past Bwlch Melynwyn). Before the bottom of the slope is reached, contour W then NW to the shallow shoulder on the north side of Elidir Fach. Descend the North Ridge to the access road junction below the Marchlyn Bach Reservoir. Once on the main access road follow it WNW to the road near Talywaen.

Strenuousness ●●●○○

Navigation ●●●○○

Technicality ●●●●○

595m
(1925ft)

Talywaen on the east side of Deiniolen
GR SH593631

Moorland, rocky corrie, rounded ridge, steep scree and narrow summit ridge

2 hours
3.2km
(2 miles)

If time allows, a detour up and down the access road to Marchlyn Mawr Reservoir is worth making to view the impressive Cwm Marchlyn.

Cwm Cywion Route ELIDIR FAWR

'Challenging and quiet' ★★

Summary: The remote and little-visited Cwm Cywion provides a handy approach to Elidir Fawr from the Ogwen Valley.

Ascent: From Ogwen Cottage take the Cwm Idwal Path SE then SW to Llyn Idwal. Cross the footbridge at the northeast end of the lake and follow the vague path which snakes up to the base of the northeast ridge of Y Garn. Before the base of the ridge is reached leave the path and contour round the steep slopes NW into Cwm Cywion. Continue NW up through Cwm Cywion to Llyn Cywion then ascend the headwall, still generally NW, to Bwlch y Cywion. Cross the col and make the short descent to join the path on the southwest side of Foel-goch. Turn R and follow it N then W around the head of Cwm Dudodyn to Bwlch y Marchlyn. From the col, climb the steep narrow ridge WSW to the summit of Elidir Fawr.

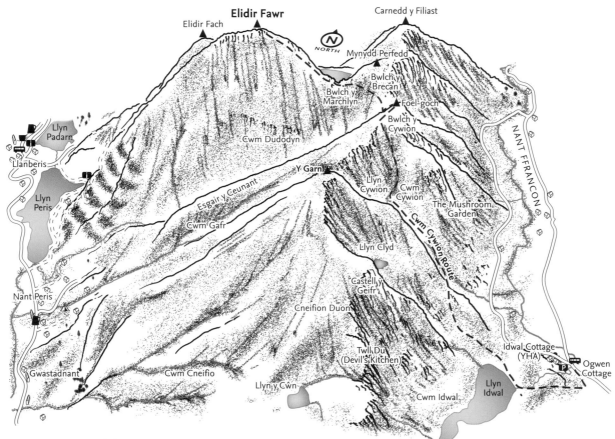

Descent: Descend the path and then the ridge ENE to Bwlch y Marchlyn. Cross the exposed col then contour E then S around the head of Cwm Dudodyn. On the southwest side of the summit slopes of Foel-goch make the short ascent E to Bwlch y Cywion. Cross the col and make the steep descent SE to Llyn Cywion. Continue descending SE through Cwm Cywion and contour around to the bottom of the northeast ridge of Y Garn. At the base of the ridge join the vague path and follow it ESE to the footbridge at the northeast end of Llyn Idwal. Cross it and join the Ogwen Cottage Path, which is followed NE then NW to the buildings and car park at Ogwen Cottage.

3 hours
5.4km
(3.4 miles)

760m
(2493ft)

Broad craggy corrie, mountain lake, steep rocky slope, high open corrie, rounded mountain ridge, exposed col and narrow summit ridge

Strenuousness
●●●●○○

Navigation
●●●●●

Technicality
●●●●○

Scramble/Winter climb
●●●○/●○

Ogwen Cottage
(Pen y Benglog),
GR SH649603

Y Garn Link ELIDIR FAWR

'Stunning views' ★★

Summary: Pleasant high-level walk between two fine mountains with excellent views into the more remote corries of the Glyders massif.

Route: Descend the path and then the ridge ENE down to Bwlch y Marchlyn. Cross the exposed col then contour E then S around the head of Cwm Dudodyn. Past Foel-goch, continue generally S to the col on the northwest side of Y Garn. Across the col trend SE and climb the steep summit slopes to Y Garn.

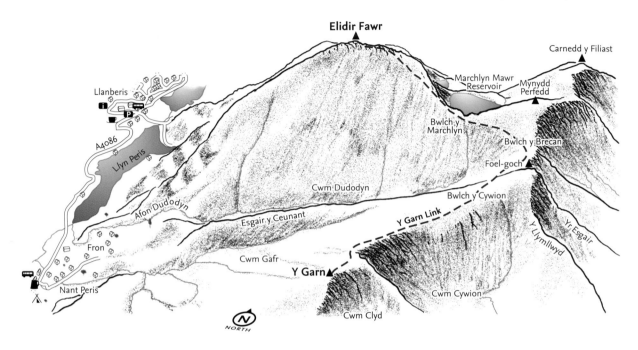

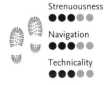

Strenuousness
●●●●○

Navigation
●●●●○

Technicality
●●●○○

Elidir Fawr,
GR SH612613

1.5 hours
4km
(2.5 miles)

280m
(919ft)

High mountain ridge, exposed
col and narrow summit ridge

Traversing Bwlch y Brecan en route for Y Garn

Cwm Dudodyn Path ELIDIR FAWR

'Quiet with a fine finish'

Summary: Cwm Dudodyn's southerly aspect and its verdant interior make it an inviting place to explore. Looks can be misleading though, for although it provides a pleasant enough approach to Elidir Fawr it is longer than it would first appear and its headwall is very steep grassland.

Ascent: From Nant Peris take the lane NE then NW to join a track. Continue generally NW along it as it climbs to the start of the Cwm Dudodyn Path. Follow the path as it zigzags up to the Afon Dudodyn. The path follows the Afon Dudodyn NE, first on the south bank then over a footbridge onto the north bank. Continue NE ascending the length of Cwm Dudodyn. At the head of Cwm Dudodyn turn NW and climb the very steep grassy slope to Bwlch y Marchlyn. From the col climb the steep narrow ridge WSW to the summit of Elidir Fawr.

Descent: Descend the path and then the ridge ENE down to Bwlch y Marchlyn. From the col turn SE to descend the steep grassy slope into Cwm Dudodyn. Follow the vague path SW alongside the Afon Dudodyn to a footbridge. Cross it and head W along the path to the top of a series of zigzags. Descend the zigzags and pick up the track then the lane down into Nant Peris.

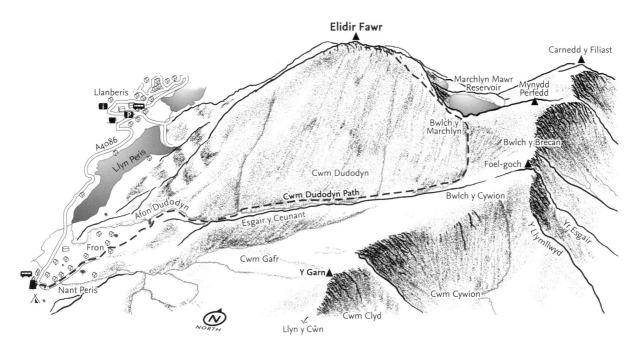

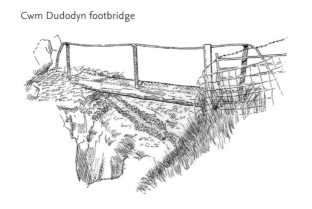

Cwm Dudodyn footbridge

Strenuousness
●●●●○○

Navigation
●●●●○○

Technicality
●●●●○○

820m
(2690ft)

Steep pasture, steep-sided corrie
and narrow rocky summit

Nant Peris,
GR SH605584

2.5 hours
5km
(3.1 miles)

Tryfan

915m (3002ft)

There can be few mountains which more readily fit the description of one of Britain's Highest Peaks than Tryfan. This fine 'shark's fin' of a mountain is separated from its neighbours, the Glyders, by the gulf of Bwlch Tryfan. Displaying nothing but steep crags and ridges from whichever angle it is viewed, it epitomises the classic mountain. This is ironic as Tryfan only just scrapes past the magic 3000ft mark.

Set in a high, prominent position between Cwm Tryfan and Cwm Bochlwyd on the south side of the Ogwen Valley, it is just possible to view all of Tryfan's facets and features from the valley floor. Because of its open nature, Tryfan generates a friendly atmosphere and it is a welcome and familiar sight, providing a key landmark when either travelling along the valley road or walking on the surrounding hills.

This friendly face can be a little misleading, however. All the routes cross ground which is rocky and involves sections of scrambling. The classic line on Tryfan, and the classic route of its type in Wales, is the North Ridge. It climbs directly from the A5 by the side of Llyn Ogwen to the summit rocks providing over 3500ft of almost continuous scrambling. For those with a thirst for scrambling, a popular expedition is to ascend the North Ridge then descend the easier South Ridge to Bwlch Tryfan from where an ascent of Bristly Ridge gives access to the Glyders massif.

Tryfan is not only a popular mountain with walkers; climbers are understandably drawn to its fine crags as well. The two main areas of interest are the slabs of Milestone Buttress at the foot of the North Ridge and the three main buttresses and associated gullies of the east face. Access to the east face is gained along Heather Terrace – a distinct diagonal break which rises steadily from north to south across their base.

Tryfan's East Face

When you arrive

Ordnance Survey: Explorer OL17 (1:25 000); Landranger 115 (1:50 000).
Harvey Mountain Maps: Snowdonia North (1:25 000)
British Mountain Maps: Snowdonia (1:40 000)

Tourist Information Centres: Caernarfon; Llanberis; Betws-y-Coed; Bangor.

Youth Hostels: Llanberis Pass: *Pen-y-pass*; Llanberis; Ogwen Valley: *Idwal Cottage*; Capel Curig.
Hotels and B&B: Nantgwryd: *Pen-y-Gwryd Hotel*; Nant Peris; Llanberis; Bethesda; Ogwen Valley; Capel Curig.
Camp sites: Llanberis Pass: *Nant Peris, Gwastadnant*; Llanberis: *Deiniolen*; Bethesda: *Ogwen Bank*; Ogwen Valley: *Gwern Gof Uchaf*; Capel Curig.

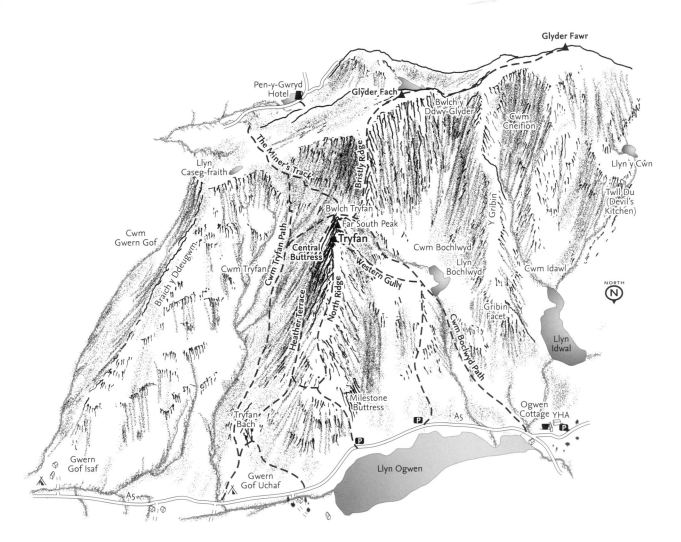

Glyder Fawr

Pen-y-Gwryd
Hotel

Glyder Fach

Bwlch y
Dawy-Glyder

Cwm
Cneifion

The Miner's Track

Bristly Ridge

Llyn y Cŵn

Llyn
Caseg-fraith

Twll Du
(Devil's Kitchen)

Bwlch Tryfan

Far South Peak

Tryfan

Y Gribin

Cwm
Gwern Gof

Cwm Tryfan Path

**Central
Buttress**

Cwm Bochlwyd

Braich y Ddeugwm

Cwm Tryfan

Western Gully

Llyn
Bochlwyd

Cwm Idawl

Heather Terrace

North Ridge

NORTH
N

Gribin
Facet

Cwm Bochlwyd Path

Llyn
Idwal

Milestone
Buttress

Ogwen
Cottage YHA

Tryfan
Bach

P

A5

P

Gwern
Gof Isaf

P

Gwern
Gof Uchaf

Llyn Ogwen

A5

The Miner's Track TRYFAN

'Devious and exciting' ★★

Summary: Works a devious course around the east flank of Glyder Fach to gain Tryfan's South Ridge via a traverse around the head of Cwm Tryfan. A surprisingly direct route, which avoids any major re-ascent crossing the main Glyders ridge.

Ascent: From the side of the A4086 take the footpath NW to the footbridge. Cross it and follow the path NE as it climbs steadily up the south and east flanks of Glyder Fach. As the crest of the main ridge line is reached the path turns N.

Follow it across the col to the top of the steep slope at the head of Cwm Tryfan. Drop down the slope and follow the path NW around the headwall to Bwlch Tryfan. From the col take the path N up the South Ridge of Tryfan (avoiding the Far South Peak on its west side) and scramble up Tryfan's crest to the summit blocks.

Descent: From the summit blocks follow the path down the South Ridge (avoiding the Far South Peak on its west side) to Bwlch Tryfan. From the col descend SE and follow The Miner's Track as it skirts around the head of Cwm Tryfan to the bleak col on the east side of Glyder Fach. Descend S then SW from the col to the footbridge across the Nant Gwryd. Once across head SE to the A4086.

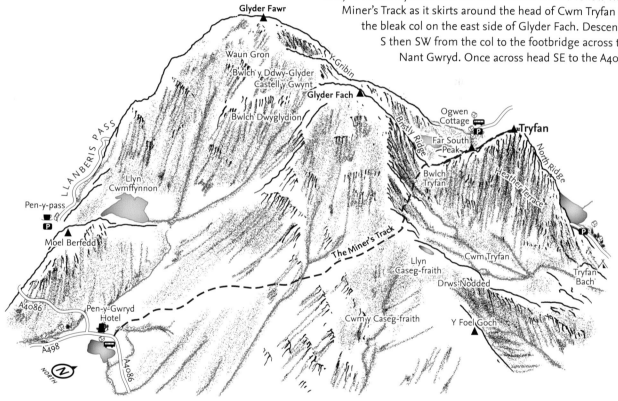

Strenuousness

● ● ○ ○ ○

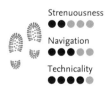

Navigation

● ● ● ○ ○

Technicality

● ● ● ● ○

A4086 near the Pen-y-Gwryd Hotel, GR SH660559

715m (2346ft)

2.5 hours 4.2km (2.6 miles)

Open rocky mountainside, bleak col, scree and boulders, high col, rocky ridge and rocky summit

'Adam and Eve' – Tryfan's summit rocks

Glyders Link (Bristly Ridge) TRYFAN

'Challenging scramble' ★★★

Summary: Steep and imposing, the pinnacled crest of Bristly Ridge presents a daunting sight. It is justifiably popular as it provides an adventurous scramble – the most direct link between Tryfan and Glyder Fach. Although it is only a Grade 1 scramble its difficulties should not be underestimated as there are a number of harder alternative lines which are easy to wander onto.

Route: From Tryfan's summit blocks follow the path down the South Ridge (avoiding the Far South Peak on its west side) to Bwlch Tryfan. Cross the col and ascend the scree to the mouth of a gully system at the base of Bristly Ridge. Follow the gully, avoiding the difficult sections on the L, to gain the crest of the ridge via a short traverse R (when wet the gully system can be particularly difficult). Follow the crest over the undulations of the pinnacles (all the steep sections can be avoided) to join the main Glyders ridge on the east side of Glyder Fach. Turn R and follow the main ridge path WSW over Glyder Fach and over Bwlch y Ddwy-Glyder to Glyder Fawr.

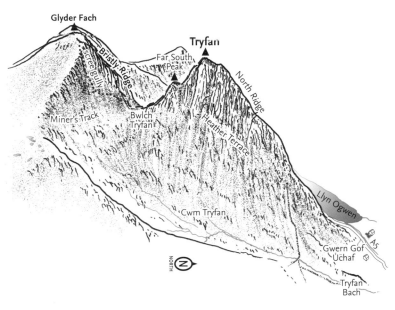

The last few moves at the top of Bristly Ridge with the south ridge of Tryfan in the background

Strenuousness
●●●●○

Navigation
●●●●●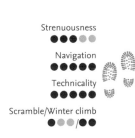

Technicality
●●●●●

Scramble/Winter climb
●●●○/●●

Tryfan's summit,
GR SH663593

1–1.5 hours
3km (1.9 miles) –
to Glyder Fach

355m
(1165ft)

Rocky ridge, high col, narrow rocky
ridge, high mountain ridge and
stony summit slopes

The difficulties of Bristly Ridge can
be avoided by following the scree
path on the east side of the ridge

Cwm Bochlwyd Path TRYFAN

'Magnificent corrie walk' ★★

Summary: The path climbing steadily across the floor of Cwm Bochlwyd gives the easiest approach to Tryfan, although the South Ridge section involves some simple scrambling.

Ascent: From Ogwen Cottage take the Cwm Idwal Path SE to a fork at the first bend. Take the left branch and continue SE to Cwm Bochlwyd. Cross the Nant Bochlwyd and climb SE to Bwlch Tryfan. At the col turn L and take the path N up the South Ridge of Tryfan (avoiding the Far South Peak on its west side) and scramble up Tryfan's crest to the summit blocks.

Descent: From the summit blocks follow the path down the South Ridge (avoiding the Far South Peak on its west side) to Bwlch Tryfan. From the col descend NW and follow the path down to Llyn Bochlwyd. Cross the Nant Bochlwyd and continue NW down to Ogwen Cottage.

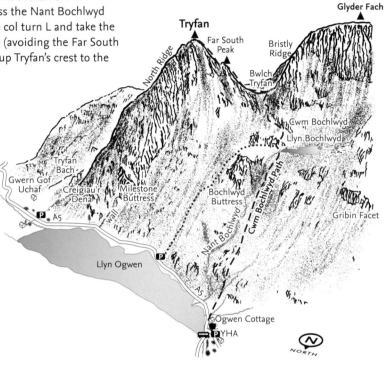

Strenuousness
●●●○○

Navigation
●●●○○

Technicality
●●●●○

Ogwen Cottage
(Pen y Benglog),
GR SH649603

2 hours
2.7km
(1.7 miles)

590m
(1936ft)

Rocky slope, broad open corrie, high col, rocky ridge and rocky summit

Cwm Bochlwyd can also be gained from the A5 via the path that starts at GR SH657601

Passing Llyn Bochlwyd en route for Bwlch Tryfan

Western Gully TRYFAN

'Quick way'

Summary: A broad scree-filled gully which climbs directly up the west face of Tryfan. An unremitting slog in ascent, best saved for descent.

 **Ascent:** From Ogwen Cottage take the Cwm Idwal Path SE to a fork at the first bend. Take the left branch and continue SE to Cwm Bochlwyd. Cross the Nant Bochlwyd then climb E directly up the slope to the mouth of Western Gully, which is followed to Tryfan's summit slope.

 **Descent:** From the summit blocks head N then turn almost immediately W and descend the path steeply down the scree. Out of the gully and on to the lower slopes keep descending W to the north end of Llyn Bochlwyd. Cross the Nant Bochlwyd and head NW down to Ogwen Cottage.

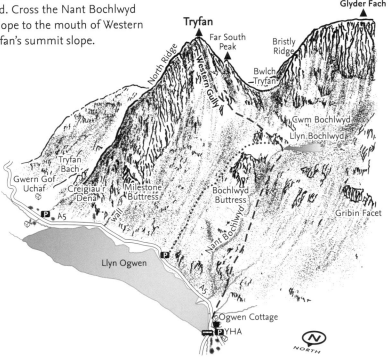

Broken ground on the western flank of Tryfan

Strenuousness

Navigation

Technicality

Ogwen Cottage
(Pen y Benglog),
GR SH649603

2 hours
2.2km
(1.4 miles)

585m
(1919ft)

Rocky slope, broad open
corrie, broad scree-filled
gully and rocky summit

Cwm Bochlwyd can also be gained
from the A5 via the path that starts
at GR SH657601

North Ridge TRYFAN

'Much loved scramble' ★ ★ ★

Summary: Unremitting line direct from the road to the summit rocks. An entertaining scramble with numerous variations both easy and difficult – a classic route.

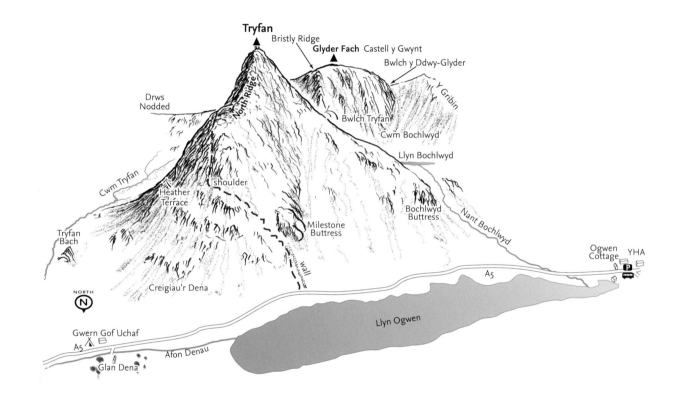

Ascent: From the stile on the A5 take the path alongside the wall as it climbs S then SE, to join the North Ridge proper. The ridge is deceptively broad, the most interesting scrambling being found on the crest. Follow the ridge directly over the subsidiary summits to the summit blocks 'Adam and Eve'.

Tryfan
Bristly Ridge
Glyder Fach Castell y Gwynt
Bwlch y Ddwy-Glyder
Drws Nodded
North Ridge
y Gribin
Bwlch Tryfan
Cwm Bochlwyd
Cwm Tryfan
Llyn Bochlwyd
shoulder
Heather Terrace
Milestone Buttress
Bochlwyd Buttress
Nant Bochlwyd
Ogwen Cottage
YHA
Tryfan Bach
Wall
A5
NORTH
Creigiau'r Dena
Gwern Gof Uchaf
A5
Llyn Ogwen
Afon Denau
Glan Dena

Strenuousness
● ● ● ● ○ ○

Navigation
● ● ● ● ●

Technicality
● ● ● ● ●

Scramble/Winter climb
● ● ○ ○ ● / ○ ○

590m
(1936ft)

A5 at the side of Llyn Ogwen, GR SH663602

Steep craggy ridge

2 hours
1.2km
(0.75 miles)

The line up the ridge can be varied and some sections can attain grade 2/3 scramble

Tryfan's East Face with the North Ridge taking the right-hand skyline

Central Buttress TRYFAN

'Route finding challenge' ★

Summary: Exploiting the easy sections of Little Gully and North Gully, this scramble up Tryfan's Central Buttress makes a superb expedition. The start can be tricky to find but once located the route is easy to follow with short but entertaining technical sections and fine views across the east face.

Ascent: From the A5 take the track E towards Gwern Gof Uchaf. Before the farm, turn R and head SW towards Tryfan Bach. Below the slabs of Tryfan Bach turn R and follow the narrow winding path that climbs W, then SW, to Heather Terrace (avoid the narrower terrace below Heather Terrace – it is easy to confuse the two). Once on Heather Terrace follow it as it climbs steadily SSW across the base of Tryfan's east-face crags. It crosses a number of gully lines which can be confusing; the start of Little Gully is marked by a split block through which Heather Terrace passes (just after crossing the bed of North Gully). Scramble up the ramp on the left side of Little Gully then up its bed to a col. Cross the col and follow the groove system and ledge into the upper reaches of North Gully. Take the zigzags up the amphitheatre then traverse L across its head, finally climbing the headwall to the summit.

Split block on Heather Terrace that marks the start of Central Buttress

Strenuousness
●●●●○○

Navigation
●●●●● 👟👟

Technicality
●●●●● 👟

590m (1936ft)

Scramble/Winter climb
●●●○/●●

Rough pasture, steep rock and heather covered mountainside, steep shallow gully, rock amphitheatre, steep headwall and rocky summit

From the A5 opposite Glan Dena, GR SH667605 ▶

The north end of Heather Terrace can be gained from Bwlch Tryfan or via The Miner's Track ⚠

2.5 hours
1.9km
(1.2 miles)

Heather Terrace TRYFAN

'Classic rock traverse' ★★

Summary: Essentially a climbers' access route to the base of Tryfan's east face it also provides a useful route to or from the South Ridge.

Ascent: From the A5 take the track E towards Gwern Gof Uchaf. Before the farm turn R and head SW towards Tryfan Bach. Below the slabs of Tryfan Bach turn R and follow the narrow winding path that climbs W then SW to Heather Terrace (avoid the narrower terrace below Heather Terrace – it is easy to confuse the two). Once on Heather Terrace follow it as it climbs steadily SSW across the base of Tryfan's east-face crags and then climbs W up to the col between the South Ridge and the Far South Peak. At the col turn R and take the path N up the South Ridge scrambling up its crest to the summit blocks.

Descent: From the summit blocks follow the path down the South Ridge to the col on the north side of the Far South Peak. From the col descend E to the top of Heather Terrace. Follow the terrace as it swings NNE then descends across the base of the east face. At the end of Heather Terrace turn NE and descend steeply to join the Cwm Tryfan Path by Tryfan Bach. Join it and continue NE along it down to Gwern Gof Uchaf. Before the farm turn L and take the track W to the A5.

Cairn at the top of Heather Terrace on the col between Tryfan and Far South Peak GR SH663592

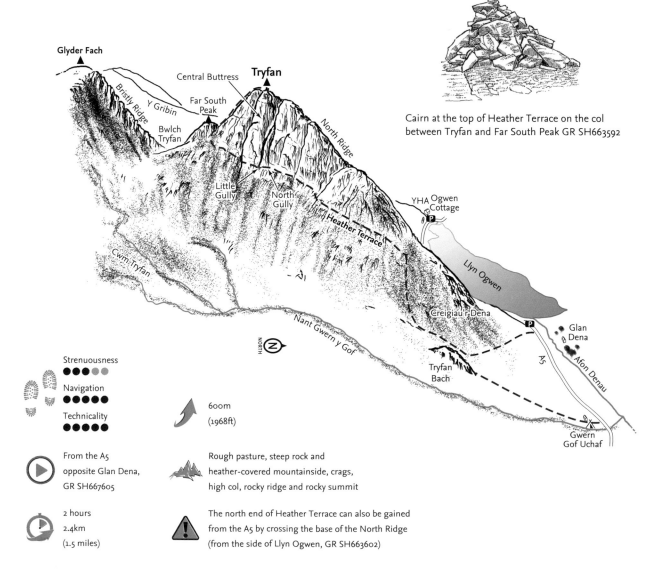

Strenuousness
● ● ● ● ○

Navigation
● ● ● ● ●

Technicality
● ● ● ● ●

600m
(1968ft)

From the A5 opposite Glan Dena, GR SH667605

Rough pasture, steep rock and heather-covered mountainside, crags, high col, rocky ridge and rocky summit

2 hours
2.4km
(1.5 miles)

The north end of Heather Terrace can also be gained from the A5 by crossing the base of the North Ridge (from the side of Llyn Ogwen, GR SH663602)

Cwm Tryfan Path TRYFAN

'Stunning views' ★★

Summary: A rough corrie in the shadow of Tryfan's impressive east face provides a lonely route to Bwlch Tryfan at the base of the South Ridge.

Ascent: From the A5 take the track E toward Gwern Gof Uchaf. Before the farm turn R and head SW towards Tryfan Bach. Pass below the slabs of Tryfan Bach and continue generally SW to enter the rough bounds of Cwm Tryfan. Follow the narrow path as it works its way to the corrie head then climbs W to Bwlch Tryfan. At the col turn R and take the path N up the South Ridge (avoiding the Far South Peak on its west side) and scramble up Tryfan's crest to the summit blocks.

Descent: From the summit blocks follow the path down the South Ridge (avoiding the Far South Peak on its west side) to Bwlch Tryfan. From the col descend E to the head of Cwm Tryfan, then turn NNE and make the steady descent by the narrow path along the corrie floor to Tryfan Bach. Pass the slabs of Tryfan Bach and head NE towards Gwern Gof Uchaf. Before the farm turn L and take the track W to the A5.

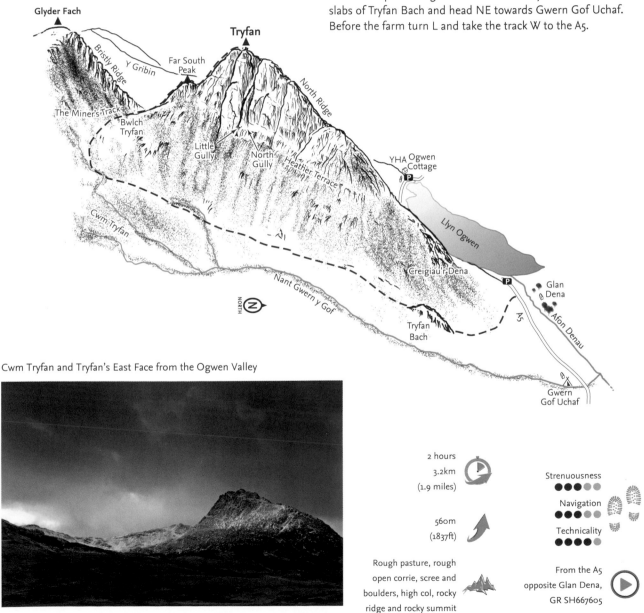

Cwm Tryfan and Tryfan's East Face from the Ogwen Valley

2 hours
3.2km
(1.9 miles)

560m
(1837ft)

Rough pasture, rough open corrie, scree and boulders, high col, rocky ridge and rocky summit

Strenuousness
●●●●○○

Navigation
●●●○○

Technicality
●●●●○

From the A5 opposite Glan Dena, GR SH667605

Challenge Walks

Extended walks stitching groups of summits together has a long tradition among British hill walkers. The roots of this practice probably date back to the original fell walkers in the Lake District, who would take advantage of the height gained reaching one summit to then go on and reach adjoining summits across linking cols. For some, these walks are an enjoyable and efficient way of bagging as many summits as possible; for others they have become physical and mental challenges in their own right. Whichever way you look at it, there can be no denying the quality of these challenge walks, and those that are included in this book offer some of the greatest rewards.

In crossing Britain's highest mountains there are innumerable permutations to the challenge style of walk, and planning and executing your own variations can be very enjoyable. Stitching together various link-ups from the routes detailed in the main chapters with additions of your own choice should provide many adventures. However, if you complete all the four established classic challenge walks, you will summit all of Britain's highest mountains. The classic challenge walks described here are for those who want to fast-track and climb groups of summits in one hit, or those that just want an excuse to visit old favourites again.

The highest peaks of England and Wales can each be tackled in long expeditions, while the peaks of Scotland form two distinct groups and are best taken on at separate times. A well-known challenge walk, the Three Peaks challenge, also involves the three highest peaks of England, Wales and Scotland, but there are a number of negative side-effects including disturbance to local communities, litter, and unnecessary calls to mountain rescue, created by the imposed constraint of a twenty-four hour time limit. The peaks are a wonderful undertaking, but in the light of the problems caused, it can only be recommended when it is pursued in a more sustainable manner, either over a longer period of time or by taking public transport to travel between the peaks.

The National Three Peaks

The National Three Peaks

'Better done over 3 days!' ★★★

Summary: In the summer of 1926 three members of the Lake District Fell and Rock Climbing Club set out to climb all three of Britain's highest mountains, Ben Nevis, Scafell Pike and Snowdon, in under twenty-four hours and thus was born the 'National Three Peaks'. This challenge was described as a 'motor-mountaineering stunt' in the Club's 1926 journal (which can be viewed online at www.frcc.co.uk). At the time, roads in mountainous regions were little more than dirt tracks and the high speeds achievable on today's motorways were many decades away.

Route: The routes taken up the three peaks were the normal, easy routes; the challenge was not the walking – it was covering the intervening road sections as fast as possible. Difficult driving conditions, interspersed with frequent punctures, mechanical failure and refuelling all had to be dealt with – this was what made the adventure. Skip forward to today, with our fast, reliable cars, motorways and tarmacked mountain roads and this challenge has been totally removed. In order to reinvigorate the challenge, a growing number of walkers are adopting a more sustainable and lower-impact approach by raising the bar and using public transport. This, of course, removes the artificial notion of the twenty-four hour time limit, which in reality was only justifiable with the 1926 road network. It does, however, greatly improve the quality of the challenge, both in terms of routes taken on the peaks and the experience of the journey in-between them. In addition, there is the Three Peaks Yacht Race every year which involves a fairly specialist mix of sailors and fell runners, and another variation of the challenge involves cycling between the mountains.

Half the fun of completing the National Three Peaks challenge by public transport is in the planning. Almost all the routes up each of the three detailed in this book are given so you can mix and match for ascent and descent, and decide whether your valley approach is by bus or train. The routes detailed in this section are really just options and you can have fun just deciding which options to take.

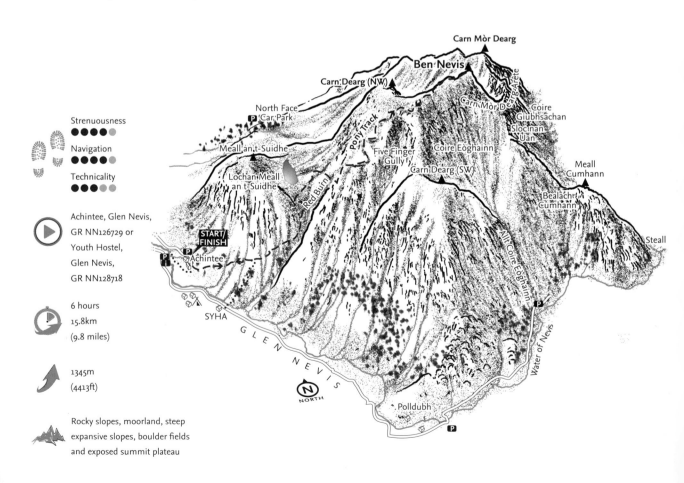

Strenuousness ●●●●○

Navigation ●●●●○

Technicality ●●●○○

Achintee, Glen Nevis, GR NN126729 or Youth Hostel, Glen Nevis, GR NN128718

6 hours
15.8km
(9.8 miles)

1345m
(4413ft)

Rocky slopes, moorland, steep expansive slopes, boulder fields and exposed summit plateau

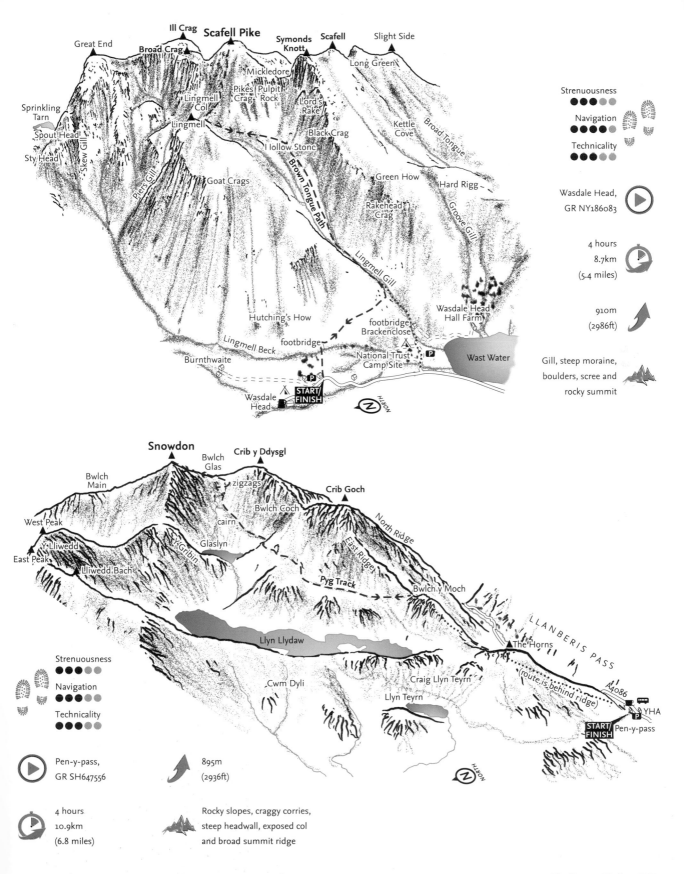

Ill Crag

Scafell Pike

Great End

Broad Crag

Symonds Knott

Scafell

Slight Side

Mickledore

Long Green

Pikes Crags

Pulpit Rock

Lord's Rake

Lingmell Col

Kettle Cove

Sprinkling Tarn

Lingmell

Black Crag

Broad Tongue

Spout Head

Hollow Stone

Sty Head

Skew Gill

Brown Tongue Path

Green How

Hard Rigg

Piers Gill

Goat Crags

Rakehead Crag

Groove Gill

Lingmell Gill

Hutching's How

Wasdale Head Hall Farm

footbridge

Brackenclose

Lingmell Beck

footbridge

National Trust Camp Site

Burnthwaite

Wast Water

Wasdale Head

START/FINISH

NORTH

Strenuousness
● ● ● ○ ○

Navigation
● ● ● ● ○

Technicality
● ● ● ○ ○

Wasdale Head,
GR NY186083

4 hours
8.7km
(5.4 miles)

910m
(2986ft)

Gill, steep moraine,
boulders, scree and
rocky summit

Snowdon

Bwlch Glas

Crib y Ddysgl

Bwlch Main

zigzags

Crib Goch

West Peak

Bwlch Coch

North Ridge

Y Lliwedd

cairn

K Gribin

East Ridge

East Peak

Lliwedd Bach

Glaslyn

Pyg Track

Bwlch y Moch

LLANBERIS PASS

Llyn Llydaw

The Horns

(route is behind ridge)

A4086

Cwm Dyli

Craig Llyn Teyrn

YHA

Llyn Teyrn

START/FINISH

Pen-y-pass

NORTH

Strenuousness
● ● ● ○ ○

Navigation
● ● ● ○ ○

Technicality
● ● ● ● ○

Pen-y-pass,
GR SH647556

895m
(2936ft)

4 hours
10.9km
(6.8 miles)

Rocky slopes, craggy corries,
steep headwall, exposed col
and broad summit ridge

Scafell and Scafell Pike – the col between these two peaks classically typifies the difficulties encountered on Britain's highest challenge walks

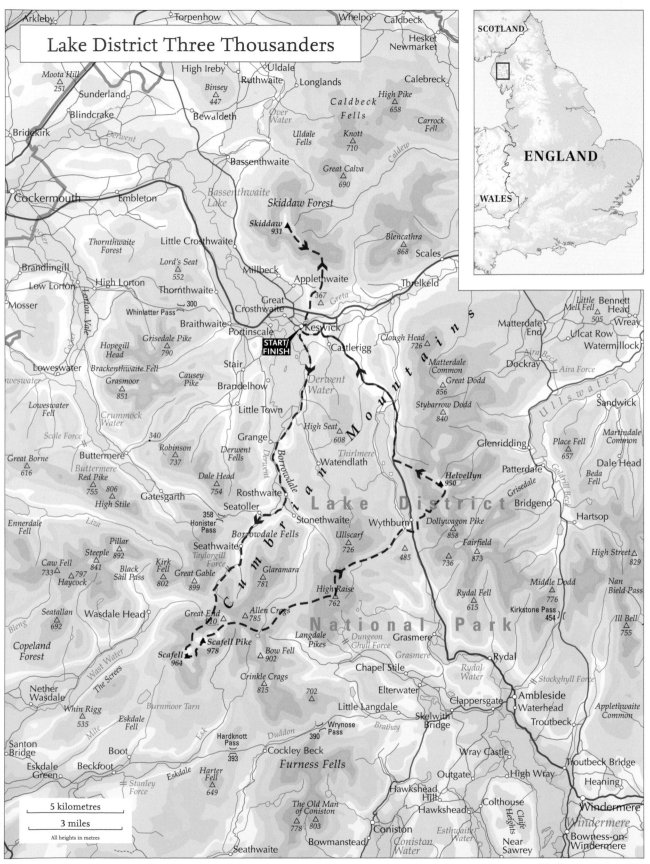

Lake District Three Thousanders

SCOTLAND

ENGLAND

WALES

Lake District Three Thousanders

'Lake District tour de force' ★ ★ ★

Summary: Although the Lake District has the fewest number of three thousanders, and those that it has are among the most modest in height, the walk that links them is perhaps the toughest of all the challenge walks. This is down in part to their scattered positions among the Lake District fells and also to the fact that the land that lies in between is challenging mountain terrain.

Route: To link the four main summits and the four further subsidiary tops involves covering a considerable intervening distance and tackling a diverse range of obstacles. The challenge is also heightened by the lack of contact with valley comforts; once you get away from Borrowdale there are no options for refuelling until you get back to Keswick. In addition, it is fairly committing, as once you get into the Scafells, options for short-cuts are limited and it is a very long walk back to Keswick!

The first recorded round of the Lakes Three Thousanders was by Dr Arthur Wakefield in 1911. Later, the Ramblers' Association (RA) adopted the walk as an annual challenge with checkpoints and support. This was abandoned following concerns about rock fall which affected the key passage of Lord's Rake. The RA-organised walk was staged close to Midsummer's Day and had a cut off of twenty-two hours. It started in the early hours of the morning at Moot Hall in Keswick, the smoother and more easily walked slopes of Skiddaw being tackled in darkness with the aim of being on the summit at dawn. This allowed, depending on pace, for the rest of the walk to be completed during daylight. This approach is a good model to work to; however, the cut-off of twenty-two hours is long gone and many people now do the route over a couple of days, backpacking.

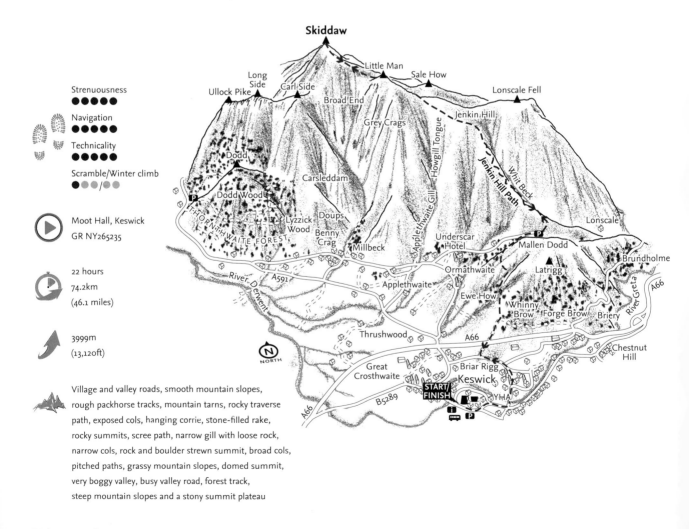

Strenuousness ● ● ● ● ●

Navigation ● ● ● ● ●

Technicality ● ● ● ● ●

Scramble/Winter climb ● ○ ○ / ○ ○

Moot Hall, Keswick
GR NY265235

22 hours
74.2km
(46.1 miles)

3999m
(13,120ft)

Village and valley roads, smooth mountain slopes, rough packhorse tracks, mountain tarns, rocky traverse path, exposed cols, hanging corrie, stone-filled rake, rocky summits, scree path, narrow gill with loose rock, narrow cols, rock and boulder strewn summit, broad cols, pitched paths, grassy mountain slopes, domed summit, very boggy valley, busy valley road, forest track, steep mountain slopes and a stony summit plateau

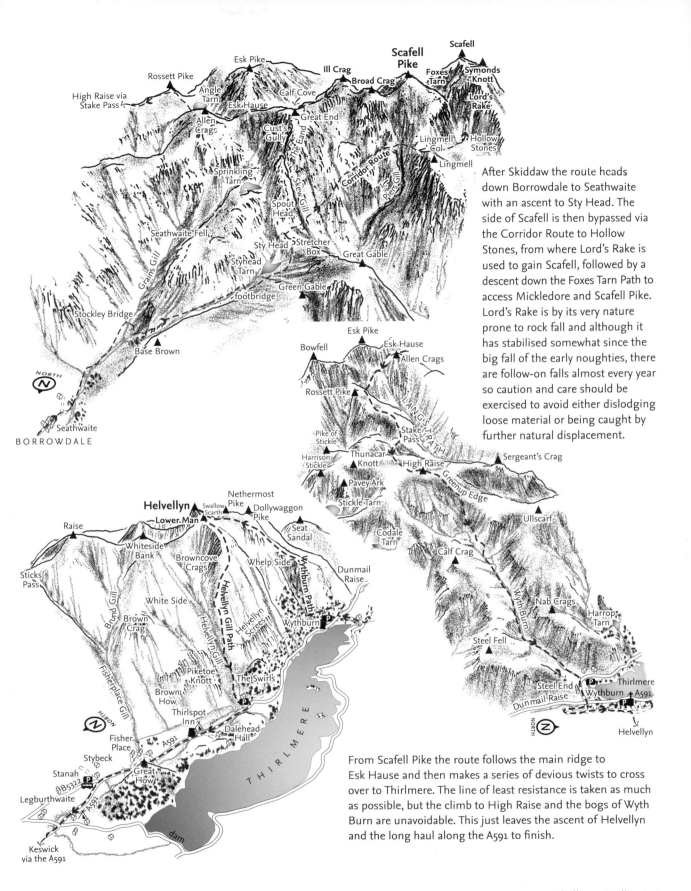

After Skiddaw the route heads down Borrowdale to Seathwaite with an ascent to Sty Head. The side of Scafell is then bypassed via the Corridor Route to Hollow Stones, from where Lord's Rake is used to gain Scafell, followed by a descent down the Foxes Tarn Path to access Mickledore and Scafell Pike. Lord's Rake is by its very nature prone to rock fall and although it has stabilised somewhat since the big fall of the early noughties, there are follow-on falls almost every year so caution and care should be exercised to avoid either dislodging loose material or being caught by further natural displacement.

From Scafell Pike the route follows the main ridge to Esk Hause and then makes a series of devious twists to cross over to Thirlmere. The line of least resistance is taken as much as possible, but the climb to High Raise and the bogs of Wyth Burn are unavoidable. This just leaves the ascent of Helvellyn and the long haul along the A591 to finish.

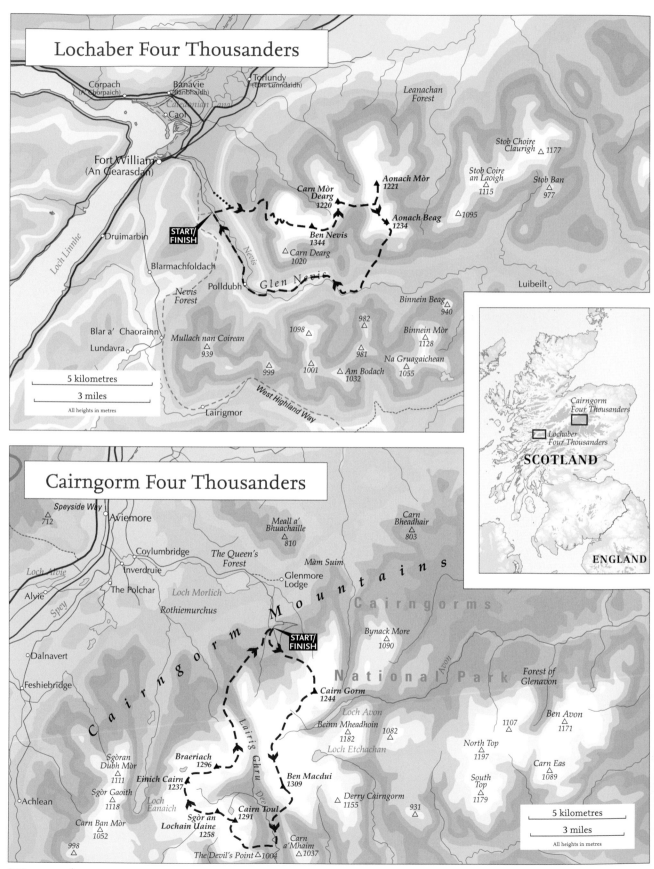

Lochaber Four Thousanders

Corpach
(A'Chorpaich)
Banavie
(Banbhaidh)
Torlundy
(Torr Lunndaidh)
Caol
Caledonian Canal
Leanachan Forest

Stob Choire Claurigh △ 1177

Stob Coire an Laoigh △ 1115

Stob Ban △ 977

Fort William
(An Gearasdan)

Aonach Mòr 1221

Carn Mòr Dearg 1220

△ 1095

Aonach Beag 1234

START/ FINISH

Druimarbin

Ben Nevis 1344

△ Carn Dearg 1020

Loch Linnhe

Blarmachfoldach

Polldubh

Glen Nevis

Nevis

Luibeilt

Binnein Beag △ 940

Nevis Forest

△ 982

Binnein Mòr △ 1128

Blar a' Chaorainn

Mullach nan Coirean △ 939

△ 1098

△ 981

Na Gruagaichean △ 1055

Lundavra

△ 999

△ 1001

△ Am Bodach 1032

5 kilometres

3 miles

All heights in metres

Lairigmor

West Highland Way

Cairngorm Four Thousanders

Speyside Way
△ 712

Aviemore

Meall a' Bhuachaille △ 810

Carn Bheadhair △ 803

Coylumbridge

Inverdruie

The Queen's Forest

Màm Suim

Glenmore Lodge

Loch Alvie

The Polchar

Loch Morlich

Rothiemurchus

Alvie

Spey

Cairngorm Mountains

Cairngorms

Dalnavert

Bynack More △ 1090

START/ FINISH

Feshiebridge

National Park

Avon

Forest of Glenavon

Cairn Gorm 1244

Loch Avon

Beinn Mheadhoin 1182

△ 1082

△ 1107

Ben Avon △ 1171

Loch Etchachan

Braeriach 1296

Lairig Ghru

North Top △ 1197

Sgòran Dubh Mòr △ 1111

Einich Cairn 1237

Ben Macdui 1309

Carn Eas △ 1089

Sgòr Gaoith △ 1118

Loch Eanaich

Derry Cairngorm △ 1155

South Top △ 1179

Achlean

Cairn Toul 1291

△ 931

Carn Ban Mòr △ 1052

Sgòr an Lochain Uaine 1258

△ 998

The Devil's Point △ 1004

Carn a'Mhaim △ 1037

5 kilometres

3 miles

All heights in metres

SCOTLAND

Cairngorm Four Thousanders

Lochaber Four Thousanders

ENGLAND

Lochaber Four Thousanders

'Big climbs and dramatic scrambles' ★★★

Summary: This route is an unashamed abridgement of the classic Lochaber Traverse that crosses from Glen Nevis to Spean Bridge, taking in Ben Nevis, Carn Mòr Dearg, Aonach Mòr, Aonach Beag and the long line of summits that make up the The Grey Corries. The original route is a fine undertaking but when combined with an overnight either up high or at the Lairig Leacach Bothy, it is a memorable expedition.

Route: This shorter version of the classic route focuses purely on the 4000ft mountains but it also has the advantage of easier logistics, as it starts and finishes in Glen Nevis, eliminating the need to arrange transport at separate start and finish points. Shorter as it is, however, it is still a major undertaking and provides one of Scotland's finest mountain days, encompassing a superb mixture of dramatic rock scenery, entertaining scrambling and a sustained feel of mountain grandeur.

To be comfortable undertaking this route you should be happy moving confidently up and down grade 1 scrambling ground and dealing with prolonged exposure. You should also be confident at route finding, as there are a number of key passages that can be confusing even in good conditions, for which it is essential to make the correct choice. Snow-free conditions and long daylight hours are important for success but be aware that Ben Nevis in particular and even parts of the Aonachs' main ridge can hold snow well into the summer months.

The Carn Mòr Dearg Arête and the East Ridge of Carn Mòr Dearg hold the bulk of the scrambling, while the steep, loose ascent of Seang Aonach Mòr represents the most risky ground. There are opportunities to escape past the Carn Mòr Dearg Arête: northeast from Carn Mòr Dearg, at the col between Carn Mòr Dearg and the Aonachs, and north off the summit of Aonach Mòr. This last option, however, does involve a long haul back to Glen Nevis.

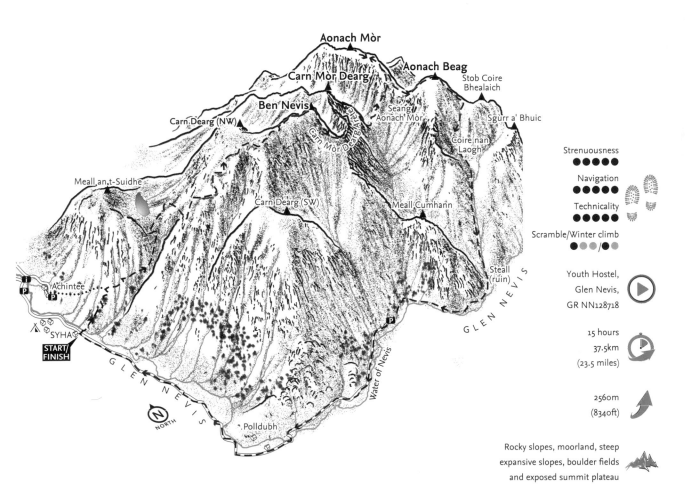

Strenuousness
●●●●●

Navigation
●●●●●

Technicality
●●●●●

Scramble/Winter climb
●●○○/●●

Youth Hostel,
Glen Nevis,
GR NN128718

15 hours
37.5km
(23.5 miles)

2560m
(8340ft)

Rocky slopes, moorland, steep
expansive slopes, boulder fields
and exposed summit plateau

Cairngorm Four Thousanders

'Sub-arctic adventure' ★ ★ ★

Summary: When the great snow beds recede into their last shady hollows, and the pink flush of moss campion fringes the gravel beds, the high sub-arctic plateau of the Cairngorms is a magical place to be. Crystal-clear air elongates the views and the sheer scale of the corries, glens and pink buttressed crags come starkly into view. It is at this time in early summer when the Cairngorms are at their best, and it is at this time that the magnificent challenge of walking all the 4000ft summits in one go is an absolute must.

Route: This walk can be done in one day if you are fleet of foot, travel light and have the weather on your side. There are two really big ascents, and the descent into the Lairig Ghru is steep and unrelenting, but if you are fit and mentally prepared this approach can be rewarding. Equally, if you fancy taking your time, the walk can easily be split over two days with a halfway overnight stop at Corrour Bothy. The bothy can be busy particularly at weekends so a bivi bag or light tent as a backup is advisable.

The plateau is effectively split into two by the deep trench cut by the Lairig Ghru. Both sides offer a similar style of terrain and similar walking, with undulating plateau separating slightly higher summits and deep corries ringed with crags forming the edges. In mist, route finding on the plateau (even when the snow has gone in summer) can be tricky as the paths are vague. In the glens and on the approaches, landmarks are a bit more frequent and so things are a bit easier. This is a very remote route and although there are escape options most are long and involve careful navigation to safely negotiate. Weather can also be a problem with blizzard and whiteout conditions possible even in summer.

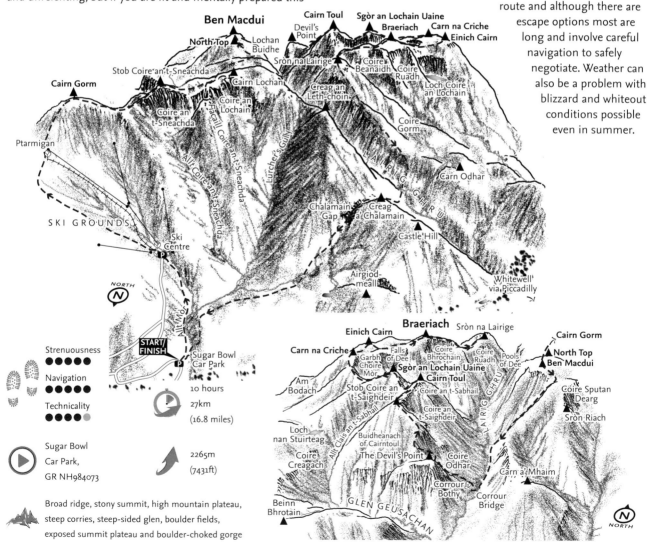

Strenuousness ● ● ● ● ●

Navigation ● ● ● ● ●

Technicality ● ● ● ● ●

Sugar Bowl Car Park, GR NH984073

10 hours

27km (16.8 miles)

2265m (7431ft)

Broad ridge, stony summit, high mountain plateau, steep corries, steep-sided glen, boulder fields, exposed summit plateau and boulder-choked gorge

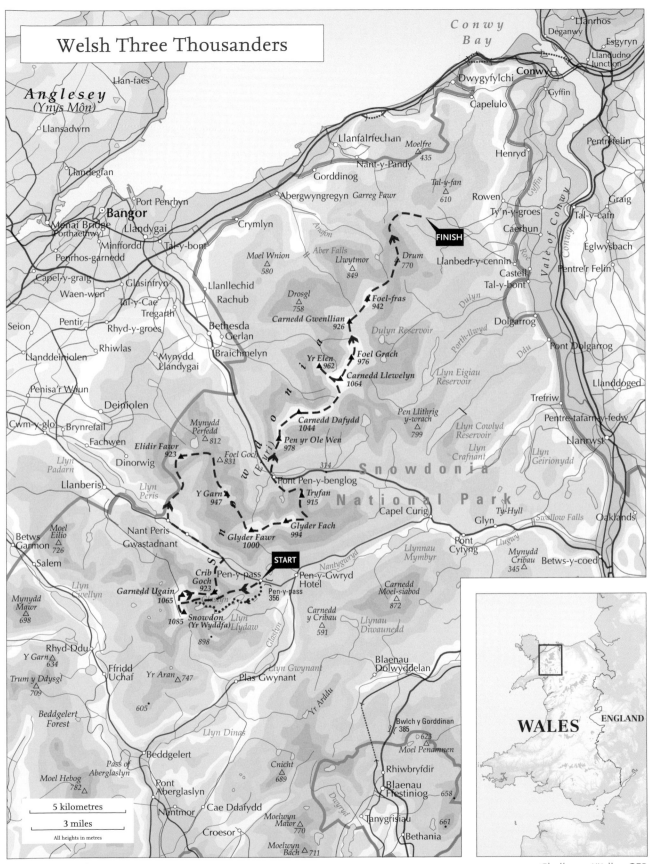

Welsh Three Thousanders

FINISH

START

Anglesey
(Ynys Môn)

Conwy Bay

WALES

ENGLAND

5 kilometres

3 miles

All heights in metres

Welsh Three Thousanders

'Snowdonia in one hit' ★ ★ ★

Summary: With fifteen 3000ft tops in one hit, the Welsh Three Thousanders walk weighs in as a particularly efficient way of walking up lots of mountains. These bare facts though are only a small part of the story, as this grand crossing not only takes in the bulk of Snowdonia's mountains, it also carries you through, past, and over all the most impressive elements of the range's landscape. In one walk you get to bag the shapeliest summits, the finest ridges, the most beautiful lakes and the wildest corners.

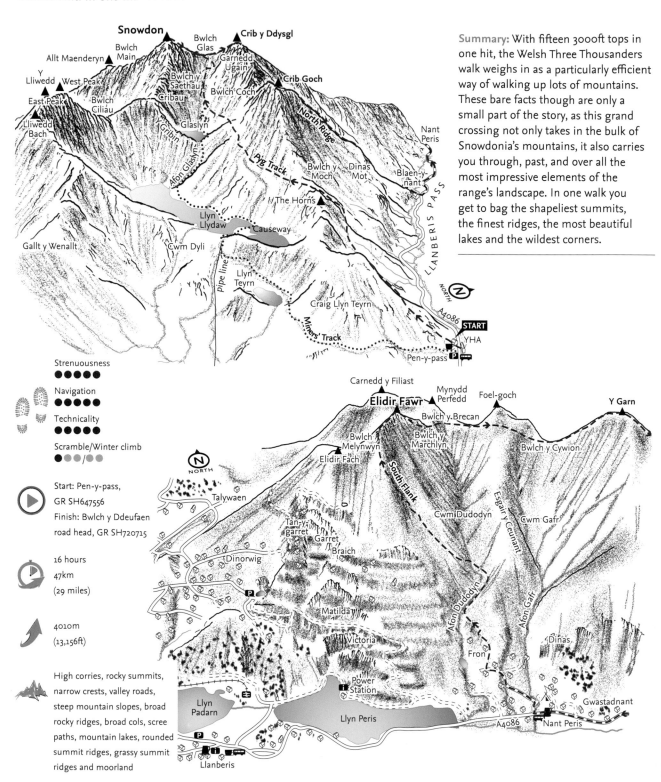

Strenuousness
●●●●●

Navigation
●●●●●

Technicality
●●●●●

Scramble/Winter climb
●●●/●●

Start: Pen-y-pass, GR SH647556
Finish: Bwlch y Ddeufaen road head, GR SH720715

16 hours
47km
(29 miles)

4010m
(13,156ft)

High corries, rocky summits, narrow crests, valley roads, steep mountain slopes, broad rocky ridges, broad cols, scree paths, mountain lakes, rounded summit ridges, grassy summit ridges and moorland

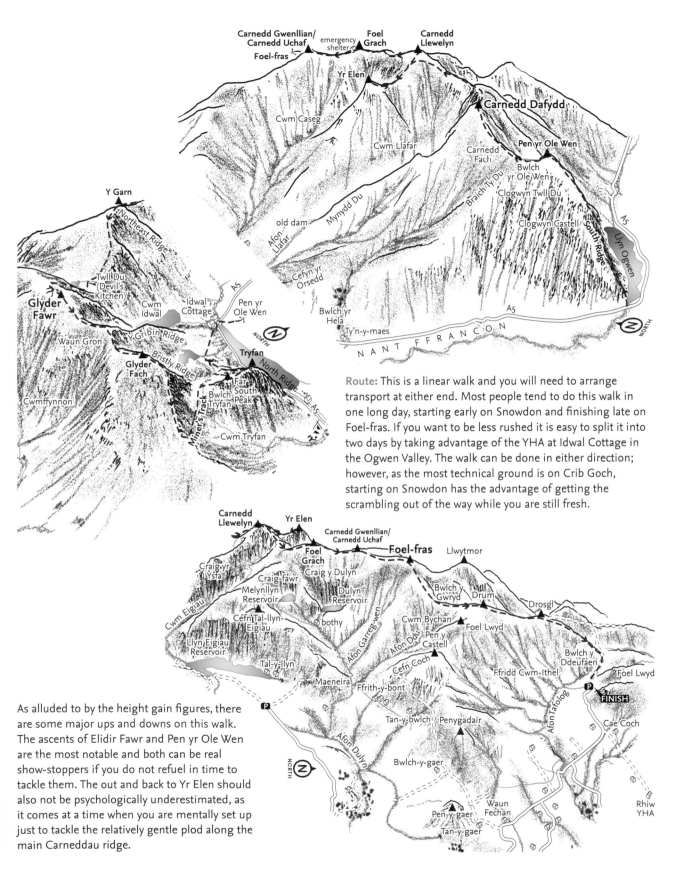

Route: This is a linear walk and you will need to arrange transport at either end. Most people tend to do this walk in one long day, starting early on Snowdon and finishing late on Foel-fras. If you want to be less rushed it is easy to split it into two days by taking advantage of the YHA at Idwal Cottage in the Ogwen Valley. The walk can be done in either direction; however, as the most technical ground is on Crib Goch, starting on Snowdon has the advantage of getting the scrambling out of the way while you are still fresh.

As alluded to by the height gain figures, there are some major ups and downs on this walk. The ascents of Elidir Fawr and Pen yr Ole Wen are the most notable and both can be real show-stoppers if you do not refuel in time to tackle them. The out and back to Yr Elen should also not be psychologically underestimated, as it comes at a time when you are mentally set up just to tackle the relatively gentle plod along the main Carneddau ridge.

Index of Peaks and Routes

Main peaks are in **bold** type with associated routes listed below

Acknowledgements

The preparation of this guidebook would have been impossible without the unstinting assistance of many people – I am grateful to them all: Robin Ashcroft, Bob Atkins, Tom Bailey, Chris Betts, Tori Dodd, Phil Girvin, Simon Ingram, Stuart Johnston, Ed Kenyon, Geoff Langman, Hanna Lindon, Claire Maxted, David Ogle, Louise Parker, Neil S Price, Guy Procter, Harry Salisbury, Phoebe Smith, Matt Swaine, Graham Thompson. Very special thanks go to Loraine Ashcroft, Flora Ashcroft, Harry Ashcroft and Audrey Ashcroft.

Credits

Front cover Mountain view from the summit of Snowdon Shutterstock © peresanz
Front endpaper Scafell Pike and Scafell from Wasdale Head © Jeremy Ashcroft
Back endpaper Striding Edge under full winter conditions © Jeremy Ashcroft
Back cover Crossing the head of Coire Domhain © Trail/Tom Bailey

4 © Trail/Tom Bailey
6 © Trail/Tom Bailey
7 © Trail/Tom Bailey
10 © Trail/Tom Bailey
12 © Jeremy Ashcroft
13 © Trail/Tom Bailey
15 © Jeremy Ashcroft
17 © Trail/Tom Bailey
21 © Jeremy Ashcroft
23 © Jeremy Ashcroft
25 Shutterstock © Stewart Smith Photography
29 © Jeremy Ashcroft
31 © Jeremy Ashcroft
33 © Trail/Tom Bailey
34 © Jeremy Ashcroft
36 Shutterstock © Stewart Smith Photography
37 © Jeremy Ashcroft
39 © Jeremy Ashcroft
42 © Jeremy Ashcroft
43 © Jeremy Ashcroft
44 © Trail/Tom Bailey
46 Shutterstock © Peter Guess
49 Shutterstock © george green
51 © Jeremy Ashcroft
52 © Jeremy Ashcroft
56 Flickr © alpiniste **CC BY-SA 2.0**
71 © Trail/Tom Bailey
73 © Neil S Price
75 Flickr © uplandaccess **CC BY 2.0**
77 Flickr © Nick Bramhall **CC BY-SA 2.0**
79 Flickr © Nick Bramhall **CC BY-SA 2.0**
80 Flickr © Nick Bramhall **CC BY-SA 2.0**

81 Flickr © Nick Bramhall **CC BY-SA 2.0**
82 Flickr © Andrew Last **CC BY 2.0**
87 Flickr © Nick Bramhall **CC BY-SA 2.0**
89 Flickr © Nick Bramhall **CC BY-SA 2.0**
91 Flickr © stusmith_uk **CC BY-ND 2.0**
92 Flickr © Nick Bramhall **CC BY-SA 2.0**
94 Flickr © Nick Bramhall **CC BY-SA 2.0**
96 © Trail/Tom Bailey
101 Flickr © sustainablerural **CC BY 2.0**
102 Flickr © GariochT **CC BY-ND 2.0**
103 Flickr © Nick Bramhall **CC BY-SA 2.0**
104 © Trail/Tom Bailey
106 Shutterstock © Iain Frazier
108 Shutterstock © N Mrtgh
109 Shutterstock © Gail Johnson
110 Shutterstock © Brendan Howard
113 © Jeremy Ashcroft
120 Flickr © tom hartley **CC BY-ND 2.0**
121 Shutterstock © Ian Ratcliffe
124 Shutterstock © hajes
128 Shutterstock © John A Cameron
131 Flickr © alpiniste **CC BY-SA 2.0**
133 Flickr © stusmith_uk **CC BY-ND 2.0**
134 Flickr © msquirrell **CC BY 2.0**
137 © Jeremy Ashcroft
138 © Trail/Tom Bailey
139 © Jeremy Ashcroft
143 Flickr © msquirrell **CC BY 2.0**
145 © Jeremy Ashcroft
149 © Trail/Tom Bailey
151 Shutterstock © Gail Johnson
155 © Trail/Tom Bailey
159 © Trail/Tom Bailey
164 Flickr © Matthew Black **CC BY-SA 2.0**
166 © Jeremy Ashcroft
169 © Jeremy Ashcroft
171 © Jeremy Ashcroft
172 © Jeremy Ashcroft
174 © Trail/Tom Bailey
175 Flickr © erwlas **CC BY 2.0**
177 © Trail/Tom Bailey
178 © Trail/Tom Bailey
181 © Jeremy Ashcroft
182 Flickr © martin_vmorris **CC BY-SA 2.0**
184 © Neil S Price

185 Shutterstock © stocker1970
188 © Neil S Price
189 © Neil S Price
190 © Trail/Tom Bailey
193 © Neil S Price
194 © Trail/Tom Bailey
196 Flickr © Nathan Jones **CC BY-SA 2.0**
197 Flickr © Nathan Jones **CC BY-SA 2.0**
199 Flickr © Denis Egan **CC BY 2.0**
201 © Neil S Price
203 Flickr © virtualjacki **CC BY-ND 2.0**
204 Flickr © Ted and Jen **CC BY 2.0**
207 Flickr © erwlas **CC BY 2.0**
208 Flickr © Stray Croc **CC BY-SA 2.0**
209 Shutterstock © David Hughes
210 Flickr © erwlas **CC BY 2.0**
211 Flickr © alh1 **CC BY-ND 2.0**
212 © Jeremy Ashcroft
215 Shutterstock © Gail Johnson
216 Flickr © erwlas **CC BY 2.0**
217 © Trail/Tom Bailey
219 Flickr © erwlas **CC BY 2.0**
220 Flickr © erwlas **CC BY 2.0**
221 Flickr © erwlas **CC BY 2.0**
223 Shutterstock © Gail Johnson
228 Flickr © Ted and Jen **CC BY 2.0**
230 © Trail/Tom Bailey
233 © Trail/Tom Bailey
234 © Neil S Price
235 © Neil S Price
236 Shuttterstock © James LePage
239 Shutterstock © Max Earey
244 © Trail/Tom Bailey

CC BY 2.0
This file is licensed under the Creative Commons Attribution 2.0 Generic license.
CC BY-SA 2.0
This file is licensed under the Creative Commons Attribution-ShareAlike 2.0 Generic license.
CC BY-ND 2.0
This file is licensed under the Creative Commons Attribution-NoDerivs 2.0 Generic license.